THE LOEB CLASSICAL LIBRARY

FOUNDED BY JAMES LOEB

EURIPIDES

LCL 12

EURIPIDES

CYCLOPS · ALCESTIS · MEDEA

EDITED AND TRANSLATED BY

DAVID KOVACS

HARVARD UNIVERSITY PRESS

CAMBRIDGE, MASSACHUSETTS

LONDON, ENGLAND

1994

Library of Congress Cataloging-in-Publication Data

Euripides.
Euripides / edited and translated by David Kovacs.
p.   cm. — (Loeb classical library; L12)
Includes bibliographical references.
Contents: Cyclops — Alcestis — Medea.
ISBN 0–674–99560–0
1. Euripides—Translations into English.
2. Greek drama (Tragedy)—Translations into English.
3. Alcestis (Greek mythology)—Drama.
4. Cyclops (Greek mythology)—Drama.
5. Medea (Greek mythology)—Drama.
I. Kovacs, David.   II. Title.   III. Series.
PA3975.A2   1994   93–821
882′.01—dc20   CIP

Typeset by Chiron, Inc, Cambridge, Massachusetts.
Printed in Great Britain by St Edmundsbury Press Ltd,
Bury St Edmunds, Suffolk, on acid-free paper.
Bound by Hunter & Foulis Ltd, Edinburgh, Scotland.

CONTENTS

INTRODUCTION   1

BIBLIOGRAPHY   43

ABBREVIATIONS   49

CYCLOPS
 introduction   53
 text and translation   59

ALCESTIS
 introduction   151
 text and translation   159

MEDEA
 introduction   285
 text and translation   293

For Frank and Irene Kovacs

PREFACE

I have incurred a number of debts of gratitude in writing this volume, which it is a pleasure to acknowledge here. My thanks for financial assistance go to the Marguerite Eyer Wilbur Foundation, the Earhart Foundation, and the Perseus Project of Harvard University for grants allowing me to spend the 1990 spring semester in Oxford, and to the University of Virginia for a semester's leave the previous semester and two summer research grants. I am grateful to the governing body of Christ Church, Oxford, for making me an honorary member during my stay there. In addition, this book benefitted immensely from discussions or correspondence with Angus Bowie, Godfrey Bond, Malcolm Heath, Richard Kannicht, Mary Lefkowitz, Hugh Lloyd-Jones, David Lewis, Jon D. Mikalson, and Oliver Taplin, but especially from the generosity of James Diggle and Charles Willink and the stylistic criticisms of George Goold.

Further work was made possible in two subsequent years by a grant from the National Endowment for the Humanities, an independent federal agency. I am grateful for its support.

This volume is dedicated to my parents in profound gratitude.

David Kovacs

University of Virginia

INTRODUCTION

The Life of Euripides

For the biography of Euripides, as for those of ancient
writers in general, reliable evidence is in short supply.[1]
During his lifetime no one saw fit to write about him as a
person, and by the time curiosity about him developed,
the means to satisfy it had nearly all vanished. There were,
to be sure, the public records, inscribed on stone, of his
entries in the tragic competitions giving year, plays, and
the order in the final awarding of prizes, and perhaps one
or two records on stone of his participation in non-
dramatic events, such as the festival of Apollo Delios he
participated in when he was a boy in his home deme of
Phlya. But there was little beyond this: no one who wrote
about him could quote letters from or to him, and few
genuine reminiscences from Euripides' family or contem-
poraries survived into the fourth century to be passed on
by Aristotle or Philochorus. Practically the only evidence

---

[1] I refer throughout by author's name to the following: Dieter-
ich, "Euripides," *RE* VI (1907), 1242–81; Jacoby, *FGrH*, vol. 3 b
(Supp.); Wilamowitz, *Einleitung in die griechische Tragödie* (Ber-
lin, 1907) [= *Euripides: Herakles*, vol. I (Berlin, 1895, reprinted
Darmstadt, 1959)]. Numerals preceded by T refer to the section
Testimonia Vitae et Artis Selecta, the principal ancient notices of
Euripides' life, published separately in my *Euripidea*, Supplement
to *Mnemosyne* 132 (Leiden, 1994).

1

dating from Euripides' lifetime was the work of Aristophanes and other poets of Old Comedy, much of which is available to us as well. The poets of Old Comedy certainly did not write with the intention of providing information about their comic targets, and their evidence is difficult to assess, though, as we will see, this did not stop biographers from using Old Comedy as a source for the life of Euripides, with sometimes ludicrous results. It is important for the assessment of Euripides' work to be clear about the limitations of our knowledge of his life. There is a demonstrable tendency in Euripidean criticism to bring to the interpretation of the plays information about the poet's intellectual and artistic affinities derived from the biographical tradition. It will emerge from the present discussion that this tradition is highly unreliable, and that on such questions the only defensible stance is agnosticism: we simply do not know anything about Euripides' life that can furnish an interpretive key to his works.

The main biographical tradition is represented in four brief, summary Lives (the *Genos Euripidou kai bios* found in many manuscripts of the plays, an article in the *Suda*, a sketch by Thomas Magister, and one in Aulus Gellius[2]) and fragments of a longer *Life of Euripides* by Satyrus.[3]

---

[2] The *Genos* [= T 1] is to be found on pp. 1–6 of Schwartz's edition of the scholia, Thomas Magister [= T 3] on pp. 11–13 of Dindorf's edition. The *Suda* article [= T 2] is E 3695 (ii 468 in Adler's edition), and the Aulus Gellius sketch [= T 5] is at 15.20.

[3] The papyrus fragments of Satyrus' *Life of Euripides* [= T 4] are P. Oxy. 1176, *The Oxyrhynchus Papyri* 9 (1912), 124–82, most recently published, with commentary, by G. Arrighetti, *Studi Classici e Orientali* 13 (1964).

Much of what these sources claim to know is obviously not factual at all and can be categorized under four heads.[4] Often these lives report as fact the jokes or even the plots of Old Comedy, as when we are told that Euripides' mother sold vegetables, an Aristophanic joke we have good reason to doubt is based on fact, or when Satyrus tells us that the women conspired at the Thesmophoria to kill Euripides, which is the plot of Aristophanes' *Thesmophoriazusae*.[5] A second category of pseudo-evidence is material about the poet's life derived from his plays. The story about the infidelity of his wife, for example, "explains" why he wrote his first *Hippolytus*,[6] and the anecdote about this wife's second husband ends with a slightly altered quotation from his *Electra*. A common procedure is to cite a "fact" about Euripides (e.g. "He wrote his plays in a cave looking out to sea") and then to cite as a consequence of this "fact" something which may in reality be its sole warrant (e.g. "and that is why he takes the majority of his metaphors from the sea").[7] A third category is stories of a mythological character, such as the oracle allegedly given to Euripides' father.[8] A fourth is material that can be shown on independent grounds to be fabrication, such as the statement, irreconcilable with the

---

[4] On the prevalence of the non-factual in ancient biography see J. Fairweather, "Fiction in the Biographies of Ancient Writers," *Ancient Society* 5 (1974), 231–75 and M. Lefkowitz, *The Lives of the Greek Poets* (Baltimore, 1981).

[5] Fr. 39 X [= T 4.13].

[6] *Genos* [= T 1.24].

[7] *Genos* [= T 1.22].

[8] See the *Genos* [= T 1.3], Aulus Gellius [= T 5.2], and Oenomaus quoted in Eusebius *Praep. Evang.* 5.33, 227C [= T 13].

chronology of Anaxagoras' career, that Euripides turned to the writing of tragedy after he saw the philosopher get into trouble for his teaching.[9] Such evidence can be easily discarded. Not much in the Lives survives this process.

Another stream of tradition comes from sources that are concerned with history or with the lives of others and that mention Euripides in passing. A number of notices that one cannot always dismiss out of hand are transmitted in Aristotle, Plutarch, and others in connection with events and persons of a more public and political nature. This material will all be assessed separately as it bears on the various phases and aspects of Euripides' life.

Of the dates of his life, the death date is the easiest to determine. Aristophanes' comedy *Frogs* was put on at the Lenaea in the archonship of Callias (406/5), i.e. in January of 405. The plot begins with Dionysus in the Underworld, where he has gone because he has been suddenly seized by a longing for the tragic poetry of Euripides, recently dead. It culminates in the contest between Aeschylus and Euripides for the throne of tragedy. Before that contest, we are told that Euripides came down to Hades and challenged Aeschylus. It is subsequently related that Sophocles came down and did not challenge him but plans to challenge Euripides if he should prove the winner. In view of this not quite explicit chronology, it is reasonable to suppose that Sophocles died in the first half of Callias' year, the latter half of 406, as in fact the Marmor Parium and other sources tell us. It is also reasonable to infer that Euripides died not much earlier, in the archonship of Antigenes (407/6). We are told in the *Genos* that when the news of Euripides' death was brought to Athens Sopho-

---

[9] See the *Suda* [= T 2.5].

cles, himself dressed in mourning, brought on his chorus in the *proagon*, or opening ceremonies, without their customary garlands. This notice sounds genuine. If it is, this would be the Dionysia of 407/6, i.e. March of 406. This death date is confirmed by the entry on the Marmor Parium,[10] which dates Euripides' death to 407/6. The rest of the biographical tradition puts his death a year later, for reasons we shall see.

Euripides was born, we are told by all but one source,[11] in the year of Salamis, the archonship of Calliades (480/79), and in most sources he was born on the very day of the battle and on the island of Salamis itself. The date is very probably one of antiquity's fictitious "synchronisms," by which exact dates that are hard to remember are replaced by nearby dates that are easier. Such synchronisms are characteristic of a whole school of biographical and chronological writing associated with the names of Apollodorus and Eratosthenes. This particular synchronism has several advantages. First, the three great tragic poets are all brought into relation with Salamis, since Aeschylus fought in it and Sophocles (we are told) was a young lad and danced a paean in honor of the victory. Second, such a synchronism puts his birth in the archonship of Calliades, his first tragic competition in that of Callias (456/5), and his death (by a further synchronism) in the archonship of another Callias (406/5) at the easily remembered age of seventy-five.[12] Coincidences of this

---

[10] *FGrH* 239 A 63 [= T 67].

[11] See the *Genos* [= T 1.2], the *Suda* [= T 2.3], Plutarch, *Quaest. Conv.* 717C [= T 7], and Diogenes Laertius 2.45 [= T 8].

[12] Cf. Eratosthenes, *FGrH* 241 F 12, quoted in the *Genos* [= T 1.17].

kind do happen, and it is no scholastic synchronism but a well-documented fact that Thomas Jefferson and John Adams both died on July 4th, 1826, exactly fifty years after the signing of the Declaration of American Independence. But it would be mistaken to place too much reliance on the date of Euripides' birth. Some of this skepticism inevitably infects the notice about his place of birth as well.

The one dissenting voice is the Marmor Parium,[13] which gives a date of 485/4 for Euripides' birth. This too is suspicious as it is the date of Aeschylus' first victory in the tragic competitions. Since, however, the Marmor Parium is the only source to give 407/6 for Euripides' death, a date corroborated by other evidence, in contrast to the synchronistic 406/5 of the other sources, it may be telling the truth about his birth as well. The most we can say with certainty is that he was born at a date not too far from 480 and that he was in his seventies at the time of his death.

Euripides belonged to the deme of Phlya, north of Mount Hymettus, part of the Athenian "tribe" of Cecropis.[14] With only one dissenting voice the tradition makes him the son of a merchant or huckster father, Mnesarchus or Mnesarchides, and a vegetable-seller mother, Cleito. The lone dissenter is Philochorus, the fourth-century historian, who "demonstrates" that Cleito came "of very noble family."[15] Just what his demonstration relied on we cannot tell. Nor can we tell whether he said anything about Euripides' father or whether he did not need to because the parallel tradition about him had

[13] *FGrH* 239 A 50 [= T 6].

[14] Harpocration, s.v. **Φλυέα** (i 302 Dindorf) [= T 11] and Theophrastus, quoted in Athenaeus 10.24, 424EF [= T 12].

[15] *FGrH* 328 F 218, quoted in the *Suda* [= T 2.2].

not yet developed. We find vegetables mentioned in connection with Euripides' mother numerous times in the comedies of Aristophanes, and it is clearly a familiar joke. There is no reason in theory why she could not have sold vegetables (though just why Aristophanes thought his audience would find the joke funny after so many repetitions is hard to see). Yet even apart from the evidence of Philochorus, there are other things in the record, as we shall see, that make the story of Euripides' humble origins seem unlikely.[16]

The *Suda*, which quotes the valuable notice of Philochorus about Euripides' mother, also tells us that his parents were exiled, settled as resident aliens in Boeotia and then in Attica.[17] Although the phrasing is consistent with their being Athenians to start with, this is more likely to be a somewhat confusingly abridged version of the story told by Nicolaus of Damascus,[18] in which the father, a Boeotian, is unable to pay his debts in Boeotia (colorful details about the Boeotian punishment for insolvency are the occasion for the story) and then comes to Athens. In spite of the local color, this report seems lacking in foundation.[19]

We are told that Euripides as a boy was torch bearer in

[16] F. Schachermeyr, "Zur Familie des Euripides," *Antidosis. Festschrift für Walther Kraus* (Wien-Köln-Graz, 1972), pp. 306–26, points out that Comedy seems to confine allegations of menial occupation to *arrivistes* and suggests that Euripides' parents, while well-off, derived their income from trade.

[17] See the beginning of the *Suda* article [= T 2.1].

[18] *FGrH* 90 F 103(v), quoted in Stobaeus iv 159 Wachsmuth-Hense [= T 10].

[19] For a different view see Schachermeyr, above, n. 16.

a procession in honor of Apollo Zosterios and served as wine pourer for the young men of prominent families who danced in honor of Delian Apollo.[20] These seem reliable reports. No one would make up such notices, and at least the second of them cites an inscription on stone in Euripides' home deme of Phlya. Services such as these suggest a family well established in the community and provide evidence against the Boeotian-immigrant story. Ancient Greek *poleis* granted citizenship to people from other *poleis* only very rarely, and there is no good reason to think that a bankrupt settler from Boeotia could have been accepted as an Athenian citizen in good standing, much less that his son could have been chosen to participate in a religious ritual with "the sons of the chief men of Athens." The origin of this story, as Wilamowitz saw,[21] is not far to seek. Someone wished to explain why Euripides was called Euripides, after the Euripus, which runs between the Boeotian coast and the island of Euboea, rather than, say, Cephisiades, after the river that runs through Attica. He came up with the idea that his father must originally have been a Boeotian. It remained only to think of a reason he might have left his native land.

Somewhat less easily dismissed are two *separate* connections with the island of Salamis. He is said to have been born on Salamis on the very day of the battle and also to have fitted out a cave on the island, where he retired to be alone and write.[22] Our authority for the second of

[20] See the *Genos* [= T 1.7] and Theophrastus, quoted in Athenaeus 10.24, 424E [= T 12].

[21] Wilamowitz, p. 8.

[22] See the *Genos* [= T 1.22], Thomas Magister [= T 3.2], Satyrus, fr. 39 IX [= T 4.12], Aulus Gellius 15.20.5 [= T 5.5].

these is Philochorus; and later travellers, such as Aulus
Gellius, were shown an unattractive grotto on the island as
the cave of Euripides. Either his birth on Salamis or his
possession of land there is possible in itself. The popula-
tion of Athens voted in 480 to leave the city, except for a
few defenders left on the Acropolis, and were settled in
Trozen, Aegina, and Salamis (Hdt. 8.41), so that if Euri-
pides' mother gave birth to him during the Persian inva-
sion, he might plausibly have been born on the island.
Alternatively, if his date of birth was moved to coincide
with that of the battle of Salamis, there is good reason for
anyone telling the story to give Salamis as the place of
birth.

We also cannot disprove the idea that Euripides or his
father may have *possessed* land on the island, though the
difficulties are greater than Wilamowitz was prepared to
admit.[23] When Euripides was a boy, his parents were
prominent members of their deme of Phlya, which sug-
gests that they lived there. If Euripides' family was as
prominent as the Philochorus and Theophrastus tes-
timonia suggest, they would scarcely have qualified for a
cleruchy on Salamis, and while they might have acquired
property there by other means, the supposition has little to
recommend it.

Various sources list the philosophers with whom Euri-
pides is supposed to have studied. The *Genos* in one place
gives Anaxagoras, Prodicus, Protagoras, and Socrates, in
another Archelaus the natural philosopher and Anaxa-
goras; the *Suda* "Prodicus in rhetoric, Socrates in ethics
and philosophy, and also Anaxagoras"; Thomas Magister

[23] See Jacoby, p. 584, n. 7 on fr. 218, and n. 5 on fr. 219;
Wilamowitz, p. 6.

"Anaxagoras, Prodicus, and certain others." Satyrus' fragments emphasize connections with Anaxagoras. Finally a series of anecdotes and comic quotations put him on friendly or even collaborative terms with Socrates.

That Euripides is said to have studied with almost every one of the leading intellectuals of the fifth century is remarkable. Suspicion is deepened by chronological inconsistencies: our sources all place his education before the beginning of his dramatic career in 455,[24] while some, at least, of the thinkers mentioned as his teachers were not active until a good while after 455. (Socrates, for example, was a lad of fourteen in 455, while Prodicus came to Athens in the late 430s at the earliest.) The story that Euripides decided to write plays instead of philosophy because he saw Anaxagoras run into danger presupposes an impossibly early chronology for Anaxagoras' trial, and there is no evidence that he visited Athens early enough to be Euripides' teacher in this sense. It is unlikely that these notices are factual.

We are also told that Protagoras gave his first public reading, his agnostic treatise *On the Gods*, in Euripides' house, a fact that would suggest personal connection and sympathy between the poet and the philosopher.[25] The anecdote is not in itself incredible, but our source goes on to say "Others say it was at the house of Megacleides, others in the Lyceum." While it is possible that he gave a public reading of the work in more than one place, it seems likely that the famous name of Euripides has simply

---

[24] See the *Genos* [= T 1.4, 1.33], the *Suda* [= T 2.4–5], Thomas Magister [= T 3.4–5], and Aulus Gellius [= T 5.4–5].

[25] Diogenes Laertius 9.54 [= T 15].

replaced the obscure name of Megacleides.[26]

The connection with Socrates appears insistently in several forms,[27] and it is the one that impressed Nietzsche, who regarded Euripides and Socrates as accomplices in the murder of tragedy. In fact, however, none of the pieces of evidence on which Nietzsche relied to connect the two men emerges from scrutiny with its credit intact.[28] The allegation of a connection between these two men probably arises from the jokes of Old Comedy, which "explains" Euripides' intellectualist manner as the influence of Socrates, a subject to which we shall return below.

Allegations of atheism seem likewise to be derived from Old Comedy. Euripides, like Socrates in the *Clouds*, is represented as having his own gods (*Frogs* 889–94) or none (*Thesmophoriazusae* 449–56). Most of the tradition ignores or contradicts this allegation, presumably because the plays themselves lend so little support to it.[29] But one

[26] We cannot now identify Megacleides.

[27] Satyrus, frr. 38 IV + 39 I [= T 4.6] and 39 II [= T 4.7], Diogenes Laertius 2.18 [= T 17], Aelian *Varia Historia* 2.13 [= T 18], Cicero, *Tusculan Disputations* 4.63 [= T 19], and Diogenes Laertius 2.22 [= T 21].

[28] See Albert Henrichs, "The Last of the Detractors: Friedrich Nietzsche's Condemnation of Euripides," *GRBS* 27 (1986), 385–90. Note in addition that Aelian's story of Socrates attending the theater when Euripides' plays were being performed "in the new tragedy section" is fourth-century in origin: before 386 there were no regular presentations of "old" tragedies, so that "the new tragedy section" is anachronistic.

[29] See Satyrus, fr. 39 II [= T 4.7], Plutarch, *How the Young Man Should Study Poetry* 4, 19E [= T 45], and Seneca, *Epistula* 115.15 [= T 46]. See also M. Lefkowitz, "Was Euripides an

11

late notice, Aëtius quoted in pseudo-Plutarch *de plac. phil.* 880DE [= T 23], shows that this obstacle was not insurmountable. According to this report, Euripides was forced by fear of the Areopagus to present his atheistic views indirectly by making Sisyphus his mouthpiece.[30] The fragment of *Sisyphus* he quotes (*TrGF* 43 F 19) explains the gods as the invention of a clever man who wanted to prevent lawlessness. The play is probably by Critias rather than Euripides, and the views of the play's leading character are in any case not necessarily those the author is espousing.

Euripides was clearly influenced by the fifth century's prominent intellectuals, as were also, to a lesser degree, Sophocles and Herodotus. But we have no reliable evidence of personal contact or that he was in any special sense a student or associate of philosophers. Whether Aristophanes regarded him as such and whether his contemporary Athenians shared such a view is a question to be treated below.

As far as we know, Euripides held no office in the Athenian state and took no part, aside from duties expected of everyone, in public life. (A notice in Aristotle, *Rhetoric* 2.6.20, 1384 b 13–17 [= T 94], that seems to make him ambassador to the Syracusans is likely to refer

---

Atheist?" *SIFC* 5 (1987), 149–66.

[30] It is to be noted that during the dramatic career of Euripides the Areopagus did not exercise the kind of authority in cases of impiety presupposed by this notice: see R. W. Wallace, *The Areopagus Council to 307 B.C.* (Baltimore and London, 1989), pp. 106–112, who shows that from 462/1 to 355 the Areopagus had no general oversight or jurisdiction in religious matters, and that the story about Euripides reflects later practice.

to someone else.[31]) It is almost exclusively as tragic poet that he was known to his contemporaries. Here we have sources that can be relied on, for the contestants in each year's tragic contests, together with the plays they entered and their rank in the awarding of prizes, were inscribed on stone in a public place. These lists are the ultimate source for the information preserved in the manuscripts of the tragic poets and elsewhere about the circumstances of their plays' first performances. Aristotle and members of his school made their own copies of these notices for their investigations into the history of the theater, and it is from this compilation, called the *Didascaliai*, that such information as we have derives. The work of the Peripatetic school was continued by the researches of the Alexandrian scholars such as Aristophanes of Byzantium, who gathered copies of as many plays as they could find and produced a *Collected Works* that is the basis for the medieval manuscript tradition.

Information about Euripides' total dramatic output in the biographical tradition[32] goes back to the Alexandrians. The Alexandrians collected plays and also drew up lists of titles for the three dramatic poets, including the names of works that did not happen to survive. They knew the titles of ninety-two plays under the name of Euripides and seemed to have possessed copies of seventy-eight plays.[33] Seventy of these were tragedies and only eight were satyr

[31] See Wilamowitz, *Hermes* 34 (1899), 617–18, D. M. Lewis, *BSA* 50 (1955), 17–19, and J. K. Davies, *Athenian Propertied Families* (Oxford, 1971), pp. 202–3.

[32] See the *Genos* [= T 1.16, 1.38] and the *Suda* [= T 2.11–12].

[33] For a discussion of the various figures transmitted in the Lives and an attempt to reconcile them, see Dieterich, p. 1247.

plays.[34] Out of the total number of titles, three tragedies (*Tennes*, *Rhadamanthys*, *Peirithous*) and one satyr play (possibly a *Sisyphus*, the Euripidean *Sisyphus* of 415 not surviving) were regarded as dubious or certainly spurious.

Euripides was awarded the first prize only four times during his life and once posthumously. (The one posthumous victory means the first performance by his literary executor, Euripides the Younger, of the three plays he had written but not performed at the time of his death. Not included in the total are the many first prizes won by revivals of Euripidean plays in the centuries after his death.) This seems a surprisingly low figure—four first prizes in approximately twenty-two contests, less than one in five—especially in light of the enormous popularity of his plays with later generations. It has been taken to imply a pronounced suspicion or hostility of the Athenian public toward Euripides. A number of studies, however, have shown that this is not the inevitable reading of the evidence.[35] It is clear that Euripides must have been

---

[34] This is far short of the one play in four we might expect. Although there is one recorded case, *Alcestis* of 438, where a tragedy was produced in the fourth place, it seems more likely that the disproportion was caused by the lower survival rate of Euripides' satyr plays. Euripides may simply not have excelled in this genre (the surviving *Cyclops*, at any rate, is not among his strongest performances) and therefore his satyr plays, not being in great demand, were not much copied. We know the name of one, *The Reapers* of 431, that did not survive to Alexandria. (See the Hypothesis to *Medea*.)

[35] See P. T. Stevens, "Euripides and the Athenians," *JHS* 76 (1956), 87–94; V. Martin, "Euripide et Ménandre face à leur public," in *Entretiens sur l'Antiquité Classique* VI, 243–83; C. Franco,

"granted a chorus" (allowed to compete) almost every time he requested one, which would not have been the case if Euripides and his audience had been living on terms of mutual hostility. We cannot say why he received the first prize only four times. Sometimes, of course, he was bested by the phenomenally successful Sophocles. But there was a great profusion of tragic talent in the fifth century, and we should not let our prejudice in favor of works that happen to survive blind us to the fact that much that perished may have been of high quality. In 431, for example, Euphorion, Aeschylus' son, defeated not only Euripides but also Sophocles. It would be unwise in such circumstances to assume that the third prize represents hostility.

One instructive example in this regard is the notice we have in Aelian about the contest of 415, in which Euripides' *Alexandros, Palamedes, Trojan Women,* and *Sisyphus* were defeated by a certain Xenocles.[36] Aelian, writing in the second century A.D., expresses amazement that Xenocles, "whoever *that* may be," should have defeated Euripides, "and that too when Euripides was competing with such good plays." He goes on to say that either the judges were deficient in taste or they were bribed, neither of which is a supposition worthy of the Athenians. It does not occur to him to think, as do many modern critics of the play, that the *Trojan Women* represented an indictment of Athenian policy at Melos,

---

"Euripide e gli Ateniensi" in *La polis e il suo teatro*, ed. E. Corsino, Saggi & materiali univ. VII, Serie di antichità e tradizione class. VI (Padova, 1986), pp. 111–25.

[36] Aelian, *Varia Historia* 2.8 [= T 31].

and that the Athenians were annoyed at Euripides for criticizing their policy.[37] In this he is not unusual: no ancient testimonium connects Euripides' lack of success, either on particular occasions or in general, with the Athenian perception of him as a critic, an outsider, or an artistic or moral revolutionary.

We are told that his dramatic career began in 455, and that among the plays produced on this occasion was a play that probably treated the Medea myth, *The Daughters of Pelias*. The date is presumably taken from the *Didascaliai* and therefore reliable. (Note that actual events have produced the sort of synchronism we might otherwise be tempted to ascribe to the school of Apollodorus, for that same year saw the death of Aeschylus.) Euripides came in third. We are also told that a first prize was awarded to Euripides for the first time in 441.

The dates of some of the plays that have survived are preserved, mostly in the *hypotheseis* or plot summaries, condensed from Alexandrian scholarship, that are prefixed to the plays in our medieval manuscripts. The rest of the surviving plays can be approximately dated on the basis of style. In particular, on the evidence of the securely dated plays we can establish that Euripides made increasing use throughout his career of the license of substituting two short syllables for a long syllable in iambic trimeter, which allows us an approximate relative chronology. The surviving plays with their known or conjectured dates are given below.

[37] For difficulties with the view that *Trojan Women* reflects the slaughter of the Melians a few months earlier, see A. M. van Erp Taalman Kip, "Euripides and Melos," *Mnemosyne* 40 (1987), 414–19.

438	*Alcestis*	second prize
431	*Medea*	third prize
c. 430	*Children of Heracles*	
428	*Hippolytus*	first prize
c. 425	*Andromache*	not produced in Athens
c. 424	*Hecuba*	
c. 423	*Suppliant Women*	
c. 420	*Electra*	
c. 416	*Heracles*	
415	*Trojan Women*	second prize
c. 414	*Iphigenia among the Taurians*	
c. 413	*Ion*	
412	*Helen*	
c. 410	*Phoenician Women*	second prize
408	*Orestes*	
posthumous	*Bacchae and Iphigenia at Aulis*	first prize
unknown	*Cyclops*	

Rhesus is probably not by Euripides. For a discussion of the dating of lost plays, see M. Cropp and G. Fick, *Resolutions and Chronology in Euripides, BICS* Supplement 43 (1985).

Two nondramatic poems are plausibly ascribed to Euripides. We have fragments[38] of a victory ode in honor

---

[38] *Vita Alcibiadis* 11.1 [= T 49, *PMG* 755] and *Vita Demosthenis* 1 [= T 50, *PMG* 756]. For a discusssion of authorship and style see C. M. Bowra, "Euripides' Epinicion for Alcibiades," *Historia* 9 (1961), 67–79, reprinted in *On Greek Margins* (Oxford, 1970), pp. 134–48.

of Alcibiades, who in 416 entered seven chariots in the Olympic Games and won three prizes. Plutarch expresses doubt about the ode's authorship, and it may well be by someone else. Attested without any doubts or alternative authorship is an epitaph in honor of the Athenians who died in Sicily probably composed a very short time after the disaster in Syracuse. It mentions the eight victories the Athenians won before the gods withdrew their impartiality and turned against them.[39] The only substantial argument against the attribution to Euripides is the belief that the poet, being a critic of Athenian policy, could not have been invited to write it or accepted if asked. But the biographical tradition says nothing to substantiate this assumption, and there is very little in the plays that is even *prima facie* evidence for it. There seems no good reason to doubt Plutarch.

We learn from a brief notice in Aristotle that Euripides was involved in a lawsuit arising out of the Athenian tax system.[40] Wealthy citizens were called on to perform "liturgies," expensive public duties such as serving as *choregus* (financial sponsor) in the production of tragedies or comedies. If a citizen felt that he was being asked to do more such liturgies than someone else better able to pay, he could challenge this person in a suit called an *antidosis*.[41] The other party in Euripides' case, Hygiainon,

[39] Plutarch, *Vita Niciae* 7 [= T 51]. For a discussion of these eight victories and their relation to official counting of "trophies" raised, see C. O. Zuretti, "Un epicedio di Euripide," *Rendiconti dell' Istituto Lombardo*, serie II, 55 (1922), 527–32.

[40] *Rhet.* 3.15, 1416 a 28–35 [= T 59].

[41] For a description of the workings of this system, see M. Christ, "Liturgy Avoidance and *Antidosis* in Classical Athens,"

alleged that Euripides' sworn statements were suspect, and he cited *Hippolytus* 612, "My tongue is sworn, my mind remains unsworn," to show that in his plays Euripides had championed perjury. Euripides' reply does not take this charge at all seriously and merely points to the first-prize verdict the Athenian public had already rendered on the play, suggesting that if Hygiainon persisted, this same theater-public, in their capacity as jurors, would make their opinion known once more. It should be noted that Euripides is here reliably shown to be a man of financial means, as one would expect someone to be who had the leisure to write plays for uncertain financial rewards.

Various anecdotes are told about Euripides' marital troubles.[42] We are told that he married twice (in some sources first Melito, then Choirile, in others the order is reversed), that he found his first wife unfaithful and was moved to write his first (and unsuccessful) *Hippolytus* in order to expose the moral failings of the female sex; that he then married a second time and found his second wife equally unfaithful. Wilamowitz was clearly right to conclude that the two wives are doublets, and that there is nothing to distinguish Melito from Choirile. Moreover, Choirile's name looks very much like something from Old Comedy (it suggests the slang term for the female sexual organ, though the name was actually borne by at least one Athenian woman), and there is reason to believe that her name and her adultery are comic invention.

The comic poets gave the name of one of the men who

---

[42] See the *Genos* [= T 1.13, 1.24], the *Suda* [= T 2.7–8], and Thomas Magister [= T 3.10].

allegedly cuckolded Euripides, Cephisophon, and said also that he helped Euripides write his plays.[43] I have given reasons elsewhere for thinking that the description of him as a slave is mistaken and that Thomas Magister may be right in calling him Euripides' actor.[44] Other men named as Euripides' artistic collaborators are Socrates, his father-in-law Mnesilochus (if the text is correct), and Timocrates of Argos, who with Cephisophon is credited with Euripides' lyrics.[45] These allegations of collaboration are literary judgments in biographical form. Euripides' dialogue is argumentative and rhetorical: therefore Socrates, the embodiment of loquacity, must have helped him write it.[46] Euripides' lyrics, by contrast, are written in a style much more removed from ordinary speech than his generally clear and lucid trimeters: they are therefore the work of Cephisophon or Timocrates.

Some time after 408, the year of *Orestes*, Euripides went to Macedon to the court of Archelaus. The motives are variously given. He is said to have been unwilling to endure mockery, either because of his wife's infidelity[47] or because of the ill will of his fellow citizens and his annoyance at competing with inferior poets.[48] Alternatively he

[43] See the *Genos* [= T 1.5, 1.29], Thomas Magister [= T 3.12], Satyrus fr. 39 XII–XIII [= T 4.14–15], and Aristophanes *Frogs* 944 and 1407–9 with scholia [= T 58].

[44] *ZPE* 84 (1990), 15–18.

[45] See the *Genos* [= T 1.5] and the comic poets Teleclides, Callias, and Aristophanes quoted in Diogenes Laertius 2.18 [= T 17].

[46] See, for example, *Frogs* 1491–99 [= T 77].

[47] See the *Suda* [= T 2.8].

[48] See Satyrus, fr. 39 XV [= T 4.17].

20

is said to have gone in a spirit of lofty disdain for his lack of success in the competitions.[49] None of these motives is anything but a guess, and we should notice that other artists, among them Timotheus the lyric poet, Zeuxis the sculptor, and Agathon the tragic dramatist, accepted invitations from Archelaus at about this time. It is usually assumed that Euripides intended never to return to Athens and that, disenchanted with his city or its policies or its prospects, he had said farewell. This is more than we know. We certainly cannot rule out the possibility that, just as Aeschylus went to Sicily to enjoy the hospitality of Hieron with no thought of remaining permanently, so Euripides and his fellow artists intended to make a temporary visit.[50] Euripides' departure may have been self-imposed exile, but we have no reliable evidence that it was.

The funerary inscription on his cenotaph in Athens, possibly of contemporary date, says that he was buried in Macedon, and we are justified in concluding that he died there. According to a tradition already current around the end of the fourth century, he met a violent end. Some said that he was killed by dogs, either accidentally let loose on him or deliberately set on him by enemies or rivals when he was either coming home late from a party or sitting quietly in a grove. Alternatively, he was torn apart by women while off to a tryst either with Archelaus' own boy-beloved or with another man's wife. The likelihood that one or another of these stories is the truth does not seem very high.

[49] See the *Genos* [= T 1.35].
[50] This comparison is made in Pausanias 1.2.2.

Euripides in Old Comedy

When the biographical tradition alleges that Euripides was devoted to a philosophical outlook that cast tragedy's religious foundations into question and was an anti-traditionalist in his art, it is likely that it is relying on Old Comedy. The witness of the biographers therefore has no independent value, and we must turn instead to Old Comedy itself, whose evidence we must examine with some care. What does Old Comedy tell us about how the poet was perceived by his contemporaries?

This evidence is more difficult to assess than is generally recognized. First, the amount of truth in a comic portrait can be extremely low.[51] For a joke to be worth making in Old Comedy, there need be only a slight resemblance between the actual person and his comic representation.[52] There are elements in Old Comedy's portrait of Euripides, such as misogyny, which scholars rightly discount, and there are other elements about which we can feel no confidence. Second, the picture of the poet varies a great deal from play to play and is sometimes more respectful than disrespectful.

In *Acharnians* of 425, Aristophanes makes fun of cer-

[51] One cannot even conclude that either the comic poet or his victim regarded a comic attack as an act of hostility or that a first prize for the play implies that the audience too hold an unfavorable view of the target in real life. See M. Heath, *Political Comedy in Aristophanes* (Göttingen, 1987) for examples.

[52] K. J. Dover, *Greek Homosexuality* (London and Cambridge, Mass., 1978), pp. 144–45, discusses the case of Cleisthenes, who, because he had a skimpy beard, was pilloried for twenty years, first as a eunuch and then as an effeminate.

tain palpable features of Euripidean tragedy, such as its
use of ragged heroes, its homely and less elevated atmo-
sphere, and its style, rich in pointed antithesis and para-
dox.[53] The audience of 425 would certainly have regarded
some of these traits as comic exaggeration of the style of
the real Euripides. The only pre-425 Greek tragedy we
possess whose script calls for rags is Aeschylus' *Persians*,
but Euripides' frequent use of this motif may have seemed
remarkable. It should be noted that the treatment of
Euripides here is without any overtones of philosophical
or religious idiosyncrasy, and though his style is held up to
(comparatively gentle) ridicule, there is no suggestion that
he is other than a respected tragic poet.

In *Clouds* (first version 423, our text an incomplete
revision of unknown date) Euripides is a questioner of
received morality. Young Pheidippides is sent by his
debt-ridden father to study with Socrates, who is to teach
the lad the dishonest rhetoric necessary to free his father
from his debts. After Pheidippides has imbibed the
Socratic mix of quack science, atheism, and pettifoggery,
he gets into an argument with his father about poetry and
finally assaults him physically. The young man has no
more use for Aeschylus and is all agog for Euripides, one
of whose speeches he recites at dinner, a tale of incest
between a brother and sister (presumably the prologue to
Aeolus). By implication here, a taste for Euripides goes
with sophistry and immoralism. Whether the Athenian
audience actually thought of Euripides, at least at times, in
these terms is unclear. If so, it will have been because in
his plays more scope is given to immoral characters

---

[53] For verbal antithesis comparable with *Acharnians* 396, cf.
Alcestis 141.

to justify their actions, and in the popular mind this may have created an impression of licentiousness, which a series of anecdotes reflects and attempts to refute.[54] But it is equally possible that the audience did not regard the charge as actually justified but found it funny because there was just enough in the plays to make it comically plausible. Just as we should not infer from this play that Socrates in the 420s was or was thought to be a quack scientist and a teacher of dishonest rhetoric, so it would be rash to conclude that Euripides at this period was or was thought to be a questioner of conventional morality. It is worth noting that non-comic writers on Euripides, however much influenced by comedy in other respects, attribute to Euripides a high moral purpose, quite the reverse of the slippery relativism comedy taxes him with.[55] The evidence is insufficient to show that Euripides questioned, or was thought to question, fundamental moral notions such as the tabu on incest.

The prologue to *Wasps* of 422 gives the audience a list of subjects and tricks it must not expect from Aristophanes: low comedy from Megara, slaves scattering nuts among the audience, Heracles being duped out of his dinner, or "Euripides being wantonly maltreated." The reference cannot be to Aristophanes' own treatment of the poet—the verb implies behavior that is shocking or inde-

---

[54] See Plutarch, *de audiendis poetis* 33C and 19E [= T 44, 45], Seneca, *Ep.* 115.14–15 [= T 46], and Plutarch, *Amatorius* 756BC [= T 47].

[55] For example, Satyrus gives no indication that he took Comedy's charge of immoralism seriously but on the contrary represents Euripides as urging a high moral standard: see fr. 39 II–IV [= T 4.7–9].

cent and would not be used of one's own actions—and must refer to comedies by other poets. Two things can be reasonably inferred: first, other comic poets besides Aristophanes launched comic attacks on Euripides, and second, such attacks could be described (in comic terms) as wanton outrage.

In *Thesmophoriazusae* (411), the women of Athens, meeting at the women's festival of the Thesmophoria, plan to punish the poet for maligning their sex in his plays. Euripides, having got wind of the plot, persuades a kinsman to disguise himself as a woman, infiltrate the meeting, and plead his cause. Two speeches are made in condemnation of Euripides. The first woman complains that Euripides has created deep suspicion against women in the minds of men by his general abuse of the sex and by his portrayal of their artful and devious ways. Men are on the lookout for lovers and ready to suspect the worst when their wives wreath a garland or a pot is broken. It is impossible to smuggle false heirs into the house, and men are too nosy about the running of the household. Thanks to Euripides, women's life is a misery, for all their usual tricks have been foiled. The second speaker makes a different charge. She, a poor widow who supports herself by making garlands, complains that her business has been cut to less than half since Euripides in his tragedies persuaded the men of Athens that the gods did not exist.

It is reasonable to ask whether Euripides was widely viewed in the fifth century as a misogynist.[56] It is not

---

[56] *Lys.* 283–84 and 368–69 [= T 75] might be evidence that this perception was more widely shared if we could be sure that they are not merely a reference to *Thesmophoriazusae*: both plays

impossible that the combination of women in dubious situations or of uncertain principle (Creusa in the *Ion*, or the Phaedra of the lost *Hippolytus*, for example) with certain generalizations about women (e.g. *Med.* 407–9, *Andr.* 269–72) created in the Athenian audience a belief that Euripides hated the entire sex. But it is equally possible that the audience laughed because there was just enough in the plays to make the idea comically plausible. So too with atheism: the Athenians did not necessarily think that lines such as *Heracles* 339–47 or *Trojan Women* 469–71 proved Euripides an atheist: they might well have laughed precisely because the charge was false though (in comic terms) colorable.

The most extensive comic treatment of Euripides is *Frogs* of 405. Here the god Dionysus, in whose honor the dramatic festivals were held, decides to go to the Underworld to fetch Euripides, who has recently died. As he explains to his half-brother Heracles, he needs a tragic poet and is not satisfied with the current crop. Arriving in Hades he finds a quarrel in progress between Aeschylus, who holds the throne of tragedy in the Underworld, and Euripides, who is the recently arrived challenger. Euripides, he is told, gave demonstrations of his art to the footpads, cutpurses, parricides, and burglars, who are in plentiful supply in the Underworld, and they were so taken with his dodgy and clever art that they thought him the rightful occupant of the throne. (Euripides, as in *Clouds*, is the poet most admired by the morally reprobate.) The rest of the play is the contest between the two poets,

---

were presented in 411, one at the Lenaea, the other at the Dionysia, but there is no clear evidence which preceded which.

allowing for extended comic characterization of each.

Frogs incidentally allows us to see clearly how slight the resemblance between comic portrait and reality can be. Aeschylus is portrayed as the Grand Old Man of tragedy, the embodiment of everything old-fashioned and good, solemn and improving. This makes comic sense, for Aeschylus belonged to an earlier generation of poets, and his style sounded grand and old-fashioned. It is comically congruent with these traits that he should also be a moralist, a praiser of bygone days, a prig, and the advocate of an exaggerated sense of tragic decorum. Aristophanes' Aeschylus regards poetry principally as a means of moral improvement, implies that he never put any immoral characters on the stage, and claims that plays such as *Seven Against Thebes* were written to produce martial valor. All this makes comic sense, but most of it is far from the truth. He taxes Euripides with putting slaves on the stage with speaking parts and with introducing into tragedy the common, humble, and everyday. But in fact speaking slaves are not unknown to Aeschylean tragedy, and his plays do not shy away from topics, such as Cilissa's discussion of toilet-training at *Libation Bearers* 753–60, that even Euripides does not touch.[57] Aeschylean tragedy was never as grand and elevated, nor Aeschylus as priggish and moraliz-

---

[57] A lost play of Aeschylus (fr. 180 Radt) mentions that necessary but lowly item, the chamber pot. The Herald in *Agamemnon* is not above mentioning bed bugs among the hardships at Troy (560–62). The Queen in *Persians* fears that Xerxes, returning home in disgrace, will suffer shame because of his ragged clothing (845–51). According to Athenaeus [Aeschylus T 117a Radt], it was Aeschylus who first put drunkenness on the tragic stage.

ing, as Aristophanes for comic purposes pretends they were. It is unsafe to assume that the portrait of Euripides is any closer to reality.

The Aristophanic Euripides is as new-fangled as his Aeschylus is old-fashioned. The real Euripides, of course, had made innovations in the tragic art, and on many points of style he stands at the opposite pole to the practice of Aeschylus. It makes comic sense, however, that as the representative of the new manner he should also be given other traits that may not correspond to the real Euripides any more than priggish moralism or exaggerated decorum belonged to the real Aeschylus. Where Aeschylus was a moralist, Euripides is portrayed as an immoralist admired by the criminal classes. Where Aeschylus is pious, he is an atheist. Where Aeschylus champions the heroic and believes in tragic decorum, Euripides is the spokesman for *verismo* and dwells with artistic satisfaction on the ordinary and everyday. It is quite possible that the comic poet has here given himself a great deal of latitude to portray both the tragic poets in ways that do not necessarily correspond to the way they are or are perceived.

Aristophanes' Euripides prays to his own private divinities, "Upper Air, my nourishment, and the Tongue's Pivot, and Sensibility, and Keen-smelling Nostrils" (892–93), a charge, in effect, of atheism. He claims to have eschewed the deceitful grandeur of Aeschylus, putting tragedy on a reducing diet and making it speak plainly (937–47). This certainly touches on an important aspect of Euripides' style, the comparative absence, in its dialogue portions, of the poetic ornament characteristic, in their separate ways, of Aeschylus and Sophocles. He claims that he gave women, slaves, girls, and crones speaking parts, this being more democratic, and taught them all to babble (948–52). Part of this corresponds with the plays we have: Euripidean tragedy "babbles" in that it is more discursive and argumentative than Aeschylean or Sophoclean tragedy. Women or slaves with speaking roles, however, were certainly not his invention. Euripides also claims to have introduced the things of ordinary daily life into his plays in preference to the imaginary and heroic, with the result that the Athenians became much sharper and more alert about their household affairs (959–63, 971–79). This is reminiscent of the First Woman's complaint in *Thesm.* 395ff that thanks to Euripides men are now too nosy about the household, but Euripidean tragedy, as far as our evidence goes, is not homelier than that of Aeschylus.[58]

Aeschylus criticizes him for putting bad women, "whores like Phaedra and Sthenoboea," on the stage in violation of the principle that "the poet ought to conceal what is wicked and not bring it on or produce (lit. teach) it" (1053–54). Adulterous women, of course, had been brought on by Aeschylus and, at least in the case of Clytaemestra, given scope to defend themselves. Euripides is not allowed to point out the inconsistency between Aeschylus' principles and his practice. Instead, the discussion is made to shift to the topic of Aeschylus' elevated tragic language. Aeschylus says this is appropriate for heroes, since they also wear more august clothing. He proceeds to tax Euripides with putting his heroes on in rags. When Euripides asks him what is wrong with characters in rags, he replies that now the rich adopt the ploy of wearing rags to get out of performing trierarchies, one of

[58] See above, n. 57.

the expensive "liturgies" imposed on the wealthy. Euripides' talkativeness is responsible, he says, for emptying the gymnasia and for causing a rash of insubordination among the ranks in the navy.

The rest of the contest consists of captious or silly criticisms of each other's prologues, parodies of each other's lyric style (Aeschylus' turgid and unintelligible, Euripides' flighty and prettified), and other such comic business. Then Dionysus announces that he will take back with him to the Upper World the poet who gives the best advice, and the two take turns assessing Alcibiades and the Athenian situation in general. (Neither is clearly the winner here.) When Euripides reminds Dionysus that he had sworn to take him back with him (the oath is here invented for the sake of the comic line to follow), Dionysus replies that it was his tongue alone that swore and pronounces in favor of Aeschylus.

It is often alleged that Aristophanes saw in Euripides a threat to the tragic art and to the moral tone of society in general, and that he saw Aeschylus and other poets of his generation as the only effective antidote. But it is by no means certain that the *Frogs* is to be read in so earnest a fashion, and much suggests that the audience would have known that in portraying this contest of opposites Aristophanes was not bound, even in the most general way, by the truth.

To sum up, the Euripides of Aristophanes is a man with the following characteristics: (1) prosaic, talky, and arid in his dialogue, his style being that either of the courtroom pleader or of the philosopher;[59] (2) fond of putting on the

[59] For the courtroom pleader, see *Peace* 528–34 [= T 74]. For

stage characters who are lame and dressed in rags; (3) determined to make tragedy less elevated by introducing common and ordinary people and things, humble objects usually banished from tragedy, and slaves with speaking parts; (4) decadent and modernist in his lyrics, with a pronounced tendency toward metrical innovation and the predominance of musical over verbal considerations;[60] (5) a hater of women, who enjoys portraying heroines of dubious principle in order to discredit their sex; (6) an underminer of received morality, who portrays shocking or immoral actions (incest, adultery, perjury) in a favorable light and whose natural admirers are the immoralist Sophists and the criminal classes; and (7) unorthodox in his religious views, believing in new-fangled divinities and not the traditional gods of the city.

On certain points, principally stylistic, this characterization, allowances being made for comic exaggeration, is an accurate one, and it is likely that Euripides' contemporaries perceived truth in it. Thus verbal dexterity and argumentativeness, tending toward dry and intellectual rhetoric, is arguably a feature of Euripidean tragedy, and we may be sure that this characteristic was not lost on his first audience. Euripides' lyrics—especially those of the last decade of his life—may well have struck contemporaries, like the lyrics of Timotheus, as disagreeably novel in their musical and metrical treatment. The com-

---

Euripides as Socratic, see also *Frogs* 1491–95 [= T 77] and Diogenes Laertius 2.18 [= T 17, Teleclides frr. 41–42, Callias fr. 15, Aristophanes fr. 392 K.-A.].

[60] See *Frogs* 1309–63.

mon and everyday make their appearance in *Electra* and
may well have appeared elsewhere. Here, however, a
strong contrast with other tragic poets can be made only
by pretending that Aeschylus and Sophocles are grander
and more sublime, further removed from ordinary life,
than they in fact are.

When we come to the other traits, however, there is
room for serious doubt about how Euripides was per-
ceived. Immoralism, atheism, and misogyny are charges
several times repeated yet ones that cannot be substanti-
ated—and are often convincingly contradicted—from
non-comic sources or the plays themselves, while the plays
contain just enough to make these charges comically
colorable. On the question whether anyone in the audi-
ence really viewed Euripides in those terms agnosticism is
the best verdict our evidence allows.

Fourth-Century Judgments of Euripides' Art

The fourth century, the age of the orator, supplies prose
evidence of a kind entirely lacking for the fifth century,
evidence strongly suggesting that Old Comedy's presenta-
tion of Euripides as morally and artistically shocking was
not accepted as truth by the populace at large. The orators
provide the most valuable evidence of acceptable senti-
ment, for an Athenian orator, addressing a large popular
jury or assembly, takes pains to avoid saying things that his
fellow citizens would regard as unorthodox or idiosyn-
cratic.[61] In light of this, it is significant that three different
orators, Aeschines, Demosthenes, and Lycurgus, quote

---

[61] On this point, see K. J. Dover, *Greek Popular Morality in
the Time of Plato and Aristotle* (Oxford, 1974), pp. 5–14.

him with approval, together with other poets, for moral principles on which they expect their audience to act.[62] Lycurgus even goes out of his way to praise Euripides' poetry in *general* as a moral exemplar. These orators quote Euripides in the same contexts and for the same purposes as they cite Homer, Solon, or Sophocles. It is noteworthy that no orator cites wisdom from anyone tainted with philosophy: no utterance of Socrates, Anaxagoras, or Protagoras is ever held up for approval. It was this same Lycurgus who arranged for a public copy to be made of the works of Aeschylus, Sophocles, and Euripides, further indication that Euripides' presence in this company was not regarded as anomalous.[63]

A similar story is suggested by the two references in Plato. The *Republic* shows Plato to be hostile to traditional poetry, both epic and tragedy, but one might have expected him to make an exception in the case of a poet of Socratic sympathies, as Old Comedy alleges Euripides to be. Instead, one reference (*Phaedrus* 268 C) couples him with Sophocles while the second (*Republic* 568 A) makes him the particularly egregious representative of errors common to the tragic poets in general.

Fragments of fourth-century comedy attest admiration for Euripides, though they are too general to show the reason for the admiration.[64] Much more interesting than the explicit praise is Menander, *Aspis* 399–428, where Daos,

---

[62] Aeschines 1.128 and 151–52 (quoting *Phoenix* and *Sthenoboea*), Demosthenes 19.246, and Lycurgus 100–101.

[63] See pseudo-Plutarch, *Vitae Decem Oratorum* 841F [= T 83].

[64] See Philemon, fr. 118 K.-A. [= T 1.31] and Axionicus, quoted in Athenaeus 4.76, 175B [= T 81].

soliloquizing for Smicrines' benefit on his master's supposed death, quotes one tragedian after another on the instability of human life, citing in swift succession lines from Euripides, Chaeremon, Aeschylus, anonymous, Carcinus, Euripides, and Chaeremon. This same common tragic theme is regarded, apparently, as characteristic of Euripides by Nicostratus (fr. 28 K.-A.) and Philippides (fr. 18 K.-A.).

Aristotle is also an important witness. As every reader of the *Poetics* knows, his favorite tragic poet was Sophocles. What is equally apparent is who his second-favorite was. Although he criticizes Euripides for bad management of his plot, irrelevant choruses, inept use of irrational events, and ending his plays by external contrivance,[65] he cites him again and again as a model for dramatists to follow.[66] Aeschylus is rarely cited for this purpose,[67] and the conclusion emerges that the *Poetics* is founded largely upon the dramatic practice of Sophocles and Euripides, supplemented by a handful of later figures.[68] In a contest between the two, Sophocles would be the winner, but Euripides would not be far behind. To judge from his recommendations, Aristotle did not share the view of Aristophanes' Aeschylus, who charges that Euripides denatured the tragic art by talky rhetoric, by low realism

[65] 1453 a 22–30, 1456 a 25–30, 1461 b 19–21, 1454 a 37–b 2 [= T 82].

[66] 1452 b 3–8, 1453 b 28, 1454 a 5, 1454 a 8, 1454 b 31, 1455 a 18, 1455 b 14, 1456 a 17, 1458 b 20.

[67] 1455 a 4, 1456 a 2, 1456 a 17.

[68] Theodectes (1452 a 27, 1455 a 9, 1455 b 29), Astydamas (1453 b 33), Agathon (1451 b 21, 1454 b 14), Dicaeogenes (1455 a 1), Polyidus (1455 a 6).

inconsistent with tragic decorum, and by making the gods and moral standards into a constant problem. We must conclude either that his recommendation of Euripides was a concession to the taste of the fourth century, a taste that seemed to enjoy the pathetic and the exciting in Euripidean tragedy; or that he really thought that Euripides and Sophocles had a great deal more in common than many modern scholars, taking their cue from Aristophanic comedy, have allowed. Our evidence does not permit us to eliminate either possibility.[69]

Euripidean criticism has in general relied heavily on the biographical tradition and on Aristophanes to find a fixed point from which to work. A recent and by no means atypical book on Euripides, for example, begins its discussion with the assumption that Euripidean drama is to be understood as the deliberate affronting of Sophoclean norms and proceeds to talk about "the tactics of shock."[70]

[69] The history of the reception of Euripides in later antiquity would require a book to itself. For particular points see W. Elsperger, "Reste und Spuren antiker Kritik gegen Euripides," *Philologus* Suppl. 11 (1907–10), 1–176; L. E. Lord, *The Literary Criticism of Euripides in the Earlier Scholia and the Relation of This Criticism to Aristotle's Poetics and to Aristophanes*, diss. Yale (Göttingen, 1908); H. Funke, "Euripides," *Jahrbücher für Antike und Christentum* 8/9 (1965/6), 233–79; H. Kuch, "Zur Euripides-Rezeption im Hellenismus," *Klio* 60 (1978), 191–202. See also Crantor, quoted in Diogenes Laertius 4.26 [= T 84], Plutarch, *De recta ratione audiendi* 45B [= T 85], pseudo-Longinus, *De sublimitate* 15.3 and 40.2–3 [= T 86], Quintilian 10.1.67–69 [= T 87], Dio of Prusa 35.15 [= T 88(b)], Archimedes, *Anthol. Pal.* 7.50 [= T 89], and Lucian 59.1 [= T 93].

[70] A. N. Michelini, *Euripides and the Tragic Tradition* (Madison, 1987).

The assumption is that Euripides shocked his contemporaries and that it was his intention to do so. In sharp contrast is the judgment of another scholar, that Euripides "remains, in most of his work, a poet of the traditional tragic genre, a genre which carries on the pessimistic emphasis on man's limits and frailties which characterizes much of archaic Greek literature and myth."[71] The assessment of these views and the spectrum of views between them can best be carried out on the basis of the plays themselves, considered against the background of Greek literature and society from Homer to Euripides' day.

Editorial Principles

All the medieval manuscripts and ancient papyrus fragments of the plays of Euripides are ultimately descended from the *Collected Works of Euripides* edited by the scholars of Alexandria ca. 200 B.C. These scholars searched out copies of all of Euripides' plays they could find (some plays did not survive to the age of Alexandrian scholarship) and prepared a critical edition, noting variant readings and the absence of certain verses from some copies. They also wrote commentaries on at least a few of the plays. The edition contained seventy-eight of the ninety-two plays ascribed to Euripides.

The Alexandrian edition was in wide circulation for several centuries, and writers up to the middle of the third century A.D. are able to quote numerous plays now lost to

[71] D. J. Mastronarde, "The Optimistic Rationalist in Euripides: Theseus, Jocasta, Teiresias," in M. Cropp et al., edd., *Greek Tragedy and Its Legacy* (Calgary, 1986), p. 207.

us. From around A.D. 250, however, quotation is chiefly from ten plays, *Hecuba, Orestes, Phoenician Women, Hippolytus, Medea, Andromache, Alcestis, Rhesus, Trojan Women*, and *Bacchae*. These ten plays, which may represent a selection, for school purposes, of plays provided with commentary, form the main tradition and are referred to as the "select" plays. These are transmitted in a number of medieval manuscripts and have scholia, or explanatory notes, in the margins. The remaining nine plays, *Helen, Electra, Children of Heracles, Heracles, Suppliant Women, Iphigenia in Aulis, Iphigenia among the Taurians, Ion*, and *Cyclops*, survive in a single manuscript, now in the Laurentian library in Florence, which preserves plays beginning with the Greek letters epsilon, eta, iota, and kappa once forming one or two codex volumes of the *Collected Works* that somehow survived to the Middle Ages. These are called the "alphabetical" plays. Apart from the occasional explanatory gloss, they have no scholia.

The present text is my own. I have not thought it necessary to collate the manuscripts again but have relied on the collations of earlier editors. My text owes a great deal to the Oxford text of James Diggle. Diggle has made substantial improvements, sometimes by adopting neglected emendations, sometimes by proposing his own, and sometimes by defending the reading of the manuscripts against attack. If I have sometimes adopted different solutions to the problems he has raised, I record my gratitude to his edition for raising them.

The editor of a Loeb text may reasonably set different goals from those of the editor of an Oxford Classical Text. I have striven to produce a text that is continuously readable, even in places where we cannot be absolutely certain of the precise wording. This means, for example, that where the context supplied enough clues to grasp the meaning of a line accidentally omitted, I have printed a supplement and translated it. (Unattributed supplements are my own.) Like other words supplied by editors, these are printed in angle brackets, but readers should note that these are to be regarded as purely illustrative. I have also made much less frequent use of the obelus, the dagger editors use to signal that, while something is clearly wrong, the author's original wording cannot be recovered with certainty. Where something plausible in sense and style was available, I have not hesitated to print it. I have discussed in a separate volume, entitled *Euripidea*, those places in *Cyclops, Alcestis,* and *Medea* where I felt the text I adopted was in need of explanation.[72] This need is particularly acute in the handful of cases where I have printed conjectures of my own not hitherto discussed in print. This I have done only when I was certain that the text was corrupt and that none of the earlier conjectures known to me was satisfactory.

The notes to the Greek pages are not intended to be an apparatus criticus. To cite all the variants and the manuscripts in which they occur would have taken far too much space, and for this information the reader is referred to Diggle's edition. Where the text rests upon the reading of one or more manuscripts, I do not usually mention other variants. In other words, these notes primarily list conjectures adopted. I have not included all of these, and where a change is very slight I have passed it

[72] See above, n. 1.

over in silence. But I include quite a few of those universally accepted by editors as a reminder that a robust faith in the reliability of manuscripts and a corresponding horror of conjecture are irrational attitudes. If conjecture were eliminated, these plays over long stretches would hover tantalizingly on the edge of intelligibility or be simply unreadable.

In order to present the essentials, I have simplified. Except for the alphabetic plays, where I cite the Laurentianus (L) and Demetrius Triclinius' corrections of it (Tr), I rarely cite individual manuscripts by their sigla. (Diggle's list of sigla at the head of each play should be consulted for these exceptional cases.) Instead, if there are variants for a word or phrase, I label the source of the first a, of the second b, etc., whether the source is one or more than one manuscript. For the united witness of all codices I use the siglum C. For citations by other authors I use t or tt (for *testimonium, -a*). For papyrus fragments and scholia I use Π and Σ respectively. (Readers should consult Diggle for further information on the papyri and the manuscript sources of the scholia.) Square brackets enclose words or lines thought to be later additions. Angle brackets mark places where letters, words, or whole lines seem to have been accidentally omitted.

The Fifth-Century Stage

It is important when reading a play to visualize its staging, as even such obvious and commonplace things as entrances and exits and their timing make an important contribution to the meaning and the effect the author intended his audience to receive.[73] We possess virtually no ancient stage directions, but scholars are in agreement that the Greek tragic poets, particularly after Aeschylus, "doubled" all the important visual cues by references or allusions to them in the words spoken by actors and Chorus. The following description, in conjunction with some photographs of ancient theaters, should help the reader to imagine the setting for the action of the text.

The action is played out before a *skene*, or stage building, usually representing the front of a house or palace. In front of this is a low stage,[74] and in front of this a circular area, tangential to the stage, called the *orchestra*, where the Chorus sing and dance. The acting area, comprising stage and orchestra, allowed three points of entry, from the *skene*, and by two entrance ramps, or *eisodoi*,[75] leading from right and left into the orchestra. In later dramatic practice, the right *eisodos* represented by convention the entrance from the country or harbor and the left *eisodos* the entrance from the city.[76] We have no evidence for the fifth century of such a convention. Rather, each play establishes its own imagined destinations for the two *eis-*

---

[73] On "visual meaning" in tragedy, see W. Steidle, *Studien zum antiken Drama* (Munich, 1968) and two books of O. Taplin, *The Stagecraft of Aeschylus* (Oxford, 1977) and *Greek Tragedy in Action* (Berkeley and Los Angeles, 1978).

[74] It is not certain that the stage was elevated over the level of the *orchestra*, though scholarly opinion seems at present more inclined in that direction.

[75] I follow Taplin, *Stagecraft*, pp. 449–51, in adopting the fifth-century term *eisodos* (*Clouds* 326, *Birds* 296) for these ramps in preference to the later term *parodos*.

[76] See Pollux 4.126–7.

odoi and uses them in a schematically consistent way, so that if a character leaves by an *eisodos*, his subsequent return will be by this same *eisodos*. In the stage directions, I call the ramps Eisodos A and Eisodos B since we cannot be sure whether the right or the left one is being used. I have marked stage directions where these are a reasonable inference from the text. The most important, of course, are entrances and exits. In cases where the choice between the *eisodoi* involves some guesswork, I have indicated doubts.

Two other features of the tragic stage, the *eccyclema* and the *mechane*, must be mentioned among the resources of the tragic poet. The *eccyclema* was a wheeled platform on which a tableau of actors could be grouped and wheeled out of the central doors of the *skene*. This seems to have been used to provide the possibility of an indoor scene in a theater which normally allowed action to take place only before the palace door. By convention the actors on the *eccyclema* are indoors (Clytaemestra, wheeled out with the corpse of Agamemnon in the bath, says "I stand where I struck him"), but the Chorus and other actors are conceived of as still outdoors, a double perspective. The *mechane* was a crane on which a god (or occasionally a mortal) could make a flying entrance or exit. The *deus ex machina*, the god or goddess who characteristically brings the action of Euripides' plays to an end, enters on this crane. Sometimes the arriving figure is winged, at others the mechane is made to represent a flying chariot. Both the roof of the *skene* and the stage could serve as the place where winged entrants could alight. The roof could also be entered from below by a stairway behind the *skene*. The roof is sometimes called the *theologeion*.[77]

The Translation

Euripides is the most argumentative of the tragic poets. His language in the dialogue passages, while recognizably different in its vocabulary and expression from prose, is comparatively bare of ornament. The lyric passages too are often rhetorical. This translation aims to bring out as clearly as possible the argument, the reasoning, of Euripidean speeches and songs, the case or brief they try to present. I have translated into prose, as literally as respect for English idiom allowed. In a few passages of *stichomythia* (line-for-line interchange), where tautness in the thrust and parry seemed particularly desirable, I have allowed myself a few lines of blank verse.

Greek tragedy had a large musical element, now lost to us. The choral odes were sung to music, accompanied by an instrumentalist playing the *auloi*, a pair of pipes with a reed mouthpiece. When the Chorus sings, their words are in lyric meter, and the language acquires a tinge of the Doric dialect. The same features, lyric meter and Doricism, mark solo song, passages sung by actors. The actors—in contrast to the Chorus—normally speak, and sung delivery almost always indicates some extraordinary state of mind, such as madness, intense grief or joy, or awareness of imminent death. All passages delivered by named characters are spoken unless specified as sung. Passages assigned to the Chorus are always sung, those assigned to the Chorus Leader always spoken.

[77] See. D. Mastronarde, "Actors on High," *CA* 9 (1990), 247–94.

SELECT BIBLIOGRAPHY

The literature on Euripides and on Greek tragedy is enormous and grows yearly. The following are standard works the present editor has found useful.

I. Complete editions of Euripides

J. Diggle, Oxford Classical Texts, 3 vols. (Oxford, 1984, 1981, 1994).

L. Méridier and others, Collection Budé (Paris, 1923–). Greek text and facing French translation of all the plays except *Rhesus*.

R. Prinz and N. Wecklein, Bibliotheca Teubneriana, 3 vols. (Leipzig, 1878–1902). Contains for each play an invaluable appendix of earlier conjectures.

II. Euripidean fragments

C. Austin, *Nova Fragmenta Euripidea in Papyris Reperta* (Berlin, 1967).

R. Kannicht, *Tragicorum Graecorum Fragmenta*, vol. 5 (Göttingen, forthcoming).

A. Nauck, *Tragicorum Graecorum Fragmenta*, 2nd ed. with a supplement by B. Snell (Hildesheim, 1964).

SELECT BIBLIOGRAPHY

D. L. Page, *Greek Literary Papyri*, Loeb Classical Library (London, 1942).

III. Scholia

E. Schwartz, *Scholia in Euripidem*, 2 vols. (Berlin, 1887–91).

IV. Commentaries

A. and J. M. Duncan, *Euripidis Opera Omnia*, 9 vols. (Glasgow, 1821). Contains a facing Latin translation and Latin commentary excerpting earlier commentaries.

F. A. Paley, *Euripides with an English Commentary*, 3 vols. (London, 1857–89).

V. Translations

D. Grene and R. Lattimore, eds., *The Complete Greek Tragedies: Euripides*, 2 vols. (Chicago, 1958–9).

U. von Wilamowitz-Moellendorff, *Griechische Tragoedien Übersetzt*, 4 vols. (Berlin, 1899–1923). Vols. 1, 3, and 4 contain *Hippolytus, Suppliant Women, Heracles, Cyclops, Alcestis, Medea, Trojan Women* and *Bacchae* in a German verse translation with notes on the Greek text.

VI. Concordances

J. T. Allen and G. Italie, *Concordance to Euripides* (Berkeley and London, 1954; rpt. Groningen, 1971).

C. Collard, *Supplement to the Allen & Italie Concordance to Euripides* (Groningen, 1971).

VII. General works on Greek tragedy and Euripides

P. Burian, ed., *Directions in Euripidean Criticism* (Durham, N.C., 1985).

A. P. Burnett, *Catastrophe Survived: Euripides' Plays of Mixed Reversal* (Oxford, 1971).

D. J. Conacher, *Euripidean Drama: Myth, Theme and Structure* (Toronto, 1967).

M. Cropp and others, edd., *Greek Tragedy and Its Legacy: Essays Presented to D. J. Conacher* (Calgary, 1986).

P. E. Easterling and B. M. W. Knox, edd., *Cambridge History of Classical Literature*, vol. I (Cambridge, 1985). Contains chapters on the individual playwrights.

Entretiens sur l'Antiquité Classique, VI: Euripide (Vandoeuvres and Geneva, 1960). Seven papers followed by discussion.

G. M. Grube, *The Drama of Euripides* (London, 1961).

J. Jones, *On Aristotle and Greek Tragedy* (London, 1962). Contains a fundamental discussion of personality in Greek tragedy.

H. D. F. Kitto, *Greek Tragedy: a Literary Study*, 3rd ed. (London, 1961).

B. M. W. Knox, *Word and Action* (Baltimore, 1979). Collected papers on drama.

W. Kranz, *Stasimon* (Berlin, 1933).

A. Lesky, *Greek Tragic Poetry*, tr. M. Dillon (New Haven, 1983). A translation of *Die tragische Dichtung der Hellenen*, 3rd ed. (Göttingen, 1972), containing discussions of all the plays and full bibliography.

G. Murray, *Euripides and His Age*, 2nd ed. (London, 1946).

M. Pohlenz, *Die griechische Tragödie*, 2nd ed., 2 vols. (Göttingen, 1954).

K. Reinhardt, "Die Sinneskrise bei Euripides," in *Tradition und Geist* (Göttingen, 1960), 223–56.

A. Rivier, *Essai sur le tragique d'Euripide*, 2nd ed. (Paris, 1975).

E. Segal, ed., *Oxford Essays in Greek Tragedy* (Oxford, 1984). Also printed as *Greek Tragedy: Modern Essays in Criticism* (New York, 1983).

B. Seidensticker, *Palintonos Harmonia: Studien zu komischen Elementen in der griechischen Tragödie* (Göttingen, 1982).

T. C. W. Stinton, *Collected Papers on Greek Tragedy* (Oxford, 1990).

T. B. L. Webster, *The Tragedies of Euripides* (London, 1967).

G. Zuntz, *The Political Plays of Euripides* (Manchester, 1963).

VIII. Theater and production

P. D. Arnott, *Greek Scenic Conventions in the Fifth Century B.C.* (Oxford, 1962).

M. Bieber, *The History of the Greek and Roman Theatre* (Princeton, 1961).

A. W. Pickard-Cambridge, *The Theatre of Dionysus in Athens* (Oxford, 1946).

—— *The Dramatic Festivals of Athens*, revised 2nd ed. with a supplement and corrections by J. Gould and D. M. Lewis (Oxford, 1988).

E. Simon, *The Ancient Theatre*, tr. by C. E. Vafopoulo-Richardson (London, 1982).

T. B. L. Webster, *Greek Theatre Production* (London, 1970).

IX. Theatrical technique

D. Bain, *Actors and Audience: A Study of Asides and Related Conventions in Greek Drama* (Oxford, 1977).

—— *Masters, Servants, and Orders in Greek Tragedy: Some Aspects of Dramatic Technique and Convention* (Manchester, 1981).

H. Erbse, *Studien zum Prolog der euripideischen Tragödie* (Berlin, 1984).

M. R. Halleran, *Stagecraft in Euripides* (London, 1985).

W. Jens, ed., *Die Bauformen der griechischen Tragödie* (Munich, 1971).

D. J. Mastronarde, *Contact and Discontinuity: Some Conventions of Speech and Action on the Greek Tragic Stage* (Berkeley, 1979).

E. R. Schwinge, *Die Verwendung der Stichomythie in den Dramen des Euripides* (Heidelberg, 1968).

W. Steidle, *Studien zum antiken Drama unter besonderer Berücksichtigung des Bühnenspiels* (Munich, 1968).

H. Strohm, *Euripides: Interpretationen zur dramatischen Form* (Munich, 1957).

O. Taplin, *The Stagecraft of Aeschylus* (Oxford, 1977).

—— *Greek Tragedy in Action* (London, 1978).

X. Meter

A. M. Dale, *The Lyric Metres of Greek Drama*, 2nd ed. (Cambridge, 1968).

SELECT BIBLIOGRAPHY

———— *Metrical Analyses of Tragic Choruses*, *BICS* Supplement 21.1 (1971), 21.2 (1981), and 21.3 (1983).

D. S. Raven, *Greek Metre* (London, 1962).

M. L. West, *Greek Metre* (Oxford, 1982).

———— *Introduction to Greek Metre* (Oxford, 1987).

XI. Textual transmission and text-critical studies

W. S. Barrett, *Euripides: Hippolytos* (Oxford, 1964) 45–90.

V. Di Benedetto, *La Tradizione manoscritta Euripidea* (Padua, 1965).

J. Jackson, *Marginalia Scaenica* (Oxford, 1955).

A. Turyn, *The Byzantine Manuscript Tradition of the Plays of Euripides* (Urbana, 1957).

G. Zuntz, *An Inquiry into the Transmission of the Plays of Euripides* (Cambridge, 1965).

XII. Bibliographical aids

L'Année Philologique (Paris, 1924–). Yearly survey of work in classical studies.

ABBREVIATIONS

AJP	*American Journal of Philology*
BICS	*Bulletin of the Institute of Classical Studies,* London
BSA	*British School at Athens*
CA	*Classical Antiquity*
CP	*Classical Philology*
CQ	*Classical Quarterly*
FGrH	*Die Fragmente der griechischen Historiker,* ed. F. Jacoby
GRBS	*Greek, Roman and Byzantine Studies*
JHS	*Journal of Hellenic Studies*
PMG	*Poetae Melici Graeci,* ed. D. L. Page
RE	*Real-Encyklopädie der classischen Altertumswissenschaft,* ed. A. Pauly, G. Wissowa, and W. Kroll
SIFC	*Studi Italiani di Filologia Classica*
TAPA	*Transactions of the American Philological Association*
WS	*Wiener Studien*
YCS	*Yale Classical Studies*
ZPE	*Zeitschrift für Papyrologie und Epigraphik*

CYCLOPS

INTRODUCTION

The date of *Cyclops* is unknown. Metrical considerations and other arguments of varying weight, discussed by R. Seaford in *Journal of Hellenic Studies* 102 (1982), 161–72, make it likely that the play belongs near the end of Euripides' career. Since Murray's edition, however, it has been traditional to put it before the tragedies.

Cyclops is the only complete surviving example of the genre satyr play. Like a comedy, the satyr play is funny, and it admits some of the indecency characteristic of Old Comedy. But like a tragedy, the satyr play has a plot based on myth, sometimes divine, sometimes heroic. The poet contrives for the presence of satyrs, often in captivity, at the place where his mythic characters perform their actions. The satyrs, divine creatures of hedonistic and cowardly nature, supply much of the humor. A play of this mythical but burlesque sort was the normal fourth play of a tragic tetralogy. (A good discussion of the genre may be found in the Introduction to Seaford's edition of *Cyclops*, Oxford, 1984.)

Cyclops is based closely on one of the most famous episodes of the *Odyssey*, Odysseus' encounter with the one-eyed giant Polyphemus. (Euripides was not the first to write a satyr play on this theme: a *Cyclops* is attributed to the early fifth-century poet Aristias.) It will come as a surprise to those who think of Homer as (comparatively) simple and Euripides as complex and sophisticated that

Euripides has simplified the complex themes and characterization of Homer to make his play. Some of his alterations in the story can be traced to the exigencies of putting it on the stage. Other changes bring out parallels with fifth-century intellectual currents. It is arresting that this much simplified story, with its clear lines of right and wrong and its transparent application to the immoralist philosophy of certain Sophists of the poet's own day, seemed interesting enough to Euripides to present at the City Dionysia.

In Homer, the main action of the play, from Odysseus' first encounter with the Cyclops until the escape of his men under the bellies of the sheep, takes place in Polyphemus' cave. In ancient drama all action (with the partial exception of scenes on the *eccyclema*) takes place out-of-doors. Odysseus' conversations with Polyphemus must take place for the most part in front of the cave, he must be able to come out to report the Cylops' feasting on his companions, and therefore there can be no great stone blocking the entrance to the cave, a prop that would have been awkward to contrive in any case. This entails one further change: in Homer, the blinding of Polyphemus was forced on Odysseus by the situation, for if he killed the monster in his sleep, he and his men would be unable to move the stone and escape. In Euripides, there is nothing to prevent Odysseus and his men from leaving once they have made Polyphemus drunk. Helping the satyrs and Silenus to escape is one reason Odysseus gives for his plan when he comes out and involves the Chorus in it, but he mentions as his first consideration "punishment for the knavish beast" (441–2). Likewise there is in theory no reason they could not kill him. It may be a part of Euripides' strategy to suggest intermittently (231, 321—but cf. contra 444, 448) that the Cyclops is immortal and can only be maimed, not killed. A further change is that the cave is imagined to have a back entrance (707), so that the Cyclops can hurl his boulders at the ships from an imagined offstage place.

Other changes are unrelated to the new medium. In Homer Odysseus' motive for seeking out the Cyclopes is curiosity and a desire for guest-gifts, and no one reading the epic can help feeling that there was something culpably rash in the whole adventure. In Euripides, Odysseus and his men approach the cave of Polyphemus because they are in need of food and water, they engage in good-faith barter with Silenus, and then are accused unfairly of stealing what they have offered to pay for. Sympathy for Odysseus is therefore strengthened, and there is no admixture of blame. The treatment of the villain is also different. Homer's Polyphemus is ogre-ish and nasty, but he is so clearly of a different world from the Greeks, so clearly a primitive creature, that it is difficult to view him consistently as one would a bad *man*, one to whom the same standards apply as to ourselves. And Homer gives him a moment of pathos when in his blindness he speaks tenderly to his favorite ram. By contrast, Euripides' Polyphemus, while primitive in some respects, is fastidious about his food, an owner of slaves, a careful manager of his household, and a sophistical arguer who can articulately *justify* his immoral behavior. Where Homer's Polyphemus neither knows nor cares about the Trojan War, in Euripides he has heard all about it and has an opinion about it. He clearly inhabits the same moral world as the Greeks but has chosen to reject a morality he knows perfectly well. When he is finally blinded, no pathos is allowed to obscure the perfect justice of the punishment.

The intellectual position Polyphemus stakes out for himself is obviously meant to call to mind analogues in the fifth century. Like certain of the Sophists, represented most fully in the Callicles of Plato's *Gorgias*, the Cyclops has "seen through" traditional morality, and he regards law as an invention of man that needlessly complicates life. (Callicles argues that the laws are the way the majority of weak men control the few whom nature has made strong. But the few ought not to heed these restraints, for nature is superior to law.) In Polyphemus' view, "the wise" make wealth their god and pay no attention to Zeus. Zeus's functions in the ordering of the world are replaced by Necessity. Polyphemus is thus portrayed as one of the aristocratic nurslings of the Sophists, contemptuous of religion and determined to throw off the yoke of conventional morality, convinced that his own view of the world is correct and that no superhuman power stands in his way. By a curious paradox appropriate to a satyr play, the one god he recognizes, Dionysus, proves to be his undoing. Zeus is implicitly involved as well.

In Homer, Odysseus' companions raise their hands in prayer to Zeus in their hour of danger, and Odysseus ponders "in the hope that I might take vengeance on him and Athena might grant me that boast." Odysseus also says that in the attack "a divinity breathed upon them great courage." And at the end he says to Polyphemus, "Therefore Zeus and the other gods have punished you." Euripides has emphasized even further the role of the gods in the punishment of the Cyclops. Polyphemus and his deeds are called "godless" throughout (26, 31, 289,

311, 348, 396, 438, 602, 693). Odysseus' appeal to the Cyclops lays stress upon the claims of piety and custom, and he alludes to the punishment of those who follow after base gain. Polyphemus' reply rejects piety explicitly. Odysseus prays repeatedly to Zeus, Athena, and other gods (350–2, 353–5, 599–600, 601–6) for vengeance on the Cyclops. In 411 the plan of making the Cyclops drunk is explicitly called an idea "divinely inspired." Finally, at the end of the play Odysseus says, "You were destined, it seems, to pay the penalty for your ungodly feast," and Polyphemus recounts an oracle showing that his punishment was predestined.

This simplicity of theme and characterization is perhaps one of the reasons the play has found few admirers. But in its general outlook it has points of contact with one of Euripides' undoubted masterpieces, *Bacchae*, which is—at least ostensibly—about the punishment of a disbeliever and the vindication of the piety and wisdom practiced by "the multitude of the ordinary" (*Bacchae* 430). (Other parallels with *Bacchae* are noted in Seaford's edition, pp. 57–9.) *Cyclops* is only intermittently funny, and it may be, as Seaford thinks, that it is untypical of the genre in its formal closeness to tragedy. The surviving fragments of other satyr plays suggest that they were both more boisterous and funnier. Perhaps the genre was exhausted by the late fifth century. Or perhaps Euripides' emphasis on more serious philosophical and religious themes obscured the levity inherent in the genre.

SELECT BIBLIOGRAPHY

Satyr play

N. C. Hourmouziades, *Satyrika* (Athens, 1974).

D. F. Sutton, *The Greek Satyr Play* (Meisenheim am Glan, 1980).

B. Seidensticker, *Satyrspiel*, Wege der Forschung 579 (Darmstadt, 1989).

Editions of Cyclops

J. Duchemin (Paris, 1945).

R. G. Ussher (Rome, 1978).

W. Biehl (Leipzig, 1983).

R. Seaford (Oxford, 1984).

Literary criticism

W. G. Arnott, "Parody and Ambiguity in Euripides' *Cyclops*," in *Antidosis: Festschrift für Walter Kraus zum 70. Geburtstag* (Vienna, 1972).

W. Wetzel, *De Euripidis fabula satyrica quae Cyclops inscribitur, cum Homerico comparata exemplo* (Wiesbaden, 1965).

D. Konstan, "An Anthropology of Euripides' *Cyclops*, *Ramus* 10 (1981), 87–103.

Dramatis Personae

ΣΙΛΗΝΟΣ	SILENUS, the father of the satyrs who make up the Chorus
ΧΟΡΟΣ	CHORUS of satyrs captured by the Cyclops
ΟΔΥΣΣΕΥΣ	ODYSSEUS
ΚΥΚΛΩΨ	The CYCLOPS, Polyphemus

A Note on Staging

The *skene* represents the cave of Polyphemus. Eisodos A is the entrance that is imagined to lead to the mountains, Eisodos B that leading to the sea. At the end of the play the cave is imagined to have a back entrance overlooking the sea.

ΚΥΚΛΩΨ

ΣΙΛΗΝΟΣ

Ὦ Βρόμιε, διὰ σὲ μυρίους ἔχω πόνους
νῦν χὥτ' ἐν ἥβῃ τοὐμὸν εὐσθένει δέμας·
πρῶτον μὲν ἡνίκ' ἐμμανὴς Ἥρας ὕπο
Νύμφας ὀρείας ἐκλιπὼν ᾤχου τροφούς·
5 ἔπειθ' ὅτ' ἀμφὶ γηγενῆ μάχην δορὸς
ἐνδέξιος σῷ ποδὶ παρασπιστὴς βεβὼς
Ἐγκέλαδον ἰτέαν ἐς μέσην θενὼν δορὶ
ἔκτεινα — φέρ' ἴδω, τοῦτ' ἰδὼν ὄναρ λέγω;
οὐ μὰ Δί', ἐπεὶ καὶ σκῦλ' ἔδειξα Βακχίῳ.
10 καὶ νῦν ἐκείνων μείζον' ἐξαντλῶ πόνον.
ἐπεὶ γὰρ Ἥρα σοι γένος Τυρσηνικὸν
λῃστῶν ἐπῶρσεν, ὡς ὁδηθείης μακράν,
<ἐγὼ> πυθόμενος σὺν τέκνοισι ναυστολῶ

5 ἔπειθ' ὅτ' Hermann: ἔπειτά γ' L
6 βεβὼς Kassel: γεγὼς L
13 <ἐγὼ> Tr

---

[a] Dionysus was driven mad by Hera (Apollodorus 3.5.1),

CYCLOPS

Enter from Polyphemus' cave SILENUS *with a rake in his hand.*

SILENUS

(apostrophizing the absent Dionysus) O Bromius, labors numberless have I had because of you, now and when I was young and able-bodied! First, when Hera drove you mad and you went off leaving behind your nurses, the mountain nymphs;[a] next, when in the battle with the Earthborn Giants[b] I took my stand protecting your right flank with my shield and, striking Enceladus with my spear in the center of his targe, killed him. (Come, let me see, did I dream all this? No, by Zeus, for I also displayed the spoils to Dionysus.)

But now I am enduring a labor greater than those. For when Hera raised the Tuscan pirates[c] against you to have you sold as a slave to a far country, I learned of it and took

doubtless out of resentment of his father Zeus's love for Semele, Dionysus' mother.

[b] The Giants were the mighty sons of Ge (Earth), who was impregnated by the blood of Ouranos (Heaven). They rose against the Olympian gods and were defeated.

[c] Dionysus held captive on shipboard and astounding his captors by wreathing their ship with vines and ivy is a theme of vase painting and of the seventh Homeric Hymn.

σέθεν κατὰ ζήτησιν. ἐν πρύμνῃ δ' ἄκρᾳ
15 αὐτὸς βεβὼς ηὔθυνον ἀμφῆρες δόρυ,
παῖδες δ' <ἐπ'> ἐρετμοῖς ἥμενοι γλαυκὴν ἅλα
ῥοθίοισι λευκαίνοντες ἐζήτουν σ', ἄναξ.
ἤδη δὲ Μαλέας πλησίον πεπλευκότας
ἀπηλιώτης ἄνεμος ἐμπνεύσας δορὶ
20 ἐξέβαλεν ἡμᾶς τήνδ' ἐς Αἰτναίαν πέτραν,
ἵν' οἱ μονῶπες ποντίου παῖδες θεοῦ
Κύκλωπες οἰκοῦσ' ἄντρ' ἔρημ' ἀνδροκτόνοι.
τούτων ἑνὸς ληφθέντες ἐσμὲν ἐν δόμοις
δοῦλοι· καλοῦσι δ' αὐτὸν ᾧ λατρεύομεν
25 Πολύφημον· ἀντὶ δ' εὐίων βακχευμάτων
ποίμνας Κύκλωπος ἀνοσίου ποιμαίνομεν.

παῖδες μὲν οὖν μοι κλειτύων ἐν ἐσχάτοις
νέμουσι μῆλα νέα νέοι πεφυκότες,
ἐγὼ δὲ πληροῦν πίστρα καὶ σαίρειν στέγας
30 μένων τέταγμαι τάσδε, τῷδε δυσσεβεῖ
Κύκλωπι δείπνων ἀνοσίων διάκονος.
καὶ νῦν, τὰ προσταχθέντ', ἀναγκαίως ἔχει
σαίρειν σιδηρᾷ τῇδέ μ' ἁρπάγῃ δόμους,
ὡς τόν τ' ἀπόντα δεσπότην Κύκλωπ' ἐμὸν
35 καθαροῖσιν ἄντροις μῆλά τ' ἐσδεχώμεθα.

ἤδη δὲ παῖδας προσνέμοντας εἰσορῶ
ποίμνας. τί ταῦτα; μῶν κρότος σικινίδων
ὁμοῖος ὑμῖν νῦν τε χὦτε Βακχίῳ
κῶμος συνασπίζοντες Ἀλθαίας δόμους

---

15 βεβὼς Diggle: λαβὼν L   16 <ἐπ'> Seidler
39 κῶμος Diggle: κῶμοι L

62

ship with my sons to find you. Taking my stand right at the stern, I myself steered the double-oared ship, and my sons, sitting at the oars, made the gray sea whiten with their rowing as they searched for you, lord. But as we were rounding Cape Malea, an east wind blew down on the ship and cast us to land near this crag of Aetna, where Neptune's one-eyed sons, the man-slaying Cyclopes, dwell in their remote caves. One of these has caught us and keeps us as slaves in his house: the master we serve is called Polyphemus. And instead of our bacchic revels we now herd the flocks of this godless Cyclops.

And so my sons, being young, are shepherding the young sheep on the distant slopes, while my orders are to remain behind, fill the watering troughs, and sweep this house, assisting this godless Cyclops at his unholy meals. And now—duty is duty—I must sweep the house with this iron rake so that I may receive my absent master, the Cyclops, and his sheep in a clean cave.

Enter by Eisodos A the CHORUS *of satyrs, with attendants, driving sheep before them.*

But now I see my sons driving the flocks this way. What is this, lads? Can it be that you have the same rhythm to your lively dance[a] as when you went revelling at Bacchus' side to the house of Althaea,[b] swaggering in to

---

[a] The *sikinnis* is a fast-paced dance characteristic of satyrs and the satyr play.

[b] According to one version of her story, Dionysus was the father by her of Deianeira, wife of Heracles. This may have been treated in an earlier satyr play.

40   προσῇτ᾽ ἀοιδαῖς βαρβίτων σαυλούμενοι;

ΧΟΡΟΣ

στρ.

παῖ γενναίων μὲν πατέρων
γενναίων δ᾽ ἐκ τοκάδων,
πᾷ δή μοι νίσῃ σκοπέλους;
οὐ τᾷδ᾽ ὑπήμενος αὔ-
45   ρα καὶ ποιηρὰ βοτάνα;
δινᾶέν δ᾽ ὕδωρ ποταμῶν
ἐν πίστραις κεῖται πέλας ἄν-
τρων, οὗ σοι βλαχαὶ τεκέων.

μεσῳδ.

ψύττ᾽· οὐ τᾷδ᾽, οὔ;
50   οὐ τᾴδε νεμῇ κλειτὺν δροσεράν;
ὠή, ῥίψω πέτρον τάχα σου·
ὕπαγ᾽ ὦ ὕπαγ᾽ ὦ κεράστα
μηλοβότα στασιωρέ,
Κύκλωπος ἀγροβάτα.

ἀντ.

55   σπαργῶντας μαστοὺς χάλασον·
δέξαι θηλαῖσι τροφὰς
ἃς λείπεις ἀρνῶν θαλάμοις.
ποθοῦσί σ᾽ ἁμερόκοι-
τοι βλαχαὶ σμικρῶν τεκέων.
60   εἰς αὐλὰν πότ᾽ ἀμφιλαφῆ
ποιηροὺς λιποῦσα νομοὺς
Αἰτναίων εἴσει σκοπέλων;

the music of the lyre?

CHORUS

(*addressing an errant ram*) Son of a noble sire and a noble dam, by what road, tell me, are you heading for the crags? Is not *this* the way to gentle breezes and green grass? The water of eddying rivers stands in the drinking troughs near the cave where your bleating young are sheltered.

Shoo! This way, this way! Feed along the dewy slope here! You there, I shall soon throw a stone at you. On with you, on with you, hornèd one, guardian of the sheepfold that belongs to the herdsman, the Cyclops who treads the wild.

(*addressing a ewe*) Unloose your swollen udders. Take to your teats the young lambs you left behind inside the cave. The little bleating ones, who have slept all day, are missing you. When will you leave the grassy haunts of Aetna behind and enter your vast pen?

---

[41] παῖ Dindorf: πᾷ δή μοι L (cf. 43)

[42] δ' L. Dindorf: τ' L

[44] αὐλὰ Musgrave

[46] δ' Wecklein: θ' L

[48] οὖ Casaubon: οὔ Tr[1]: rasuram L

[53] στασιωρὲ Wilamowitz: -òν L

[56] τροφὰς Wieseler: σπορὰς L

[60] ἀμφιλαφῆ Hartung: ἀμφιβαλεῖς Tr: ἀμφιβαίνεις L

[62] εἴσει Seidler: εἴσω L

ἐπῳδ.

οὐ τάδε Βρόμιος, οὐ τάδε χοροὶ
βακχεῖαί τε θυρσοφόροι,
65 οὐ τυμπάνων ἀλαλαγ-
μοὶ κρήναις παρ' ὑδροχύτοις,
οὐκ οἴνου χλωραὶ σταγόνες·
οὐδ' ἐν Νύσᾳ μετὰ Νυμ-
φᾶν ἴακχον ἴακχον ᾠ-
70 δὰν μέλπω πρὸς τὰν Ἀφροδί-
ταν, ἃν θηρεύων πετόμαν
βάκχαις σὺν λευκόποσιν.
ὦ φίλος ὦναξ Βακχεῖε, ποῖ οἰ-
75 οπολῶν ξανθὰν χαίταν σείεις;
ἐγὼ δ' ὁ σὸς πρόπολος
Κύκλωπι θητεύω
τῷ μονοδέρκτᾳ δοῦλος ἀλαίνων
80 σὺν τᾷδε τράγου χλαίνᾳ μελέᾳ
σᾶς χωρὶς φιλίας.

ΣΙΛΗΝΟΣ

σιγήσατ', ὦ τέκν', ἄντρα δ' ἐς πετρηρεφῆ
ποίμνας ἀθροῖσαι προσπόλους κελεύσατε.

ΧΟΡΟΣ

χωρεῖτ'· ἀτὰρ δὴ τίνα, πάτερ, σπουδὴν ἔχεις;

---

64 βακχεῖαί Wilamowitz: βάκχαι L
73 ὦ φίλος ὦναξ post Kovacs Willink: ὦ φίλος ὦ φίλε L
74 οἰοπολῶν Nauck: -πολεῖς L
77 Κύκλωπι θητεύω Fritzsche: θ- Κ- L

No Dionysus is here, no dances, no wand-bearing Bacchic worship, no ecstatic noise of drums by the gushing springs of water, no fresh drops of wine. Nor can I join the Nymphs on Mount Nysa in singing the song "Iacchos Iacchos" to Aphrodite, whom I swiftly pursued in the company of white-footed Bacchants. Ah me, lord Dionysus, where are you going without your companions, shaking your golden hair? I, your attendant, serve this one-eyed Cyclops, a slave in exile, dressed in this wretched goat-skin cloak and deprived of your friendship.

SILENUS

Silence, my sons! Order your attendants to drive the flocks into the rocky cave!

CHORUS LEADER

(*to the attendants*) Do as he says.

They go into the cave with the animals.

But what is your concern, father?

ΣΙΛΗΝΟΣ

85   ὁρῶ πρὸς ἀκταῖς ναὸς Ἑλλάδος σκάφος
κώπης τ' ἄνακτας σὺν στρατηλάτῃ τινὶ
στείχοντας ἐς τόδ' ἄντρον· ἀμφὶ δ' αὐχέσιν
τεύχη φέρονται κενά, βορᾶς κεχρημένοι,
κρωσσούς θ' ὑδρηλούς. ὦ ταλαίπωροι ξένοι·
90   τίνες ποτ' εἰσίν; οὐκ ἴσασι δεσπότην
Πολύφημον οἷός ἐστιν ἄξενόν τε γῆν
τήνδ' ἐμβεβῶτες καὶ Κυκλωπίαν γνάθον
τὴν ἀνδροβρῶτα δυστυχῶς ἀφιγμένοι.
ἀλλ' ἥσυχοι γίγνεσθ', ἵν' ἐκπυθώμεθα
95   πόθεν πάρεισι Σικελὸν Αἰτναῖον πάγον.

ΟΔΥΣΣΕΥΣ

ξένοι, φράσαιτ' ἂν νᾶμα ποτάμιον πόθεν
δίψης ἄκος λάβοιμεν εἴ τέ τις θέλει
βορὰν ὀδῆσαι ναυτίλοις κεχρημένοις;
   <ἔα·>
τί χρῆμα; Βρομίου πόλιν ἔοιγμεν ἐσβαλεῖν·
100 Σατύρων πρὸς ἄντροις τόνδ' ὅμιλον εἰσορῶ.
χαίρειν προσεῖπον πρῶτα τὸν γεραίτατον.

ΣΙΛΗΝΟΣ

χαῖρ', ὦ ξέν'· ὅστις δ' εἶ φράσον πάτραν τε σήν.

ΟΔΥΣΣΕΥΣ

Ἴθακος Ὀδυσσεύς, γῆς Κεφαλλήνων ἄναξ.

<hr>

91 ἄξενόν τε γῆν Jacobs: ἄξενον στέγην L
99 <ἔα·> Wecklein
101 προσεῖπον Fix: προσεῖπα L

CYCLOPS

SILENUS

I see a Greek ship on the beach, and sailors who ply the
oar coming to this cave with someone who must be their
commander. About their necks they carry empty vessels,
since it is food they need, and pails for water. O unlucky
strangers! Who can they be? They know not what our
master Polyphemus is like, nor that this ground they stand
on is no friend to guests, and that they have arrived with
wretched bad luck at the man-eating jaws of the Cyclops.
But hold your peace so that we may learn where they have
come from to Sicilian Aetna's crag.

Enter by Eisodos B ODYSSEUS *with his men.*

ODYSSEUS

Strangers, could you tell me where we might find a stream
of water to slake our thirst, and whether anyone is willing
to sell provisions to needy sailors?

    Why, what is this? We seem to have marched into
Dionysus' town. For here's a throng of satyrs near the
cave. My first words to the eldest: Greeting!

SILENUS

Greeting, stranger! But tell me your name and country.

ODYSSEUS

Odysseus, of Ithaca, lord of Cephallene.

ΣΙΛΗΝΟΣ

οἶδ' ἄνδρα, κρόταλον δριμύ, Σισύφου γένος.

ΟΔΥΣΣΕΥΣ

105 ἐκεῖνος αὐτός εἰμι· λοιδόρει δὲ μή.

ΣΙΛΗΝΟΣ

πόθεν Σικελίαν τήνδε ναυστολῶν πάρει;

ΟΔΥΣΣΕΥΣ

ἐξ Ἰλίου γε κἀπὸ Τρωικῶν πόνων.

ΣΙΛΗΝΟΣ

πῶς; πορθμὸν οὐκ ᾔδησθα πατρῴας χθονός;

ΟΔΥΣΣΕΥΣ

ἀνέμων θύελλαι δεῦρό μ' ἥρπασαν βίᾳ.

ΣΙΛΗΝΟΣ

110 παπαῖ· τὸν αὐτὸν δαίμον' ἐξαντλεῖς ἐμοί.

ΟΔΥΣΣΕΥΣ

ἦ καὶ σὺ δεῦρο πρὸς βίαν ἀπεστάλης;

ΣΙΛΗΝΟΣ

λῃστὰς διώκων <γ'> οἳ Βρόμιον ἀνήρπασαν.

ΟΔΥΣΣΕΥΣ

τίς δ' ἥδε χώρα καὶ τίνες ναίουσί νιν;

ΣΙΛΗΝΟΣ

Αἰτναῖος ὄχθος Σικελίας ὑπέρτατος.

105 αὐτός L. Dindorf: οὗτός L
112 <γ'> Wecklein

SILENUS

I know of the man, the wheedling chatterer, Sisyphus' son.[a]

ODYSSEUS

The very same. But spare me these aspersions.

SILENUS

From what land have you sailed here to Sicily?

ODYSSEUS

From Ilium and from the fighting at Troy.

SILENUS

What? Did you not know your way home?

ODYSSEUS

I was driven here by windstorms against my will.

SILENUS

O dear! The fate you suffer is the same as mine.

ODYSSEUS

Did you also come here against your will?

SILENUS

Yes, chasing the pirates who had carried off Dionysus.

ODYSSEUS

What is this country, and who are its inhabitants?

SILENUS

This is Mount Aetna, highest in Sicily.

[a] One version of Odysseus' ancestry, alluded to several times in tragedy, makes Anticleia, Odysseus' mother, marry Laertes when she is already pregnant by Sisyphus.

ΟΔΥΣΣΕΥΣ

115 τείχη δὲ ποῦ 'στι καὶ πόλεως πυργώματα;

ΣΙΛΗΝΟΣ

οὐκ ἔστ'· ἔρημοι πρῶνες ἀνθρώπων, ξένε.

ΟΔΥΣΣΕΥΣ

τίνες δ' ἔχουσι γαῖαν; ἢ θηρῶν γένος;

ΣΙΛΗΝΟΣ

Κύκλωπες, ἄντρ' ἔχοντες, οὐ στέγας δόμων.

ΟΔΥΣΣΕΥΣ

τίνος κλύοντες; ἢ δεδήμευται κράτος;

ΣΙΛΗΝΟΣ

120 μονάδες· ἀκούει δ' οὐδὲν οὐδεὶς οὐδενός.

ΟΔΥΣΣΕΥΣ

σπείρουσι δ' — ἢ τῷ ζῶσι; — Δήμητρος στάχυν;

ΣΙΛΗΝΟΣ

γάλακτι καὶ τυροῖσι καὶ μήλων βορᾷ.

ΟΔΥΣΣΕΥΣ

Βρομίου δὲ πῶμ' ἔχουσιν, ἀμπέλου ῥοάς;

ΣΙΛΗΝΟΣ

ἥκιστα· τοιγὰρ ἄχορον οἰκοῦσι χθόνα.

ΟΔΥΣΣΕΥΣ

125 φιλόξενοι δὲ χὥσιοι περὶ ξένους;

116 ἔστ' Schenk: εἰσ' L
120 μονάδες V. Schmidt: νομάδες L

CYCLOPS

ODYSSEUS

But where are the walls and city battlements?

SILENUS

There are none. No men dwell in these headlands, stranger.

ODYSSEUS

Who then are the land's inhabitants? Wild beasts?

SILENUS

Cyclopes, who live in caves, not houses.

ODYSSEUS

Who is their ruler? Or do the people govern?

SILENUS

They are solitaries: no one is anyone's subject.

ODYSSEUS

Do they sow Demeter's grain? Or how do they live?

SILENUS

On milk and cheese and the flesh of sheep.

ODYSSEUS

Do they possess Dionysus' drink, that flows from the vine?

SILENUS

Not at all! Hence the land they dwell in knows no dancing.

ODYSSEUS

Are they god-fearing and hospitable toward strangers?

ΣΙΛΗΝΟΣ
γλυκύτατά φασι τὰ κρέα τοὺς ξένους φορεῖν.

ΟΔΥΣΣΕΥΣ
τί φῇς; βορᾷ χαίρουσιν ἀνθρωποκτόνῳ;

ΣΙΛΗΝΟΣ
οὐδεὶς μολὼν δεῦρ᾽ ὅστις οὐ κατεσφάγη.

ΟΔΥΣΣΕΥΣ
αὐτὸς δὲ Κύκλωψ ποῦ 'στιν; ἦ δόμων ἔσω;

ΣΙΛΗΝΟΣ
130 φροῦδος, πρὸς Αἴτνῃ θῆρας ἰχνεύων κυσίν.

ΟΔΥΣΣΕΥΣ
οἶσθ᾽ οὖν ὃ δρᾶσον, ὡς ἀπαίρωμεν χθονός;

ΣΙΛΗΝΟΣ
οὐκ οἶδ᾽, Ὀδυσσεῦ· πᾶν δέ σοι δρῴημεν ἄν.

ΟΔΥΣΣΕΥΣ
ὄδησον ἡμῖν σῖτον, οὗ σπανίζομεν.

ΣΙΛΗΝΟΣ
οὐκ ἔστιν, ὥσπερ εἶπον, ἄλλο πλὴν κρέας,

ΟΔΥΣΣΕΥΣ
135 ἀλλ᾽ ἡδὺ λιμοῦ καὶ τόδε σχετήριον.

ΣΙΛΗΝΟΣ
καὶ τυρὸς ὀπίας ἔστι καὶ βοὸς γάλα.

131 δρᾶσον Canter: δράσεις L

CYCLOPS

SILENUS

Most delicious, they maintain, is the flesh of strangers.

ODYSSEUS

What? Do they feast on men?

SILENUS

Everyone who has come here has been slaughtered.

ODYSSEUS

The Cyclops himself, where is he? In his house?

SILENUS

He has gone off hunting wild beasts on Mount Aetna with his dogs.

ODYSSEUS

Do you know what you must do so that we can leave this land?

SILENUS

No, Odysseus. But I will do everything I can for you.

ODYSSEUS

Sell us some bread, the thing we lack.

SILENUS

As I told you, we have nothing but meat.

ODYSSEUS

That too is a pleasant way to put an end to hunger.

SILENUS

And there is curdled cheese and also cows' milk.

EURIPIDES

ΟΔΥΣΣΕΥΣ

ἐκφέρετε· φῶς γὰρ ἐμπολήμασιν πρέπει.

ΣΙΛΗΝΟΣ

σὺ δ᾽ ἀντιδώσεις, εἰπέ μοι, χρυσὸν πόσον;

ΟΔΥΣΣΕΥΣ

οὐ χρυσὸν ἀλλὰ πῶμα Διονύσου φέρω.

ΣΙΛΗΝΟΣ

140   ὦ φίλτατ᾽ εἰπών, οὗ σπανίζομεν πάλαι.

ΟΔΥΣΣΕΥΣ

καὶ μὴν Μάρων μοι πῶμ᾽ ἔδωκε, παῖς θεοῦ.

ΣΙΛΗΝΟΣ

ὃν ἐξέθρεψα ταῖσδ᾽ ἐγώ ποτ᾽ ἀγκάλαις;

ΟΔΥΣΣΕΥΣ

ὁ Βακχίου παῖς, ὡς σαφέστερον μάθῃς.

ΣΙΛΗΝΟΣ

ἐν σέλμασιν νεώς ἐστιν ἢ φέρεις σύ νιν;

ΟΔΥΣΣΕΥΣ

145   ὅδ᾽ ἀσκὸς ὃς κεύθει νιν, ὡς ὁρᾷς, γέρον.

ΣΙΛΗΝΟΣ

οὗτος μὲν οὐδ᾽ ἂν τὴν γνάθον πλήσειέ μου.

ΟΔΥΣΣΕΥΣ

<τοῦτον μὲν οὖν τὸν ἀσκὸν οὐκ ἂν ἐκπίοις.>

146 post h. v. lac. indic. Nauck, Kirchhoff

CYCLOPS

ODYSSEUS

Bring them out: daylight befits merchandise.

SILENUS

But you, tell me, how much gold will you give in exchange?

ODYSSEUS

It is not gold I carry but rather Dionysus' drink.

SILENUS

What good news you bring! The very thing we have lacked so long!

ODYSSEUS

Yes, Maron, the god's own son, gave me the drink.

SILENUS

The lad I once raised in these very arms?

ODYSSEUS

Dionysus' son, to make my meaning plainer.

SILENUS

Is it on board ship, or do you have it with you?

Odysseus produces a wineskin.

ODYSSEUS

This is the wineskin that holds it, as you can see, old sir.

SILENUS

This would not even be a mouthful for me.

ODYSSEUS

<You would not be able to drink this wineskin dry.>

ΣΙΛΗΝΟΣ

\<φύει γὰρ ἀσκὸς οἶνον ἐξ αὑτοῦ πάλιν ;\>

ΟΔΥΣΣΕΥΣ

ναί, δὶς τοσόν πῶμ' ὅσον ἂν ἐξ ἀσκοῦ ῥυῇ.

ΣΙΛΗΝΟΣ

καλήν γε κρήνην εἶπας ἡδεῖάν τ' ἐμοί.

ΟΔΥΣΣΕΥΣ

βούλῃ σε γεύσω πρῶτον ἄκρατον μέθυ ;

ΣΙΛΗΝΟΣ

150 δίκαιον · ἦ γὰρ γεῦμα τὴν ὠνὴν καλεῖ.

ΟΔΥΣΣΕΥΣ

καὶ μὴν ἐφέλκω καὶ ποτῆρ' ἀσκοῦ μέτα.

ΣΙΛΗΝΟΣ

φέρ' ἐγκάναξον, ὡς ἀναμνησθῶ πιών.

ΟΔΥΣΣΕΥΣ

ἰδού.

ΣΙΛΗΝΟΣ

παπαιάξ, ὡς καλὴν ὀσμὴν ἔχει.

ΟΔΥΣΣΕΥΣ

εἶδες γὰρ αὐτήν ;

ΣΙΛΗΝΟΣ

οὐ μὰ Δί', ἀλλ' ὀσφραίνομαι.

---

[148] τ' Reiske: γ' L
[152] ἐγκάναξον Valckenaer, Pierson: ἐκπάταξον L
[153] ὀσμὴν] χροιὰν Kovacs: φυὴν Willink

SILENUS

<What? Does the skin produce new wine of itself?>[a]

ODYSSEUS

Yes, twice as much as has flowed out of the skin.

SILENUS

What a lovely spring you speak of! What pleasure it gives me!

ODYSSEUS

Would you like me to give you a taste of it neat first?

SILENUS

That's fair enough: a taste invites a purchase.

Odysseus produces a drinking vessel.

ODYSSEUS

See, I've brought a cup with me.

SILENUS

Splash some in so that I can remember what it's like to drink.

ODYSSEUS

Done.

SILENUS

Oh my, oh my! What a fine bouquet it has!

ODYSSEUS

What? Have you caught it?

SILENUS

No, by Zeus, I smell it!

[a] The supplements are, of course, mere guesses. A miraculous wineskin is perfectly in keeping with the spirit of a satyr play: compare the wine miracle ascribed to Dionysus at *Ba*. 705.

79

ΟΔΥΣΣΕΥΣ

155 γεῦσαί νυν, ὡς ἂν μὴ λόγῳ 'παινῇς μόνον.

ΣΙΛΗΝΟΣ

βαβαί· χορεῦσαι παρακαλεῖ μ' ὁ Βάκχιος.
ἆ ἆ ἆ.

ΟΔΥΣΣΕΥΣ

μῶν τὸν λάρυγγα διεκάναξέ σου καλῶς;

ΣΙΛΗΝΟΣ

ὥστ' εἰς ἄκρους γε τοὺς ὄνυχας ἀφίκετο.

ΟΔΥΣΣΕΥΣ

160 πρὸς τῷδε μέντοι καὶ νόμισμα δώσομεν.

ΣΙΛΗΝΟΣ

χάλα τὸν ἀσκὸν μόνον· ἔα τὸ χρυσίον.

ΟΔΥΣΣΕΥΣ

ἐκφέρετέ νυν τυρεύματ' ἢ μήλων τόκον.

ΣΙΛΗΝΟΣ

δράσω τάδ', ὀλίγον φροντίσας γε δεσποτῶν.
ὡς ἐκπιεῖν κἂν κύλικα βουλοίμην μίαν,
165 πάντων Κυκλώπων ἀντιδοὺς βοσκήματα,
ῥῖψαί τ' ἐς ἅλμην Λευκάδος πέτρας ἄπο
ἅπαξ μεθυσθεὶς καταβαλών τε τὰς ὀφρῦς.

---

[164] κἂν Paley: γ' ἂν L
βουλοίμην editio Aldina: μαινοίμην L
[167] καταχαλῶν anonymus apud append. Weckl.

Odysseus hands him the cup.

ODYSSEUS

Taste it, then, so that your praise of it may not be mere words.

SILENUS

Oo la la! Bacchus invites me to the dance! Tra la, tra la, tra la!

ODYSSEUS

Didn't it gurgle nicely down your throat?

SILENUS

Yes, all the way down to the ends of my toes!

ODYSSEUS

But we will give you some money in addition.

SILENUS

Just keep pouring the wine. Never mind the gold!

ODYSSEUS

Then bring out cheese or lamb.

SILENUS

I will do just that and pay little heed to my master. I would like to drink down a single cup of this wine, giving all the Cyclopes' flocks in exchange for it, and then to leap from the Leucadian cliff[a] into the brine, good and drunk with

---

[a] Leucas, a small island in the Ionian sea off the west coast of Greece, has chalk cliffs rising sharply from the sea. The leap from this cliff into the sea is used in Anacreon, fr. 376 *PMG*, as an image of the loss of self-control encountered when one is "drunk with love." Sappho is said to have leapt from the cliff for the love of Phaon.

ὡς ὅς γε πίνων μὴ γέγηθε μαίνεται·
ἵν' ἔστι τουτί τ' ὀρθὸν ἐξανιστάναι
170 μαστοῦ τε δραγμὸς καὶ παρεσκευασμένον
ψαῦσαι χεροῖν λειμῶνος ὀρχηστύς θ' ἅμα
κακῶν τε λῆστις. εἶτ' ἐγὼ <οὐ> κυνήσομαι
τοιόνδε πῶμα, τὴν Κύκλωπος ἀμαθίαν
κλαίειν κελεύων καὶ τὸν ὀφθαλμὸν μέσον;

ΧΟΡΟΣ
175 ἄκου', Ὀδυσσεῦ· διαλαλήσωμέν τί σοι.

ΟΔΥΣΣΕΥΣ
καὶ μὴν φίλοι γε προσφέρεσθε πρὸς φίλον.

ΧΟΡΟΣ
ἐλάβετε Τροίαν τὴν Ἑλένην τε χειρίαν;

ΟΔΥΣΣΕΥΣ
καὶ πάντα γ' οἶκον Πριαμιδῶν ἐπέρσαμεν.

ΧΟΡΟΣ
οὔκουν, ἐπειδὴ τὴν νεᾶνιν εἵλετε,
180 ἅπαντες αὐτὴν διεκροτήσατ' ἐν μέρει,
ἐπεί γε πολλοῖς ἥδεται γαμουμένη,
τὴν προδότιν; ἦ τοὺς θυλάκους τοὺς ποικίλους
περὶ τοῖν σκελοῖν ἰδοῦσα καὶ τὸν χρύσεον
κλῳὸν φοροῦντα περὶ μέσον τὸν αὐχένα
185 ἐξεπτοήθη, Μενέλεων ἀνθρώπιον
λῷστον λιποῦσα. μηδαμοῦ γένος ποτὲ
φῦναι γυναικῶν ὤφελ', εἰ μὴ 'μοὶ μόνῳ.

[170] παρεσκευασμένον Blaydes: -μένου L
[172] <οὐ> Matthiae

82

my eyebrows cast down. The man who does not enjoy drinking is mad: in drink one can raise *this* to a stand, catch a handful of breast and look forward to stroking her boscage, there's dancing and forgetfulness of cares. Shall I not kiss such a drink and tell the bonehead Cyclops—and the eye in the middle of his head, too—to go hang?

Exit SILENUS into the cave.

CHORUS LEADER
Listen, Odysseus. We would like a little chat with you.

ODYSSEUS
Of course, since you are my friends and I am yours.

CHORUS LEADER
Did you capture Troy and take Helen prisoner?

ODYSSEUS
Yes, and we sacked the whole house of the sons of Priam.

CHORUS LEADER
Once you had caught the girl, didn't you all then take turns banging her, since she takes pleasure in having more than one mate? The traitor! She saw the parti-colored breeches on the man's legs and the gold necklace around his neck and went all aflutter after them, leaving behind that fine little man Menelaus. O would that the female sex were nowhere to be found—but in my lap!

Enter SILENUS from the cave.

ΣΙΛΗΝΟΣ

ἰδού· τάδ' ὑμῖν ποιμνίων βοσκήματα,
ἄναξ Ὀδυσσεῦ, μηκάδων ἀρνῶν τροφαί,
190   πηκτοῦ γάλακτός τ' οὐ σπάνια τυρεύματα.
φέρεσθε· χωρεῖθ' ὡς τάχιστ' ἄντρων ἄπο,
βότρυος ἐμοὶ πῶμ' ἀντιδόντες εὐίου.

   οἴμοι· Κύκλωψ ὅδ' ἔρχεται· τί δράσομεν;

ΟΔΥΣΣΕΥΣ

ἀπολώλαμέν τἄρ', ὦ γέρον· ποῖ χρὴ φυγεῖν;

ΣΙΛΗΝΟΣ

195   ἔσω πέτρας τῆσδ', οὗπερ ἂν λάθοιτέ γε.

ΟΔΥΣΣΕΥΣ

δεινὸν τόδ' εἶπας, ἀρκύων μολεῖν ἔσω.

ΣΙΛΗΝΟΣ

οὐ δεινόν· εἰσὶ καταφυγαὶ πολλαὶ πέτρας.

ΟΔΥΣΣΕΥΣ

οὐ δῆτ'· ἐπεί τἂν μεγάλα γ' ἡ Τροία στένοι,
εἰ φευξόμεσθ' ἕν' ἄνδρα, μυρίον δ' ὄχλον
200   Φρυγῶν ὑπέστην πολλάκις σὺν ἀσπίδι.
ἀλλ', εἰ θανεῖν δεῖ, κατθανούμεθ' εὐγενῶς
ἢ ζῶντες αἶνον τὸν πάρος συσσώσομεν.

ΚΥΚΛΩΨ

ἄνεχε πάρεχε· τί τάδε; τίς ἡ ῥᾳθυμία;
τί βακχιάζετ'; οὐχὶ Διόνυσος τάδε,

---

[188] ποιμνίων Scaliger: ποιμένων L
[193n] Sileno continuat L. Dindorf: ὀδ. L
[203n] Κυ. Tyrwhitt: σι. L

84

CYCLOPS

SILENUS

Here, my lord Odysseus, are your flocks, the nurslings of the bleating sheep, and a goodly number of cheeses made of curdled milk. Take them. Go away quickly from the cave, but first give me the drink of the Bacchic vine.

Oh no! Here comes the Cyclops. What are we to do?

ODYSSEUS

Then we are done for, old man. Where should we flee to?

SILENUS

Inside this cave, where you could avoid being seen.

ODYSSEUS

A dangerous suggestion, this, going into the net.

SILENUS

No danger: there are many hiding places in the cave.

ODYSSEUS

I shall not do it. Troy would groan loudly if I were to run from a single man when I stood my ground so often, shield in hand, against a throng of Trojans without number. Rather, if I must die, I will die nobly—or live on and also retain my old reputation.

Enter the CYCLOPS *with retinue by Eisodos A.*

CYCLOPS

Give way, make way! What is going on here? What means this slackness? Why this Bacchic holiday? Here is no

205 οὐ κρόταλα χαλκοῦ τυμπάνων τ᾽ ἀράγματα.
πῶς μοι κατ᾽ ἄντρα νεόγονα βλαστήματα ;
ἢ πρός τε μαστοῖς εἰσι χὖπὸ μητέρων
πλευρὰς τρέχουσι, σχοινίνοις τ᾽ ἐν τεύχεσιν
πλήρωμα τυρῶν ἐστιν ἐξημελγμένον ;
210 τί φατε ; τί λέγετε ; τάχα τις ὑμῶν τῷ ξύλῳ
δάκρυα μεθήσει. βλέπετ᾽ ἄνω καὶ μὴ κάτω.

ΧΟΡΟΣ

ἰδού· πρὸς αὐτὸν τὸν Δί᾽ ἀνακεκύφαμεν
τά τ᾽ ἄστρα, καὶ τὸν Ὠρίωνα δέρκομαι.

ΚΥΚΛΩΨ

ἄριστόν ἐστιν εὖ παρεσκευασμένον ;

ΧΟΡΟΣ

215 πάρεστιν. ὁ φάρυγξ εὐτρεπὴς ἔστω μόνον.

ΚΥΚΛΩΨ

ἦ καὶ γάλακτός εἰσι κρατῆρες πλέῳ ;

ΧΟΡΟΣ

ὥστ᾽ ἐκπιεῖν γέ σ᾽, ἢν θέλῃς, ὅλον πίθον.

ΚΥΚΛΩΨ

μήλειον ἢ βόειον ἢ μεμιγμένον ;

ΧΟΡΟΣ

ὃν ἂν θέλῃς σύ· μὴ 'μὲ καταπίῃς μόνον.

---

[207] τε L. Dindorf: γε L
[213] τά τ᾽ ἄστρα t: καὶ τἄστρα L

Dionysus, no bronze castanets, no rattle of drums. How fare my newborn lambs in the cave? Are they at the teat and running to their mothers' sides? The milk for cheeses—has it been put in rush buckets? What say you? This club will soon make someone cry. Look up, not down!

CHORUS LEADER
(*looking up at Polyphemus*) There! My head is turned up toward Zeus himself and the stars, and I see Orion!

CYCLOPS
Is my dinner well prepared?

CHORUS LEADER
It is: just be sure your gullet is ready.

CYCLOPS
Are the mixing bowls filled with milk as well?

CHORUS LEADER
So much that you can drink an entire storage jar if you like.

CYCLOPS
Cows' milk or sheep's or a mixture of both?

CHORUS LEADER
Whatever you like. Just don't swallow *me* down.

ΚΥΚΛΩΨ

220 ἥκιστ᾽· ἐπεί μ᾽ ἂν ἐν μέσῃ τῇ γαστέρι
πηδῶντες ἀπολέσαιτ᾽ ἂν ὑπὸ τῶν σχημάτων.

ἔα· τίν᾽ ὄχλον τόνδ᾽ ὁρῶ πρὸς αὐλίοις;
λῃσταί τινες κατέσχον ἢ κλῶπες χθόνα;
ὁρῶ γέ τοι τούσδ᾽ ἄρνας ἐξ ἄντρων ἐμῶν
225 στρεπταῖς λύγοισι σῶμα συμπεπλεγμένους
τεύχη τε τυρῶν συμμιγῆ γέροντά τε
πληγαῖς μέτωπον φαλακρὸν ἐξῳδηκότα.

ΣΙΛΗΝΟΣ

ὤμοι, πυρέσσω συγκεκομμένος τάλας.

ΚΥΚΛΩΨ

ὑπὸ τοῦ; τίς ἐς σὸν κρᾶτ᾽ ἐπύκτευσεν, γέρον;

ΣΙΛΗΝΟΣ

230 ὑπὸ τῶνδε, Κύκλωψ, ὅτι τὰ σ᾽ οὐκ εἴων φέρειν.

ΚΥΚΛΩΨ

οὐκ ᾖσαν ὄντα θεόν με καὶ θεῶν ἄπο;

ΣΙΛΗΝΟΣ

ἔλεγον ἐγὼ τάδ᾽· οἱ δ᾽ ἐφόρουν τὰ χρήματα,
καὶ τόν γε τυρὸν οὐκ ἐῶντος ἤσθιον
τούς τ᾽ ἄρνας ἐξεφοροῦντο· δήσαντες δὲ σὲ
235 κλῳῷ τριπήχει, κατὰ τὸν ὀφθαλμὸν μέσον

227 μέτωπον Tyrwhitt: πρόσωπον L
233 γε] τε Kaibel
235 κατὰ Canter: κᾶτα L

88

CYCLOPS

I wouldn't think of it: you would be the death of me with
your dance steps, leaping around inside my belly.

Hey! What is this crowd I see near my cave? Have
some pirates or robbers landed here? I *do* see lambs here
from my cave, their bodies bound with twisted willow-
withes, and my cheese buckets all in disarray, and an old
man with his bald head swollen with blows.[a]

SILENUS

Oh! Oh! Wretched me! What a fever I have got from
being beaten up!

CYCLOPS

By whom? Who has been pummeling your head, old
man?

SILENUS

These men, because I would not let them take your pro-
perty.

CYCLOPS

Did they not know that I am a god and descended from
gods?

SILENUS

I told them so, but they went on plundering your posses-
sions, and, what is more, they started in on the cheese,
though I tried to stop them, and began to carry off the
sheep. And they said that they would collar you like a
dangerous dog and right under your very eye violently pull

---

[a] We must suppose that the Cyclops here misdiagnoses the
effect of the wine on Silenus, who then improvises his story to
agree with the Polyphemus' mistake.

τὰ σπλάγχν᾽ ἔφασκον ἐξαμήσεσθαι βίᾳ,
μάστιγί τ᾽ εὖ τὸ νῶτον ἀπολέψειν σέθεν,
κἄπειτα συνδήσαντες ἐς θἀδώλια
τῆς ναὸς ἐμβαλόντες ἀποδώσειν τινὶ
240 πέτρους μοχλεύειν, ἢ ᾿ς μυλῶνα καταβαλεῖν.

ΚΥΚΛΩΨ

ἄληθες; οὔκουν κοπίδας ὡς τάχιστ᾽ ἰὼν
θήξεις μαχαίρας καὶ μέγαν φάκελον ξύλων
ἐπιθεὶς ἀνάψεις; ὡς σφαγέντες αὐτίκα
πλήσουσι νηδὺν τὴν ἐμὴν ἀπ᾽ ἄνθρακος
245 θερμὴν διδόντες δαῖτα τῷ κρεανόμῳ,
τὰ δ᾽ ἐκ λέβητος ἑφθὰ καὶ τετηκότα.
ὡς ἔκπλεώς γε δαιτός εἰμ᾽ ὀρεσκόου·
ἅλις λεόντων ἐστί μοι θοινωμένῳ
ἐλάφων τε, χρόνιος δ᾽ εἴμ᾽ ἀπ᾽ ἀνθρώπων βορᾶς.

ΣΙΛΗΝΟΣ

250 τὰ καινά γ᾽ ἐκ τῶν ἠθάδων, ὦ δέσποτα,
ἥδιόν᾽ ἐστίν. οὐ γὰρ οὖν νεωστί γε
ἄλλοι πρὸς οἴκους σοὺς ἀφίκοντο ξένοι.

ΟΔΥΣΣΕΥΣ

Κύκλωψ, ἄκουσον ἐν μέρει καὶ τῶν ξένων.
ἡμεῖς βορᾶς χρήζοντες ἐμπολὴν λαβεῖν
255 σῶν ἆσσον ἄντρων ἤλθομεν νεὼς ἄπο.
τοὺς δ᾽ ἄρνας ἡμῖν οὗτος ἀντ᾽ οἴνου σκύφου
ἀπημπόλα τε κἀδίδου πιεῖν λαβὼν
ἑκὼν ἑκοῦσι, κοὐδὲν ἦν τούτων βίᾳ.

---

236 ἐξαμήσεσθαι Duport: -σασθαι L

out your guts, flay your back nicely with a whip, then bind
you hand and foot and throw you onto the rowing benches
of their ship and sell you to someone who needs to move
heavy rocks or throw you into a mill.

CYCLOPS

Is that so? *(to a servant)* You there, go on the double and
sharpen my carving knives and start a big bundle of wood
blazing on the hearth. *(The servant goes into the cave.)*
They shall be slaughtered at once and fill my belly, giving
the server a feast hot from the coals and the rest boiled
and tender from the cauldron. I have had my fill of moun-
tain fare: I have dined enough on lions and deer and have
gone far too long without a meal of man's flesh.

SILENUS

After ordinary fare, good master, something new is all the
pleasanter. It has been some time since strangers arrived
at your house.

ODYSSEUS

Cyclops, listen in turn to us strangers as well. We came
from our ship to your cave wishing to buy food. And this
fellow, since he had got something to drink, sold and ten-
dered us these sheep for a cup of wine, willing seller to
willing buyers: there was no violence in this business. But

---

237 ἀπολέψειν Ruhnken: ἀποθλίψειν L
240 ἢ ’ς μυλῶνα Ruhnken: ἢ πυλῶνα L
245 διδόντες Heath: ἔδοντες L
247 εἰμ’ ὀρεσκόου Stephanus: ἱμεροσκόου L
251 οὖν Reiske: αὖ L
252 οἴκους σοὺς Heimsoeth: ἄντρα τὰ σ’ L

ἀλλ᾽ οὗτος ὑγιὲς οὐδὲν ὧν φησιν λέγει,
260 ἐπεί γ᾽ ἐλήφθη σοῦ λάθρᾳ πωλῶν τὰ σά.

ΣΙΛΗΝΟΣ

ἐγώ; κακῶς γ᾽ ἄρ᾽ ἐξόλοι᾽.

ΟΔΥΣΣΕΥΣ
                    εἰ ψεύδομαι.

ΣΙΛΗΝΟΣ

μὰ τὸν Ποσειδῶ τὸν τεκόντα σ᾽, ὦ Κύκλωψ,
μὰ τὸν μέγαν Τρίτωνα καὶ τὸν Νηρέα,
μὰ τὴν Καλυψὼ τάς τε Νηρέως κόρας,
265 μὰ θαἰερὰ κύματ᾽ ἰχθύων τε πᾶν γένος,
ἀπώμοσ᾽, ὦ κάλλιστον ὦ Κυκλώπιον,
ὦ δεσποτίσκε, μὴ τὰ σ᾽ ἐξοδᾶν ἐγὼ
ξένοισι χρήματ᾽. ἢ κακῶς οὗτοι κακοὶ
οἱ παῖδες ἀπόλοινθ᾽, οὓς μάλιστ᾽ ἐγὼ φιλῶ.

ΧΟΡΟΣ

270 αὐτὸς ἔχ᾽. ἔγωγε τοῖς ξένοις τὰ χρήματα
περνάντα σ᾽ εἶδον· εἰ δ᾽ ἐγὼ ψευδῆ λέγω,
ἀπόλοιθ᾽ ὁ πατήρ μου· τοὺς ξένους δὲ μὴ ἀδίκει.

ΚΥΚΛΩΨ

ψεύδεσθ᾽· ἔγωγε τῷδε τοῦ Ῥαδαμάνθυος
μᾶλλον πέποιθα καὶ δικαιότερον λέγω.
275 θέλω δ᾽ ἐρέσθαι· πόθεν ἐπλεύσατ᾽, ὦ ξένοι;
ποδαποί; τίς ὑμᾶς ἐξεπαίδευσεν πόλις;

now every word this fellow says is a lie since he has been caught selling your goods behind your back.

SILENUS

What, me? Damnation take you!

ODYSSEUS

Yes, if I'm lying.

SILENUS

By your father Poseidon, Cyclops, by great Triton and Nereus, by Calypso and Nereus' daughters, by the holy sea swell and the whole tribe of fishes, I swear—o my handsome, o my dear Cyclops, o sweet master—that I was not trying to sell your property to the strangers. If I am lying, may utter damnation take these sons of mine, the apple of my eye!

CHORUS LEADER

On your head, rather! I saw you selling the goods to these strangers. If I am lying, then damnation take my father! But do no wrong to the strangers.

CYCLOPS

(to the Chorus leader) You lie. For my part, I put more trust in this man and think he is more honest than Rhadamanthys.[a] But I want to ask you a question. Where have you sailed from, strangers? What is your country? What city was it that brought you up?

[a] Legendary ruler of Crete and judge in the Underworld famous for his justice.

---

260 γ᾽ ἐλήφθη Heath: κατελήφθη L
261 γ᾽ ἄρ᾽ Kirchhoff: γὰρ L   265 θαλερὰ Franke: θ᾽ ἱερὰ L
273 τῷδε Canter: τοῦδε L   274 μᾶλλον Kirchhoff: πολλὰ L

ΟΔΥΣΣΕΥΣ

Ἰθακήσιοι μὲν τὸ γένος, Ἰλίου δ' ἄπο,
πέρσαντες ἄστυ, πνεύμασιν θαλασσίοις
σὴν γαῖαν ἐξωσθέντες ἥκομεν, Κύκλωψ.

ΚΥΚΛΩΨ

280 ἦ τῆς κακίστης οἳ μετήλθεθ' ἁρπαγὰς
Ἑλένης Σκαμάνδρου γείτον' Ἰλίου πόλιν;

ΟΔΥΣΣΕΥΣ

οὗτοι, πόνον τὸν δεινὸν ἐξηντληκότες.

ΚΥΚΛΩΨ

αἰσχρὸν στράτευμά γ', οἵτινες μιᾶς χάριν
γυναικὸς ἐξεπλεύσατ' ἐς γαῖαν Φρυγῶν.

ΟΔΥΣΣΕΥΣ

285 θεοῦ τὸ πρᾶγμα· μηδέν' αἰτιῶ βροτῶν.
    ἡμεῖς δέ σ', ὦ θεοῦ ποντίου γενναῖε παῖ,
ἱκετεύομέν τε καὶ ψέγομεν ἐλευθέρως·
μὴ τλῇς πρὸς οἴκους σοὺς ἀφιγμένους φίλους
κτανεῖν βοράν τε δυσσεβῆ θέσθαι γνάθοις·
290 οἳ τὸν σόν, ὦναξ, πατέρ' ἔχειν ναῶν ἕδρας
ἐρρυσάμεσθα γῆς ἐν Ἑλλάδος μυχοῖς·
ἱερᾶς τ' ἄθραυστος Ταινάρου μένει λιμὴν
Μαλέας τ' ἄκρας κευθμῶνες ἥ τε Σουνίου

---

²⁸⁷ ψέγομεν scripsi, cl. Andr. 419, Su. 565, Aesch. Cho. 989,
Soph. O.T. 338: λέγομεν L
²⁸⁸ οἴκους Heimsoeth: ἄντρα L

ODYSSEUS

We are men of Ithaca by birth, and it is from Ilium, after sacking the city, that we have come to your land, Cyclops, blown off course by sea storms.

CYCLOPS

Are you the ones who went to punish Ilium on the Scamander for the theft of the worthless Helen?

ODYSSEUS

Yes, we are the ones who endured that terrible toil.

CYCLOPS

Disgraceful expedition, sailing to Phrygia for the sake of one woman!

ODYSSEUS

It was the doing of a god: blame no mortal for it.

But, o noble son of the seagod, we at once entreat you and give you our frank censure: do not have the hardness to kill benefactors who have come to your house and to make of them a godless meal for your jaws. It was we who kept your father safe in the possession of his temple seats in every corner of Greece: the harbor of sacred Taenarum and the recesses of Cape Malea remain inviolate, safe is the rock of Sunium rich in silver, sacred to the goddess

---

290 ναῶν Canter: νεῶν L
292 ἱερᾶς Kassel: ἱερεύς L
293 ἄκρας Seaford: ἄκροι L

δίας Ἀθάνας σῶς ὑπάργυρος πέτρα
295 Γεραίστιοί τε καταφυγαί· τά θ᾽ Ἑλλάδος
†δύσφρον᾽ ὀνείδη† Φρυξὶν οὐκ ἐδώκαμεν.
ὧν καὶ σὺ κοινοῖ· γῆς γὰρ Ἑλλάδος μυχοὺς
οἰκεῖς ὑπ᾽ Αἴτνῃ, τῇ πυριστάκτῳ πέτρᾳ.
    νόμος δὲ θνητοῖς, εἰ λόγους ἀποστρέφῃ,
300 ἱκέτας δέχεσθαι ποντίους ἐφθαρμένους
ξένιά τε δοῦναι καὶ πέπλους ἐπαρκέσαι·
<τούτων δίκαιόν σου τυχεῖν ἡμᾶς, ἄναξ,>
οὐκ ἀμφὶ βουπόροισι πηχθέντας μέλη
ὀβελοῖσι νηδὺν καὶ γνάθον πλῆσαι σέθεν.
ἅλις δὲ Πριάμου γαῖ᾽ ἐχήρωσ᾽ Ἑλλάδα,
305 πολλῶν νεκρῶν πιοῦσα δοριπετῆ φόνον,
ἀλόχους τ᾽ ἀνάνδρους γραῦς τ᾽ ἄπαιδας ὤλεσεν
πολιούς τε πατέρας. εἰ δὲ τοὺς λελειμμένους
σὺ συμπυρώσας δαῖτ᾽ ἀναλώσεις πικράν,
ποῖ τρέψεταί τις; ἀλλ᾽ ἐμοὶ πιθοῦ, Κύκλωψ·
310 πάρες τὸ μάργον σῆς γνάθου, τὸ δ᾽ εὐσεβὲς
τῆς δυσσεβείας ἀνθελοῦ· πολλοῖσι γὰρ
κέρδη πονηρὰ ζημίαν ἠμείψατο.

ΣΙΛΗΝΟΣ

παραινέσαι σοι βούλομαι· τῶν γὰρ κρεῶν
μηδὲν λίπῃς τοῦδ᾽, ἤν τε τὴν γλῶσσαν δάκῃς,
315 κομψὸς γενήσῃ καὶ λαλίστατος, Κύκλωψ.

---

296 δύσφορά γ᾽ apogr. Par.: δύσφορον ὄνειδος per parenthesim
Diggle
    301 πέπλους Blaydes: πέπλοις L

Athena, safe are Geraestus' refuges. We did not suffer the great disgrace of surrendering Greek possessions to the Trojans.[a] In these events you also have a share, dwelling as you do in the far reaches of Hellas, under Aetna, the rock that drips with fire.

But if you are deaf to these considerations, there is a law among mortals that one must receive shipwrecked suppliants, give them the gifts hospitality requires, and provide them with clothing. <It is this treatment we ought to receive from you,> rather than to have our limbs pierced with spits for roasting beef and to fill your maw and belly. Priam's land has wrought enough bereavement on Greece, drinking down the spear-shed blood of many corpses. She has widowed wives and brought old women and greybeards childless to the grave. If you mean to cook and consume those left, making a grim feast, where shall anyone turn for refuge? Listen to me, Cyclops: give up this gluttony and choose to be godly instead of impious: for many have found that base gain brings punishment in its train.

SILENUS

I want to give you some advice: don't leave untouched a single bit of this man's flesh. And if you chew on his tongue, you will become clever and glib, Cyclops.

[a] I translate Diggle's conjecture.

---

302 ante h. v. lac. stat. et suppl. Kassel

ΚΥΚΛΩΨ

ὁ πλοῦτος, ἀνθρωπίσκε, τοῖς σοφοῖς θεός,
τὰ δ᾽ ἄλλα κόμποι καὶ λόγων εὐμορφία.
ἄκρας δ᾽ ἐναλίας αἷς καθίδρυται πατὴρ
χαίρειν κελεύω· τί τάδε προυστήσω λόγῳ;

320 Ζηνὸς δ᾽ ἐγὼ κεραυνὸν οὐ φρίσσω, ξένε,
οὐδ᾽ οἶδ᾽ ὅ τι Ζεύς ἐστ᾽ ἐμοῦ κρείσσων θεός.
<ἀλλ᾽ εἴ τι τοῦδε καὶ πάροιθ᾽ ἐφρόντισα,>
οὔ μοι μέλει τὸ λοιπόν· ὡς δ᾽ οὔ μοι μέλει
ἄκουσον· ὅταν ἄνωθεν ὄμβρον ἐκχέῃ,

325 ἐν τῇδε πέτρᾳ στέγν᾽ ἔχων σκηνώματα,
ἢ μόσχον ὀπτὸν ἤ τι θήρειον δάκος
δαινύμενος ἐστιῶ τι γαστέρ᾽ ὑπτίαν,
εἶτ᾽ ἐκπιὼν γάλακτος ἀμφορέα πλέων
κρούω, Διὸς βρονταῖσιν εἰς ἔριν κτυπῶν.

330 ὅταν δὲ βορέας χιόνα Θρήκιος χέῃ,
δοραῖσι θηρῶν σῶμα περιβαλὼν ἐμὸν
καὶ πῦρ ἀναίθων, χιόνος οὐδέν μοι μέλει.
ἡ γῆ δ᾽ ἀνάγκῃ, κἂν θέλῃ κἂν μὴ θέλῃ,
τίκτουσα ποίαν τἀμὰ πιαίνει βοτά.

335 ἀγὼ οὔτινι θύω πλὴν ἐμοί, θεοῖσι δ᾽ οὔ,
καὶ τῇ μεγίστῃ, γαστρὶ τῇδε, δαιμόνων.
ὡς τοὐμπιεῖν γε καὶ φαγεῖν τοὐφ᾽ ἡμέραν,
Ζεὺς οὗτος ἀνθρώποισι τοῖσι σώφροσιν,
λυπεῖν δὲ μηδὲν αὑτόν. οἳ δὲ τοὺς νόμους

340 ἔθεντο ποικίλλοντες ἀνθρώπων βίον,
κλαίειν ἄνωγα· τὴν <δ᾽> ἐμὴν ψυχὴν ἐγὼ
οὐ παύσομαι δρῶν εὖ, κατεσθίων γε σέ.

CYCLOPS

Little man, the wise regard wealth as the god to worship;
all else is just prating and fine-sounding sentiments. As for
the headlands where my father's temples are built, I pay
them no heed. Why did you bother to put them in your
speech? As for Zeus's thunderbolt, I do not shudder at
that, stranger, nor do I know any respect in which he is my
superior as a god. <If I ever thought about him before,> I
am not concerned about him for the future. How it is that
I am not concerned you may hear. When Zeus sends his
rain from above, taking my water-tight shelter in this cave
and dining on roasted calf or some wild animal, I put on a
feast for my upturned belly, then drinking dry a whole
storage vat of milk, I drum on it, making a din to rival
Zeus's thunder. And when the north wind out of Thrace
pours snow on us, I wrap my body in the skins of beasts,
pile up a great blazing fire, and pay no heed to the snow.
The Earth brings forth grass willy-nilly to feed my flock.
These I sacrifice to no one but myself—never to the
gods—and to my belly, the greatest of divinities. To guz-
zle and eat day by day and to give oneself no pain—this is
Zeus in the eyes of men of sense. As for those who have
passed laws and complicated men's lives, they can go hang.
For my part, I shall not forgo giving pleasure to my
heart—by eating you. Guest-presents you shall have—you

---

317 εὐμορφία Nauck:-ίαι L   318 αἷς Paley: ἆς L
322 ante h. v. lac. statui   324 ἔχων Reiske: ἔχω L
326 ἑστιῶ τι scripsi: ἐν στέγοντι L: εὖ τέγγων τε Reiske
327 εἶτ᾽ ἐκπιὼν Musgrave: ἐπεκπιὼν L
πλέων W. Gilbert: πέπλον L: πίθον Hartung: πέδον Musgrave
336 τοὐμπιεῖν Reiske: τοῦ πιεῖν L
340 <δ᾽> Barnes   341 γε Hermann: τε L

ξένια δὲ λήψῃ τοιάδ᾽, ὡς ἄμεμπτος ὦ,
πῦρ καὶ πατρῷον ἅλα λέβητά θ᾽, ὃς ζέσας
σὴν σάρκα δυσφάρωτον ἀμφέξει καλῶς.
345   ἀλλ᾽ ἕρπετ᾽ εἴσω, τοῦ κατ᾽ αὔλιον θεοῦ
ἵν᾽ ἀμφὶ βωμὸν στάντες εὐωχῆτέ με.

ΟΔΥΣΣΕΥΣ

αἰαῖ, πόνους μὲν Τρωικοὺς ὑπεξέδυν
θαλασσίους τε, νῦν δ᾽ ἐς ἀνδρὸς ἀνοσίου
ὠμὴν κατέσχον ἀλίμενόν τε καρδίαν.
350   ὦ Παλλάς, ὦ δέσποινα Διογενὲς θεά,
νῦν νῦν ἄρηξον· κρείσσονας γὰρ Ἰλίου
πόνους ἀφῖγμαι κἀπὶ κινδύνου βάθη.
σύ τ᾽, ὦ φαεννὰς ἀστέρων οἰκῶν ἕδρας
Ζεῦ ξένι᾽, ὅρα τάδ᾽· εἰ γὰρ αὐτὰ μὴ βλέπεις,
355   ἄλλως νομίζῃ, Ζεὺς τὸ μηδὲν ὢν, θεός.

ΧΟΡΟΣ

στρ.

Εὐρείας λάρυγγος, ὦ Κύκλωψ,
ἀναστόμου τὸ χεῖλος· ὡς ἕτοιμά σοι

---

343 ἅλα post Nauck (λίβα) scripsi: τόνδε L: τόδε Hermann
θ᾽ Nauck: γ᾽ L   344 δυσφάρωτον Barnes: δυσφόρητον L
345 τοῦ ... θεοῦ Blaydes: τῷ ... θεῷ L
346 βωμὸν Stephanus: κῶμον L
349 ὠμὴν Reiske: γνώμην L
352 βάθη Musgrave: βάθρα L
353 φαεννὰς Kassel: -ῶν L
356 λάρυγγος Seaford cl. 158, Eubul. fr. 139.2: φάρυγγος L

shall not blame me there—guest-presents of this kind: fire to warm you, salt[a] inherited from my father, and a bronze pot, which when it has reached a boil will clothe your ill-clad body nicely. Now go inside in order that you may stand around the altar of the god who dwells within and give me sumptuous entertainment.

ODYSSEUS

Oh, alas, I have escaped hardships at Troy and on the sea only to put in now at the fierce and harborless heart of this godless man!

O Pallas Athena, Zeus's divine daughter, now, now is the time to help me! For I have come into trouble greater than at Troy and to the very uttermost of danger. And you, Zeus, Protector of Guests, who dwell in the bright realm of the stars, look on these things! For if you take no note of them, men mistakenly worship you as a god when you are in fact Zeus the worthless.

The CYCLOPS *herds* ODYSSEUS *and his men into the cave.* SILENUS *follows.*

CHORUS

Open the gate, O Cyclops, of your yawning throat: the limbs of your guests, boiled, roasted, or hot from the coals,

[a] Conjecturally restored. The giving of salt was the proverbial emblem of hospitality, and Polyphemus has plenty from his father Poseidon. He will use it, however, to season his guest for eating.

ἑφθὰ καὶ ὀπτὰ καὶ ἀνθρακιᾶς ἄπο <θερμὰ>
χναύειν βρύκειν
κρεοκοπεῖν μέλη ξένων
360 δασυμάλλῳ ἐν αἰγίδι κλινομένῳ.

μεσῳδ.

μή 'μοὶ μὴ προσδίδου·
μόνος μόνῳ γέμιζε πορθμίδος σκάφος.
χαιρέτω μὲν αὖλις ἅδε,
χαιρέτω δὲ θυμάτων
365 ἀποβώμιος ἃν ἀνέχει θυσίαν
Κύκλωψ Αἰτναῖος ξενικῶν
κρεῶν κεχαρμένος βορᾷ.

ἀντ.

370 νηλής, τλᾶμον, ὅστε δωμάτων
371 ἐφεστίους ἱκτῆρας ἐκθύει ξένους,
373 ἑφθά τε δαινύμενος, μυσαροῖσί τ' ὀδοῦσιν
372 κόπτων βρύκων
374 θέρμ' ἀπ' ἀνθράκων κρέα
        < . . . . >

ΟΔΥΣΣΕΥΣ

375 ὦ Ζεῦ, τί λέξω, δείν' ἰδὼν ἄντρων ἔσω
        κοὐ πιστά, μύθοις εἰκότ' οὐδ' ἔργοις βροτῶν;

358 <θερμὰ> Hermann   βρύκειν Casaubon: βρύχ- L
360 κλινομένῳ Reiske: καινόμενα L
362 γέμιζε Wecklein: κόμιζε L
365 ἀνέχει Spengel: ἔχει L
370 τλᾶμον Wecklein: ὦ τλᾶμον L   ὅστε scripsi: ὅστις L

102

are ready for you to gnaw, rend, and devour as you recline dressed in a soft-fleeced goatskin.

Do not, do not, I say, give me any share of them! You yourself alone freight your vessel's hold! Away with this house! Away with the godless sacrifice of victims which Aetna's Cyclops celebrates, taking his pleasure in the flesh of his guests!

Hard-hearted one, pitiless is the man who sacrifices strangers who have taken refuge at his hearth, and who feasts on them boiled and with teeth defiled tears and devours their flesh warm from the coals < . . . . . . >!

Enter ODYSSEUS from the cave.

ODYSSEUS

O Zeus, what am I to say when I have seen in the cave terrible things, incredible things such as one meets only in stories, not in the deeds of mortals?

---

371 ἱκτῆρας Bothe: ξενικοὺς ἱκτῆρας L
ξένους Kirchhoff: δόμων L
373 ante 372 trai. Hermann   μυσαροῖσί τ᾽ Kirchhoff: -οῖσιν L
374 θέρμ᾽ Hermann: ἀνθρώπων θέρμ᾽ L   post h.v. lac.
stat. Haupt

ΧΟΡΟΣ

τί δ᾿ ἔστ᾿, Ὀδυσσεῦ; μῶν τεθοίναται σέθεν
φίλους ἑταίρους ἀνοσιώτατος Κύκλωψ;

ΟΔΥΣΣΕΥΣ

δισσούς γ᾿ ἀθρήσας κἀπιβαστάσας χεροῖν,
380   οἳ σαρκὸς εἶχον εὐτραφέστατον πάχος.

ΧΟΡΟΣ

πῶς, ὦ ταλαίπωρ᾿, ἦτε πάσχοντες τάδε;

ΟΔΥΣΣΕΥΣ

ἐπεὶ πετραίαν τήνδ᾿ ἐσήλθομεν στέγην,
ἀνέκαυσε μὲν πῦρ πρῶτον, ὑψηλῆς δρυὸς
κορμοὺς πλατείας ἐσχάρας βαλὼν ἔπι,
385   τρισσῶν ἁμαξῶν ὡς ἀγώγιμον βάρος,
392   καὶ χάλκεον λέβητ᾿ ἐπέζεσεν πυρί,
ἔπειτα φύλλων ἐλατίνων χαμαιπετῆ
ἔστρωσεν εὐνὴν πλησίον πυρὸς φλογί.
κρατῆρα δ᾿ ἐξέπλησεν ὡς δεκάμφορον,
μόσχους ἀμέλξας, λευκὸν ἐσχέας γάλα,
390   σκύφος τε κισσοῦ παρέθετ᾿ εἰς εὖρος τριῶν
391   πήχεων, βάθος δὲ τεσσάρων ἐφαίνετο,
393   ὀβελούς τ᾿, ἄκρους μὲν ἐγκεκαυμένους πυρί,
ξεστοὺς δὲ δρεπάνῳ τἄλλα, παλιούρου κλάδων,
395   †Αἰτναῖά τε σφαγεῖα πελέκεων γνάθοις†.
ὡς δ᾿ ἦν ἔτοιμα πάντα τῷ θεοστυγεῖ

---

377 τεθοίναται Reiske: γε θοινᾶται L
382 στέγην Musgrave: χθόνα L
392 huc trai. Paley (post 395 Hartung)

CHORUS LEADER

What is it, Odysseus? Can it really be that the godless
Cyclops has feasted on your dear companions?

ODYSSEUS

Yes. He spotted and weighed in his hands the two who
had the fattest flesh.

CHORUS LEADER

Poor man, how came your comrades to suffer this fate?

ODYSSEUS

When we entered this rocky hall, he first made the fire
blaze up, heaping onto the hearth thick logs from a mighty
oak, enough to load three wagons, and he set the bronze
kettle to boil on the fire. Then near the blaze he spread
out a bed of fir branches upon the ground. After he had
milked the heifers, he filled to the brim a great mixing
bowl, holding about ninety gallons, with white milk, and
he set next to it a cup of ivy wood four-and-a-half feet from
rim to rim and what looked like a good six feet to the bot-
tom; then spits made of buckthorn wood, their ends burnt
in the fire but the rest of them scraped with a scythe,
< . . . . . . >.[a] When that vile and murderous cook had

[a] In addition to the unintelligible 395, there is probably also a
lacuna here.

---

387 ἔστρωσεν Pierson: ἔστησεν L
394 κλάδων Scaliger: κλάδῳ L: κλάδους Kirchhoff
395 ante h. v. lac. indic. Boissonade, post h. v. Fix

"Αιδου μαγείρῳ, φῶτε συμμάρψας δύο

399 τὸν μὲν λέβητος ἐς κύτος χαλκήλατον
398 ἔσφαζ᾽ ἑταίρων τῶν ἐμῶν ῥυθμῷ τινι,
400 τὸν δ᾽ αὖ, τένοντος ἁρπάσας ἄκρου ποδός,
     παίων πρὸς ὀξὺν στόνυχα πετραίου λίθου
     ἐγκέφαλον ἐξέρρανε· καὶ διαρταμῶν
     λάβρῳ μαχαίρᾳ σάρκας ἐξώπτα πυρί,
     τὰ δ᾽ ἐς λέβητ᾽ ἐφῆκεν ἕψεσθαι μέλη.

405 ἐγὼ δ᾽ ὁ τλήμων δάκρυ ἀπ᾽ ὀφθαλμῶν χέων
     ἐχριμπτόμην Κύκλωπι κἀδιακόνουν·
     ἄλλοι δ᾽ ὅπως ὄρνιθες ἐν μυχοῖς πέτρας
     πτήξαντες εἶχον, αἷμα δ᾽ οὐκ ἐνῆν χροΐ.
     ἐπεὶ δ᾽ ἑταίρων τῶν ἐμῶν πλησθεὶς βορᾶς

410 ἀνέπεσε, φάρυγος αἰθέρ᾽ ἐξανεὶς βαρύν,
     ἐσῆλθέ μοί τι θεῖον· ἐμπλήσας σκύφος
     Μάρωνος αὐτῷ τοῦδε προσφέρω πιεῖν,
     λέγων τάδ᾽· Ὦ τοῦ ποντίου θεοῦ Κύκλωψ,
     σκέψαι τόδ᾽ οἷον Ἑλλὰς ἀμπέλων ἄπο

415 θεῖον κομίζει πῶμα, Διονύσου γάνος.
     ὁ δ᾽ ἔκπλεως ὢν τῆς ἀναισχύντου βορᾶς
     ἐδέξατ᾽ ἔσπασέν <τ᾽> ἄμυστιν ἑλκύσας
     κἀπήνεσ᾽ ἄρας χεῖρα· Φίλτατε ξένων,
     καλὸν τὸ πῶμα δαιτὶ πρὸς καλῇ δίδως.

420 ἡσθέντα δ᾽ αὐτὸν ὡς ἐπῃσθόμην ἐγώ,
     ἄλλην ἔδωκα κύλικα, γιγνώσκων ὅτι
     τρώσει νιν οἶνος καὶ δίκην δώσει τάχα.
     καὶ δὴ πρὸς ᾠδὰς εἷρπ᾽. ἐγὼ δ᾽ ἐπεγχέων
     ἄλλην ἐπ᾽ ἄλλῃ σπλάγχν᾽ ἐθέρμαινον ποτῷ.

everything ready, he snatched up two of my companions. He cut the throat of the first over the cauldron with a sweep of the arm and drained him of blood, the second he seized by the tendon at the end of his foot, struck him against the sharp edge of a rock, and dashed out his brains. Then butchering them with a fierce blade he roasted their fleshy parts in the fire and put their arms and legs in the cauldron to boil. I stood near the Cyclops in my wretchedness, tears streaming from my eyes, and attended him at his work. The others cowered like birds in the recesses of the cave, their faces pale and bloodless.

But when, sated with the meal he had made of my companions, he fell on his back and belched a foul stench from his maw, I was struck with a heaven-sent thought. I filled a cup with this Maron wine and offered it to him to drink with these words: "O Cyclops, son of the sea god, come see what kind of divine drink this is that Greece provides from its vines, the gleaming cup of Dionysus." And he, his belly full to bursting with that execrable meal, took it and downed it in one long draught, then raising his hand in admiration he said, "Dearest friend, you give me fine drink on top of a fine meal." Seeing it had given him pleasure, I gave him another cup, knowing that wine would be his undoing and he would soon pay the penalty. In due course he proceeded to sing, and I plied him with one cup after another and heated his heart with drink.

397 Ἄιδου Stephanus: δίδου L
399 ante 398 trai. Seaford
401 στόνυχα Scaliger: γ᾽ ὄνυχα L
402 διαρταμῶν Paley: καθαρπάσας L: καταρτάσας Shackle
410 ἐξανεὶς Porson: ἐξιεὶς L   417 <τ᾽> Barnes

425 ᾄδει δὲ παρὰ κλαίουσι συνναύταις ἐμοῖς
ἄμουσ᾽, ἐπηχεῖ δ᾽ ἄντρον. ἐξελθὼν δ᾽ ἐγὼ
σιγῇ σὲ σῶσαι κἄμ᾽, ἐὰν βούλῃ, θέλω.
ἀλλ᾽ εἴπατ᾽ εἴτε χρῄζετ᾽ εἴτ᾽ οὐ χρῄζετε
φεύγειν ἄμεικτον ἄνδρα καὶ τὰ Βακχίου
430 ναίειν μέλαθρα Ναΐδων νυμφῶν μέτα.
ὁ μὲν γὰρ ἔνδον σὸς πατὴρ τάδ᾽ ᾔνεσεν·
ἀλλ᾽ ἀσθενὴς γὰρ κἀποκερδαίνων ποτοῦ
ὥσπερ πρὸς ἰξῷ τῇ κύλικι λελημμένος
πτέρυγας ἀλύει· σὺ δέ (νεανίας γὰρ εἶ)
435 σώθητι μετ᾽ ἐμοῦ καὶ τὸν ἀρχαῖον φίλον
Διόνυσον ἀνάλαβ᾽, οὐ Κύκλωπι προσφερῆ.

ΧΟΡΟΣ

ὦ φίλτατ᾽, εἰ γὰρ τήνδ᾽ ἴδοιμεν ἡμέραν
Κύκλωπος ἐκφυγόντες ἀνόσιον κάρα.
ὡς διὰ μακροῦ γε †τὸν σίφωνα τὸν φίλον
440 χηρεύομεν τόνδ᾽ οὐκ ἔχομεν καταφαγεῖν.†

ΟΔΥΣΣΕΥΣ

ἄκουε δή νυν ἣν ἔχω τιμωρίαν
θηρὸς πανούργου σῆς τε δουλείας φυγήν.

ΧΟΡΟΣ

λέγ᾽, ὡς Ἀσιάδος οὐκ ἂν ἥδιον ψόφον
κιθάρας κλύοιμεν ἢ Κύκλωπ᾽ ὀλωλότα.

430 Ναΐδων Casaubon: δαναιδων L
439–40 τὸν φίλον χηρεύομεν / σίφωνα τόνδε Diggle: fort τὸν
φίλον θηρεύομεν (Scaliger) σίφωνα τόνδε κἀκφυγεῖν οὐκ εἴχομεν

108

Now hard by my weeping crew he sings his tuneless songs while the cavern echoes with it. I have crept out with the intention of saving you and me, if you agree. So tell me whether or not you want to be quit of this savage and live in the halls of Dionysus together with the Naiads. Your father assented to this in the cave, but since he is weak and has been enjoying the wine too much, he sticks fast to the cup like a bird caught in bird lime, flapping his wings in vain. But since you are young, escape with me and get back your old friend Dionysus, quite a different sort from the Cyclops.

CHORUS LEADER
Dearest of friends, if only we might see that day and escape from the impious Cyclops! For a long time now my poor siphon here has been widowed, with no place to lay its head.[a]

ODYSSEUS
Then listen to the punishment I have contrived for the knavish beast and how you may escape from slavery.

CHORUS LEADER
Say on! I would not enjoy hearing the sound of the Asian lyre more than the news of the Cyclops' death!

[a] I give what many think is the approximate sense. Also possible is "For a long time now I have been in quest of that dear wine spigot but could not escape."

109

ΟΔΥΣΣΕΥΣ

445 ἐπὶ κῶμον ἕρπειν πρὸς κασιγνήτους θέλει
Κύκλωπας ἡσθεὶς τῷδε Βακχίου ποτῷ.

ΧΟΡΟΣ

ξυνῆκ᾽· ἔρημον ξυλλαβὼν δρυμοῖσί νιν
σφάξαι μενοινᾷς ἢ πετρῶν ὦσαι κάτα.

ΟΔΥΣΣΕΥΣ

οὐδὲν τοιοῦτον· δόλιος ἡ προθυμία.

ΧΟΡΟΣ

450 πῶς δαί; σοφόν τοί σ᾽ ὄντ᾽ ἀκούομεν πάλαι.

ΟΔΥΣΣΕΥΣ

κώμου μὲν αὐτὸν τοῦδ᾽ ἀπαλλάξαι, λέγων
ὡς οὐ Κύκλωψι πῶμα χρὴ δοῦναι τόδε,
μόνον δ᾽ ἔχοντα βίοτον ἡδέως ἄγειν.
ὅταν δ᾽ ὑπνώσσῃ Βακχίου νικώμενος,
455 ἀκρεμὼν ἐλαίας ἔστιν ἐν δόμοισί τις,
ὃν φασγάνῳ τῷδ᾽ ἐξαποξύνας ἄκρον
ἐς πῦρ καθήσω· κᾆθ᾽ ὅταν κεκαυμένον
ἴδω νιν, ἄρας θερμὸν ἐς μέσην βαλῶ
Κύκλωπος ὄψιν ὄμμα τ᾽ ἐκτήξω πυρί.
460 ναυπηγίαν δ᾽ ὡσεί τις ἁρμόζων ἀνὴρ
διπλοῖν χαλινοῖν τρύπανον κωπηλατεῖ,
οὕτω κυκλώσω δαλὸν ἐν φαεσφόρῳ
Κύκλωπος ὄψει καὶ συναυανῶ κόρας.

---

447 δρυμοῖσί Tyrwhitt: ῥυθμοῖσί L
449 προθυμία Musgrave: ᾽πιθυμία L
458-9 βαλῶ . . . ὄμμα τ᾽ Pierson: βαλὼν . . . ὄμματ᾽ L

CYCLOPS

ODYSSEUS

He wants to go to his brother Cyclopes for a revel since he is delighted with this drink of Dionysus.

CHORUS LEADER

I take your drift. You are eager to catch him by himself in the woods and cut his throat or push him off a cliff.

ODYSSEUS

No, nothing like that. My desire is for something cunning.

CHORUS LEADER

What is it then? We have long heard about your cleverness.

ODYSSEUS

To begin with, I want to keep him from going on this revel by telling him he shouldn't give the other Cyclopes this drink but keep it to himself and live a life of pleasure. But when he falls asleep, overcome by Dionysus, there is an olive stake in his hall, whose tip, when I have sharpened it with this sword of mine, I shall put into the fire. Then when I see it burnt, I shall lift it hot and poke it into the Cyclops' face and melt his eye with the fire. And just as a ship's joiner whirls his auger with a pair of thongs, so I shall drill the brand into the Cyclops' orb of vision and burn out his eyeball.

ΧΟΡΟΣ

ἰοὺ ἰού·

465 γέγηθα μαινόμεσθα τοῖς εὑρήμασιν.

ΟΔΥΣΣΕΥΣ

κἄπειτα καὶ σὲ καὶ φίλους γέροντά τε
νεὼς μελαίνης κοῖλον ἐμβήσας σκάφος
διπλαῖσι κώπαις τῆσδ' ἀποστελῶ χθονός.

ΧΟΡΟΣ

ἔστ' οὖν ὅπως ἂν ὡσπερεὶ σπονδῆς θεοῦ
470 κἀγὼ λαβοίμην τοῦ τυφλοῦντος ὄμματα
δαλοῦ; φόνου γὰρ τοῦδε κοινωνεῖν θέλω.

ΟΔΥΣΣΕΥΣ

δεῖ γοῦν· μέγας γὰρ δαλός, οὗ ξυλληπτέον.

ΧΟΡΟΣ

ὡς κἂν ἁμαξῶν ἑκατὸν ἀραίμην βάρος,
εἰ τοῦ Κύκλωπος τοῦ κακῶς ὀλουμένου
475 ὀφθαλμὸν ὥσπερ σφηκιὰν ἐκθύψομεν.

ΟΔΥΣΣΕΥΣ

σιγᾶτέ νυν· δόλον γὰρ ἐξεπίστασαι·
χὤταν κελεύω, τοῖσιν ἀρχιτέκτοσιν
πείθεσθ'. ἐγὼ γὰρ ἄνδρας ἀπολιπὼν φίλους
τοὺς ἔνδον ὄντας οὐ μόνος σωθήσομαι.
480 [καίτοι φύγοιμ' ἂν κἀκβέβηκ' ἄντρου μυχῶν·
ἀλλ' οὐ δίκαιον ἀπολιπόντ' ἐμοὺς φίλους
ξὺν οἷσπερ ἦλθον δεῦρο σωθῆναι μόνον.]

CYCLOPS

CHORUS LEADER
Hurrah! I am driven frantic with joy by your inventions!

ODYSSEUS
Then I shall put you and my friends and your old father on board my black ship, and with paired oars I shall set off from this land.

CHORUS LEADER
Is there any way that I too could put my hand, as men do with a libation to the gods, to the brand that will blind the Cyclops? I want to have a part in this bloodletting.

ODYSSEUS
You must, for the brand is big and you must help to hold it.

CHORUS LEADER
I could lift the weight of a hundred wagons if we are going to smoke out that cursed Cyclops' eye like a wasps' nest!

ODYSSEUS
Then hold your tongue—you now know my plan—and when I give the word, do what the master builder tells you. I shall not leave behind my friends in the cave and save myself alone. [And yet I could flee, and I have come out of the cave, but it is not right to leave behind my friends with whom I came here and save myself alone.]

---

475 ἐκθύψομεν Hertlein: ἐκθρύψ- L
480–82 del. anonymus (1872), tum Conradt

ΧΟΡΟΣ

ἄγε, τίς πρῶτος, τίς δ᾽ ἐπὶ πρώτῳ
ταχθεὶς δαλοῦ κώπην ὀχμάσαι
485 Κύκλωπος ἔσω βλεφάρων ὤσας
λαμπρὰν ὄψιν διακναίσει;

           ᾠδὴ ἔνδοθεν

σίγα σίγα. καὶ δὴ μεθύων
ἄχαριν κέλαδον μουσιζόμενος
490 σκαιὸς ἀπῳδὸς καὶ κλαυσόμενος
χωρεῖ πετρίνων ἔξω μελάθρων.
φέρε νυν κώμοις παιδεύσωμεν
τὸν ἀπαίδευτον·
πάντως μέλλει τυφλὸς εἶναι.

στρ. α
495 μάκαρ ὅστις εὐιάζει
βοτρύων φίλαισι πηγαῖς
ἐπὶ κῶμον ἐκπετασθεὶς
φίλον ἄνδρ᾽ ὑπαγκαλίζων
ἐπὶ δεμνίοισί τ᾽ ἄνθος
500 χλιδανᾶς ἔχων ἑταίρας,
μυρόχριστον λιπαρὸς βό-
στρυχον, αὐδᾷ δέ· Θύραν τίς οἴξει μοι;

484 ὀχμάσαι Musgrave: ὀχμάσας L
492 νυν Diggle: νιν L
495 μάκαρ Hermann: μακάριος L
499 δεμνίοισί τ᾽ ἄνθος Meineke: δεμνίοις τε ξανθὸν L
501 μυρόχριστον Musgrave: μυρόχριστος L

114

CYCLOPS

CHORUS LEADER

Who shall be stationed first, who next to first, to hold fast the grip of the firebrand, thrust it beneath the Cyclops' brow, and grind to powder his bright eye?

Singing within.[a]

Hush! Hush! For now the Cyclops, drunk and making graceless melody, comes forth from the rocky cave, a singer who is inept and who shall pay dearly. Come, let us with our revelling songs impart some culture to this lout. In any case he shall be blind.

Enter the CYCLOPS *from the cave, leaning on* SILENUS.

CHORUS

Happy the man who shouts the Bacchic cry, off to the revel, the well-beloved juice of the vine putting the wind in his sails. His arm is around his trusty friend, and he has waiting for him the fresh, young body of his voluptuous mistress upon her bed, and with his locks gleaming with myrrh he says, "Who will open the door for me?"

[a] An ancient stage direction preserved in the text.

ΚΥΚΛΩΨ

στρ. β

παπαπαῖ· πλέως μὲν οἴνου,
γάνυμαι <δὲ> δαιτὸς ἥβᾳ,
505 σκάφος ὁλκὰς ὣς γεμισθεὶς
ποτὶ σέλμα γαστρὸς ἄκρας.
ὑπάγει μ᾽ ὁ φόρτος εὔφρων
ἐπὶ κῶμον ἦρος ὥραις
ἐπὶ Κύκλωπας ἀδελφούς.
510 φέρε μοι, ξεῖνε, φέρ᾽, ἀσκὸν ἔνδος μοι.

ΧΟΡΟΣ

στρ. γ

καλὸν ὄμμασιν δεδορκὼς
καλὸς ἐκπερᾷ μελάθρων
<κελαδῶν·> Φιλεῖ τις ἡμᾶς.
λύχνα δ᾽ ἀμμένειν ἔασον·
515 †χρόα χὼς† τέρεινα νύμφα
δροσερῶν ἔσωθεν ἄντρων.
στεφάνων δ᾽ οὐ μία χροιὰ
περὶ σὸν κρᾶτα τάχ᾽ ἐξομιλήσει.

ΟΔΥΣΣΕΥΣ

Κύκλωψ, ἄκουσον· ὡς ἐγὼ τοῦ Βακχίου
520 τούτου τρίβων εἴμ᾽, ὃν πιεῖν ἔδωκά σοι.

ΚΥΚΛΩΨ

ὁ Βάκχιος δὲ τίς; θεὸς νομίζεται;

ΟΔΥΣΣΕΥΣ

μέγιστος ἀνθρώποισιν ἐς τέρψιν βίου.

CYCLOPS

(*sung*) Ooh la la! I'm loaded up with wine, my heart skips with the cheer of the feast. My hull is full right up to the top deck of my belly. This cheerful cargo brings me out to revel, in the springtime, to the houses of my brother Cyclopes. Come now, my friend, come now, give me the wineskin.

CHORUS

With a lovely glance he steps forth in beauty from the halls <crying,> "Someone loves me." Don't wait for the hour of lamplighting: < . . . . . . > and a slender nymph are within a dewy cave. But it is crowns of more than one hue that will soon hold converse with your brow.

ODYSSEUS

Hear me, Cyclops, since I am acquainted with this Dionysus whom I gave you to drink.

CYCLOPS

Who is Dionysus? Is he worshipped as a god?

ODYSSEUS

Yes, the best source of joy in life for mortals.

---

504 <δὲ> Tr   ἥβα post Lobeck Diggle: -ης L
507 φόρτος Seymour: χόρτος L
512 καλὸς Scaliger: -ὸν L
513 <κελαδῶν ·> Diggle, e.g.
514 ἀμμένειν ἔασον Diggle: ἀμμένει δαΐα σὸν L
515 ῥόδα φῶς Diggle

ΚΥΚΛΩΨ

ἐρυγγάνω γοῦν αὐτὸν ἡδέως ἐγώ.

ΟΔΥΣΣΕΥΣ

τοιόσδ' ὁ δαίμων· οὐδένα βλάπτει βροτῶν.

ΚΥΚΛΩΨ

525   θεὸς δ' ἐν ἀσκῷ πῶς γέγηθ' οἴκους ἔχων;

ΟΔΥΣΣΕΥΣ

ὅπου τιθῇ τις, ἐνθάδ' ἐστὶν εὐπετής.

ΚΥΚΛΩΨ

οὐ τοὺς θεοὺς χρῆν σῶμ' ἔχειν ἐν δέρμασιν.

ΟΔΥΣΣΕΥΣ

τί δ', εἴ σε τέρπει γ'; ἢ τὸ δέρμα σοι πικρόν;

ΚΥΚΛΩΨ

μισῶ τὸν ἀσκόν· τὸ δὲ ποτὸν φιλῶ τόδε.

ΟΔΥΣΣΕΥΣ

530   μένων νυν αὐτοῦ πῖνε κεὐθύμει, Κύκλωψ.

ΚΥΚΛΩΨ

οὐ χρή μ' ἀδελφοῖς τοῦδε προσδοῦναι ποτοῦ;

ΟΔΥΣΣΕΥΣ

ἔχων γὰρ αὐτὸς τιμιώτερος φανῇ.

ΚΥΚΛΩΨ

διδοὺς δὲ τοῖς φίλοισι χρησιμώτερος.

⁵²⁵ οἴκους Canter: οἴνους L
⁵²⁷ χρῆν Nauck: χρὴ L

118

CYCLOPS
At any rate, I belch him out with pleasure.

ODYSSEUS
Such is this god. No mortal will he harm.

CYCLOPS
But how can a god love to dwell in a wineskin?

ODYSSEUS
Wherever you put him, there he is at ease.

CYCLOPS
The gods ought not to clothe themselves in skins.

ODYSSEUS
Why, if he gives delight? Do you mind the skin?

CYCLOPS
I hate the wineskin. But this drink I love.

ODYSSEUS
Stay here and drink then, Cyclops. Take your cheer.

CYCLOPS
Shall I not give my brothers some to drink?

ODYSSEUS
Keep it yourself and you will be more honored.

CYCLOPS
By giving it I'm more helpful to my kin.

ΟΔΥΣΣΕΥΣ

πυγμὰς ὁ κῶμος λοιδορόν τ' ἔριν φιλεῖ.

ΚΥΚΛΩΨ

535 μεθύω μέν, ἔμπας δ' οὔτις ἂν ψαύσειέ μου.

ΟΔΥΣΣΕΥΣ

ὦ τᾶν, πεπωκότ' ἐν δόμοισι χρὴ μένειν.

ΚΥΚΛΩΨ

ἠλίθιος ὅστις μὴ πιὼν κῶμον φιλεῖ.

ΟΔΥΣΣΕΥΣ

ὃς δ' ἂν μεθυσθείς γ' ἐν δόμοις μείνῃ σοφός.

ΚΥΚΛΩΨ

τί δρῶμεν, ὦ Σιληνέ; σοὶ μένειν δοκεῖ;

ΣΙΛΗΝΟΣ

540 δοκεῖ· τί γὰρ δεῖ συμποτῶν ἄλλων, Κύκλωψ;

ΟΔΥΣΣΕΥΣ

καὶ μὴν λαχνῶδές γ' οὖδας ἀνθηρᾶς χλόης.

ΣΙΛΗΝΟΣ

καὶ πρός γε θάλπος ἡλίου πίνειν καλόν.
κλίθητί νύν μοι πλευρὰ θεὶς ἐπὶ χθονός.

ΚΥΚΛΩΨ

ἰδού.

545 τί δῆτα τὸν κρατῆρ' ὄπισθ' ἐμοῦ τίθης;

541n Οδ. Mancini: κυ. L
541 γ' οὖδας Porson: τοὖδας L

120

ODYSSEUS
Revelling often ends in fists and quarrelling.

CYCLOPS
Besotted though I am, no man shall touch me!

ODYSSEUS
Good friend, it's best when drunk to stay at home.

CYCLOPS
Foolish the man who drinks and does not revel.

ODYSSEUS
But he who's drunk and stays at home is wise.

CYCLOPS
What shall we do, Silenus? Shall we stay?

SILENUS
Yes, stay: what need of other banqueters?

ODYSSEUS
What's more, the ground is soft with flowery boscage.

SILENUS
What's more, it's nice to drink when the sun's so hot.
Please lie down, then, recline upon the ground.

The Cyclops lies down. Silenus puts the mixing bowl behind him.

CYCLOPS
Done! Why are you putting the bowl behind me?

ΣΙΛΗΝΟΣ

ὡς μὴ παριών τις καταβάλῃ.

ΚΥΚΛΩΨ

πίνειν μὲν οὖν
κλέπτων σὺ βούλῃ· κάθες αὐτὸν ἐς μέσον.
σὺ δ᾽, ὦ ξέν᾽, εἰπὲ τοὔνομ᾽ ὅ τι σε χρὴ καλεῖν.

ΟΔΥΣΣΕΥΣ

Οὖτιν· χάριν δὲ τίνα λαβών σ᾽ ἐπαινέσω;

ΚΥΚΛΩΨ

550   πάντων σ᾽ ἑταίρων ὕστερον θοινάσομαι.

ΣΙΛΗΝΟΣ

καλόν γε τὸ γέρας τῷ ξένῳ δίδως, Κύκλωψ.

ΚΥΚΛΩΨ

οὗτος, τί δρᾷς; τὸν οἶνον ἐκπίνεις λάθρᾳ;

ΣΙΛΗΝΟΣ

οὔκ, ἀλλ᾽ ἔμ᾽ οὗτος ἔκυσεν ὅτι καλὸν βλέπω.

ΚΥΚΛΩΨ

κλαύσῃ, φιλῶν τὸν οἶνον οὐ φιλοῦντα σέ.

ΣΙΛΗΝΟΣ

555   οὐ μὰ Δί᾽, ἐπεί μού φησ᾽ ἐρᾶν ὄντος καλοῦ.

546 παριών Reiske: παρών L
551n Σι. Lenting: ὀδ. L
555 οὐ Diggle: ναὶ L

SILENUS

So no one passing by may knock it over.

CYCLOPS

No, you mean to steal some and drink it. Put it down between us. But you, stranger, tell me what name I must call you.

ODYSSEUS

Noman. What favor shall I get and thank you for?

CYCLOPS

Of all your company I shall eat you last.

SILENUS

Fine present, Cyclops, you have given your guest!

Silenus helps himself quietly to some wine.

CYCLOPS

You! What are you doing? Drinking on the sly?

SILENUS

No, the wine kissed me for my handsome looks.

CYCLOPS

You'll regret you loved the wine which loves not you.

SILENUS

No, by Zeus, for it says it has fallen for my beauty.

ΚΥΚΛΩΨ

ἔγχει, πλέων δὲ τὸν σκύφον δίδου μόνον.

ΣΙΛΗΝΟΣ

πῶς οὖν κέκραται; φέρε διασκεψώμεθα.

ΚΥΚΛΩΨ

ἀπολεῖς· δὸς οὕτως.

ΣΙΛΗΝΟΣ

οὐ μὰ Δί᾽, οὐ πρὶν ἄν γέ σε
στέφανον ἴδω λαβόντα γεύσωμαί τέ τι.

ΚΥΚΛΩΨ

560   οἰνοχόος ἄδικος.

ΣΙΛΗΝΟΣ

<ναὶ> μὰ Δί᾽, ἀλλ᾽ οἶνος γλυκύς.
ἀπομακτέον δέ σούστὶν ὡς λήψῃ πιεῖν.

ΚΥΚΛΩΨ

ἰδού, καθαρὸν τὸ χεῖλος αἱ τρίχες τέ μου.

ΣΙΛΗΝΟΣ

θές νυν τὸν ἀγκῶν᾽ εὐρύθμως κᾆτ᾽ ἔκπιε,
ὥσπερ μ᾽ ὁρᾷς πίνοντα — χὥσπερ οὐκέτι.

---

558 οὐ (prius) Wecklein: ναὶ L
560 οἰνοχόος Canter: ὦ οἰνοχόος L   <ναὶ> editio Aldina:
rasura in L
561 ἀπομακτέον Cobet: -μυκτέον L   σούστὶν Wilamowitz: σοι
L
564 οὐκέτι Nauck: οὐκ ἐμέ L

CYCLOPS

Just pour, give me the cup when you have filled it!

SILENUS

How is the mixture? Let me have a look.

CYCLOPS

You'll be the death of me! Just hand it over!

SILENUS

Not until I see you crowned (*gives him a garland to put on*) and have had a little taste.

CYCLOPS

This wine pourer's a crook.

SILENUS

Yes, but the wine is sweet. But time to wipe your mouth: here comes a drink.

CYCLOPS

I've wiped it off: my lips and beard are clean.

SILENUS

Lie gracefully on your elbow and drink it off, just as you see me drink—or see me not!

He drinks, tipping the wine cup up so as to be invisible behind it.

ΚΥΚΛΩΨ

565 ἆ ἆ, τί δράσεις;

ΣΙΛΗΝΟΣ
ἡδέως ἠμύστισα.

ΚΥΚΛΩΨ
λάβ᾽, ὦ ξέν᾽, αὐτὸς οἰνοχόος τέ μοι γενοῦ.

ΟΔΥΣΣΕΥΣ
γιγνώσκεται γοῦν ἄμπελος τἠμῇ χερί.

ΚΥΚΛΩΨ
φέρ᾽ ἔγχεόν νυν.

ΟΔΥΣΣΕΥΣ
ἐγχέω, σίγα μόνον.

ΚΥΚΛΩΨ
χαλεπὸν τόδ᾽ εἶπας, ὅστις ἂν πίνῃ πολύν.

ΟΔΥΣΣΕΥΣ
570 ἰδού· λαβὼν ἔκπιθι καὶ μηδὲν λίπῃς·
συνεκθανεῖν δὲ σπῶντα χρὴ τῷ πώματι.

ΚΥΚΛΩΨ
παπαῖ, σοφόν γε τὸ ξύλον τῆς ἀμπέλου.

ΟΔΥΣΣΕΥΣ
κἂν μὲν σπάσῃς γε δαιτὶ πρὸς πολλῇ πολύν,
τέγξας ἄδιψον νηδύν, εἰς ὕπνον βαλεῖ,
575 ἢν δ᾽ ἐλλίπῃς τι, ξηρανεῖ σ᾽ ὁ Βάκχιος.

566 λάβ᾽ ὦ . . . τέ μοι Dobree: λαβὼν . . . γέ μου L

CYCLOPS

Hey, what are you up to?

SILENUS

Nicely down the hatch!

CYCLOPS

Stranger, take charge of the wine and be my wine pourer.

ODYSSEUS

At least my hand has some acquaintance with the vine.

CYCLOPS

Come, pour then.

ODYSSEUS

See, I'm pouring. Just be quiet.

CYCLOPS

That's hard advice for a man who's downed a lot.

ODYSSEUS

(*handing him the cup*) There: take it and drain it off now.
No heel taps. The toper and his wine must end together.

CYCLOPS

Oh my, how clever is the grapevine's wood!

ODYSSEUS

And if you swig deep after a full meal and drink till your
belly loses its thirst, it will put you to sleep. But if you leave
some, Dionysus will give you a parching thirst.

---

⁵⁷¹ σπῶντα Casaubon: σιγῶντα L
⁵⁷³ σπάσῃς Dobree: -σῃ L
⁵⁷⁴ βαλεῖ Musgrave: -εῖς L

127

ΚΥΚΛΩΨ

ἰοὺ ἰού·
ὡς ἐξένευσα μόγις· ἄκρατος ἡ χάρις.
ὁ δ' οὐρανός μοι συμμεμειγμένος δοκεῖ
τῇ γῇ φέρεσθαι, τοῦ Διός τε τὸν θρόνον
580 λεύσσω τὸ πᾶν τε δαιμόνων ἁγνὸν σέβας.
οὐκ ἂν φιλήσαιμ'· αἱ Χάριτες πειρῶσί με.
ἅλις· Γανυμήδη τόνδ' ἔχων ἀναπαύσομαι
κάλλιον ἢ τὰς Χάριτας. ἥδομαι δέ πως
τοῖς παιδικοῖσι μᾶλλον ἢ τοῖς θήλεσιν.

ΣΙΛΗΝΟΣ
585 ἐγὼ γὰρ ὁ Διός εἰμι Γανυμήδης, Κύκλωψ;

ΚΥΚΛΩΨ
ναὶ μὰ Δί', ὃν ἁρπάζω γ' ἐγὼ 'κ τῆς Δαρδάνου.

ΣΙΛΗΝΟΣ
ἀπόλωλα, παῖδες· σχέτλια πείσομαι κακά.

ΚΥΚΛΩΨ
μέμφῃ τὸν ἐραστὴν κἀντρυφᾷς πεπωκότι;

ΣΙΛΗΝΟΣ
οἴμοι· πικρότατον οἶνον ὄψομαι τάχα.

ΟΔΥΣΣΕΥΣ
590 ἄγε δή, Διονύσου παῖδες, εὐγενῆ τέκνα,
ἔνδον μὲν ἀνήρ· τῷ δ' ὕπνῳ παρειμένος
τάχ' ἐξ ἀναιδοῦς φάρυγος ὠθήσει κρέα.

583 κάλλιον ἢ Spengel: κάλλιστα νὴ L
586 τῆς Hermann: τοῦ L   588 πεπωκότι Scaliger: -ότα L

The Cyclops has a long drink.

CYCLOPS

Calloo, callay! How close I was to drowning in it! This is
pleasure unalloyed. I think I see the heaven and the earth
swimming around together, I see Zeus's throne and the
whole revered company of the gods. Shall I not kiss them?
The Graces are trying to seduce me. No more! With this
Ganymede here I shall go off to bed with greater glory
than with the Graces. And somehow I take more pleasure
in boys than in women.

SILENUS

What, am I Zeus's boy Ganymede, Cyclops?

CYCLOPS

Yes, by Zeus, and I am abducting him from Dardanus'
house!

SILENUS

Oh, I am done for, my sons! A terrible fate is in store for
me!

CYCLOPS

Do you not like your lover and turn up your nose at one
who's drunk?

SILENUS

Oh me! My glimpse of the wine will soon prove all too
bitter!

Exit the CYCLOPS, with the reluctant SILENUS, into the cave.

ODYSSEUS

Come, Dionysus' children, noble offspring, the man's
within and soon, relaxed in sleep, he'll belch his meat out
from his shameless maw. Inside the hall the firebrand is

129

δαλὸς δ' ἔσωθεν αὐλίων πνέων καπνὸν
παρευτρέπισται, κοὐδὲν ἄλλο πλὴν πυροῦν
595 Κύκλωπος ὄψιν· ἀλλ' ὅπως ἀνὴρ ἔσῃ.

ΧΟΡΟΣ

πέτρας τὸ λῆμα κἀδάμαντος ἔξομεν.
χώρει δ' ἐς οἴκους πρίν τι τὸν πατέρα παθεῖν
ἀπάλαμνον· ὥς σοι τἀνθάδ' ἐστὶν εὐτρεπῆ.

ΟΔΥΣΣΕΥΣ

Ἥφαιστ', ἄναξ Αἰτναῖε, γείτονος κακοῦ
600 λαμπρὸν πυρώσας ὄμμ' ἀπαλλάχθηθ' ἅπαξ,
σύ τ', ὦ μελαίνης Νυκτὸς ἐκπαίδευμ', Ὕπνε,
ἄκρατος ἐλθὲ θηρὶ τῷ θεοστυγεῖ,
καὶ μὴ 'πὶ καλλίστοισι Τρωικοῖς πόνοις
αὐτόν τε ναύτας τ' ἀπολέσῃτ' Ὀδυσσέα
605 ὑπ' ἀνδρὸς ᾧ θεῶν οὐδὲν ἢ βροτῶν μέλει.
ἢ τὴν τύχην μὲν δαίμον' ἡγεῖσθαι χρεών,
τὰ δαιμόνων δὲ τῆς τύχης ἐλάσσονα.

ΧΟΡΟΣ

λήψεται τὸν τράχηλον
ἐντόνως ὁ καρκίνος
610 τοῦ ξενοδαιτυμόνος· πυρὶ γὰρ τάχα
φωσφόρους ὀλεῖ κόρας.
ἤδη δαλὸς ἠνθρακωμένος
615 κρύπτεται ἐς σποδιάν, δρυὸς ἄσπετον
ἔρνος. ἀλλ' ἴτω Μάρων,
πρασσέτω,
μαινομένου 'ξελέτω βλέφαρον

130

ready, sending forth smoke, and there is nothing left to do but to burn out the Cyclops' eye. But now you must show your manhood.

CHORUS LEADER

Our hearts shall be like rock or adamant! But go into the house before my father suffers some awful disaster. From this quarter all is ready for you.

ODYSSEUS

Hephaestus, lord of Aetna, burn out the bright eye of this pest, your neighbor, and be quit of him for good! And you, Sleep, child of black Night, come with undiluted force against this god-detested beast! After his glorious deeds at Troy do not let Odysseus, himself and his men, die at the hands of a man who heeds not gods or men. Otherwise, we will have to regard Chance as God and the gods as weaker than Chance.

Exit ODYSSEUS into the cave.

CHORUS

The tongs will firmly grasp the neck of the guest-eater: for by fire he will soon lose his shining eye. Already the fire-brand, burnt to charcoal, is hid in the ashes, huge offshoot of its tree. But let the Maron wine come, let it act, let it

---

⁵⁹³ πνέων Diggle: ὠθεῖ L
⁵⁹⁴ κοὐδὲν Kirchhoff: δ' οὐδὲν L
⁵⁹⁸ ἀπάλαμνον Canter: ἀπαλλαγμὸν L
⁶⁰⁴ ναύτας Tr: ναῦς L
⁶¹⁸ μαινομένου 'ξελέτω Hermann: μαινόμενος ἐξελέτω L

Κύκλωπος, ὡς πίῃ κακῶς.
620 κᾆτ᾽ ἐγὼ
τὸν φιλοκισσοφόρον Βρόμιον
ποθεινὸν εἰσιδεῖν θέλω,
Κύκλωπος λιπὼν ἐρημίαν·
ἆρ᾽ ἐς τοσόνδ᾽ ἀφίξομαι;

ΟΔΥΣΣΕΥΣ

625 σιγᾶτε πρὸς θεῶν, θῆρες, ἡσυχάζετε,
συνθέντες ἄρθρα στόματος· οὐδὲ πνεῖν ἐῶ,
οὐ σκαρδαμύσσειν οὐδὲ χρέμπτεσθαί τινα,
ὡς μὴ 'ξεγερθῇ τὸ κακόν, ἔστ᾽ ἂν ὄμματος
ὄψις Κύκλωπος ἐξαμιλληθῇ πυρί.

ΧΟΡΟΣ

σιγῶμεν ἐγκάψαντες αἰθέρα γνάθοις.

ΟΔΥΣΣΕΥΣ

630 ἄγε νυν ὅπως ἅψεσθε τοῦ δαλοῦ χεροῖν
ἔσω μολόντες· διάπυρος δ᾽ ἐστὶν καλῶς.

ΧΟΡΟΣ

οὔκουν σὺ τάξεις οὕστινας πρώτους χρεὼν
καυτὸν μοχλὸν λαβόντας ἐκκάειν τὸ φῶς
Κύκλωπος, ὡς ἂν τῆς τύχης κοινώμεθα;

ΧΟΡΟΣ Α

635 ἡμεῖς μέν ἐσμεν μακροτέρω πρὸ τῶν θυρῶν
ἑστῶτες ὠθεῖν ἐς τὸν ὀφθαλμὸν τὸ πῦρ.

620 κᾆτ᾽ ἐγὼ Willink: κἀγὼ L
633 καυτὸν Hermann: καὶ τὸν L

132

extract the eye of the mad Cyclops so that he may prove to have drunk to his cost! After that I long to see the lovely ivy-garlanded Dionysus and to leave behind the Cyclops' lonely dwelling. Shall I ever attain such joy?

Enter ODYSSEUS from the cave.

ODYSSEUS
Silence, you savages, for heaven's sake quiet! Let your lips be shut fast! I forbid anyone even to breathe or to blink or to clear his throat lest the monster wake up before the Cyclops' eye can have its contest with the fire.

CHORUS LEADER
We hold our peace, gulping down the air with our mouths.

ODYSSEUS
Come then, you must go inside and put your hands to the firebrand. It is now glowing nicely.

CHORUS LEADER
Won't you say who are to be the first to grasp the charred stake and burn out the Cyclops' eye, so that we may share in whatever fate chance holds?

LEADER OF CHORUS A
We stand too far from the door to push the fire into the Cyclops' eye.

ΧΟΡΟΣ Β

ἡμεῖς δὲ χωλοί γ᾽ ἀρτίως γεγενήμεθα.

ΧΟΡΟΣ Α

ταὐτὸν πεπόνθατ᾽ ἆρ᾽ ἐμοί· τοὺς γὰρ πόδας
ἑστῶτες ἐσπάσθημεν οὐκ οἶδ᾽ ἐξ ὅτου.

ΟΔΥΣΣΕΥΣ

640   ἑστῶτες ἐσπάσθητε;

ΧΟΡΟΣ Α

καὶ τά γ᾽ ὄμματα
μέστ᾽ ἐστὶν ἡμῖν κόνεος ἢ τέφρας ποθέν.

ΟΔΥΣΣΕΥΣ

ἄνδρες πονηροὶ κοὐδὲν οἵδε σύμμαχοι.

ΧΟΡΟΣ

ὁτιὴ τὸ νῶτον τὴν ῥάχιν τ᾽ οἰκτίρομεν
καὶ τοὺς ὀδόντας ἐκβαλεῖν οὐ βούλομαι
645   τυπτόμενος, αὕτη γίγνεται πονηρία;
ἀλλ᾽ οἶδ᾽ ἐπῳδὴν Ὀρφέως ἀγαθὴν πάνυ,
ὥστ᾽ αὐτόματον τὸν δαλὸν ἐς τὸ κρανίον
στείχονθ᾽ ὑφάπτειν τὸν μονῶπα παῖδα γῆς.

ΟΔΥΣΣΕΥΣ

πάλαι μὲν ἤδη σ᾽ ὄντα τοιοῦτον φύσει,
650   νῦν δ᾽ οἶδ᾽ ἄμεινον. τοῖσι δ᾽ οἰκείοις φίλοις
χρῆσθαί μ᾽ ἀνάγκη. χειρὶ δ᾽ εἰ μηδὲν σθένεις,
ἀλλ᾽ οὖν ἐπεγκέλευέ γ᾽, ὡς εὐψυχίαν
φίλων κελευσμοῖς τοῖσι σοῖς κτησώμεθα.

LEADER OF CHORUS B

And we have just now become lame.

LEADER OF CHORUS A

The same thing has happened to me. As I was standing
here I sprained my feet, I can't think how.

ODYSSEUS

You got a sprain while standing?

LEADER OF CHORUS A

Yes, and somehow my eyes have become full of dust and
ash.

ODYSSEUS

These allies of mine are cowardly and worthless.

CHORUS LEADER

Just because I take pity on my back and my spine and have
no desire to have my teeth knocked out, is that cowardice?
But I know an incantation of Orpheus so wonderful that
the firebrand all on its own will march up to his skull and
set the one-eyed son of earth on fire.

ODYSSEUS

For a long time I have known that your nature was like
this, but now I know it better. I must make use of my own
friends. But if you have no strength in your arm, at least
cheer us on so that with your encouragement we may find
our friends brave.

Exit ODYSSEUS into the cave.

---

641 μέστ' ἐστὶν Scaliger: μέτεσιν L   ἡμῖν Barnes: ἡμῶν L
647 ὥστ' Blaydes; ὡς L
649 ἤδη Heath: ἤδειν L

135

ΧΟΡΟΣ

δράσω τάδ᾽. ἐν τῷ Καρὶ κινδυνεύσομεν.
655   κελευσμάτων δ᾽ ἕκατι τυφέσθω Κύκλωψ.

ἰὼ ἰώ·
ὠθεῖτε γενναιότατα,
σπεύδετ᾽, ἐκκαίετ᾽ ὀφρὺν
θηρὸς τοῦ ξενοδαίτα.
τύφετ᾽ ὦ, καίετ᾽ ὦ
660   τὸν Αἴτνας μηλονόμον.
τόρνευ᾽ ἕλκε, μὴ 'ξοδυνη-
θεὶς δράσῃ τι μάταιον.

ΚΥΚΛΩΨ

ὤμοι, κατηνθρακώμεθ᾽ ὀφθαλμοῦ σέλας.

ΧΟΡΟΣ

καλός γ᾽ ὁ παιάν· μέλπε μοι τόνδ᾽ αὖ, Κύκλωψ.

ΚΥΚΛΩΨ

665   ὤμοι μάλ᾽, ὡς ὑβρίσμεθ᾽, ὡς ὀλώλαμεν.
ἀλλ᾽ οὔτι μὴ φύγητε τῆσδ᾽ ἔξω πέτρας
χαίροντες, οὐδὲν ὄντες· ἐν πύλαισι γὰρ
σταθεὶς φάραγγος τῆσδ᾽ ἐναρμόσω χέρας.

ΧΟΡΟΣ

τί χρῆμ᾽ ἀυτεῖς, ὦ Κύκλωψ;

ΚΥΚΛΩΨ

ἀπωλόμην.

CYCLOPS

CHORUS LEADER

I shall do so and let a mercenary run my risk. If encouragements can do it, let the Cyclops be burned!

CHORUS

Hurrah, hurrah! Thrust bravely, hurry, burn out the eyebrow of the guest-eating monster! Burn, incinerate the herdsman of Aetna! Whirl and pull, whirl and pull, lest in pain he do you some desperate harm!

Enter the CYCLOPS from the cave with bloodied mask.

CYCLOPS

Alas! My bright eye is all turned to cinder!

CHORUS LEADER

A lovely song: please sing it for me again, Cyclops!

CYCLOPS

Alas, alack! How I have been maltreated, how undone! But you will never escape this cave unpunished, you worthless wretches! For I shall take my stand in the entrance and fit my hands to it.

CHORUS LEADER

Why do you shout so, Cyclops?

CYCLOPS

I am ruined!

---

656 ὠθεῖτε γενναιότατα Diggle: γ- ὠ- L

657 ὀφρὺν Hermann: τὰν ὀφρὺν L

661 μὴ 'ξοδυνη- apogr. Par.: μή σ' ἐξοδυνη- L

664 αὖ Markland: ὦ L

668 τῆσδ' Nauck: τάσδ' L

ΧΟΡΟΣ

670 αἰσχρός γε φαίνῃ.

ΚΥΚΛΩΨ

κἀπὶ τοῖσδέ γ᾽ ἄθλιος.

ΧΟΡΟΣ

μεθύων κατέπεσες ἐς μέσους τοὺς ἄνθρακας;

ΚΥΚΛΩΨ

Οὖτίς μ᾽ ἀπώλεσ᾽.

ΧΟΡΟΣ

οὐκ ἄρ᾽ οὐδείς <σ᾽> ἠδίκει.

ΚΥΚΛΩΨ

Οὖτίς με τυφλοῖ βλέφαρον.

ΧΟΡΟΣ

οὐκ ἄρ᾽ εἶ τυφλός.

ΚΥΚΛΩΨ

†ὡς δὴ σύ†.

ΧΟΡΟΣ

καὶ πῶς σ᾽ οὖτις ἂν θείη τυφλόν;

ΚΥΚΛΩΨ

675 σκώπτεις. ὁ δ᾽ Οὖτις ποῦ ᾽στιν;

ΧΟΡΟΣ

οὐδαμοῦ, Κύκλωψ.

672 <σ᾽> Battierius
674 fort. ὡς δριμύ vel ὡς εἰλύ (εἰλύ· μέλαν Hesychius)
σ᾽ οὖτις Canter: σύ· τίς σ᾽ L

138

CHORUS LEADER

You *do* look ugly.

CYCLOPS

And miserable as well!

CHORUS LEADER

Did you fall in a drunken stupor into the coals?

CYCLOPS

Noman destroyed me.

CHORUS LEADER

No one, then, has wronged you.

CYCLOPS

Noman has blinded my eye.

CHORUS LEADER

So you are *not* blind.

CYCLOPS

<How sharp the pain!>^a

CHORUS LEADER

And how could nobody make you blind?

CYCLOPS

You mock me. But this Noman, where is he?

CHORUS LEADER

Nowhere, Cyclops.

---

^a The transmitted words are unintelligible and none of the conjectures is wholly satisfactory. This translation gives one possible sense.

ΚΥΚΛΩΨ

ὁ ξένος ἵν᾿ ὀρθῶς ἐκμάθῃς μ᾿ ἀπώλεσεν,
ὁ μιαρός, ὅς μοι δοὺς τὸ πῶμα κατέκλυσεν.

ΧΟΡΟΣ

δεινὸς γὰρ οἶνος καὶ παλαίεσθαι βαρύς.

ΚΥΚΛΩΨ

πρὸς θεῶν, πεφεύγασ᾿ ἢ μένουσ᾿ ἔσω δόμων;

ΧΟΡΟΣ

680 οὗτοι σιωπῇ τὴν πέτραν ἐπήλυγα
λαβόντες ἑστήκασι.

ΚΥΚΛΩΨ

ποτέρας τῆς χερός;

ΧΟΡΟΣ

ἐν δεξιᾷ σου.

ΚΥΚΛΩΨ

ποῦ;

ΧΟΡΟΣ

πρὸς αὐτῇ τῇ πέτρᾳ.

ἔχεις;

ΚΥΚΛΩΨ

κακόν γε πρὸς κακῷ· τὸ κρανίον
παίσας κατέαγα.

---

677 κατέκλυσεν Canter: κατέκαυσε L

CYCLOPS

Know well, it was my guest who destroyed me, the abominable guest, who drowned me with the drink he gave me.

CHORUS LEADER

Yes, wine is a dangerous thing and hard to wrestle against.

CYCLOPS

Tell me, for heaven's sake, have they fled or are they still in the house?

CHORUS LEADER

They are standing here quietly under the overhang of the cliff.

CYCLOPS

To my left or my right?

CHORUS LEADER

To your right.

The Cyclops moves from the entrance. ODYSSEUS *and his men accompanied by* SILENUS *slip silently out.*

CYCLOPS

Where?

CHORUS LEADER

Right next to the cliff. Have you got them?

The Cyclops collides with the rock cliff.

CYCLOPS

Yes, got pain on top of pain! I've hit my head and broken it.

141

ΧΟΡΟΣ

καί σε διαφεύγουσί γε.

ΚΥΚΛΩΨ

685   οὐ τῇδέ πη, τῇδ᾽ εἶπας;

ΧΟΡΟΣ

οὔ· ταύτῃ λέγω.

ΚΥΚΛΩΨ

πῇ γάρ;

ΧΟΡΟΣ

περιάγου κεῖσε, πρὸς τἀριστερά.

ΚΥΚΛΩΨ

οἴμοι γελῶμαι· κερτομεῖτέ μ᾽ ἐν κακοῖς.

ΧΟΡΟΣ

ἀλλ᾽ οὐκέτ᾽, ἀλλὰ πρόσθεν οὗτός ἐστι σοῦ.

ΚΥΚΛΩΨ

ὦ παγκάκιστε, ποῦ ποτ᾽ εἶ;

ΟΔΥΣΣΕΥΣ

τηλοῦ σέθεν

690   φυλακαῖσι φρουρῶ σῶμ᾽ Ὀδυσσέως τόδε.

ΚΥΚΛΩΨ

πῶς εἶπας; ὄνομα μεταβαλὼν καινὸν λέγεις.

685 τῇδέ πη Blaydes: τῇδ᾽ ἐπεὶ L
686 περιάγου κεῖσε Nauck: περιάγουσί σε L
690 σῶμ᾽ Canter: δῶμ᾽ L

142

CHORUS LEADER
And what's more, they've given you the slip.

CYCLOPS
Didn't you say somewhere over here?

CHORUS LEADER
No. I mean over here.

CYCLOPS
And where is that?

CHORUS LEADER
Turn round this way, to your left.

CYCLOPS
Oh, you are mocking me, deceiving me in my troubles!

CHORUS LEADER
I shall no more. He's right in front of you.

CYCLOPS
Knave, where in the world are you?

ODYSSEUS
At some distance, where I can keep the person of Odysseus here safe from harm.

CYCLOPS
What? This is a new name you use.

ΟΔΥΣΣΕΥΣ

ὅπερ μ᾽ ὁ φύσας ὠνόμαζ᾽ †Ὀδυσσέα†,
δώσειν δ᾽ ἔμελλες ἀνοσίου δαιτὸς δίκας·
κακῶς γὰρ ἂν Τροίαν γε διεπυρώσαμεν
695   εἰ μή σ᾽ ἑταίρων φόνον ἐτιμωρησάμην.

ΚΥΚΛΩΨ

αἰαῖ· παλαιὸς χρησμὸς ἐκπεραίνεται·
τυφλὴν γὰρ ὄψιν ἐκ σέθεν σχήσειν μ᾽ ἔφη
Τροίας ἀφορμηθέντος. ἀλλὰ καὶ σέ τοι
δίκας ὑφέξειν ἀντὶ τῶνδ᾽ ἐθέσπισεν,
700   πολὺν θαλάσσῃ χρόνον ἐναιωρούμενον.

ΟΔΥΣΣΕΥΣ

κλαίειν σ᾽ ἄνωγα· καὶ δέδραχ᾽ ὅπερ λέγεις.
ἐγὼ δ᾽ ἐπ᾽ ἀκτὰς εἶμι καὶ νεὼς σκάφος
ἥσω 'πὶ πόντον Σικελὸν ἔς τ᾽ ἐμὴν πάτραν.

ΚΥΚΛΩΨ

οὐ δῆτ᾽, ἐπεί σε τῆσδ᾽ ἀπορρήξας πέτρας
705   αὐτοῖσι συνναύταισι συντρίψω βαλών.
ἄνω δ᾽ ἐπ᾽ ὄχθον εἶμι, καίπερ ὢν τυφλός,
δι᾽ ἀμφιτρῆτος τῆσδε προσβαίνων ποδί.

692 μ᾽ Nauck: γ᾽ L   Ὀδυσσέα] fort. ὀργῆς χάριν
694 διεπυρώσαμεν Fix: -σάμην L
701 λέγεις Paley: -ω L
707 ποδί] πέτρας Kirchhoff

144

CYCLOPS

ODYSSEUS

The very one my father gave me, [Odysseus,][a] and you were destined, it seems, to pay the penalty for your ungodly feast. For my burning Troy to the ground would have been a sorry deed if I had not punished you for the murder of my companions.

CYCLOPS

Oh, oh, an ancient prophecy is now being fulfilled! It said that I would be blinded at your hands when you had set out from Troy. But it also prophesied that you would pay the penalty for this by drifting about on the sea for a long time.

ODYSSEUS

You can go hang, say I! And I have already done what you say I shall do. But now I shall go to the beach and launch my ship homeward over the Sicilian Sea.

Exit ODYSSEUS and his men by Eisodos B.

CYCLOPS

Oh no you won't: I shall break off a piece of this crag, hurl it, and crush you, companions and all, to bits. I'm going up to the hilltop, blind though I am, by climbing through my tunnel.[b]

---

[a] The repeated name looks suspicious. It may have ousted an expression like "(a name) derived from anger," an allusion to the derivation of Odysseus' name from ὀδύσσασθαι, to be angry at or to hate.

[b] The cave is imagined to have a back entrance looking over the sea.

ΧΟΡΟΣ

ἡμεῖς δὲ συνναῦταί γε τοῦδ᾽ Ὀδυσσέως
ὄντες τὸ λοιπὸν Βακχίῳ δουλεύσομεν.

CYCLOPS

Exit CYCLOPS into the cave.

CHORUS LEADER

As for us, we shall be shipmates with Odysseus and ever after serve in Dionysus' train.

Exit CHORUS and SILENUS by Eisodos B

ALCESTIS

INTRODUCTION

The story of Admetus—how Apollo, in gratitude for his kindness, tricked the Fates into granting him a reprieve from his fated day of death provided he could find a substitute, how his wife Alcestis agreed to die in his place, and how Heracles brought her back from Hades—had been the subject of an *Alcestis* by the early tragic poet Phrynichus, and the story is alluded to in Aeschylus, *Eumenides* 723ff. We have only one line, corrupt at that, from Phrynichus' play, but one of the themes inherent in the story, whether or not given prominence by Phrynichus, is visible in the Aeschylus passage, where the Erinyes complain to Apollo that he once erased the distinction between mortals and immortals by his favor to Admetus. Although this is a rhetorical exaggeration—Admetus gets postponement of death, not immortality—it indicates clearly what the story of Admetus is about. It is about suspension of the ordinary conditions of mortal existence.

Euripides developed this aspect of the myth to the full in the earliest of his extant tragedies and one of the most beautiful and satisfying plays he wrote. Whatever had been made of it before, in his hands it became one of those myths—like the stories in Grimm of three miraculous wishes or the myths of Midas or Tithonus—that console us for the disappointments of ordinary life and the fact of mortality by showing the disasters that would happen if these conditions of mortal existence were

151

suspended. Admetus is particularly favored in that he gets to postpone the day of his death. Yet the fact that he must lose his wife to enjoy this favor means, as he learns, that he would have been better off dying. The paradox of the story is that, while a woman who would die in her husband's stead would be the best of wives, the loss of so good a woman would render desolate and unlivable the remaining life she made possible for her husband. When his wife is restored to him at the end by the intervention of Heracles, Admetus has recovered not only her but also a juster appreciation of ordinary mortal existence.

Apollo's prologue sets forth both situation and theme. Apollo had been condemned to a period of servitude to a mere mortal, Admetus of Pherae, because both the god and his son Asclepius rebelled against the order of things established by Zeus. (Asclepius used his skill in medicine to raise the dead, a clear violation of the distinction between mortals and immortals. And when Zeus killed him with the thunderbolt, Apollo retaliated on the Cyclopes, who forged these weapons for Zeus.) To repay Admetus' kindness Apollo has won for his mortal master a reprieve from his fated early death provided he can find someone to die in his place. The god Death enters to claim Alcestis as Admetus' substitute. Apollo tells Death that he will be robbed of her by Heracles, who is on his way to fetch the horses of Diomedes. Apollo, god of prophecy, has the facts correct, but since he has never been a mortal, he cannot gauge the human realities of the situation he has created. These are played out in the sequel.

Alcestis is presented to us first in a messenger speech delivered by a maidservant, and then in person in her death scene before the palace. She loves her husband, but her decision to die for him is motivated, as her final speech to him suggests, by more practical considerations. She does not want to live apart from him with his orphaned children, she says. This would be her lot if she allowed him to die. If she dies, however, and Admetus does not remarry, the family, minus the mother, is intact. (The situation is quite different if Alcestis lives and Admetus dies. She presumably would have to remarry, and then her children by Admetus would take second place to the children her new husband gave her.) Her decision is not wildly quixotic but based on a calculus she and Admetus both accept.

For his part, Admetus is not content merely to accept the condition that he not remarry. To show that he loves Alcestis and realizes the value of her sacrifice, he promises her several other things she had not asked for: he vows perpetual mourning for her and forswears all music; and although her demand to him was only that he not remarry, Admetus swears perpetual celibacy and promises that his only sexual pleasure will be to embrace a statue of his dead wife. Alcestis says farewell to her children and her husband and dies. Their young son sings an affecting lament, and the picture before us is of a family united in grief.

After they go in and the Chorus sing an ode in praise of Alcestis, promising her immortality in song, Heracles arrives. Since the audience know from Apollo's prophecy that he will bring Alcestis back from the dead, they are in a position to see the significance of his arrival immediately after Alcestis' death, namely that the final dramatic movement of the play, from unhappiness to joy, has already been set in train, even though subjectively Admetus' fortunes have not yet reached their lowest ebb.

Heracles is reluctant to enter a house of mourning, and Admetus deceives him into thinking that Alcestis is still alive and it is some other woman who has died. This deception is necessary to the plot in three ways: first, Heracles must accept Admetus' hospitality if he is to figure in the sequel; second, Admetus' action in entertaining Heracles even when he is in mourning is regarded by Heracles as a piece of extraordinary generosity, and its repayment becomes the motive for his rescue of Alcestis; third, the deception (which he regards as well-meant and only *pretends* to take offense at) motivates his kindly deception of Admetus at the end of the play. Whether the concealing of Alcestis' death from Heracles was a traditional feature of the story or an invention of our poet, Euripides manages it in such a way that, after the audience's immediate shock at Admetus' deceptiveness, they are led by the Chorus's shocked question, Admetus' reply, and the Chorus's admiring ode on Admetus' hospitality to regard it not as evidence of moral obtuseness but as of a piece with his admirable treatment of Apollo.

Although the happy ending is already in train, Admetus must sink to further depths of grief. Just as the funeral procession is about to start off, Admetus' father Pheres comes to pay his respects. A hideous quarrel ensues, in which Admetus reproaches Pheres for not dying in his place and sparing Alcestis the necessity of doing so, and Pheres calls him a coward for not dying himself. Then returning from the funeral Admetus confronts his empty house, the misery of his longing for his dead wife, and the handle he has given (as his quarrel with his father showed) to anyone who wishes to call him a coward. Apollo's favor to him is no favor at all, for his wife's lot, he now sees, is more fortunate than his own.

The re-entrance of Heracles with the veiled Alcestis brings Admetus' fortunes, subjectively, to their very lowest ebb before transporting him, in the twinkling of an eye, from abject misery to inexpressible joy, a perfect Aristotelian *peripeteia* from bad fortune to good. Heracles pretends he has won a woman in a wrestling match and insists on entrusting her to Admetus' safekeeping; Admetus can see that the woman resembles his dead wife, he repeatedly refuses to take her in and reacts with shock to the hints of Heracles that he might find solace in her arms. When Heracles insists that he take her in by the hand, the point of Admetus' greatest misery is reached. That is the moment when Heracles removes the veil, and in an instant Admetus' misery turns to happiness. Heracles' deception of Admetus is a kindly return for Admetus' deception of him, for he proves his devotion to his dead wife while she is standing by unbeknownst to him.

The return of Alcestis means that ordinary life, lived under the usual conditions of mortality, is restored once more for Admetus and Alcestis, and significantly it is a son of Zeus who is the author of the restoration. Apollo's boon by itself was no boon. Heracles, son of Zeus, had spoken in his drunken discourse to the Manservant (773–802) of the nature of mortal life, that no one knows whether he will be alive tomorrow and so we must make good use of today. At the play's end he restores the order of Zeus, and Admetus declares "the new life we have now taken on is better than the old" (1157–8). The five anapestic lines at the very end express not only the unexpectedness of the events of this play but also the essential character of mor-

155

tal life, in which confident expectation is often defeated and it is wise to expect the unexpected.

Once the thematic of the play is grasped, the question of the characterization of Admetus, to which much attention is often devoted, becomes of secondary importance. Some critics judge Admetus' acceptance of his wife's sacrifice much more harshly than others. Some find in his hospitality something weighty to set down in his favor, while others regard it as superficial. Admetus is demonstrably neither a hero nor a knave, but the story requires only that he be neither. Just how bad a figure he cuts during the course of the play will be variously judged by various temperaments, with the indulgent applying fairy-tale and the censorious real-life standards of judgment. It is clear that for the working of this story his conduct must not be utterly clear of reproach, but clear also that we must not regard his happiness at the end as a monstrously unjust rewarding of the utterly unworthy. The important thing about Admetus is not his character in itself but his remarkable situation. When the ordinary rules of mortality are suspended, no one except Alcestis cuts a very noble figure.

Alcestis was the fourth play of four, a place occupied in all other known instances by a satyr play such as *Cyclops*. The play is, however, a tragedy in the ancient sense: Greek tragedies with happy endings, while not as common as the other sort, were written by all three of the fifth century's great tragic poets. The occasional comic elements, such as Heracles drunk, do not detract from the seriousness of the play or its tragic focus on the limits of human life.

SELECT BIBLIOGRAPHY

Editions

A. M. Dale (Oxford, 1954).
A. Garzya (Leipzig, 1980).
D. J. Conacher (Warminster, 1988)

Literary criticism

W. Arrowsmith, introduction to his translation (New York & London, 1974).
A. P. Burnett, "The Virtues of Admetus," *CP* 60 (1965), 240–55.
J. W. Gregory, "Euripides' *Alcestis*," *Hermes* 107 (1979), 259–70.
W. Smith, "The Ironic Structure in *Alcestis*," *Phoenix* 14 (1960), 126–45.
W. Steidle, *Studien zum antiken Drama* (Munich, 1968), pp. 29–32, 132–51.
J. R. Wilson, ed., *Twentieth-Century Interpretations of Euripides' 'Alcestis'* (Englewood Cliffs, 1968).

Dramatis Personae

ΑΠΟΛΛΩΝ	APOLLO
ΘΑΝΑΤΟΣ	DEATH
ΧΟΡΟΣ	CHORUS of men of Pherae
ΘΕΡΑΠΑΙΝΑ	MAIDSERVANT
ΑΛΚΗΣΤΙΣ	ALCESTIS, wife of Admetus
ΑΔΜΗΤΟΣ	ADMETUS, king of Pherae
ΠΑΙΣ	CHILD, son of Admetus and Alcestis
ΗΡΑΚΛΗΣ	HERACLES
ΦΕΡΗΣ	PHERES, father of Admetus
ΘΕΡΑΠΩΝ	MANSERVANT

A Note on Staging

The *skene* represents the palace of Admetus at Pherae in Thessaly. Eisodos A is the entrance-way imagined to lead from the countryside, Eisodos B that from the town.

159

ΑΛΚΗΣΤΙΣ

ΑΠΟΛΛΩΝ

Ὦ δώματ' Ἀδμήτει', ἐν οἷς ἔτλην ἐγὼ
θῆσσαν τράπεζαν αἰνέσαι θεός περ ὤν.
Ζεὺς γὰρ κατακτὰς παῖδα τὸν ἐμὸν αἴτιος
Ἀσκληπιόν, στέρνοισιν ἐμβαλὼν φλόγα·
5   οὗ δὴ χολωθεὶς τέκτονας Δίου πυρὸς
κτείνω Κύκλωπας· καί με θητεύειν πατὴρ
θνητῷ παρ' ἀνδρὶ τῶνδ' ἄποιν' ἠνάγκασεν.
ἐλθὼν δὲ γαῖαν τήνδ' ἐβουφόρβουν ξένῳ,
καὶ τόνδ' ἔσῳζον οἶκον ἐς τόδ' ἡμέρας.
10 ὁσίου γὰρ ἀνδρὸς ὅσιος ὢν ἐτύγχανον
παιδὸς Φέρητος, ὃν θανεῖν ἐρρυσάμην,
Μοίρας δολώσας· ᾔνεσαν δέ μοι θεαὶ
Ἄδμητον Ἅιδην τὸν παραυτίκ' ἐκφυγεῖν,
ἄλλον διαλλάξαντα τοῖς κάτω νεκρόν.
15 πάντας δ' ἐλέγξας καὶ διεξελθὼν φίλους,
[πατέρα γεραιάν θ' ἥ σφ' ἔτικτε μητέρα,]
οὐχ ηὗρε πλὴν γυναικὸς ὅστις ἤθελεν
θανὼν πρὸ κείνου μηκέτ' εἰσορᾶν φάος·

16 del. Dindorf   17 ὅστις Reiske: ἥτις C
18 θανὼν Reiske: θανεῖν C

160

ALCESTIS

Enter APOLLO *from the palace of Admetus. He is wearing a quiver and carrying a bow.*

APOLLO

House of Admetus! In you I brought myself to taste the bread of menial servitude, god though I am. Zeus was the cause: he killed my son Asclepius, striking him in the chest with the lightning bolt, and in anger at this I slew the Cyclopes who forged Zeus's fire. As my punishment for this Zeus compelled me to be a serf in the house of a mortal. I came to this land and served as herdsman to my host, and I have kept this house safe from harm to this hour. I am myself godly, and in Admetus, son of Pheres, I found a godly man. And so I rescued him from death by tricking the Fates. These goddesses promised me that Admetus could escape an immediate death by giving in exchange another corpse to the powers below. But when he had sounded all his near and dear in turn, [his father and the aged mother who bore him,] he found no one but his wife who was willing to die for him and look no more on the

ἢ νῦν κατ' οἴκους ἐν χεροῖν βαστάζεται
20   ψυχορραγοῦσα· τῇδε γάρ σφ' ἐν ἡμέρᾳ
θανεῖν πέπρωται καὶ μεταστῆναι βίου.
ἐγὼ δέ, μὴ μίασμά μ' ἐν δόμοις κίχῃ,
λείπω μελάθρων τῶνδε φιλτάτην στέγην.
ἤδη δὲ τόνδε Θάνατον εἰσορῶ πέλας,
25   ἱερέα θανόντων, ὅς νιν εἰς Ἅιδου δόμους
μέλλει κατάξειν· συμμέτρως δ' ἀφίκετο,
φρουρῶν τόδ' ἦμαρ ᾧ θανεῖν αὐτὴν χρεών.

ΘΑΝΑΤΟΣ

ἆ ἆ·
τί σὺ πρὸς μελάθροις; τί σὺ τῇδε πολεῖς,
30   Φοῖβ'; ἀδικεῖς αὖ τιμὰς ἐνέρων
ἀφοριζόμενος καὶ καταπαύων;
οὐκ ἤρκεσέ σοι μόρον Ἀδμήτου
διακωλῦσαι, Μοίρας δολίῳ
σφήλαντι τέχνῃ; νῦν δ' ἐπὶ τῇδ' αὖ
35   χέρα τοξήρη φρουρεῖς ὁπλίσας,
ἣ τόδ' ὑπέστη, πόσιν ἐκλύσασ'
αὐτὴ προθανεῖν Πελίου παῖς;

ΑΠΟΛΛΩΝ

θάρσει· δίκην τοι καὶ λόγους κεδνοὺς ἔχω.

ΘΑΝΑΤΟΣ

τί δῆτα τόξων ἔργον, εἰ δίκην ἔχεις;

19–20 ἤν ... ψυχορραγοῦσαν Usener cl. 201: post 19 lac. stat.
Kirchhoff

sun's light. She is now on the point of death, held up by
the arms of her family within the house, for it is on this day
that she is fated to die. And I, to avoid the pollution of
death in the house, am departing from this palace I love so
well.

Enter DEATH by an Eisodos (A?).

Ah, I see that Death, the sacrificer of the dead, is already
drawing near. He is about to take her down to the house
of Hades. He has arrived punctually, watching for today
when she must die.

DEATH

Ah! What are you doing at the palace? Why do you loiter
about here, Phoebus? Are you engaged in more injustice,
curtailing and annulling the prerogatives of the gods
below? Was it not enough that you prevented the death of
Admetus, tripping up the Fates by cunning trickery? Are
you now standing guard, bow in hand, over *her*, Pelias'
daughter, who promised to free her husband by dying in
his stead?

APOLLO

Fear not: I have nothing, I assure you, but justice and rea-
sonable words.

DEATH

If justice, then what need for your bow and arrows?

163

ΑΠΟΛΛΩΝ

40 σύνηθες αἰεὶ ταῦτα βαστάζειν ἐμοί.

ΘΑΝΑΤΟΣ

καὶ τοῖσδέ γ᾽ οἴκοις ἐκδίκως προσωφελεῖν.

ΑΠΟΛΛΩΝ

φίλου γὰρ ἀνδρὸς συμφοραῖς βαρύνομαι.

ΘΑΝΑΤΟΣ

καὶ νοσφιεῖς με τοῦδε δευτέρου νεκροῦ;

ΑΠΟΛΛΩΝ

ἀλλ᾽ οὐδ᾽ ἐκεῖνον πρὸς βίαν σ᾽ ἀφειλόμην.

ΘΑΝΑΤΟΣ

45 πῶς οὖν ὑπὲρ γῆς ἐστι κοὐ κάτω χθονός;

ΑΠΟΛΛΩΝ

δάμαρτ᾽ ἀμείψας, ἣν σὺ νῦν ἥκεις μέτα.

ΘΑΝΑΤΟΣ

κἀπάξομαί γε νερτέραν ὑπὸ χθόνα.

ΑΠΟΛΛΩΝ

λαβὼν ἴθ᾽· οὐ γὰρ οἶδ᾽ ἂν εἰ πείσαιμί σε.

ΘΑΝΑΤΟΣ

κτείνειν γ᾽ ὃν ἂν χρῇ; τοῦτο γὰρ τετάγμεθα.

ΑΠΟΛΛΩΝ

50 οὔκ, ἀλλὰ τοῖς μέλλουσι θάνατον ἀμβαλεῖν.

ΘΑΝΑΤΟΣ

ἔχω λόγον δὴ καὶ προθυμίαν σέθεν.

[50] ἀμβαλεῖν Bursian: ἐμβ- C

ALCESTIS

APOLLO

It is my custom always to carry them.

DEATH

Yes, and also to give unjust assistance to this house.

APOLLO

Certainly, since I am grieved by the misfortunes of my dear friend.

DEATH

Will you then rob me of a second corpse?

APOLLO

But not even the first did I take from you by force.

DEATH

Then how is he still on earth and not beneath the ground?

APOLLO

By giving in exchange the wife you have now come to fetch.

DEATH

Yes, and I will take her down below.

APOLLO

Take her and go: I doubt if I can persuade you.

DEATH

To kill my fated victims? Yes, for those are my orders.

APOLLO

No, to postpone death for the doomed.

DEATH

I now understand your purpose and your desire.

ΑΠΟΛΛΩΝ

ἔστ᾽ οὖν ὅπως Ἄλκηστις ἐς γῆρας μόλοι;

ΘΑΝΑΤΟΣ

οὐκ ἔστι· τιμαῖς κἀμὲ τέρπεσθαι δόκει.

ΑΠΟΛΛΩΝ

οὔτοι πλέον γ᾽ ἂν ἢ μίαν ψυχὴν λάβοις.

ΘΑΝΑΤΟΣ

55   νέων φθινόντων μεῖζον ἄρνυμαι γέρας.

ΑΠΟΛΛΩΝ

κἂν γραῦς ὄληται, πλουσίως ταφήσεται.

ΘΑΝΑΤΟΣ

πρὸς τῶν ἐχόντων, Φοῖβε, τὸν νόμον τίθης.

ΑΠΟΛΛΩΝ

πῶς εἶπας; ἀλλ᾽ ἦ καὶ σοφὸς λέληθας ὤν;

ΘΑΝΑΤΟΣ

ὠνοῖντ᾽ ἂν οἷς πάρεστι γηραιοὶ θανεῖν.

ΑΠΟΛΛΩΝ

60   οὔκουν δοκεῖ σοι τήνδε μοι δοῦναι χάριν.

ΘΑΝΑΤΟΣ

οὐ δῆτ᾽· ἐπίστασαι δὲ τοὺς ἐμοὺς τρόπους.

ΑΠΟΛΛΩΝ

ἐχθρούς γε θνητοῖς καὶ θεοῖς στυγουμένους.

ΘΑΝΑΤΟΣ

οὐκ ἂν δύναιο πάντ᾽ ἔχειν ἃ μή σε δεῖ.

[59] γηραιοὶ Hermann: -οὺς C

APOLLO
Well, is there any way Alcestis might reach old age?

DEATH
There is none. I too, you must know, get pleasure from my office.

APOLLO
You will not, of course, get more than one life in any case.

DEATH
I win greater honor when the victims are young.

APOLLO
And yet if she dies old, she will receive a rich burial.

DEATH
The law you are trying to establish, Phoebus, is to the advantage of the rich.

APOLLO
What do you mean? Can I have failed to appreciate what a thinker you are?

DEATH
Those with means could buy death at an advanced age.

APOLLO
You are not inclined, I take it, to grant me this favor.

DEATH
No, indeed. You know my character.

APOLLO
Yes, hateful to mortals and rejected by the gods.

DEATH
You may not have all that you should not have.

ΑΠΟΛΛΩΝ

ἦ μὴν σὺ παύσῃ καίπερ ὠμὸς ὢν ἄγαν·
65 τοῖος Φέρητος εἶσι πρὸς δόμους ἀνὴρ
Εὐρυσθέως πέμψαντος ἵππειον μετὰ
ὄχημα Θρήκης ἐκ τόπων δυσχειμέρων,
ὃς δὴ ξενωθεὶς τοῖσδ' ἐν Ἀδμήτου δόμοις
βίᾳ γυναῖκα τήνδε σ' ἐξαιρήσεται.
70 κοὔθ' ἡ παρ' ἡμῶν σοι γενήσεται χάρις
δράσεις θ' ὁμοίως ταῦτ' ἀπεχθήσῃ τ' ἐμοί.

ΘΑΝΑΤΟΣ

πόλλ' ἂν σὺ λέξας οὐδὲν ἂν πλέον λάβοις·
ἡ δ' οὖν γυνὴ κάτεισιν εἰς Ἅιδου δόμους.
στείχω δ' ἐπ' αὐτὴν ὡς κατάρξωμαι ξίφει·
75 ἱερὸς γὰρ οὗτος τῶν κατὰ χθονὸς θεῶν
ὅτου τόδ' ἔγχος κρατὸς ἁγνίσῃ τρίχα.

ΧΟΡΟΣ

— τί ποθ' ἡσυχία πρόσθεν μελάθρων;
τί σεσίγηται δόμος Ἀδμήτου;
— ἀλλ' οὐδὲ φίλων πέλας <ἔστ'> οὐδείς,
80 ὅστις ἂν εἴποι πότερον φθιμένην
χρὴ βασίλειαν πενθεῖν ἢ ζῶσ'
ἔτι φῶς λεύσσει Πελίου τόδε παῖς
Ἄλκηστις, ἐμοὶ πᾶσί τ' ἀρίστη
δόξασα γυνὴ
85 πόσιν εἰς αὐτῆς γεγενῆσθαι.

---

64 πείσῃ F. W. Schmidt   79 <ἔστ'> Monk
81 χρὴ βασίλειαν πενθεῖν Blomfield: β- π- χ- C
82 λεύσσει Πελίου τόδε Bothe: τ- λ- π- C

ALCESTIS

APOLLO

I swear to you that, ruthless as you are, you will yet cease from your hateful ways. The man to make you do so is coming to the house of Pheres sent by Eurystheus to fetch the horses and chariot from the wintry land of Thrace. He, entertained as a guest in this house of Admetus, shall take the woman from you by force. You shall do precisely as I have asked and yet get no gratitude from me but hatred instead.

Exit APOLLO by an Eisodos (A?).

DEATH

Your plentiful talk will gain you nothing. The woman is going down in any case to the house of Hades. I go to her to take the first sacrificial cutting of her hair. For when this sword has consecrated the hair of someone's head, he is the sacred property of the gods below.

Exit DEATH into the palace. Enter the CHORUS by Eisodos B. They divide into two semi-choruses.

LEADER OF CHORUS A

What means this stillness before the palace? Why is the house of Admetus wrapped in silence?

LEADER OF CHORUS B

What is more, there are not even any of his kin about who might say whether the queen has died and one should mourn her or whether Pelias' daughter still lives and looks on the light, Alcestis, the best of wives to her husband, as I and everyone regard her.

στρ. α

— κλύει τις ἢ στεναγμὸν ἢ
χειρῶν κτύπον κατὰ στέγας
ἢ γόον ὡς πεπραγμένων ;
— οὐ μὰν οὐδέ τις ἀμφιπόλων
90 στατίζεται ἀμφὶ πύλας.
εἰ γὰρ μετακοίμιος ἄτας,
ὦ Παιάν, φανείης.
— οὐ τὰν φθιμένας γ᾽ ἐσιώπων.
οὐ γὰρ δήπου
φροῦδός γε δόμων νέκυς ἤδη.
95— πόθεν ; οὐκ αὐχῶ. τί σε θαρσύνει ;
— πῶς ἂν ἔρημον τάφον Ἄδμητος
κεδνῆς ἂν ἔπραξε γυναικός ;

ἀντ. α

— πυλῶν πάροιθε δ᾽ οὐχ ὁρῶ
πηγαῖον ὡς νομίζεται
100 χέρνιβ᾽ ἐπὶ φθιτῶν πύλαις.
χαίτα τ᾽ οὔτις ἐπὶ προθύροις
τομαῖος, ὃ δὴ νεκύων
πένθει πρέπει, †οὐδὲ νεολαία†
δουπεῖ χεὶρ γυναικῶν.
105— καὶ μὴν τόδε κύριον ἦμαρ
— τί τόδ᾽ αὐδάσεις ;

91 μετακοίμιος Zacher: -κύμιος C (cf. Aesch. Cho. 1076)
94 δήπου φροῦδός γε δόμων Willink: δὴ φροῦδός γ᾽ ἐξ οἴκων fere
C
96 post h. v. lac. stat. Hartung, <μετά θ᾽ ἡσυχίας> e.g. suppl.
Oldfather cl. Σ   102 ὃ Diggle: ἆ C
170

CHORUS A

Does anyone hear a groan or a cry or the thud of hands striking the breast within the house, as if all were over?

CHORUS B

No, nor is there even a slave stationed at the gates. O God of Healing, may you come bringing respite from disaster!

CHORUS A

If she had died, there would not be silence. For of course the body has not been carried from the house already.

LEADER OF CHORUS B

How do you know? I am not sure. What makes you so confident?

LEADER OF CHORUS A

How would Admetus have held the funeral of his good wife without mourners?

CHORUS A

I do not see before the gates the lustral basin which custom places at the doors of those who have died. On the porch there is no cut lock of hair, which befits mourning for the dead, nor do the hands of women beat resoundingly.

CHORUS B

And yet this is the fated day . . .

CHORUS A

What is this you mean to say?

---

¹⁰³ πρέπει Blaydes: πιτνεῖ C   οὐ νέῳ ῞Αιδᾳ Willink: fort. οὐδὲ συναίμων
¹⁰⁶ αὐδάσεις Hermann: αὐδᾷς C

171

— ᾧ χρή σφε μολεῖν κατὰ γαίας.
— ἔθιγες ψυχῆς, ἔθιγες δὲ φρενῶν.
— χρὴ τῶν ἀγαθῶν διακναιομένων
110   πενθεῖν ὅστις
     χρηστὸς ἀπ᾿ ἀρχῆς νενόμισται.

στρ. β

     ἀλλ᾿ οὐδὲ ναυκληρίαν
     ἔσθ᾿ ὅποι τις αἴας
     στείλας, ἢ Λυκίαν
115   εἴτ᾿ ἐφ᾿ ἕδρας ἀνύδρους Ἀμμωνιάδας,
     δυστάνου παραλῦσαι
     ψυχάν· μόρος γὰρ ἀπότομος
     πλάθει. θεῶν δ᾿ ἐπ᾿ ἐσχάραν
120   οὐκέτ᾿ ἔχω τίνα μηλοθύταν πορευθῶ.

ἀντ. β

     μόνος δ᾿ ἄν, εἰ φῶς τόδ᾿ ἦν
     ὄμμασιν δεδορκὼς
     Φοίβου παῖς, προλιπεῖν
125   ἦνεν ἕδρας σκοτίους Ἅιδα τε πύλας·
     δμαθέντας γὰρ ἀνίστη,
     πρὶν αὐτὸν εἷλε διόβολον
     πλῆκτρον πυρὸς κεραυνίου.
130   νῦν δὲ βίου τίν᾿ ἔτ᾿ ἐλπίδα προσδέχωμαι;

     [πάντα γὰρ ἤδη †τετέλεσται βασιλεῦσιν†,
     πάντων δὲ θεῶν ἐπὶ βωμοῖς
     αἱμόρραντοι θυσίαι πλήρεις,
135   οὐδ᾿ ἔστι κακῶν ἄκος οὐδέν.]

ALCESTIS

CHORUS B
... when she must go beneath the earth.

LEADER OF CHORUS A
You have touched my heart, you have touched my soul.

LEADER OF CHORUS B
When the noble are afflicted, those who all their lives have
been deemed loyal must mourn.

The semi-choruses unite.

CHORUS
There is no shrine on earth where one might send even by
ship, either Lycia or the waterless seat of Ammon, to save
the life of the ill-starred queen. Death inexorable draws
nigh. And I know not to what sacrificial hearth of the gods
I am to go.

Only Phoebus' son, if he still looked upon the light of
the sun, would cause her to leave behind the gloomy realm
and the portals of Hades. For he used to raise the dead,
until the two-pronged goad of the lightning-fire killed
him. But now what hope can I still cherish that she will
live?

[For all is over for the royal family. At the altars of all
the gods are sacrifices dripping profusely with blood, and
there is no cure for disaster.]

---

114 Λυκίαν Monk: -ίας C   115–16 ἐφ᾽ ἕδρας ἀνύδρους /
Ἀμμ- Nauck: ἐπὶ τὰς ἀνύδρους Ἀμμωνιάδας ἕδρας C

120 οὐκέτ᾽ ἔχω Hartung; οὐκ ἔχω C   124 προλιπεῖν scripsi:
προλιπὼν a: προλιποῦσ᾽ b   125 ἧνεν Willink (ἤνυσ᾽ iam ego,
cl. Soph. O.T. 720): ἧλθεν C   130 βίου τίν᾽ ἔτ᾽ Hartung: τίν᾽
ἔτι βίου C   132–5 del. Wheeler

— ἀλλ' ἥδ' ὀπαδῶν ἐκ δόμων τις ἔρχεται
δακρυρροοῦσα· τίνα τύχην ἀκούσομαι;
πενθεῖν μέν, εἴ τι δεσπόταισι τυγχάνει,
συγγνωστόν· εἰ δ' ἔτ' ἐστὶν ἔμψυχος γυνὴ
140 εἴτ' οὖν ὄλωλεν εἰδέναι βουλοίμεθ' ἄν.

ΘΕΡΑΠΑΙΝΑ
καὶ ζῶσαν εἰπεῖν καὶ θανοῦσαν ἔστι σοι.

ΧΟΡΟΣ
καὶ πῶς ἂν αὑτὸς κατθάνοι τε καὶ βλέποι;

ΘΕΡΑΠΑΙΝΑ
143 ἤδη προνωπής ἐστι καὶ ψυχορραγεῖ.

ΧΟΡΟΣ
146 ἐλπὶς μὲν οὐκέτ' ἐστὶ σώζεσθαι βίον;

ΘΕΡΑΠΑΙΝΑ
147 πεπρωμένη γὰρ ἡμέρα βιάζεται.

ΧΟΡΟΣ
148 οὔκουν ἐπ' αὐτῇ πράσσεται τὰ πρόσφορα;

ΘΕΡΑΠΑΙΝΑ
149 κόσμος γ' ἕτοιμος, ᾧ σφε συνθάψει πόσις.

ΧΟΡΟΣ
144 ὦ τλῆμον, οἵας οἷος ὢν ἁμαρτάνεις.

ΘΕΡΑΠΑΙΝΑ
145 οὔπω τόδ' οἶδε δεσπότης, πρὶν ἂν πάθῃ.

146–9 ante 144 trai. Lueders

ALCESTIS

Enter a MAIDSERVANT *from the palace.*

CHORUS LEADER
But here comes one of the servants out of the house weeping. What turn of events will I hear from her? *(Addressing her)* If anything has befallen your master, it would be pardonable for you to grieve, but I would like to know whether the queen yet lives or has died.

MAIDSERVANT
You might call her both living and dead.

CHORUS LEADER
And how could the same person be both dead and alive?

MAIDSERVANT
She is already sinking and on the point of death.

CHORUS LEADER
Is there then no hope that her life may be saved?

MAIDSERVANT
No: her fated day presses on.

CHORUS LEADER
Are the necessary preparations then being made?

MAIDSERVANT
The finery in which her husband will bury her is ready.

CHORUS LEADER
Unhappy man, being so good a husband to lose so good a wife!

MAIDSERVANT
My master will not know his loss until it happens.

ΧΟΡΟΣ

150 ἴστω νυν εὐκλεής γε κατθανουμένη
γυνή τ' ἀρίστη τῶν ὑφ' ἡλίῳ μακρῷ.

ΘΕΡΑΠΑΙΝΑ

πῶς δ' οὐκ ἀρίστη; τίς δ' ἐναντιώσεται;
τί χρὴ λέγεσθαι τὴν ὑπερβεβλημένην
γυναῖκα; πῶς δ' ἂν μᾶλλον ἐνδείξαιτό τις
155 πόσιν προτιμῶσ' ἢ θέλουσ' ὑπερθανεῖν;
καὶ ταῦτα μὲν δὴ πᾶσ' ἐπίσταται πόλις·
ἃ δ' ἐν δόμοις ἔδρασε θαυμάσῃ κλύων.
ἐπεὶ γὰρ ᾔσθεθ' ἡμέραν τὴν κυρίαν
ἥκουσαν, ὕδασι ποταμίοις λευκὸν χρόα
160 ἐλούσατ', ἐκ δ' ἑλοῦσα κεδρίνων δόμων
ἐσθῆτα κόσμον τ' εὐπρεπῶς ἠσκήσατο,
καὶ στᾶσα πρόσθεν Ἑστίας κατηύξατο·
Δέσποιν', ἐγὼ γὰρ ἔρχομαι κατὰ χθονός,
πανύστατόν σε προσπίτνουσ' αἰτήσομαι,
165 τέκν' ὀρφανεῦσαι τἀμά· καὶ τῷ μὲν φίλην
σύζευξον ἄλοχον, τῇ δὲ γενναῖον πόσιν·
μηδ' ὥσπερ αὐτῶν ἡ τεκοῦσ' ἀπόλλυμαι
θανεῖν ἀώρους παῖδας, ἀλλ' εὐδαίμονας
ἐν γῇ πατρῴᾳ τερπνὸν ἐκπλῆσαι βίον.
170 πάντας δὲ βωμούς, οἳ κατ' Ἀδμήτου δόμους,
προσῆλθε κἀξέστεψε καὶ προσηύξατο,
πτόρθων ἀποσχίζουσα μυρσίνης φόβην,
ἄκλαυτος ἀστένακτος, οὐδὲ τοὐπιὸν
κακὸν μεθίστη χρωτὸς εὐειδῆ φύσιν.
175 κἄπειτα θάλαμον ἐσπεσοῦσα καὶ λέχος

ALCESTIS

CHORUS LEADER

Let her know then that she will die glorious and the noblest woman by far under the sun.

MAIDSERVANT

Most assuredly the noblest! Who will say she is not? What should we call the woman who surpasses her? How could any woman give greater proof that she gives her husband the place of honor than by being willing to die for him? This, of course, the whole city knows, but what she did within the house you will be amazed to hear. When she learned that the fated day had come, she bathed her fair skin in fresh water, and taking her finery from its chambers of cedar she dressed herself becomingly. And standing in front of the hearth goddess' altar she made her prayer: "Lady, since I am going now beneath the earth, as my last entreaty I ask you to care for my orphaned children: marry my son to a loving wife and give my daughter a noble husband. And may they not, like their mother, perish untimely but live out their lives in happiness in their ancestral land!"

She went to all the altars in Admetus' house and garlanded them, breaking off a spray of myrtle for each, and prayed. There was no tear in her eye or groan in her voice, nor was the lovely color of her skin changed by her looming misfortune. Then she entered the bedchamber. Here

---

153 λέγεσθαι Broadhead: γενέσθαι C

ἐνταῦθα δὴ 'δάκρυσε καὶ λέγει τάδε ·
Ὦ λέκτρον, ἔνθα παρθένε' ἔλυσ' ἐγὼ
κορεύματ' ἐκ τοῦδ' ἀνδρός, οὗ θνήσκω πάρος,
χαῖρ' · οὐ γὰρ ἐχθαίρω σ' · ἀπώλεσας δέ με
180   μόνον · προδοῦναι γάρ σ' ὀκνοῦσα καὶ πόσιν
θνήσκω. σὲ δ' ἄλλη τις γυνὴ κεκτήσεται,
σώφρων μὲν οὐκ ἂν μᾶλλον, εὐτυχὴς δ' ἴσως.
      κυνεῖ δὲ προσπίτνουσα, πᾶν δὲ δέμνιον
ὀφθαλμοτέγκτῳ δεύεται πλημμυρίδι.
185   ἐπεὶ δὲ πολλῶν δακρύων εἶχεν κόρον,
στείχει προνωπὴς ἐκπεσοῦσα δεμνίων,
καὶ πολλὰ θαλάμων ἐξιοῦσ' ἐπεστράφη
κἄρριψεν αὑτὴν αὖθις ἐς κοίτην πάλιν.
παῖδες δὲ πέπλων μητρὸς ἐξηρτημένοι
190   ἔκλαιον · ἡ δὲ λαμβάνουσ' ἐς ἀγκάλας
ἠσπάζετ' ἄλλοτ' ἄλλον ὡς θανουμένη.
πάντες δ' ἔκλαιον οἰκέται κατὰ στέγας
δέσποιναν οἰκτίροντες, ἡ δὲ δεξιὰν
προύτειν' ἑκάστῳ, κοὔτις ἦν οὕτω κακὸς
195   ὃν οὐ προσεῖπε καὶ προσερρήθη πάλιν.
τοιαῦτ' ἐν οἴκοις ἐστὶν Ἀδμήτου κακά.
καὶ κατθανὼν τἂν ᾤχετ', ἐκφυγὼν δ' ἔχει
τοσοῦτον ἄλγος, οὔποθ' οὗ λελήσεται.

ΧΟΡΟΣ
ἦ που στενάζει τοισίδ' Ἄδμητος κακοῖς,
200   ἐσθλῆς γυναικὸς εἰ στερηθῆναί σφε χρή;

178 πάρος Wilamowitz; πέρι C: cf. *Hcld.* 536
180 μόνον Markland: μόνην C

178

at last she wept and said, "O marriage bed, where I yielded up my virginity to my husband, the man for whose sake I am now dying, farewell! I do not hate you, although it is you alone that cause my death: it is because I shrank from abandoning you and my husband that I now die. Some other woman will possess you, luckier, perhaps, than I but not more virtuous."

She fell on the bed and kissed it and moistened all the bedclothes with a flood of tears. When she had had enough of weeping, she tore herself from the bed and walked bent with weakness, and again and again, as she was going out of the chamber, she turned back and threw herself upon the bed once more. Now the children were hanging onto their mother's gown and weeping, and she, taking them into her arms, gave them each her last kiss. All the servants in the house were weeping and bewailing their mistress. She reached out her hand to each of them, and none was so lowly that she did not address him and receive his blessing in return. Such are the troubles in Admetus' house. And if he had died he would be gone, but since he has escaped death, he lives with such grief as he shall never forget.

CHORUS LEADER

Admetus, I suppose, is groaning at this misfortune, that he must lose so noble a wife?

---

187 θαλάμων Nauck: θάλαμον C
197 ᾤχετ' F. W. Schmidt: ὤλετ' C
198 οὔποθ' οὐ Nauck: οὔποτ' οὐ a: οὖ ποτ' οὐ b

ΘΕΡΑΠΑΙΝΑ

κλαίει γ' ἄκοιτιν ἐν χεροῖν φίλην ἔχων
καὶ μὴ προδοῦναι λίσσεται, τἀμήχανα
ζητῶν· φθίνει γὰρ καὶ μαραίνεται νόσῳ.
παρειμένη δέ, χειρὸς ἄθλιον βάρος,
<κεῖται, τὸ σῶμα δ' οὐκέτ' ὀρθῶσαι σθένει.>
205 ὅμως δέ, καίπερ σμικρὸν ἐμπνέουσ' ἔτι,
βλέψαι πρὸς αὐγὰς βούλεται τὰς ἡλίου
ὡς οὔποτ' αὖθις, ἀλλὰ νῦν πανύστατον
[ἀκτῖνα κύκλον θ' ἡλίου προσόψεται].
ἀλλ' εἶμι καὶ σὴν ἀγγελῶ παρουσίαν·
210 οὐ γάρ τι πάντες εὖ φρονοῦσι κοιράνοις,
ὥστ' ἐν κακοῖσιν εὐμενεῖς παρεστάναι·
σὺ δ' εἶ παλαιὸς δεσπόταις ἐμοῖς φίλος.

ΧΟΡΟΣ

στρ.

— ἰὼ Ζεῦ, τίς ἂν πᾷ πόρος κακῶν
γένοιτο καὶ λύσις τύχας
ἃ πάρεστι κοιράνοις;
215— <αἰαῖ>· εἰσί τις; ἢ τέμω
τρίχα, καὶ μέλανα στολμὸν πέπλων
ἀμφιβαλώμεθ' ἤδη;
— δῆλα μέν, φίλοι, δῆλά γ', ἀλλ' ὅμως
θεοῖσιν εὐχώμεσθα· θεῶν δύναμις μεγίστα.

204 post h.v. lac. indic. Elmsley
208 del. Lachmann (207–8 [= Hec. 411–12] iam Valckenaer)
215 <αἰαῖ>· εἰσί τις; Wilamowitz: ἔξεισί τις C
219 θεῶν Hermann: θεῶν γὰρ C

MAIDSERVANT

Yes, he weeps, holding his beloved wife in his arms, and he begs her not to abandon him, asking for the impossible. For she is waning and wasting with her malady. And now, her body limp, a pitiful burden in his arms, <she lies unable to raise herself up>. Still, although she has scarcely any breath within her, she wishes once more to look on the light of the sun since it is now for the last time and never again that she does so [she will look upon the ray and orb of the sun]. But I will go and announce your arrival: for by no means does everyone wish their rulers well and stand by to show goodwill to them in their misfortune. But you are a friend of long standing to my masters.

Exit MAIDSERVANT into the palace.

CHORUS A

O Zeus, what way out of disaster could there be, what release from the fate that visits our royal family?

CHORUS B

Alas! Will someone come forth from the palace? Shall I cut my hair in mourning now and put on black apparel?

CHORUS A

Her fate is plain, my friends, all too plain, but still let us pray to the gods: the gods' power is supreme.

220— ὦναξ Παιάν,
  ἔξευρε μηχανάν τιν' Ἀδμήτῳ κακῶν.
— πόριζε δὴ πόριζε· καὶ
  πάρος γάρ <τι> τῷδ' ἐφηῦρες καὶ νῦν
  λυτήριος ἐκ θανάτου
225 γενοῦ, φόνιον δ' ἀπόπαυσον Ἅιδαν.
ἀντ.
— παπαῖ <φεῦ, παπαῖ φεῦ· ἰὼ ἰώ,>
  ὦ παῖ Φέρητος, οἷ' ἔπρα-
  ξας δάμαρτος σᾶς στερείς.
— αἰαῖ· ἄξια καὶ σφαγᾶς
  τάδε, καὶ πλέον ἢ βρόχῳ δέραν
  οὐρανίῳ πελάσσαι.
230— τὰν γὰρ οὐ φίλαν ἀλλὰ φιλτάταν
  γυναῖκα κατθανοῦσαν ἐν ἄματι τῷδ' ἐπόψῃ.
— ἰδοὺ ἰδού,
  ἅδ' ἐκ δόμων δὴ καὶ πόσις πορεύεται.
— βόασον ὦ στέναξον ὦ
235 Φεραία χθών, τὰν ἀρίσταν <πασᾶν>
  γυναῖκα μαραινομέναν
  νόσῳ κατὰ γᾶς χθόνιον παρ' Ἅιδαν.

— οὔποτε φήσω γάμον εὐφραίνειν
  πλέον ἢ λυπεῖν, τοῖς τε πάροιθεν
240 τεκμαιρόμενος καὶ τάσδε τύχας

222 <τι> Willink   τῷδ' Heath: τοῦδ' C
226 lac. suppl. Gaisford
235 <πασᾶν> Willink

ALCESTIS

CHORUS B

Lord of Healing,[a] contrive for Admetus some escape from disaster!

CHORUS A

Yes, devise a way! For you found one for him before. Now too be his rescuer from death, check deadly Hades!

CHORUS B

Alas! <Ah, alas!> O son of Pheres, what has your fortune become now that you are bereft of your wife!

CHORUS A

Oh, this calls for death by the sword and is more than enough to put one's neck in a noose hung high.

CHORUS B

Yes, for your wife, not dear but dearest, you will this day see dead.

Enter ALCESTIS *from the palace, supported by servants, and* ADMETUS *with their two children.*

CHORUS A

Look, look! Here she comes out of the house, and her husband with her.

CHORUS B

Cry aloud, O land of Pherae, weep for the noblest of all wives wasting away to Hades with fatal sickness!

CHORUS LEADER

I shall never henceforth say that marriage causes more joy than pain. So I conclude from what has gone before and

[a] Apollo is addressed by the cult title Paian.

EURIPIDES

λεύσσων βασιλέως, ὅστις ἀρίστης
ἀπλακὼν ἀλόχου τῆσδ' ἀβίωτον
τὸν ἔπειτα χρόνον βιοτεύσει.

ΑΛΚΗΣΤΙΣ

στρ. α

Ἅλιε καὶ φάος ἁμέρας
245 οὐράνιαί τε δῖναι νεφέλας δρομαίου.

ΑΔΜΗΤΟΣ

ὁρᾷ σὲ κἀμέ, δύο κακῶς πεπραγότας,
οὐδὲν θεοὺς δράσαντας ἀνθ' ὅτου θανῇ.

ΑΛΚΗΣΤΙΣ

ἀντ. α

γαῖά τε καὶ μελάθρων στέγαι
νυμφίδιοί τε κοῖται πατρίας Ἰωλκοῦ.

ΑΔΜΗΤΟΣ

250 ἔπαιρε σαυτήν, ὦ τάλαινα, μὴ προδῷς ·
λίσσου δὲ τοὺς κρατοῦντας οἰκτῖραι θεούς.

ΑΛΚΗΣΤΙΣ

στρ. β

ὁρῶ δίκωπον ὁρῶ σκάφος ἐν
λίμνᾳ · νεκύων δὲ πορθμεὺς
ἔχων χέρ' ἐπὶ κοντῷ Χάρων
255 μ' ἤδη καλεῖ · Τί μέλλεις;
ἐπείγου · σὺ κατείργεις. τάδε τοί
με σπερχόμενος ταχύνει.

184

from looking on the fate of my king, who will lose this noble wife and live henceforth a life that is no life at all.

ALCESTIS

(sung) O sun god, light of day, eddies of whirling clouds in the sky!

ADMETUS

The sun god sees you and me, two unfortunates, who have done nothing to the gods to deserve your death.

ALCESTIS

(sung) O land and palace and maiden bed of my ancestral Iolcus!

ADMETUS

Rouse yourself up, poor woman, do not abandon me! Pray for pity to the gods who have you in their grasp!

ALCESTIS

(sung) I see the two-oared boat in the lake. Charon, the ferryman of the dead, his hand on the boat pole, calls me now: "Why are you tarrying? Make haste, you hinder my going!" He speaks impatiently, urging me on with these words.

ΑΔΜΗΤΟΣ

οἴμοι· πικρὰν γε τήνδε μοι ναυκληρίαν
ἔλεξας. ὦ δύσδαιμον, οἷα πάσχομεν.

ΑΛΚΗΣΤΙΣ

ἀντ. β

ἄγει μ' ἄγει τις· ἄγει μέ τις (οὐχ
260   ὁρᾷς;) νεκύων ἐς αὐλάν,
ὑπ' ὀφρύσι κυαναυγέσι
βλέπων πτερωτὸς Ἅιδας.
τί ῥέξεις; ἄφες. οἵαν ὁδὸν ἁ
δειλαιοτάτα προβαίνω.

ΑΔΜΗΤΟΣ

οἰκτρὰν φίλοισιν, ἐκ δὲ τῶν μάλιστ' ἐμοὶ
265   καὶ παισίν, οἷς δὴ πένθος ἐν κοινῷ τόδε.

ΑΛΚΗΣΤΙΣ

ἐπῳδ.

μέθετε μέθετέ μ' ἤδη·
κλίνατ', οὐ σθένω ποσίν.
πλησίον Ἅιδας,
σκότια δ' ἐπ' ὄσσοισι νὺξ ἐφέρπει.
270   τέκνα τέκν', οὐκέτ' ἔστι δὴ σφῷν μάτηρ.
χαίροντες, ὦ τέκνα, τόδε φάος ὁρῷτον.

262 Ἅιδαν Wilamowitz
268 Ἅιδας Willink: Ἅιδας C
269 σκότια Elmsley: -ία C
270 οὐκέτ' scripsi: οὐκέτ' οὐκέτ' vel o. δὴ o. C
271 ἔστι δὴ σφῷν μάτηρ Willink: μ. σ. ἔ. C

ADMETUS

Oh, it is a bitter ferrying you speak of! O my luckless wife,
what suffering is ours!

ALCESTIS

(*sung*) Someone is taking, is taking me (don't you see
him?) away to the court of the dead. It is winged Hades,
glowering from beneath his dark brows. What do you
want? Let me go! Ah, what a journey it is that I, unhappi-
est of women, am making!

ADMETUS

A journey to make your loved ones weep, especially the
children and me, who feel this as their common grief.

ALCESTIS

(*to the servants*) (*sung*) Let me go, let me go now! Lay me
back, I have no strength in my legs! Hades is near and
night creeps darkly over my eyes. Children, children, your
mother is no more, no more! Farewell, my children, joy
be yours as you look on the light of the sun!

ΑΔΜΗΤΟΣ

οἴμοι· τόδ' ἔπος λυπρὸν ἀκούειν
καὶ παντὸς ἐμοὶ θανάτου μεῖζον.
275 μὴ πρός <σε> θεῶν τλῇς με προδοῦναι,
μὴ πρὸς παίδων οὓς ὀρφανιεῖς,
ἀλλ' ἄνα, τόλμα.
σοῦ γὰρ φθιμένης οὐκέτ' ἂν εἴην·
ἐν σοὶ δ' ἐσμὲν καὶ ζῆν καὶ μή·
σὴν γὰρ φιλίαν σεβόμεσθα.

ΑΛΚΗΣΤΙΣ

280 Ἄδμηθ', ὁρᾷς γὰρ τἀμὰ πράγμαθ' ὡς ἔχει,
λέξαι θέλω σοι πρὶν θανεῖν ἃ βούλομαι.
ἐγώ σε πρεσβεύουσα κἀντὶ τῆς ἐμῆς
ψυχῆς καταστήσασα φῶς τόδ' εἰσορᾶν
θνήσκω, παρόν μοι μὴ θανεῖν ὑπὲρ σέθεν,
285 ἀλλ' ἄνδρα τε σχεῖν Θεσσαλῶν ὃν ἤθελον
καὶ δῶμα ναίειν ὄλβιον τυραννίδι.
κοὐκ ἠθέλησα ζῆν ἀποσπασθεῖσα σοῦ
σὺν παισὶν ὀρφανοῖσιν, οὐδ' ἐφεισάμην
ἥβης, ἔχουσ' ἐν οἷς ἐτερπόμην ἐγώ.
290 καίτοι σ' ὁ φύσας χἠ τεκοῦσα προύδοσαν,
καλῶς μὲν αὐτοῖς †κατθανεῖν ἧκον† βίου,
καλῶς δὲ σῶσαι παῖδα κεὐκλεῶς θανεῖν.
μόνος γὰρ αὐτοῖς ἦσθα, κοὔτις ἐλπὶς ἦν
σοῦ κατθανόντος ἄλλα φιτύσειν τέκνα.

273 ἀκούειν Monk: ἀκούω C
275 <σε> Porson

ALCESTIS

ADMETUS

Alas! That is a painful thing to hear and a greater woe than any death for me. I beg you by the gods, by the children you will orphan, do not have the hardness to desert me! Up, endure! For if you are gone I live no more. Whether we live or not is in your power, for it is your love we hold in reverence.

ALCESTIS

Admetus, since you see how things stand with me, I want to tell you before I die what I wish. Because I give you the place of honor and have caused you to look on the light instead of me, I am dying. I need not have died in your place but could have married the Thessalian of my choice and lived in wealth in a royal house. But I refused to live torn from your side with orphaned children and did not spare my young life, though I had much in which I took delight. Yet your father and mother abandoned you, though it well befitted them to feel they had lived enough,[a] well befitted them to save their son and die a noble death. For you were their only son, and there was no hope, with you dead, that they would have other

[a] I translate the first of my tentative conjectures. The text is almost certainly corrupt.

---

[277] fort. εἶμεν

[287] κοὐκ Lenting: οὐκ C

[291] ἧκον ἐκστῆναι Hayley: fort. κόρον ἔχειν ἧκον vel καταμελεῖν ἧκον

295 κἀγώ τ' ἂν ἔζων καὶ σὺ τὸν λοιπὸν χρόνον,
κοὔκ ἂν μονωθεὶς σῆς δάμαρτος ἔστενες
καὶ παῖδας ὠρφάνευες. ἀλλὰ ταῦτα μὲν
θεῶν τις ἐξέπραξεν ὥσθ' οὕτως ἔχειν.

εἶεν· σύ νύν μοι τῶνδ' ἀπόμνησαι χάριν·
300 αἰτήσομαι γάρ σ' ἀξίαν μὲν οὔποτε
(ψυχῆς γὰρ οὐδέν ἐστι τιμιώτερον),
δίκαια δ', ὡς φήσεις σύ· τούσδε γὰρ φιλεῖς
οὐχ ἧσσον ἢ 'γὼ παῖδας, εἴπερ εὖ φρονεῖς·
τούτους ἀνάσχου δεσπότας ἐμῶν δόμων
305 καὶ μὴ 'πιγήμῃς τοῖσδε μητρυιὰν τέκνοις,
ἥτις κακίων οὖσ' ἐμοῦ γυνὴ φθόνῳ
τοῖς σοῖσι κἀμοῖς παισὶ χεῖρα προσβαλεῖ.
μὴ δῆτα δράσῃς ταῦτά γ', αἰτοῦμαί σ' ἐγώ.
ἐχθρὰ γὰρ ἡ 'πιοῦσα μητρυιὰ τέκνοις
310 τοῖς πρόσθ', ἐχίδνης οὐδὲν ἠπιωτέρα.
καὶ παῖς μὲν ἄρσην πατέρ' ἔχει πύργον μέγαν
[ὃν καὶ προσεῖπε καὶ προσερρήθη πάλιν]·
σὺ δ', ὦ τέκνον μοι, πῶς κορευθήσῃ καλῶς;
ποίας τυχοῦσα συζύγου τῷ σῷ πατρί;
315 μή σοί τιν' αἰσχρὰν προσβαλοῦσα κληδόνα
ἥβης ἐν ἀκμῇ σοὺς διαφθείρῃ γάμους.
οὐ γάρ σε μήτηρ οὔτε νυμφεύσει ποτὲ
οὔτ' ἐν τόκοισι σοῖσι θαρσυνεῖ, τέκνον,
παροῦσ', ἵν' οὐδὲν μητρὸς εὐμενέστερον.
320 δεῖ γὰρ θανεῖν με· καὶ τόδ' οὐκ ἐς αὔριον
οὐδ' ἐς τρίτην μοι †μηνὸς† ἔρχεται κακόν,
ἀλλ' αὐτίκ' ἐν τοῖς οὐκέτ' οὖσι λέξομαι.

190

children. Had they agreed to die, you and I would now be living the remainder of our lives together, and you would not be grieving at the loss of your wife or raising your children as orphans. But some god has brought these things to pass.

Well, then. Remember to show your gratitude for this. I shall not ask you for the return my act deserves (for nothing is more precious than a life), but for what is right, as you will agree. For you love these children as much as I do, if you are in your senses. Keep them as lords of my house and do not marry again, putting over them a stepmother, who will be less noble than I and out of envy will lay a hostile hand to your children and mine. No, do not do it, I beg you. For a stepmother comes in as a foe to the former children, no kinder to them than a viper. And though a son has in his father a bulwark of defense, how will you, my daughter, grow to an honored womanhood? What sort of stepmother will you get? May she not cast some disgraceful slur on your reputation and in the prime of your youth destroy your chances of marriage! Your mother will never see you married, never stand by to encourage you in childbirth, my daughter, where nothing is better than a mother's kindness. For I must die: this calamity does not come upon me tomorrow or the day after, but this very hour I will be numbered among the

---

312 del. Pierson: cf. 195
314 τοίας Reiske, tum fort. τυχούσης
321 τρίτον μοι φέγγος Herwerden: v. del. Mekler

χαίροντες εὐφραίνοισθε· καὶ σοὶ μέν, πόσι,
γυναῖκ᾽ ἀρίστην ἔστι κομπάσαι λαβεῖν,
325 ὑμῖν δέ, παῖδες, μητρὸς ἐκπεφυκέναι.

ΧΟΡΟΣ

θάρσει· πρὸ τούτου γὰρ λέγειν οὐχ ἅζομαι·
δράσει τάδ᾽, εἴπερ μὴ φρενῶν ἁμαρτάνει.

ΑΔΜΗΤΟΣ

ἔσται τάδ᾽, ἔσται, μὴ τρέσῃς· ἐπεί σ᾽ ἐγὼ
καὶ ζῶσαν εἶχον καὶ θανοῦσ᾽ ἐμὴ γυνὴ
330 μόνη κεκλήσῃ, κοὔτις ἀντὶ σοῦ ποτε
τόνδ᾽ ἄνδρα νύμφη Θεσσαλὶς προσφθέγξεται.
οὐκ ἔστιν οὕτως οὔτε πατρὸς εὐγενοῦς
οὔτ᾽ εἶδος ἄλλως ἐκπρεπεστάτη γυνή.
ἅλις δὲ παίδων· τῶνδ᾽ ὄνησιν εὔχομαι
335 θεοῖς γενέσθαι· σοῦ γὰρ οὐκ ὠνήμεθα.
οἴσω δὲ πένθος οὐκ ἐτήσιον τὸ σὸν
ἀλλ᾽ ἔστ᾽ ἂν αἰὼν οὑμὸς ἀντέχῃ, γύναι,
στυγῶν μὲν ἥ μ᾽ ἔτικτεν, ἐχθαίρων δ᾽ ἐμὸν
πατέρα· λόγῳ γὰρ ἦσαν οὐκ ἔργῳ φίλοι.
340 σὺ δ᾽ ἀντιδοῦσα τῆς ἐμῆς τὰ φίλτατα
ψυχῆς ἔσωσας. ἆρά μοι στένειν πάρα
τοιᾶσδ᾽ ἁμαρτάνοντι συζύγου σέθεν;
    παύσω δὲ κώμους συμποτῶν θ᾽ ὁμιλίας
στεφάνους τε μοῦσάν θ᾽ ἣ κατεῖχ᾽ ἐμοὺς δόμους.
345 οὐ γάρ ποτ᾽ οὔτ᾽ ἂν βαρβίτου θίγοιμ᾽ ἔτι
οὔτ᾽ ἂν φρέν᾽ ἐξάραιμι πρὸς Λίβυν λακεῖν
αὐλόν· σὺ γάρ μου τέρψιν ἐξείλου βίου.

dead. Farewell! I wish you joy! You, my husband, have the right to boast the best of wives, and you, my children, the best of mothers.

CHORUS LEADER

Fear not (I do not hesitate to speak for him): he will do this if he has any sense.

ADMETUS

It shall be so, fear not, it shall be so. While you lived you were my wife, and in death you alone will bear that title. No Thessalian bride will ever speak to me in place of you: none is of so noble parentage or so beautiful as that. And of children I have enough. I pray to the gods that I may reap the benefit of them, as I have not of you. I shall mourn you not a year only but as long as my life shall last, hating her who bore me and loathing my father. For their love was in word, not deed. But you sacrificed what is most precious so that I might live. Do I not have cause to mourn when I have lost such a wife as you?

I shall put an end to revels and the company of banqueters and to the garlands and music which once filled my halls. I shall never touch the lyre, or lift my heart in song to the Libyan pipe. For your death takes all the joy

---

[333] ἄλλων ἐκπρεπὴς οὕτω vel ἄλλως τ᾽ ἐκπρεπὴς ἄλλη Wecklein

σοφῇ δὲ χειρὶ τεκτόνων δέμας τὸ σὸν
εἰκασθὲν ἐν λέκτροισιν ἐκταθήσεται,
350 ᾧ προσπεσοῦμαι καὶ περιπτύσσων χέρας
ὄνομα καλῶν σὸν τὴν φίλην ἐν ἀγκάλαις
δόξω γυναῖκα καίπερ οὐκ ἔχων ἔχειν·
ψυχρὰν μέν, οἶμαι, τέρψιν, ἀλλ᾽ ὅμως βάρος
ψυχῆς ἀπαντλοίην ἄν. ἐν δ᾽ ὀνείρασιν
355 φοιτῶσά μ᾽ εὐφραίνοις ἄν· ἡδὺ γὰρ φίλους
κἂν νυκτὶ λεύσσειν, ὅντιν᾽ ἂν παρῇ χρόνον.
    εἰ δ᾽ Ὀρφέως μοι γλῶσσα καὶ μέλος παρῆν,
ὥστ᾽ ἢ κόρην Δήμητρος ἢ κείνης πόσιν
ὕμνοισι κηλήσαντά σ᾽ ἐξ Ἅιδου λαβεῖν,
360 κατῆλθον ἄν, καί μ᾽ οὔθ᾽ ὁ Πλούτωνος κύων
οὔθ᾽ οὑπὶ κώπῃ ψυχοπομπὸς ἂν Χάρων
ἔσχ᾽ ἄν, πρὶν ἐς φῶς σὸν καταστῆσαι βίον.
ἀλλ᾽ οὖν ἐκεῖσε προσδόκα μ᾽, ὅταν θάνω,
καὶ δῶμ᾽ ἑτοίμαζ᾽, ὡς συνοικήσουσά μοι.
365 ἐν ταῖσιν αὐταῖς γάρ μ᾽ ἐπισκήψω κέδροις
σοὶ τούσδε θεῖναι πλευρά τ᾽ ἐκτεῖναι πέλας
πλευροῖσι τοῖς σοῖς· μηδὲ γὰρ θανών ποτε
σοῦ χωρὶς εἴην τῆς μόνης πιστῆς ἐμοί.

ΧΟΡΟΣ

καὶ μὴν ἐγώ σοι πένθος ὡς φίλος φίλῳ
370 λυπρὸν συνοίσω τῆσδε· καὶ γὰρ ἀξία.

ΑΛΚΗΣΤΙΣ

ὦ παῖδες, αὐτοὶ δὴ τάδ᾽ εἰσηκούσατε
πατρὸς λέγοντος μὴ γαμεῖν ἄλλην ποτὲ

from my life. An image of you shaped by the hand of skilled craftsmen shall be laid out in my bed. I shall fall into its arms, and as I embrace it and call your name I shall imagine, though I have her not, that I hold my dear wife in my arms, a cold pleasure, to be sure, but thus I shall lighten my soul's heaviness. And perhaps you will cheer me by visiting me in dreams. For even in sleep it is pleasant to see loved ones for however long we are permitted.

If I had the voice and music of Orpheus so that I could charm Demeter's daughter or her husband with song and fetch you from Hades, I would have gone down to the Underworld, and neither Pluto's hound nor Charon the ferryman of souls standing at the oar would have kept me from bringing you back to the light alive. But now wait for me to arrive there when I die and prepare a home where you may dwell with me. For I shall command my children here to bury me in the same coffin with you and to lay out my body next to yours. Never, even in death, may I be parted from you, the woman who alone has been faithful to me!

CHORUS LEADER

Be sure that I will share in this bitter grief with you as friend with friend. She deserves no less.

ALCESTIS

Children, you yourselves have heard your father promise

---

353 οἶδα Elmsley
362 ἔσχ᾽ ἄν Lenting: ἔσχον C

195

EURIPIDES

γυναῖκ᾽ ἐφ᾽ ὑμῖν μηδ᾽ ἀτιμάσειν ἐμέ.

ΑΔΜΗΤΟΣ
καὶ νῦν γέ φημι καὶ τελευτήσω τάδε.

ΑΛΚΗΣΤΙΣ
375 ἐπὶ τοῖσδε παῖδας χειρὸς ἐξ ἐμῆς δέχου.

ΑΔΜΗΤΟΣ
δέχομαι, φίλον γε δῶρον ἐκ φίλης χερός.

ΑΛΚΗΣΤΙΣ
σύ νυν γενοῦ τοῖσδ᾽ ἀντ᾽ ἐμοῦ μήτηρ τέκνοις.

ΑΔΜΗΤΟΣ
πολλή μ᾽ ἀνάγκη, σοῦ γ᾽ ἀπεστερημένοις.

ΑΛΚΗΣΤΙΣ
ὦ τέκν᾽, ὅτε ζῆν χρῆν μ᾽, ἀπέρχομαι κάτω.

ΑΔΜΗΤΟΣ
380 οἴμοι, τί δράσω δῆτα σοῦ μονούμενος;

ΑΛΚΗΣΤΙΣ
χρόνος μαλάξει σ᾽· οὐδέν ἐσθ᾽ ὁ κατθανών.

ΑΔΜΗΤΟΣ
ἄγου με σὺν σοί, πρὸς θεῶν, ἄγου κάτω.

ΑΛΚΗΣΤΙΣ
ἀρκοῦμεν ἡμεῖς οἱ προθνήσκοντες σέθεν.

ΑΔΜΗΤΟΣ
ὦ δαῖμον, οἴας συζύγου μ᾽ ἀποστερεῖς.

380–1 del. Wheeler

196

never to put another woman over you, never to dishonor
me.

ADMETUS

I promise and will make it good hereafter.

ALCESTIS

On those terms, then, receive the children from my hand.

ADMETUS

I receive them, a precious gift from a precious hand.

ALCESTIS

Be therefore mother to these children in my place.

ADMETUS

So I clearly must since they are bereft of you.

ALCESTIS

Children, at a time when I ought to be alive I go below.

ADMETUS

Ah, what then shall I do separated from you?

ALCESTIS

Time will heal you. One who is dead is nothing.

ADMETUS

Take me with you, by the gods, take me below.

ALCESTIS

My death in your place is enough.

ADMETUS

O fate,[a] what a wife you take from me!

---

[a] The meaning of δαίμων here could be either the "guardian
spirit" of a man, identified as the force that assigns him his lot, or
"god, divinity," with possible reference to Hades.

ΑΛΚΗΣΤΙΣ

385   καὶ μὴν σκοτεινὸν ὄμμα μου βαρύνεται.

ΑΔΜΗΤΟΣ

ἀπωλόμην ἄρ᾽, εἴ με δὴ λείψεις, γύναι.

ΑΛΚΗΣΤΙΣ

ὡς οὐκέτ᾽ οὖσαν οὐδὲν ἂν λέγοις ἐμέ.

ΑΔΜΗΤΟΣ

ὄρθου πρόσωπον, μὴ λίπῃς παῖδας σέθεν.

ΑΛΚΗΣΤΙΣ

οὐ δῆθ᾽ ἑκοῦσά γ᾽· ἀλλὰ χαίρετ᾽, ὦ τέκνα.

ΑΔΜΗΤΟΣ

390   βλέψον πρὸς αὐτούς, βλέψον.

ΑΛΚΗΣΤΙΣ

                οὐδέν εἰμ᾽ ἔτι.

ΑΔΜΗΤΟΣ

τί δρᾷς; προλείπεις;

ΑΛΚΗΣΤΙΣ

    χαῖρ᾽.

ΑΔΜΗΤΟΣ

          ἀπωλόμην τάλας.

ΧΟΡΟΣ

βέβηκεν, οὐκέτ᾽ ἔστιν Ἀδμήτου γυνή.

ΠΑΙΣ

στρ.

ἰώ μοι τύχας. μαῖα δὴ κάτω

198

ALCESTIS

ALCESTIS
Already now my vision is growing dark and dim.

ADMETUS
I am lost, then, if you are going to leave me.

ALCESTIS
No more existing: such you may call me now.

ADMETUS
Raise up your head! Do not leave your children!

ALCESTIS
I leave them all unwilling. Farewell, children!

ADMETUS
Look at them, look!

ALCESTIS
I am gone.

ADMETUS
What are you doing? Are you leaving me?

ALCESTIS
Husband, farewell!

ADMETUS
I am utterly undone.

CHORUS LEADER
She is gone. Admetus' wife is no more.

CHILD
(sung) Alas for my fate! My mother has gone below: no

395 βέβακεν, οὐκέτ᾽ ἔστιν, ὦ πάτερ, ὑφ᾽ ἁλίῳ,
προλιποῦσα δ᾽ ἐμὸν βίον ὠρφάνισεν τλάμων.
†ἴδε γὰρ ἴδε βλέφαρον καὶ†
παρατόνους χέρας.
ὑπάκουσον ἄκουσον, ὦ
400 μᾶτερ, ἀντιάζω.
ἐγώ σ᾽ ἐγώ,
μᾶτερ, <μᾶτερ,> ὁ σὸς
ποτὶ σοῖσι πίτνων καλοῦ-
μαι στόμασιν νεοσσός.

ΑΔΜΗΤΟΣ

τὴν οὐ κλύουσαν οὐδ᾽ ὁρῶσαν· ὥστ᾽ ἐγὼ
405 καὶ σφὼ βαρείᾳ συμφορᾷ πεπλήγμεθα.

ΠΑΙΣ

ἀντ.

νέος ἐγώ, πάτερ, λείπομαι φίλας
μονόστολός τε ματρός· ὦ σχέτλια δὴ παθὼν
410 ἐγὼ ἔργ᾽ ἃ σὺ σύγκασί μοι συνέτλας κούρα.
< . . . .
. . . . > ὦ πάτερ,
ἀνόνατ᾽ ἀνόνατ᾽ ἐνύμ-
φευσας οὐδὲ γήρως
ἔβας τέλος
σὺν τᾷδ᾽· ἔφθιτο γὰρ
πάρος· οἰχομένας δὲ σοῦ,
415 μᾶτερ, ὄλωλεν οἶκος.

more, Father, is she in the light of the sun, and she has left
me an orphan. Look at her eyes and slackened arms.
Listen to me, Mother, listen, I implore you, it is I, Mother,
I, your little one falling upon your lips, who call your
name!

ADMETUS

She does not hear or see. You two and I are stricken with a
heavy misfortune.

CHILD

(*sung*) I am left young and cut adrift from my dear mother.
Oh, I have suffered terrible grief, and you, dear sister,
have suffered it too. < . . . . > O father, it was all in
vain, all in vain that you wedded since you did not come to
the end of your life with her. For she died first. And since
you have gone, Mother, the house is utterly destroyed.

---

³⁹⁶ ἐμὸν Monk: ἀμὸν C

⁴⁰²⁻³ <μᾶτερ,> ὁ σὸς / ποτὶ σοῖσι πίτνων καλοῦ- / μαι Willink:
καλοῦμαι ὁ σὸς ποτὶ σοῖσι πίτνων C

⁴⁰⁹⁻¹⁰ ἔργ᾽, ἃ σὺ σύγκασί μοι συνέτλας κούρα Willink: ἔργα σύ
τε μοι σύγκασι κ- συν- fere C   post h.v. lac. stat. Hermann

ΧΟΡΟΣ

Ἄδμητ᾽, ἀνάγκη τάσδε συμφορὰς φέρειν·
οὐ γάρ τι πρῶτος οὐδὲ λοίσθιος βροτῶν
γυναικὸς ἐσθλῆς ἤμπλακες· γίγνωσκε δὲ
ὡς πᾶσιν ἡμῖν κατθανεῖν ὀφείλεται.

ΑΔΜΗΤΟΣ

420 ἐπίσταμαί τοι, κοὐκ ἄφνω κακὸν τόδε
προσέπτατ᾽· εἰδὼς δ᾽ αὔτ᾽ ἐτειρόμην πάλαι.
ἀλλ᾽, ἐκφορὰν γὰρ τοῦδε θήσομαι νεκροῦ,
πάρεστε καὶ μένοντες ἀντηχήσατε
παιᾶνα τῷ κάτωθεν ἄσπονδον θεῷ.

425 πᾶσιν δὲ Θεσσαλοῖσιν ὧν ἐγὼ κρατῶ
πένθους γυναικὸς τῆσδε κοινοῦσθαι λέγω
κουρᾷ ξυρήκει καὶ μελαμπέπλῳ στολῇ·
τέθριππά θ᾽ οἳ ζεύγνυσθε καὶ μονάμπυκας
πώλους, σιδήρῳ τέμνετ᾽ αὐχένων φόβην.

430 αὐλῶν δὲ μὴ κατ᾽ ἄστυ, μὴ λύρας κτύπος
ἔστω σελήνας δώδεκ᾽ ἐκπληρουμένας.
οὐ γάρ τιν᾽ ἄλλον φίλτερον θάψω νεκρὸν
τοῦδ᾽ οὐδ᾽ ἀμείνον᾽ εἰς ἔμ᾽· ἀξία δέ μοι
τιμῆς, ἐπεὶ τέθνηκεν ἀντ᾽ ἐμοῦ μόνη.

ΧΟΡΟΣ

στρ. α
435 ὦ Πελίου θύγατερ,
χαίρουσά μοι εἰν Ἅιδα δόμοισιν
τὸν ἀνάλιον οἶκον οἰκετεύοις.

ALCESTIS

CHORUS LEADER

Admetus, you must endure this misfortune. For you are
not the first or last of mortals to lose a noble wife. Know
that death is a debt we all must pay.

ADMETUS

I understand that, and this sorrow did not fall upon me
unexpected. I have long been worn down with the
knowledge of it. But since I shall conduct the funeral,
attend me here, and while you wait sing a hymn to the god
below, a hymn unaccompanied by libations.

I command all the Thessalians in my realm to join in
the mourning for my wife: let them cut their hair and
wear black apparel. All you who yoke teams and all single
riders, cut your horses' manes with a blade. And let there
be no sound of pipe or lyre in the city for twelve full
months. For I shall never bury one I love more or who has
been kinder to me. She deserves my honor since she died
for me as would no one else.

Exit ADMETUS *with children and retinue carrying* AL-
CESTIS' *body into the palace.*

CHORUS

O daughter of Pelias, farewell, and may you have joy even
as you dwell in the sunless house of Hades! Let Hades,

---

^{420} τοι Nauck: τε a: γε b
^{424} ἄσπονδον Σ: ἀσπόνδῳ C

ἴστω δ᾽ Ἀΐδας ὁ μελαγχαί-
τας θεὸς ὅς τ᾽ ἐπὶ κώπᾳ
440 πηδαλίῳ τε γέρων
νεκροπομπὸς ἵζει
πολὺ δὴ πολὺ δὴ γυναῖκ᾽ ἀρίσταν
λίμναν Ἀχεροντίαν πορεύ-
σας ἐλάτᾳ δικώπῳ.

ἀντ. α
445 πολλά σε μουσοπόλοι
μέλψουσι καθ᾽ ἑπτάτονόν τ᾽ ὀρείαν
χέλυν ἔν τ᾽ ἀλύροις κλέοντες ὕμνοις,
Σπάρτᾳ κυκλὰς ἁνίκα Καρνεί-
ου περινίσεται ὥρα
450 μηνός, ἀειρομένας
παννύχου σελάνας,
λιπαραῖσί τ᾽ ἐν ὀλβίαις Ἀθάναις,
τοίαν ἔλιπες θανοῦσα μολ-
πὰν μελέων ἀοιδοῖς.

στρ. β
455 εἴθ᾽ ἐπ᾽ ἐμοὶ μὲν εἴη,
δυναίμαν δέ σε πέμ-
ψαι φάος ἐξ Ἀΐδα τεράμνων
Κωκυτοῖο ῥεέθρων
ποταμίᾳ νερτέρᾳ τε κώπᾳ.
460 σὺ γάρ, ὦ μόνα ὦ φίλα γυναικῶν,
σὺ τὸν αὑτᾶς ἔτλας
πόσιν ἀντὶ σᾶς ἀμεῖψαι
ψυχᾶς ἐξ Ἅιδα. κούφα σοι

204

black-haired god, and the old man who sits at oar and tiller, ferryman of souls, be in no doubt that it is by far the best of women that he has ferried in his skiff across the lake of Acheron.

Poets shall sing often in your praise both on the seven-stringed mountain tortoise shell[a] and in songs unaccompanied by the lyre when at Sparta the month of Carnea[b] comes circling round and the moon is aloft the whole night long, and also in rich, gleaming Athens. Such is the theme for song that you have left for poets by your death.

Would that it lay in my power and I could escort you to the light from the halls of Hades by an oar plied on the nether stream of Cocytus! For you, you alone, dear among women, had the courage to redeem your husband from Hades at the price of your life. May the earth lie

[a] Hermes is said to have made the first lyre out of a tortoise shell.

[b] The Spartan month of Carnea was the time of a festival, also called Carnea. This passage is our only evidence showing that it included musical performances.

---

[448] κυκλὰς Scaliger: κύκλος C
[458] Κωκυτοῖο Willink: καὶ Κωκυτοῖο a: καὶ Κωκυτοῦ τε b
[461] αὑτᾶς Erfurdt: ἑαυτ- a σαυτ- b

χθὼν ἐπάνωθε πέσοι, γύναι. εἰ δέ τι
καινὸν ἕλοιτο πόσις λέχος, ἦ μάλ' ἂν
465   ἔμοιγ' ἂν εἴη στυγη-
θεὶς τέκνοις τε τοῖς σοῖς.

ἀντ. β

ματέρος οὐ θελούσας
πρὸ παιδὸς χθονὶ κρύ-
ψαι δέμας, οὐδὲ πατρὸς γεραιοῦ,
<τοῦδ' ἐγγὺς ἦν Ἀίδας,>
ὃν ἔτεκον δ', οὐκ ἔτλαν ῥύεσθαι,
470   σχετλίω, πολιὰν ἔχοντε χαίταν.
σὺ δ' ἐν ἥβᾳ νέα νέου
προθανοῦσα φωτὸς οἴχῃ.
τοιαύτας εἴη μοι κῦρσαι
συνδυάδος φιλίας ἀλόχου, τὸ γὰρ
ἐν βιότῳ σπάνιον μέρος· ἦ γὰρ ἂν
475   ἔμοιγ' ἄλυπος δι' αἰ-
ῶνος ἂν ξυνείη.

ΗΡΑΚΛΗΣ

ξένοι, Φεραίας τῆσδε κωμῆται χθονός,
Ἄδμητον ἐν δόμοισιν ἆρα κιγχάνω;

ΧΟΡΟΣ

ἔστ' ἐν δόμοισι παῖς Φέρητος, Ἡράκλεις.
ἀλλ' εἰπὲ χρεία τίς σε Θεσσαλῶν χθόνα
480   πέμπει, Φεραῖον ἄστυ προσβῆναι τόδε.

ΗΡΑΚΛΗΣ

Τιρυνθίῳ πράσσω τιν' Εὐρυσθεῖ πόνον.

light upon you, lady! And if your husband should take a new bride, he will be hateful in my eyes as in those of your children.

His mother was not willing to be buried in earth for her child nor was his aged father. <Death was at his door,> yet unfeeling, they could not bring themselves to rescue the child they bore, although their hair was white with age. But you died in your prime, a young bride saving a young husband. Be it my fate to find such a dear wife, since the time of our life is short! Truly, such a woman, living with me my whole life, would bring me no grief.[a]

Enter by Eisodos A HERACLES with his characteristic lion skin and club. A servant goes in to tell Admetus of the arrival.

HERACLES

Strangers, citizens of this land of Pherae, is Admetus at home?

CHORUS LEADER

Yes, Pheres' son is at home, Heracles. But tell us what brings you to Thessaly and to this city of Pherae.

HERACLES

I am performing a task for Eurystheus, king of Tiryns.

[a] The unspoken background to this statement is the belief that women are normally a bane to men: see Hesiod, *Theogony* 561–612, for the idea that women are men's punishment, sent by Zeus to afflict them.

---

469 ante h.v. lac. indic. Canter, suppl. Willink

ΧΟΡΟΣ
καὶ ποῖ πορεύῃ; τῷ συνέζευξαι πλάνῳ;

ΗΡΑΚΛΗΣ
Θρῃκὸς τέτρωρον ἅρμα Διομήδους μέτα.

ΧΟΡΟΣ
πῶς οὖν δυνήσῃ; μῶν ἄπειρος εἶ ξένου;

ΗΡΑΚΛΗΣ
485 ἄπειρος· οὔπω Βιστόνων ἦλθον χθόνα.

ΧΟΡΟΣ
οὐκ ἔστιν ἵππων δεσπόσαι σ᾽ ἄνευ μάχης.

ΗΡΑΚΛΗΣ
ἀλλ᾽ οὐδ᾽ ἀπειπεῖν μὴν πόνους οἷόν τ᾽ ἐμοί.

ΧΟΡΟΣ
κτανὼν ἄρ᾽ ἥξεις ἢ θανὼν αὐτοῦ μενεῖς.

ΗΡΑΚΛΗΣ
οὐ τόνδ᾽ ἀγῶνα πρῶτον ἂν δράμοιμ᾽ ἐγώ.

ΧΟΡΟΣ
490 τί δ᾽ ἂν κρατήσας δεσπότην πλέον λάβοις;

ΗΡΑΚΛΗΣ
πώλους ἀπάξω κοιράνῳ Τιρυνθίῳ.

ΧΟΡΟΣ
οὐκ εὐμαρὲς χαλινὸν ἐμβαλεῖν γνάθοις.

ΗΡΑΚΛΗΣ
εἰ μή γε πῦρ πνέουσι μυκτήρων ἄπο.

CHORUS LEADER

Where are you bound? What is this journey you are forced to make?

HERACLES

I go in quest of the four-horse chariot of Thracian Diomedes.

CHORUS LEADER

How can you do that? Do you not know what kind of host he is?

HERACLES

I do not. I have never yet been to Bistonia.

CHORUS LEADER

You cannot possess those horses without a fight.

HERACLES

But all the same, I cannot decline these labors.

CHORUS LEADER

Then you will either kill him and return or end your days there.

HERACLES

This is not the first such race I shall have run.

CHORUS LEADER

If you defeat their master, what will it profit you?

HERACLES

I will bring the horses back to the lord of Tiryns.

CHORUS LEADER

You will not find it easy to put a bit in their mouths.

HERACLES

Surely so, unless they breathe fire from their nostrils.

ΧΟΡΟΣ

ἀλλ᾽ ἄνδρας ἀρταμοῦσι λαιψηραῖς γνάθοις.

ΗΡΑΚΛΗΣ

495 θηρῶν ὀρείων χόρτον, οὐχ ἵππων, λέγεις.

ΧΟΡΟΣ

φάτνας ἴδοις ἂν αἵμασιν πεφυρμένας.

ΗΡΑΚΛΗΣ

τίνος δ᾽ ὁ θρέψας παῖς πατρὸς κομπάζεται;

ΧΟΡΟΣ

Ἄρεος, ζαχρύσου Θρηκίας πέλτης ἄναξ.

ΗΡΑΚΛΗΣ

καὶ τόνδε τοὐμοῦ δαίμονος πόνον λέγεις
500 (σκληρὸς γὰρ αἰεὶ καὶ πρὸς αἶπος ἔρχεται),
εἰ χρή με πᾶσιν οἷς Ἄρης ἐγείνατο
μάχην συνάψαι, πρῶτα μὲν Λυκάονι,
αὖθις δὲ Κύκνῳ, τόνδε δ᾽ ἔρχομαι τρίτον
ἀγῶνα πώλοις δεσπότῃ τε συμβαλῶν.
505 ἀλλ᾽ οὔτις ἔστιν ὃς τὸν Ἀλκμήνης γόνον
τρέσαντα χεῖρα πολεμίαν ποτ᾽ ὄψεται.

ΧΟΡΟΣ

καὶ μὴν ὅδ᾽ αὐτὸς τῆσδε κοίρανος χθονὸς
Ἄδμητος ἔξω δωμάτων πορεύεται.

ΑΔΜΗΤΟΣ

χαῖρ᾽, ὦ Διὸς παῖ Περσέως τ᾽ ἀφ᾽ αἵματος.

501 πᾶσιν Wakefield: παισὶν C

CHORUS LEADER
No, but they tear men apart with their nimble jaws.

HERACLES
This is fodder for mountain beasts, not horses.

CHORUS LEADER
You will see their feeding troughs drenched with blood.

HERACLES
Whose son does their master claim to be?

CHORUS LEADER
Ares' son, and shield-bearing lord of Thrace rich in gold.

HERACLES
Like the others this labor you have described befits my destiny (which is always hard and steep) since I am fated to do battle with all the sons of Ares: first Lycaon, then Cycnus, and now this is the third contest I enter, going off to fight horses and master alike. But no one shall ever see Alcmene's son quake at the hand of an enemy.

Enter ADMETUS *from the palace, dressed in black and hair cut in mourning.*

CHORUS LEADER
But here, Admetus, the king of this land, is himself coming out of doors.

ADMETUS
I wish you joy, son of Zeus and child of Perseus' blood.

ΗΡΑΚΛΗΣ

510 Ἄδμητε, καὶ σὺ χαῖρε, Θεσσαλῶν ἄναξ.

ΑΔΜΗΤΟΣ

θέλοιμ' ἄν· εὔνουν δ' ὄντα σ' ἐξεπίσταμαι.

ΗΡΑΚΛΗΣ

τί χρῆμα κουρᾷ τῇδε πενθίμῳ πρέπεις;

ΑΔΜΗΤΟΣ

θάπτειν τιν' ἐν τῇδ' ἡμέρᾳ μέλλω νεκρόν.

ΗΡΑΚΛΗΣ

ἀπ' οὖν τέκνων σῶν πημονὴν εἴργοι θεός.

ΑΔΜΗΤΟΣ

515 ζῶσιν κατ' οἴκους παῖδες οὓς ἔφυσ' ἐγώ.

ΗΡΑΚΛΗΣ

πατήρ γε μὴν ὡραῖος, εἴπερ οἴχεται.

ΑΔΜΗΤΟΣ

κἀκεῖνος ἔστι χἠ τεκοῦσά μ', Ἡράκλεις.

ΗΡΑΚΛΗΣ

οὐ μὴν γυνή γ' ὄλωλεν Ἄλκηστις σέθεν;

ΑΔΜΗΤΟΣ

διπλοῦς ἐπ' αὐτῇ μῦθος ἔστι μοι λέγειν.

ΗΡΑΚΛΗΣ

520 πότερα θανούσης εἶπας ἢ ζώσης ἔτι;

ΑΔΜΗΤΟΣ

ἔστιν τε κοὐκέτ' ἔστιν, ἀλγύνει δέ με.

ALCESTIS

HERACLES
Admetus, king of Thessaly, I wish you joy as well.

ADMETUS
If only I could have it! I know you wish me well.

HERACLES
Why are you wearing the shorn hair of mourning?

ADMETUS
I am about to conduct a funeral today.

HERACLES
God keep misfortune from your children!

ADMETUS
The children I begot are alive in the house.

HERACLES
Your father was of a ripe old age, if it is he that has departed.

ADMETUS
My father lives, Heracles, and my mother too.

HERACLES
Surely your wife Alcestis has not died?

ADMETUS
There is a double tale to tell of her.

HERACLES
Do you mean that she has died or is still alive?

ADMETUS
She is and is no more. It is a grief to me.

ΗΡΑΚΛΗΣ

οὐδέν τι μᾶλλον οἶδ᾿· ἄσημα γὰρ λέγεις.

ΑΔΜΗΤΟΣ

οὐκ οἶσθα μοίρας ἧς τυχεῖν αὐτὴν χρεών;

ΗΡΑΚΛΗΣ

οἶδ᾿, ἀντὶ σοῦ γε κατθανεῖν ὑφειμένην.

ΑΔΜΗΤΟΣ

525 πῶς οὖν ἔτ᾿ ἔστιν, εἴπερ ἤνεσεν τάδε;

ΗΡΑΚΛΗΣ

ἆ, μὴ πρόκλαι᾿ ἄκοιτιν, ἐς τότ᾿ ἀμβαλοῦ.

ΑΔΜΗΤΟΣ

τέθνηχ᾿ ὁ μέλλων καὶ θανὼν οὐκ ἔστ᾿ ἔτι.

ΗΡΑΚΛΗΣ

χωρὶς τό τ᾿ εἶναι καὶ τὸ μὴ νομίζεται.

ΑΔΜΗΤΟΣ

σὺ τῇδε κρίνεις, Ἡράκλεις, κείνῃ δ᾿ ἐγώ.

ΗΡΑΚΛΗΣ

530 τί δῆτα κλαίεις; τίς φίλων ὁ κατθανών;

ΑΔΜΗΤΟΣ

γυνή· γυναικὸς ἀρτίως μεμνήμεθα.

ΗΡΑΚΛΗΣ

ὀθνεῖος ἢ σοὶ συγγενὴς γεγῶσά τις;

---

527 καὶ θανὼν οὐκ ἔστ᾿ ἔτι Schwartz: χὠ θανὼν οὐκ ἔστ᾿ ἔτι a:
κοὐκέτ᾿ ἔσθ᾿ ὁ κατθανών b

HERACLES

I'm still no wiser: you speak in riddles.

ADMETUS

Do you not know what doom she is fated to suffer?

HERACLES

I know: she promised to die for you.

ADMETUS

How can she be still truly alive once she had promised that?

HERACLES

Oh, do not mourn your wife beforehand! Put it off till the day!

ADMETUS

Someone who is doomed to die is dead, has died and is no more.

HERACLES

Existence and non-existence are deemed to be separate things.

ADMETUS

You have your view on this, Heracles, and I have mine.

HERACLES

Why then are you in mourning? Who of your kin has died?

ADMETUS

A woman: it was a woman I spoke of just now.

HERACLES

Was it someone related to you by blood or not?

ΑΔΜΗΤΟΣ

ὀθνεῖος, ἄλλως δ᾽ ἦν ἀναγκαία δόμοις.

ΗΡΑΚΛΗΣ

πῶς οὖν ἐν οἴκοις σοῖσιν ὤλεσεν βίον;

ΑΔΜΗΤΟΣ

535   πατρὸς θανόντος ἐνθάδ᾽ ὠρφανεύετο.

ΗΡΑΚΛΗΣ

φεῦ.
εἴθ᾽ ηὕρομέν σ᾽, Ἄδμητε, μὴ λυπούμενον.

ΑΔΜΗΤΟΣ

ὡς δὴ τί δράσων τόνδ᾽ ὑπορράπτεις λόγον;

ΗΡΑΚΛΗΣ

ξένων πρὸς ἄλλων ἑστίαν πορεύσομαι.

ΑΔΜΗΤΟΣ

οὐκ ἔστιν, ὦναξ· μὴ τοσόνδ᾽ ἔλθοι κακόν.

ΗΡΑΚΛΗΣ

540   λυπουμένοις ὀχληρός, εἰ μόλοι, ξένος.

ΑΔΜΗΤΟΣ

τεθνᾶσιν οἱ θανόντες· ἀλλ᾽ ἴθ᾽ ἐς δόμους.

ΗΡΑΚΛΗΣ

αἰσχρὸν <δὲ> παρὰ κλαίουσι θοινᾶσθαι ξένους.

ΑΔΜΗΤΟΣ

χωρὶς ξενῶνές εἰσιν οἵ σ᾽ ἐσάξομεν.

542 <δὲ> Erfurdt

216

ADMETUS

Not by blood, but she was in other ways closely connected to the family.

HERACLES

How did she come to die in your house?

ADMETUS

After her father died, she spent her orphan years here.

HERACLES

Oh dear! I wish I had not found you in mourning, Admetus!

ADMETUS

With what intent do you utter these words?

HERACLES

I shall go to the house of some other guest-friend.

ADMETUS

No no, my lord! Heaven avert such a misfortune!

HERACLES

To mourners the arrival of a guest is vexing.

ADMETUS

Those who have died are dead: go into the house.

HERACLES

But it is disgraceful for guests to be feasted in a house of mourning.

ADMETUS

The guest rooms where we will bring you are in a separate place.

ΗΡΑΚΛΗΣ

μέθες με καί σοι μυρίαν ἕξω χάριν.

ΑΔΜΗΤΟΣ

545 οὐκ ἔστιν ἄλλου σ᾽ ἀνδρὸς ἑστίαν μολεῖν.
ἡγοῦ σὺ τῷδε δωμάτων ἐξωπίους
ξενῶνας οἴξας τοῖς τ᾽ ἐφεστῶσιν φράσον
σίτων παρεῖναι ::λῆθος, εὖ δὲ κλῄσατε
θύρας μεταύλους· οὐ πρέπει θοινωμένους
550 κλύειν στεναγμῶν οὐδὲ λυπεῖσθαι ξένους.

ΧΟΡΟΣ

τί δρᾷς; τοσαύτης συμφορᾶς προκειμένης,
Ἄδμητε, τολμᾷς ξενοδοκεῖν; τί μῶρος εἶ;

ΑΔΜΗΤΟΣ

ἀλλ᾽ εἰ δόμων σφε καὶ πόλεως ἀπήλασα
ξένον μολόντα, μᾶλλον ἄν μ᾽ ἐπῄνεσας;
555 οὐ δῆτ᾽, ἐπεί μοι συμφορὰ μὲν οὐδὲν ἂν
μείων ἐγίγνετ᾽, ἀξενώτερος δ᾽ ἐγώ.
καὶ πρὸς κακοῖσιν ἄλλο τοῦτ᾽ ἂν ἦν κακόν,
δόμους καλεῖσθαι τοὺς ἐμοὺς ἐχθροξένους.
αὐτὸς δ᾽ ἀρίστου τοῦδε τυγχάνω ξένου,
560 ὅταν ποτ᾽ Ἄργους διψίαν ἔλθω χθόνα.

ΧΟΡΟΣ

πῶς οὖν ἔκρυπτες τὸν παρόντα δαίμονα,
φίλου μολόντος ἀνδρὸς ὡς αὐτὸς λέγεις;

ΑΔΜΗΤΟΣ

οὐκ ἄν ποτ᾽ ἠθέλησεν εἰσελθεῖν δόμους,

<hr>

549 μεταύλους Brunck: μεσαύλους C

218

HERACLES

Let me go and I will be enormously grateful to you.

ADMETUS

You must not go to any other man's house.

(to a servant) Go before this man and open up the guest quarters away from the main palace; tell those responsible to provide an abundance of food. And be sure to close fast the doors of the courtyard: it is not right for guests to hear the sounds of mourning or to feel distress as they dine.

The servant goes into the palace, followed by HERACLES.

CHORUS LEADER

What are you doing? Faced with so great a misfortune, Admetus, do you have the stomach to entertain guests? Why are you so foolish?

ADMETUS

Yet if I had driven from my house and city a friend who had just arrived, would you have praised me more? No, indeed, since my misfortune would have been in no way lessened, and I would have been less hospitable. And in addition to my ills we would have the further ill that my house would be called a spurner of guests. I myself find in this man the best of hosts whenever I go to thirsty Argos.

CHORUS LEADER

Why then did you conceal your present plight when, as you say yourself, he has come as a friend?

ADMETUS

He would never have consented to enter the house if he

219

εἰ τῶν ἐμῶν τι πημάτων ἐγνώρισεν.
565   καὶ τῷ μέν, οἶμαι, δρῶν τάδ' οὐ φρονεῖν δοκῶ
οὐδ' αἰνέσει με· τἀμὰ δ' οὐκ ἐπίσταται
μέλαθρ' ἀπωθεῖν οὐδ' ἀτιμάζειν ξένους.

ΧΟΡΟΣ

στρ. α

ὦ πολυξείνου καὶ ἐλευθέρου ἀνδρὸς ἀεί ποτ' οἶκος,
570   σέ τοι καὶ ὁ Πύθιος εὐλύρας Ἀπόλλων
ἠξίωσε ναίειν,
ἔτλα δὲ σοῖσι μηλονόμας
ἐν νομοῖς γενέσθαι,
575   δοχμιᾶν διὰ κλειτύων
βοσκήμασι σοῖσι συρίζων
ποιμνίτας ὑμεναίους.

ἀντ. α

σὺν δ' ἐποιμαίνοντο χαρᾷ μελέων βαλιαί τε λύγκες,
580   ἔβα δὲ λιποῦσ' Ὄθρυος νάπαν λεόντων
ἁ δαφοινὸς ἴλα·
χόρευσε δ' ἀμφὶ σὰν κιθάραν,
Φοῖβε, ποικιλόθριξ
585   νεβρὸς ὑψικόμων πέραν
βαίνουσ' ἐλατᾶν σφυρῷ κούφῳ,
χαίρουσ' εὔφρονι μολπᾷ.

στρ. β

τοιγὰρ πολυμηλοτάταν
ἑστίαν οἰκεῖ παρὰ καλλίναον
590   Βοιβίαν λίμναν. ἀρότοις δὲ γυᾶν
καὶ πεδίων δαπέδοις

had known anything of my sorrow. And no doubt some-
one will think that in doing this I am being foolish and will
not approve of me. But my house does not know how to
reject or dishonor guests.

Exit ADMETUS into the palace.

CHORUS

O house of an ever hospitable and generous man, even
Pythian Apollo of the lovely lyre deigned to dwell in you
and submitted to become a shepherd in your pastures,
playing on his pipe mating songs for your herds on the
slanting hillsides.

Under his shepherd care, in joy at his songs, were also
spotted lynxes, and there came, leaving the vale of Othrys,
a pride of tawny lions, and the dappled fawn stepping
beyond the tall fir trees with its light foot danced to your
lyre-playing, Apollo, rejoicing in its joyful melody.

Therefore he dwells in a house rich in flocks beside
fair-flowing Lake Boebias, and for the tillage of his fields
and for his grazing lands he sets the boundary where the

---

568 πολυξείνου καὶ ἐλευθέρου Purgold: πολύξεινος καὶ ἐλεύθερος
C

574 νομοῖς Pierson: δόμοις C

589 οἰκεῖ Markland: οἰκεῖς C

ὅρον ἀμφὶ μὲν ἀελίου κνεφαίαν
ἱππόστασιν ἐς τὸ πέραν Μολοσ-
σῶν <ὀρέων> τίθεται,
595 πόντιον δ' Αἰγαῖον ἐπ' ἀκτὰν
ἀλίμενον Πηλίου κρατύνει.

ἀντ. β

καὶ νῦν δόμον ἀμπετάσας
δέξατο ξεῖνον νοτερῷ βλεφάρῳ,
τᾶς φίλας κλαίων ἀλόχου νέκυν ἐν
600 δώμασιν ἀρτιθανῆ·
τὸ γὰρ εὐγενὲς ἐκφέρεται πρὸς αἰδῶ.
ἐν τοῖς ἀγαθοῖσι δὲ πάντ' ἔνε-
στιν· σοφίας ἄγαμαι.
πρὸς δ' ἐμᾷ ψυχᾷ θράσος ἧσται
605 θεοσεβῆ φῶτα κεδνὰ πράξειν.

ΑΔΜΗΤΟΣ

ἀνδρῶν Φεραίων εὐμενὴς παρουσία,
νέκυν μὲν ἤδη πάντ' ἔχοντα πρόσπολοι
φέρουσιν ἄρδην πρὸς τάφον τε καὶ πυράν·
ὑμεῖς δὲ τὴν θανοῦσαν, ὡς νομίζεται,
610 προσείπατ' ἐξιοῦσαν ὑστάτην ὁδόν.

ΧΟΡΟΣ

καὶ μὴν ὁρῶ σὸν πατέρα γηραιῷ ποδὶ
στείχοντ', ὀπαδούς τ' ἐν χεροῖν δάμαρτι σῇ
κόσμον φέροντας, νερτέρων ἀγάλματα.

593 ἐς τὸ πέραν Pohlenz: αἰθέρα τὰν C
594 <ὀρέων> Bauer

sun stables his horses in the dark west beyond the Molossian mountains, and he rules as far as the rocky Aegean promontory of Pelion.

And now, throwing open the gates of his house, he has received a guest though his own eyes were wet, weeping for the loss of his dear wife so recently perished in his house. For his noble nature runs unbridled toward pity and respect. All that is good lives in the hearts of those who are nobly born. I marvel at his wisdom. And sure confidence sits in my heart that the god-fearing man will prosper.

Enter ADMETUS *from the palace with servants carrying Alcestis on her bier.*

ADMETUS

Men of Pherae who stand by in goodwill, the body has been prepared for burial, and my servants are carrying it on their shoulders to its resting place. Do you, then, as custom ordains, bid the dead woman farewell as she goes out on her last journey.

Enter PHERES *with retinue by Eisodos B.*

CHORUS LEADER

But look! I see your father approaching with aged step and his servants carrying finery for your wife, adornment for the dead.

---

599 φίλας editio Aldina: φιλίας C
603 ante σοφίας dist. Dale: post σοφίας C
604 θράσος Barnes: θάρσος C

ΦΕΡΗΣ

ἥκω κακοῖσι σοῖσι συγκάμνων, τέκνον·
615 ἐσθλῆς γάρ, οὐδεὶς ἀντερεῖ, καὶ σώφρονος
γυναικὸς ἡμάρτηκας. ἀλλὰ ταῦτα μὲν
φέρειν ἀνάγκη καίπερ ὄντα δύσφορα.
δέχου δὲ κόσμον τόνδε καὶ κατὰ χθονὸς
ἴτω. τὸ ταύτης σῶμα τιμᾶσθαι χρεών,
620 ἥτις γε τῆς σῆς προύθανε ψυχῆς, τέκνον,
καί μ' οὐκ ἄπαιδ' ἔθηκεν οὐδ' εἴασε σοῦ
στερέντα γήρᾳ πενθίμῳ καταφθίνειν,
πάσαις δ' ἔθηκεν εὐκλεέστερον βίον
γυναιξίν, ἔργον τλᾶσα γενναῖον τόδε.
625 ὦ τόνδε μὲν σώσασ', ἀναστήσασα δὲ
ἡμᾶς πίτνοντας, χαῖρε, κἀν Ἅιδου δόμοις
εὖ σοι γένοιτο. φημὶ τοιούτους γάμους
λύειν βροτοῖσιν, ἢ γαμεῖν οὐκ ἄξιον.

ΑΔΜΗΤΟΣ

οὔτ' ἦλθες ἐς τόνδ' ἐξ ἐμοῦ κληθεὶς τάφον
630 οὔτ' ἐν φίλοισι σὴν παρουσίαν λέγω.
κόσμον δὲ τὸν σὸν οὔποθ' ἥδ' ἐνδύσεται·
οὐ γάρ τι τῶν σῶν ἐνδεὴς ταφήσεται.
τότε ξυναλγεῖν χρῆν σ' ὅτ' ὠλλύμην ἐγώ·
σὺ δ' ἐκποδὼν στὰς καὶ παρεὶς ἄλλῳ θανεῖν
635 νέῳ γέρων ὢν τόνδ' ἀποιμώξῃ νεκρόν;
οὐκ ἦσθ' ἄρ' ὀρθῶς τοῦδε σώματος πατήρ,
οὐδ' ἡ τεκεῖν φάσκουσα καὶ κεκλημένη
μήτηρ μ' ἔτικτε, δουλίου δ' ἀφ' αἵματος
μαστῷ γυναικὸς σῆς ὑπεβλήθην λάθρᾳ.

PHERES

I have come to share in your trouble, my son. For you have lost, as no one will deny, a noble and virtuous wife. Yet you must bear this stroke, though it is hard to bear. Now take this finery, and let it be buried with her. We must show honor to her corpse seeing that she died to save your life, my son, and did not leave me childless or let me waste away in a stricken old age bereft of you. She has given the lives of all women a fairer repute by daring to do this noble deed. *(to Alcestis)* You that both saved this man's life and raised me up when I was falling: farewell! In the house of Hades may it go well with you! Marriages like this, I maintain, are a benefit to mortals: if they are not, no marriage is worthwhile.[a]

ADMETUS

I did not invite you to this funeral, nor do I count your presence here as that of a friend. As for your finery, she shall never wear it, for she needs nothing of yours for her burial. You should have shared my trouble when I was dying. You stood aside and, though you are old, allowed a young person to die: will you now come to mourn her? You were not, as it now seems clear, truly my father, nor did she who claims to have borne me and is called my mother really give me birth, but I was born of some slave and secretly put to your wife's breast. When you were put

[a] See note above on 476.

640 ἔδειξας εἰς ἔλεγχον ἐξελθὼν ὃς εἶ,
καί μ᾽ οὐ νομίζω παῖδα σὸν πεφυκέναι.
ἦ τἄρα πάντων διαπρέπεις ἀψυχίᾳ,
ὃς τηλικόσδ᾽ ὢν κἀπὶ τέρμ᾽ ἥκων βίου
οὐκ ἠθέλησας οὐδ᾽ ἐτόλμησας θανεῖν
645 τοῦ σοῦ πρὸ παιδός, ἀλλὰ τήνδ᾽ εἰάσατε
γυναῖκ᾽ ὀθνείαν, ἣν ἐγὼ καὶ μητέρα
καὶ πατέρ᾽ ἂν ἐνδίκως ἂν ἡγοίμην μόνην.
καίτοι καλόν γ᾽ ἂν τόνδ᾽ ἀγῶν᾽ ἠγωνίσω,
τοῦ σοῦ πρὸ παιδὸς κατθανών, βραχὺς δέ σοι
650 πάντως ὁ λοιπὸς ἦν βιώσιμος χρόνος.
[κἀγώ τ᾽ ἂν ἔζων χἥδε τὸν λοιπὸν χρόνον,
κοὐκ ἂν μονωθεὶς ἔστενον κακοῖς ἐμοῖς.]
    καὶ μὴν ὅσ᾽ ἄνδρα χρὴ παθεῖν εὐδαίμονα
πέπονθας· ἥβησας μὲν ἐν τυραννίδι,
655 παῖς δ᾽ ἦν ἐγώ σοι τῶνδε διάδοχος δόμων,
ὥστ᾽ οὐκ ἄτεκνος κατθανὼν ἄλλοις δόμον
λείψειν ἔμελλες ὀρφανὸν διαρπάσαι.
οὐ μὴν ἐρεῖς γέ μ᾽ ὡς ἀτιμάζοντα σὸν
γῆρας θανεῖν προύδωκας, ὅστις αἰδόφρων
660 πρὸς σ᾽ ἦ μάλιστα· κἀντὶ τῶνδέ μοι χάριν
τοιάνδε καὶ σὺ χἠ τεκοῦσ᾽ ἠλλαξάτην.
τοιγὰρ φυτεύων παῖδας οὐκέτ᾽ ἂν φθάνοις,
οἳ γηροβοσκήσουσι καὶ θανόντα σε
περιστελοῦσι καὶ προθήσονται νεκρόν.
665 οὐ γάρ σ᾽ ἔγωγε τῇδ᾽ ἐμῇ θάψω χερί·
τέθνηκα γὰρ δὴ τοὐπὶ σ᾽. εἰ δ᾽ ἄλλου τυχὼν

to the test you showed your true nature, and I do not count
myself as your son. You are, you know, truly superlative in
cowardice; for though you are so old and have come to the
end of your life, yet you refused and had not the courage
to die for your own son, but you and your wife let this
woman, who was no blood relative, do so. I shall consider
her with perfect justice to be both mother and father to
me. And yet it would have been a noble contest to enter,
dying for your son, and in any case the time you had left to
live was short. [And she and I would have lived for the rest
of our time, and I would not be grieving for my trouble,
bereft of her.]

What is more, all that is required for a man to be happy
has already befallen you: you spent the prime of your life
as a king, and you had me as son and successor to your
house, so that you were not going to die childless and leave
your house behind without heirs for others to plunder.
Surely you cannot say that you abandoned me to death
because I dishonored you in your old age, for I have always
shown you every respect. And now this is the repayment
you and my mother have made to me. You had better
hurry, therefore, and beget other children to take care of
you in old age and to dress you, when you have died, and
lay you out for burial. I for my part shall never bury you
myself. For as far as you are concerned I am dead. And if

---

647 καὶ πατέρ᾽ ἂν Weil: πατέρα τέ γ᾽ fere C: πατέρα τ᾽ ἂν
Elmsley
651–52 del. Lenting: cf. 295–6
655 ἢ γεγώς Nauck
660 ἢ Elmsley: ἢν C
665 τῆδε μὴ Weil

σωτῆρος αὐγὰς εἰσορῶ, κείνου λέγω
καὶ παῖδά μ᾽ εἶναι καὶ φίλον γηροτρόφον.
μάτην ἄρ᾽ οἱ γέροντες εὔχονται θανεῖν,
670 γῆρας ψέγοντες καὶ μακρὸν χρόνον βίου·
ἢν δ᾽ ἐγγὺς ἔλθῃ θάνατος, οὐδεὶς βούλεται
θνῄσκειν, τὸ γῆρας δ᾽ οὐκέτ᾽ ἔστ᾽ αὐτοῖς βαρύ.

ΧΟΡΟΣ

νεικῶν — ἅλις γὰρ ἡ παροῦσα συμφορά —
παῦσαι, πατρὸς δὲ μὴ παροξύνῃς φρένας.

ΦΕΡΗΣ

675 ὦ παῖ, τίν᾽ αὐχεῖς, πότερα Λυδὸν ἢ Φρύγα,
κακοῖς ἐλαύνειν ἀργυρώνητον σέθεν;
οὐκ οἶσθα Θεσσαλόν με κἀπὸ Θεσσαλοῦ
πατρὸς γεγῶτα γνησίως ἐλεύθερον;
ἄγαν ὑβρίζεις καὶ νεανίας λόγους
680 ῥίπτων ἐς ἡμᾶς οὐ βαλὼν οὕτως ἄπει.
    ἐγὼ δέ σ᾽ οἴκων δεσπότην ἐγεινάμην
κἄθρεψ᾽, ὀφείλω δ᾽ οὐχ ὑπερθνῄσκειν σέθεν·
οὐ γὰρ πατρῷον τόνδ᾽ ἐδεξάμην νόμον,
παίδων προθνῄσκειν πατέρας, οὐδ᾽ Ἑλληνικόν.
685 σαυτῷ γὰρ εἴτε δυστυχὴς εἴτ᾽ εὐτυχὴς
ἔφυς· ἃ δ᾽ ἡμῶν χρῆν σε τυγχάνειν ἔχεις.
πολλῶν μὲν ἄρχεις, πολυπλέθρους δέ σοι γύας
λείψω· πατρὸς γὰρ ταῦτ᾽ ἐδεξάμην πάρα.
τί δῆτά σ᾽ ἠδίκηκα; τοῦ σ᾽ ἀποστερῶ;
690 μὴ θνῇσχ᾽ ὑπὲρ τοῦδ᾽ ἀνδρός, οὐδ᾽ ἐγὼ πρὸ σοῦ.
χαίρεις ὁρῶν φῶς· πατέρα δ᾽ οὐ χαίρειν δοκεῖς;

I have found another savior and still look upon the sun, I am that savior's child and fond support in old age. It seems that old men, who find fault with age and length of years, pray for death insincerely. For once death comes near, none of them wishes to die, and age is no longer burdensome to them.

CHORUS LEADER

Stop your railing—the present grief is enough—and do not provoke your father!

PHERES

Son, whom do you imagine you are berating with insults, some Lydian or Phrygian slave of yours, bought with money? Do you not know that I am a freeborn Thessalian, legitimately begotten of a Thessalian father? You go too far in insult, and since you hurl brash words at me, you will not get off with impunity.

I begot you and raised you to be the master of this house, but I am not obliged to die for you. I did not inherit this as a family custom, fathers dying for sons, nor as a Greek custom either. You are fortunate or unfortunate for yourself alone. What you should in justice have received from me you have: you rule over many subjects, and I shall leave to you many acres of land, for I received the same from *my* father. What injustice have I done you? Of what am I robbing you? Do not die on my behalf, and I shall not die on yours. You enjoy looking on the light. Do you think your father does not? Truly I regard the time

---

[673] νεικῶν post Hayley ('Αδμηθ') scripsi: παύσασθ' C
[674] παῦσαι Hayley: ὦ παῖ C

ἦ μὴν πολύν γε τόν κάτω λογίζομαι
χρόνον, τὸ δὲ ζῆν σμικρὸν ἀλλ' ὅμως γλυκύ.
σὺ γοῦν ἀναιδῶς διεμάχου τὸ μὴ θανεῖν
695 καὶ ζῆς παρελθὼν τὴν πεπρωμένην τύχην,
ταύτην κατακτάς· εἶτ' ἐμὴν ἀψυχίαν
λέγεις, γυναικός, ὦ κάκισθ', ἡσσημένος,
ἢ τοῦ καλοῦ σοῦ προύθανεν νεανίου;
σοφῶς δ' ἐφηῦρες ὥστε μὴ θανεῖν ποτε,
700 εἰ τὴν παροῦσαν κατθανεῖν πείσεις ἀεὶ
γυναῖχ' ὑπὲρ σοῦ· κᾆτ' ὀνειδίζεις φίλοις
τοῖς μὴ θέλουσι δρᾶν τάδ', αὐτὸς ὢν κακός;
σίγα· νόμιζε δ', εἰ σὺ τὴν σαυτοῦ φιλεῖς
ψυχήν, φιλεῖν ἅπαντας· εἰ δ' ἡμᾶς κακῶς
705 ἐρεῖς, ἀκούσῃ πολλὰ κοὐ ψευδῆ κακά.

ΧΟΡΟΣ

πλείω λέλεκται νῦν τε καὶ τὸ πρὶν κακά·
παῦσαι δέ, πρέσβυ, παῖδα σὸν κακορροθῶν.

ΑΔΜΗΤΟΣ

λέγ', ὡς ἐμοῦ λέγοντος· εἰ δ' ἀλγεῖς κλύων
τἀληθές, οὐ χρῆν σ' εἰς ἔμ' ἐξαμαρτάνειν.

ΦΕΡΗΣ

710 σοῦ δ' ἂν προθνήσκων μᾶλλον ἐξημάρτανον.

ΑΔΜΗΤΟΣ

ταὐτὸν γὰρ ἡβῶντ' ἄνδρα καὶ πρέσβυν θανεῖν;

ΦΕΡΗΣ

ψυχῇ μιᾷ ζῆν, οὐ δυοῖν, ὀφείλομεν.

below as long and life as short but sweet for all that. At all events you have shamelessly striven to avoid death, and you live beyond your fated day by killing *her*. Can you then reproach *me* with cowardice when you, consummate coward, have been bested by a woman, who died to save you, her fine young husband? You have cleverly found out a way never to die by persuading each wife in turn to die on your behalf. Can you then cast in the teeth of your kin that they do not wish to do this when you yourself are so craven? Hold your tongue! Consider that if you love life, so do all men. If you continue to insult me, you shall hear reproaches many and true.

CHORUS LEADER

Too many reproaches have been uttered, now and previously. Old sir, stop reviling your son.

ADMETUS

Speak on, and so shall I! But if it pains you to hear the truth, you should not be wronging me.

PHERES

If I were dying on your behalf, I would be acting far more wrongly.

ADMETUS

What? Is death the same thing for a man in his prime as for an old man?

PHERES

We must live with a single life, not with two.

---

697 ψέγεις editio Hervag.
706 τὸ Wakefield: τὰ C

ΑΔΜΗΤΟΣ

καὶ μὴν Διός γε μείζονα ζώης χρόνον.

ΦΕΡΗΣ

ἀρᾷ γονεῦσιν οὐδὲν ἔκδικον παθών;

ΑΔΜΗΤΟΣ

715 μακροῦ βίου γὰρ ᾐσθόμην ἐρῶντά σε.

ΦΕΡΗΣ

ἀλλ' οὐ σὺ νεκρὸν ἀντὶ σοῦ τόνδ' ἐκφέρεις;

ΑΔΜΗΤΟΣ

σημεῖα τῆς σῆς γ', ὦ κάκιστ', ἀψυχίας.

ΦΕΡΗΣ

οὔτοι πρὸς ἡμῶν γ' ὤλετ' · οὐκ ἐρεῖς τόδε.

ΑΔΜΗΤΟΣ

φεῦ ·
εἴθ' ἀνδρὸς ἔλθοις τοῦδέ γ' ἐς χρείαν ποτέ.

ΦΕΡΗΣ

720 μνήστευε πολλάς, ὡς θάνωσι πλείονες.

ΑΔΜΗΤΟΣ

σοὶ τοῦτ' ὄνειδος · οὐ γὰρ ἤθελες θανεῖν.

ΦΕΡΗΣ

φίλον τὸ φέγγος τοῦτο τοῦ θεοῦ, φίλον.

ΑΔΜΗΤΟΣ

κακὸν τὸ λῆμα κοὐκ ἐν ἀνδράσιν τὸ σόν.

ΦΕΡΗΣ

οὐκ ἐγγελᾷς γέροντα βαστάζων νεκρόν.

ADMETUS

And may yours be longer than Zeus's!

PHERES

Do you curse your father, though he has done you no wrong?

ADMETUS

Yes, for I see you lusting for length of days.

PHERES

But is it not you who are burying this corpse in your stead?

ADMETUS

Yes, the sign of your cravenness, you coward.

PHERES

She did not die at my hands. You cannot say that.

ADMETUS

Oh! If only you might come to need my help some day!

PHERES

Woo many wives so that more may die!

ADMETUS

That is a reproach to you, for you refused to.

PHERES

Sweet is the sun god's light, sweet.

ADMETUS

Your heart is cowardly, not a man's at all.

PHERES

At least you cannot mock me as you carry my aged body out for burial.

ΑΔΜΗΤΟΣ

725 θανῇ γε μέντοι δυσκλεής, ὅταν θάνῃς.

ΦΕΡΗΣ

κακῶς ἀκούειν οὐ μέλει θανόντι μοι.

ΑΔΜΗΤΟΣ

φεῦ φεῦ· τὸ γῆρας ὡς ἀναιδείας πλέων.

ΦΕΡΗΣ

ἥδ' οὐκ ἀναιδής· τήνδ' ἐφηῦρες ἄφρονα.

ΑΔΜΗΤΟΣ

ἄπελθε κἀμὲ τόνδ' ἔα θάψαι νεκρόν.

ΦΕΡΗΣ

730 ἄπειμι· θάψεις δ' αὐτὸς ὢν αὐτῆς φονεύς,
δίκας δὲ δώσεις σοῖσι κηδεσταῖς ἔτι·
ἦ τἄρ' Ἄκαστος οὐκέτ' ἔστ' ἐν ἀνδράσιν,
εἰ μή σ' ἀδελφῆς αἷμα τιμωρήσεται.

ΑΔΜΗΤΟΣ

ἔρρων νυν αὐτὸς χἠ ξυνοικήσασά σοι,
735 ἄπαιδε παιδὸς ὄντος, ὥσπερ ἄξιοι,
γηράσκετ'· οὐ γὰρ τῷδ' ἔτ' ἐς ταὐτὸν στέγος
νεῖσθ'· εἰ δ' ἀπειπεῖν χρῆν με κηρύκων ὕπο
τὴν σὴν πατρῴαν ἑστίαν, ἀπεῖπον ἄν.
  ἡμεῖς δέ — τοὐν ποσὶν γὰρ οἰστέον κακόν —
740 στείχωμεν, ὡς ἂν ἐν πυρᾷ θῶμεν νεκρόν.

ΧΟΡΟΣ

ἰὼ ἰώ. σχετλία τόλμης,
ὦ γενναία καὶ μέγ' ἀρίστη,

ADMETUS

But die you shall, and die with no good name.

PHERES

When I am gone, I care not what men say.

ADMETUS

Oh my, how full of shamelessness is age!

PHERES

She was not shameless. What she lacked was sense.

ADMETUS

Go, and let me bury this body.

PHERES

I go. But you will bury her being yourself her murderer, and one day you will pay the penalty to your kin by marriage. Acastus is no man if he fails to punish you for his sister's death.

ADMETUS

Off with you! You and your wife, spend, as you deserve, a childless old age, though with a child alive. For you shall never come under the same roof with me. If I had to renounce your paternal hearth by public herald, I would have renounced it.

Exit PHERES and retinue by Eisodos B.

(to the Chorus) But since we must now endure the sorrow at hand, let us go to bury our dead.

CHORUS LEADER

(obeying Admetus' earlier command to bid their farewell to Alcestis) Alas, alas! O resolute in courage, heart noble

χαῖρε· πρόφρων σε χθόνιός θ' Ἑρμῆς
Ἅιδης τε δέχοιτ'. εἰ δέ τι κἀκεῖ
745 πλέον ἔστ' ἀγαθοῖς, τούτων μετέχουσ'
Ἅιδου νύμφῃ παρεδρεύοις.

ΘΕΡΑΠΩΝ

πολλοὺς μὲν ἤδη κἀπὸ παντοίας χθονὸς
ξένους μολόντας οἶδ' ἐς Ἀδμήτου δόμους,
οἷς δεῖπνα προύθηκ'· ἀλλὰ τοῦδ' οὔπω ξένον
750 κακίον' ἐς τήνδ' ἑστίαν ἐδεξάμην.
ὃς πρῶτα μὲν πενθοῦντα δεσπότην ὁρῶν
ἐσῆλθε κἀτόλμησ' ἀμείψασθαι πύλας.
ἔπειτα δ' οὔτι σωφρόνως ἐδέξατο
τὰ προστυχόντα ξένια, συμφορὰν μαθών,
755 ἀλλ', εἴ τι μὴ φέροιμεν, ὤτρυνεν φέρειν.
ποτήριον δ' ἐν χερσὶ κίσσινον λαβὼν
πίνει μελαίνης μητρὸς εὔζωρον μέθυ,
ἕως ἐθέρμην' αὐτὸν ἀμφιβᾶσα φλὸξ
οἴνου. στέφει δὲ κρᾶτα μυρσίνης κλάδοις,
760 ἄμουσ' ὑλακτῶν· δισσὰ δ' ἦν μέλη κλύειν·
ὁ μὲν γὰρ ᾖδε, τῶν ἐν Ἀδμήτου κακῶν
οὐδὲν προτιμῶν, οἰκέται δ' ἐκλαίομεν
δέσποιναν, ὄμμα δ' οὐκ ἐδείκνυμεν ξένῳ
τέγγοντες· Ἄδμητος γὰρ ὧδ' ἐφίετο.
765 καὶ νῦν ἐγὼ μὲν ἐν δόμοισιν ἑστιῶ
ξένον, πανοῦργον κλῶπα καὶ λῃστήν τινα,
ἡ δ' ἐκ δόμων βέβηκεν, οὐδ' ἐφεσπόμην
οὐδ' ἐξέτεινα χεῖρ' ἀποιμώζων ἐμὴν

749 ξένον Dobree: ξένου C
236

and generous, farewell! May Hermes of the Underworld
and Hades receive you kindly! And if in that place the
good have any advantage, may you have a share in it and sit
as attendant beside Hades' bride![a]

Exit ADMETUS, CHORUS, *and funeral procession by Eiso-
dos A. To the empty stage enter a* MANSERVANT *from the
palace.*

MANSERVANT

I have known many men from all manner of lands to come
as guests to Admetus' house, and I have served them
dinner. But never yet have I welcomed a worse guest to
our hearth than this one. In the first place, though he saw
that our master was in mourning, he was shameless
enough to enter our doors. Then he did not soberly accept
the fare that was set before him, as he might in view of our
misfortunes, but if we failed to bring anything, he ordered
it brought. Then taking an ivy-wood drinking bowl in his
hands and drinking unmixed wine, offspring of the dark
grape, until the fire in it enveloped and warmed his heart,
he garlanded his head with sprays of myrtle and howled
songs out of tune. You could hear two sorts of melody.
He was singing, paying no attention to the trouble in
Admetus' house, while we servants were bewailing our
mistress. But we did not show our faces in tears to the
stranger, for those were Admetus' orders. And now I must
feast the stranger in our house, some knavish thief or bri-
gand, while my mistress has left the house without my fol-
lowing or holding out my hand in mourning for her.

[a] Persephone.

---

[756] ποτήριον δ' ἐν χερσὶ Musgrave: ποτῆρα δ' ἐν χείρεσσι C

δέσποιναν, ἣ 'μοὶ πᾶσί τ' οἰκέταισιν ἦν
770 μήτηρ· κακῶν γὰρ μυρίων ἐρρύετο,
ὀργὰς μαλάσσουσ' ἀνδρός. ἆρα τὸν ξένον
στυγῶ δικαίως, ἐν κακοῖς ἀφιγμένον;

ΗΡΑΚΛΗΣ

οὗτος, τί σεμνὸν καὶ πεφροντικὸς βλέπεις;
οὐ χρὴ σκυθρωπὸν τοῖς ξένοις τὸν πρόσπολον
775 εἶναι, δέχεσθαι δ' εὐπροσηγόρῳ φρενί.
σὺ δ' ἄνδρ' ἑταῖρον δεσπότου παρόνθ' ὁρῶν
στυγνῷ προσώπῳ καὶ συνωφρυωμένῳ
δέχῃ, θυραίου πήματος σπουδὴν ἔχων.

δεῦρ' ἔλθ', ὅπως ἂν καὶ σοφώτερος γένῃ.
780 τὰ θνητὰ πράγμαθ' ἥντιν' οἶσθ' ἔχει φύσιν;
οἶμαι μὲν οὔ· πόθεν γάρ; ἀλλ' ἄκουέ μου.
βροτοῖς ἅπασι κατθανεῖν ὀφείλεται,
κοὐκ ἔστι θνητῶν ὅστις ἐξεπίσταται
τὴν αὔριον μέλλουσαν εἰ βιώσεται·
785 τὸ τῆς τύχης γὰρ ἀφανὲς οἷ προβήσεται,
κἄστ' οὐ διδακτὸν οὐδ' ἁλίσκεται τέχνῃ.
ταῦτ' οὖν ἀκούσας καὶ μαθὼν ἐμοῦ πάρα
εὔφραινε σαυτόν, πῖνε, τὸν καθ' ἡμέραν
βίον λογίζου σόν, τὰ δ' ἄλλα τῆς τύχης.
790 τίμα δὲ καὶ τὴν πλεῖστον ἡδίστην θεῶν
Κύπριν βροτοῖσιν· εὐμενὴς γὰρ ἡ θεός.
τὰ δ' ἄλλ' ἔασον πάντα καὶ πιθοῦ λόγοις
ἐμοῖσιν, εἴπερ ὀρθά σοι δοκῶ λέγειν.
οἶμαι μέν. οὔκουν τὴν ἄγαν λύπην ἀφεὶς
795 πίῃ μεθ' ἡμῶν [τάσδ' ὑπερβαλὼν τύχας,

238

She was like a mother to me and to the other servants, rescuing us from countless troubles and softening her husband's temper. Do I not have reason to hate the guest, who has arrived in our hour of misfortune?

Enter HERACLES from the palace.

HERACLES

You there, why do you look so grave and careworn? A servant ought not to scowl at the guest but welcome him with an affable air. But you, though you see an old friend of your master arrive, receive him with an unfriendly face and with your brows knit together, worrying about a grief that does not concern your house.

Come here so that you may be made wiser! Do you know the nature of our mortal life? I think not. How could you? But listen to me. Death is a debt all mortals must pay, and no man knows for certain whether he will still be living on the morrow. The outcome of our fortune is hid from our eyes, and it lies beyond the scope of any teaching or craft. So now that you have learned this from me, cheer your heart, drink, regard this day's life as yours but all else as Fortune's! Honor Aphrodite, too, sweetest of the gods to mortals, for she is a kindly goddess. Forget all else and take my advice, if you think what I say is correct, as I suppose you do. Lay aside your excessive grief and have some wine with me [overcoming these

---

780 πράγμαθ' ἥντιν' οἶσθ' Blaydes; πράγματ' οἶδας ἦν C
792 πάντα Markland: ταῦτα C
795–6 τάσδ' ... πυκασθείς del. Herwerden: cf. 829, 832

στεφάνοις πυκασθείς]· καὶ σάφ᾽ οἶδ᾽ ὁθούνεκα
τοῦ νῦν σκυθρωποῦ καὶ ξυνεστῶτος φρενῶν
μεθορμιεῖ σε πίτυλος ἐμπεσὼν σκύφου.
ὄντας δὲ θνητοὺς θνητὰ καὶ φρονεῖν χρεών·
800   ὡς τοῖς γε σεμνοῖς καὶ συνωφρυωμένοις
ἅπασίν ἐστιν, ὥς γ᾽ ἐμοὶ χρῆσθαι κριτῇ,
οὐ βίος ἀληθῶς ὁ βίος ἀλλὰ συμφορά.

ΘΕΡΑΠΩΝ

ἐπιστάμεσθα ταῦτα· νῦν δὲ πράσσομεν
οὐχ οἷα κώμου καὶ γέλωτος ἄξια.

ΗΡΑΚΛΗΣ

805   γυνὴ θυραῖος ἡ θανοῦσα· μὴ λίαν
πένθει· δόμων γὰρ ζῶσι τῶνδε δεσπόται.

ΘΕΡΑΠΩΝ

τί ζῶσιν; οὐ κάτοισθα τὰν δόμοις κακά;

ΗΡΑΚΛΗΣ

εἰ μή τι σός με δεσπότης ἐψεύσατο.

ΘΕΡΑΠΩΝ

ἄγαν ἐκεῖνός ἐστ᾽ ἄγαν φιλόξενος.

ΗΡΑΚΛΗΣ

810   οὐ χρῆν μ᾽ ὀθνείου γ᾽ οὕνεκ᾽ εὖ πάσχειν νεκροῦ;

ΘΕΡΑΠΩΝ

ἦ κάρτα μέντοι καὶ λίαν οἰκεῖος ἦν.

ΗΡΑΚΛΗΣ

μῶν ξυμφοράν τιν᾽ οὖσαν οὐκ ἔφραζέ μοι;

misfortunes, head crowned with garlands]! I am quite
sure that when the fit of drinking is upon you, it will bring
you round from your clotted and gloomy state of mind.
Being mortal we ought to think mortal thoughts. As for
those who are solemn and knit their brows together, their
life, in my judgment, is no life worthy of the name but
merely a disaster.

MANSERVANT

We understand this. But our present circumstances do
not call for carousing and laughter.

HERACLES

The woman who died is no relation. Do not grieve so
excessively. The lord and lady of this house are living.

MANSERVANT

How do you mean living? Do you not know of the grief in
our house?

HERACLES

Yes, unless your master has deceived me.

MANSERVANT

My master is too, too hospitable!

HERACLES

Should I not enjoy myself just because someone not your
own has died?

MANSERVANT

But she was very much our own, too much so.

HERACLES

Did he conceal from me some misfortune?

ΘΕΡΑΠΩΝ

χαίρων ἴθ᾽ · ἡμῖν δεσποτῶν μέλει κακά.

ΗΡΑΚΛΗΣ

ὅδ᾽ οὐ θυραίων πημάτων ἄρχει λόγος.

ΘΕΡΑΠΩΝ

815   οὐ γάρ τι κωμάζοντ᾽ ἂν ἠχθόμην σ᾽ ὁρῶν.

ΗΡΑΚΛΗΣ

ἀλλ᾽ ἦ πέπονθα δείν᾽ ὑπὸ ξένων ἐμῶν;

ΘΕΡΑΠΩΝ

οὐκ ἦλθες ἐν δέοντι δέξασθαι δόμοις.
[πένθος γὰρ ἡμῖν ἐστι· καὶ κουρὰν βλέπεις
μελαμπέπλους στολμούς τε.]

ΗΡΑΚΛΗΣ

[τίς δ᾽ ὁ κατθανών;]

820   μῶν ἢ τέκνων τι φροῦδον ἢ γέρων πατήρ;

ΘΕΡΑΠΩΝ

γυνὴ μὲν οὖν ὄλωλεν Ἀδμήτου, ξένε.

ΗΡΑΚΛΗΣ

τί φῄς; ἔπειτα δῆτά μ᾽ ἐξενίζετε;

ΘΕΡΑΠΩΝ

ᾐδεῖτο γάρ σε τῶνδ᾽ ἀπώσασθαι δόμων.

ΗΡΑΚΛΗΣ

ὦ σχέτλι᾽, οἵας ἤμπλακες ξυναόρου.

818–19 del. Kvičala cl. Σ ad 820

MANSERVANT

Pay it no heed. The master's troubles are our concern.

HERACLES

It is no foreign grief these words prelude.

MANSERVANT

No, for otherwise I would not have been vexed at seeing you carousing.

HERACLES

But has my host done a terrible thing to me?

MANSERVANT

You have not come at the proper time for the house to receive you. [For we are in mourning, and you see our shorn hair and our black garb.]

HERACLES

[Who is it that has died?] Is one of his children or his aged father gone?

MANSERVANT

No, stranger, it is Admetus' wife who has died.

HERACLES

What are you saying? And yet you still entertained me?

MANSERVANT

Yes, for his sense of honor kept him from thrusting you from his house.

HERACLES

O poor man, what a helpmeet you have lost!

ΘΕΡΑΠΩΝ

825 ἀπωλόμεσθα πάντες, οὐ κείνη μόνη.

ΗΡΑΚΛΗΣ

ἀλλ᾽ ᾐσθόμην μὲν ὄμμ᾽ ἰδὼν δακρυρροοῦν
κουράν τε καὶ πρόσωπον· ἀλλ᾽ ἔπειθέ με
λέγων θυραῖον κῆδος ἐς τάφον φέρειν.
βίᾳ δὲ θυμοῦ τάσδ᾽ ὑπερβαλὼν πύλας
830 ἔπινον ἀνδρὸς ἐν φιλοξένου δόμοις
πράσσοντος οὕτω. κᾆτα κωμάζω κάρα
στεφάνοις πυκασθείς; ἀλλὰ σοῦ τὸ νῦν φράσαι,
κακοῦ τοσούτου δώμασιν προσκειμένου,
ποῦ καί σφε θάπτει, ποῖ νιν εὑρήσω μολών.

ΘΕΡΑΠΩΝ

835 ὀρθὴν παρ᾽ οἶμον ἣ 'πὶ Λάρισαν φέρει
τύμβον κατόψῃ ξεστὸν ἐκ προαστίου.

ΗΡΑΚΛΗΣ

ὦ πολλὰ τλᾶσα καρδία καὶ χεὶρ ἐμή,
νῦν δεῖξον οἷον παῖδά σ᾽ ἡ Τιρυνθία
ἐγείνατ᾽ Ἠλεκτρύωνος Ἀλκμήνη Διί.
840 δεῖ γάρ με σῶσαι τὴν θανοῦσαν ἀρτίως
γυναῖκα κἀς τόνδ᾽ αὖθις ἱδρῦσαι δόμον
Ἄλκηστιν Ἀδμήτῳ θ᾽ ὑπουργῆσαι χάριν.
ἐλθὼν δ᾽ ἄνακτα τὸν μελάμπεπλον νεκρῶν
Θάνατον φυλάξω, καί νιν εὑρήσειν δοκῶ
845 πίνοντα τύμβου πλησίον προσφαγμάτων.
κἄνπερ λοχαίας αὐτὸν ἐξ ἕδρας συθεὶς
μάρψω, κύκλον γε περιβαλὼν χεροῖν ἐμαῖν,

244

MANSERVANT

We have all perished, not she alone.

HERACLES

I noticed his brimming eyes, his shorn hair, and his expression of grief, but he convinced me that he was burying someone unrelated. And against my better judgment I passed through these gates and caroused in the house of this hospitable man in his hour of grief. And can I now go on revelling, my head garlanded? But it is your task now, with such a great misfortune brought on the house, to tell me where he is burying her, where I must go to find her.

MANSERVANT

You will see from the outskirts of the city, next to the straight road that leads to Larisa, a sculpted tomb.

HERACLES

O heart and hand that have endured so much, now show what kind of son Tirynthian Alcmene, daughter of Electryon, bore to Zeus! I must save the woman who has just died and show my gratitude to Admetus by restoring Alcestis once more to this house. I shall go and look out for the black-robed lord of the dead, Death himself, and I think I shall find him drinking from the offerings near the tomb. And if once I rush from ambush and catch him in my side-crushing grip, no one shall take him from me

---

832 νῦν φράσαι (possis etiam μὴ στέγειν) scripsi: μὴ φράσαι C
833 προσκειμένου Scaliger: προκ- C
834 ποῖ Monte: ποῦ C
839 ἐγείνατ' Ἠλεκτρύωνος Gaisford: ἠλεκτρ. γείνατ' C
847 γε Diggle: δὲ C

οὐκ ἔστιν ὅστις αὐτὸν ἐξαιρήσεται
μογοῦντα πλευρά, πρὶν γυναῖκ' ἐμοὶ μεθῇ.
850 ἢν δ' οὖν ἁμάρτω τῆσδ' ἄγρας καὶ μὴ μόλῃ
πρὸς αἱματηρὸν πελανόν, εἶμι τῶν κάτω
Κόρης Ἄνακτός τ' εἰς ἀνηλίους δόμους,
αἰτήσομαί τε καὶ πέποιθ' ἄξειν ἄνω
Ἄλκηστιν, ὥστε χερσὶν ἐνθεῖναι ξένου,
855 ὅς μ' ἐς δόμους ἐδέξατ' οὐδ' ἀπήλασεν,
καίπερ βαρείᾳ συμφορᾷ πεπληγμένος,
ἔκρυπτε δ' ὢν γενναῖος, αἰδεσθεὶς ἐμέ.
τίς τοῦδε μᾶλλον Θεσσαλῶν φιλόξενος,
τίς Ἑλλάδ' οἰκῶν; τοιγὰρ οὐκ ἐρεῖ κακὸν
860 εὐεργετῆσαι φῶτα γενναῖος γεγώς.

ΑΔΜΗΤΟΣ

ἰώ,
στυγναὶ πρόσοδοι, στυγναὶ δ' ὄψεις
χήρων μελάθρων.
ἰώ μοί μοι, αἰαῖ <αἰαῖ>.
ποῖ βῶ; ποῖ στῶ; τί λέγω; τί δὲ μή;
πῶς ἂν ὀλοίμην;
865 ἦ βαρυδαίμονα μήτηρ μ' ἔτεκεν.
ζηλῶ φθιμένους, κείνων ἔραμαι,
κεῖν' ἐπιθυμῶ δώματα ναίειν.
οὔτε γὰρ αὐγὰς χαίρω προσορῶν
οὔτ' ἐπὶ γαίας πόδα πεζεύων·
870 τοῖον ὅμηρόν μ' ἀποσυλήσας
Ἅιδῃ Θάνατος παρέδωκεν.

862 <αἰαῖ> Hermann

until he releases the woman to me. But if I fail to catch this quarry and he does not come to the blood offering, I shall go down to the sunless house of Persephone and her lord in the world below and shall ask for Alcestis, and I think I shall bring her up and put her in the hands of my friend. He welcomed me into his house and did not drive me away, though he had suffered grievous misfortune. In his nobility he concealed it, out of respect for me. What Thessalian is more hospitable than he, what Greek? Therefore he must never be able to say that in his nobility he has done a kindness to a man who is ungrateful.

Exit HERACLES *by Eisodos A and the* MANSERVANT *into the palace. Re-enter* ADMETUS, CHORUS, *and funeral procession.*

ADMETUS

Oh, how hateful the approach, how hateful the sight of this bereaved house. Ah, woe is me! Where shall I go, where stay? What shall I say, what conceal? I wish I could die! It was to an ill fate that my mother bore me. I envy the dead, I long for their state, I yearn to dwell in those halls below. For I take no joy in looking on the light or in walking about on the earth. Such is the hostage Death took from me and handed over to Hades.

ΧΟΡΟΣ

πρόβα, πρόβα· βᾶθι κεῦθος οἴκων.

ΑΔΜΗΤΟΣ

αἰαί.

ΧΟΡΟΣ

πέπονθας ἄξι᾽ αἰαγμάτων.

ΑΔΜΗΤΟΣ

ἒ ἔ.

ΧΟΡΟΣ

δι᾽ ὀδύνας
ἔβας, σάφ᾽ οἶδα.

ΑΔΜΗΤΟΣ

φεῦ φεῦ.

ΧΟΡΟΣ

875   τὰν νέρθε δ᾽ οὐδὲν ὠφελεῖς.

ΑΔΜΗΤΟΣ

ἰώ μοί μοι.

ΧΟΡΟΣ

τὸ μήποτ᾽ εἰσιδεῖν φιλίας ἀλόχου
πρόσωπόν σ᾽ ἔσαντα λυπρόν.

ΑΔΜΗΤΟΣ

ἔμνησας ὅ μου φρένας ἤλκωσεν·
τί γὰρ ἀνδρὶ κακὸν μεῖζον ἁμαρτεῖν

877 σ᾽ ἔσαντα Wilamowitz: ἄντα C

248

CHORUS

Go on, go on, enter the recesses of the house.

ADMETUS

Alas!

CHORUS

Your sufferings well deserve that "alas."

ADMETUS

O pain!

CHORUS

You have been in pain, I know it.

ADMETUS

O grief!

CHORUS

But you do her who is dead no good.

ADMETUS

Alas!

CHORUS

No more to see your dead wife face to face is painful.

ADMETUS

You have stirred in my memory the wound on my heart.
What greater sorrow can a man have than the loss of his

880 πιστῆς ἀλόχου; μήποτε γήμας
ὤφελον οἰκεῖν μετὰ τῆσδε δόμους.
ζηλῶ δ᾽ ἀγάμους ἀτέκνους τε βροτῶν·
μία γὰρ ψυχή, τῆς ὑπεραλγεῖν
μέτριον ἄχθος·
885 παίδων δὲ νόσους καὶ νυμφιδίους
εὐνὰς θανάτοις κεραϊζομένας
οὐ τλητὸν ὁρᾶν, ἐξὸν ἀτέκνοις
ἀγάμοις τ᾽ εἶναι διὰ παντός.

ΧΟΡΟΣ

ἀντ. α

τύχα τύχα δυσπάλαιστος ἥκει.

ΑΔΜΗΤΟΣ

890 αἰαῖ.

ΧΟΡΟΣ
πέρας δέ γ᾽ οὐδὲν ἀλγέων τίθης.

ΑΔΜΗΤΟΣ
ἒ ἔ.

ΧΟΡΟΣ
βαρέα μὲν
φέρειν, ὅμως δὲ . . .

ΑΔΜΗΤΟΣ
φεῦ φεῦ.

ΧΟΡΟΣ
τλᾶθ᾽· οὐ σὺ πρῶτος ὤλεσας . . .

250

faithful wife? Would I had never married and lived with her in this house! I envy the unmarried and childless among mortals. For they have but a single soul, and to feel its pains is only a moderate burden. But diseases of children and wives snatched by death from their marriage beds are unendurable to see when one can live unwed and childless all one's days.

CHORUS

Fate inexorable is come.

ADMETUS

Alas!

CHORUS

But you set no limit upon grief.

ADMETUS

The pain!

CHORUS

It is grievous to bear, but still . . .

ADMETUS

O grief!

CHORUS

bear it: you are not the first to lose . . .

251

ΑΔΜΗΤΟΣ

ἰώ μοί μοι.

ΧΟΡΟΣ

γυναῖκα· συμφορὰ δ' ἑτέρους ἑτέρα
πιέζει φανεῖσα θνατῶν.

ΑΔΜΗΤΟΣ

895 ὦ μακρὰ πένθη λῦπαί τε φίλων
τῶν ὑπὸ γαίας.
τί μ' ἐκώλυσας ῥῖψαι τύμβου
τάφρον ἐς κοίλην καὶ μετ' ἐκείνης
τῆς μέγ' ἀρίστης κεῖσθαι φθίμενον;
900 δύο δ' ἀντὶ μιᾶς Ἅιδης ψυχὰς
τὰς πιστοτάτας σὺν ἂν ἔσχεν, ὁμοῦ
χθονίαν λίμνην διαβάντε.

ΧΟΡΟΣ

στρ. β

ἐμοί τις ἦν
ἐν γένει, ᾧ κόρος ἀξιόθρη-
905 νος ὤλετ' ἐν δόμοισιν
μονόπαις· ἀλλ' ἔμπας
ἔφερε κακὸν ἅλις, ἄτεκνος ὤν,
πολιὰς ἐπὶ χαίτας ἤδη
910 προπετὴς ὢν βιότου τε πόρσω.

ΑΔΜΗΤΟΣ

ὦ σχῆμα δόμων, πῶς εἰσέλθω,
πῶς δ' οἰκήσω, μεταπίπτοντος
δαίμονος; οἴμοι. πολὺ γὰρ τὸ μέσον·

ADMETUS

Alas!

CHORUS

... a wife. Different misfortunes arise to press on different mortals.

ADMETUS

Oh, how great is the pain and grief for loved ones who lie beneath the earth! Why did you keep me from throwing myself into the open grave and lying there dead with her, the best of women? Hades would have had two most faithful souls instead of one, crossing the Underworld's lake together.

CHORUS

I had a kinsman whose son, full worthy to lament, perished at home, an only child. But still, he bore his sorrow in measure, though he was without an heir and already sunk down toward gray old age and far on in years.

ADMETUS

O sad image of my house, how am I to enter, how live in you with my fortune so changed? Alas! How great the

915 τότε μὲν πεύκαις σὺν Πηλιάσιν
σύν θ᾽ ὑμεναίοις ἔστειχον ἔσω
φιλίας ἀλόχου χέρα βαστάζων,
πολυάχητος δ᾽ εἵπετο κῶμος
τήν τε θανοῦσαν κἄμ᾽ ὀλβίζων
920 ὡς εὐπατρίδαι κἀπ᾽ ἀμφοτέρων
ὄντες ἀριστέων σύζυγες εἶμεν·
νῦν δ᾽ ὑμεναίων γόος ἀντίπαλος
λευκῶν τε πέπλων μέλανες στολμοὶ
πέμπουσί μ᾽ ἔσω
925 λέκτρων κοίτας ἐς ἐρήμους.

ΧΟΡΟΣ

ἀντ. β

παρ᾽ εὐτυχῆ
σοι πότμον ἦλθεν ἀπειροκάκῳ
τόδ᾽ ἄλγος· ἀλλ᾽ ἔσωσας
βίοτον καὶ ψυχάν.
930 ἔθανε δάμαρ, ἔλιπε φιλίαν·
τί νέον τόδε; πολλοῖς ἤδη
παρέλυσεν θάνατος δάμαρτας.

ΑΔΜΗΤΟΣ

935 φίλοι, γυναικὸς δαίμον᾽ εὐτυχέστερον
τοὐμοῦ νομίζω, καίπερ οὐ δοκοῦνθ᾽ ὅμως.
τῆς μὲν γὰρ οὐδὲν ἄλγος ἅψεταί ποτε,
πολλῶν δὲ μόχθων εὐκλεὴς ἐπαύσατο.
ἐγὼ δ᾽, ὃν οὐ χρῆν ζῆν, παρεὶς τὸ μόρσιμον
940 λυπρὸν διάξω βίοτον· ἄρτι μανθάνω.

254

difference! Once I entered with pine torches from Mount
Pelion and bridal songs, holding the hand of my dear wife,
and a clamorous throng followed, praising the blessedness
of my dead wife and me, because she and I, both nobly
born, had become man and wife. Now groans of grief in
answer to those songs and black robes in place of white
escort me in to a desolate bed chamber.

CHORUS

In the midst of good fortune this grief has come to you
while you were unschooled in trouble. But you are still
alive. Your wife has died, she has left your love behind.
This is not something new. Many men ere now have been
parted from wives by death.

ADMETUS

My friends, I think my wife's lot is happier than my own,
though it may not appear so. For she will never be
touched by any grief and has ended her many troubles
with glory. But I, who ought not to be alive and have
escaped my fate, shall now live out my life in pain. Now I

---

921 ἀριστέων Dobree: ἀρίστων C
932 δάμαρτας a: -ος b: -α Dale

πῶς γὰρ δόμων τῶνδ' εἰσόδους ἀνέξομαι;
τίν' ἂν προσειπών, τοῦ δὲ προσρηθεὶς ὕπο
τερπνῆς τύχοιμ' ἂν εἰσόδου; ποῖ τρέψομαι;
ἡ μὲν γὰρ ἔνδον ἐξελᾷ μ' ἐρημία,
945 γυναικὸς εὐνὰς εὖτ' ἂν εἰσίδω κενὰς
θρόνους τ' ἐν οἷσιν ἷζε καὶ κατὰ στέγας
αὐχμηρὸν οὖδας, τέκνα δ' ἀμφὶ γούνασιν
πίπτοντα κλαίῃ μητέρ', οἱ δὲ δεσπότιν
στένωσιν οἵαν ἐκ δόμων ἀπώλεσαν.
950 τὰ μὲν κατ' οἴκους τοιάδ'· ἔξωθεν δέ με
γάμοι τ' ἐλῶσι Θεσσαλῶν καὶ ξύλλογοι
γυναικοπληθεῖς· οὐ γὰρ ἐξανέξομαι
λεύσσων δάμαρτος τῆς ἐμῆς ὁμήλικας.
ἐρεῖ δέ μ' ὅστις ἐχθρὸς ὢν κυρεῖ τάδε·
955 Ἰδοῦ τὸν αἰσχρῶς ζῶνθ', ὃς οὐκ ἔτλη θανεῖν
ἀλλ' ἣν ἔγημεν ἀντιδοὺς ἀψυχίᾳ
πέφευγεν Ἅιδην· κᾆτ' ἀνὴρ εἶναι δοκεῖ;
στυγεῖ δὲ τοὺς τεκόντας, αὐτὸς οὐ θέλων
θανεῖν. τοιάνδε πρὸς κακοῖσι κληδόνα
960 ἕξω. τί μοι ζῆν δῆτα κέρδιον, φίλοι,
κακῶς κλύοντι καὶ κακῶς πεπραγότι;

ΧΟΡΟΣ

στρ. α

ἐγὼ καὶ διὰ μούσας
καὶ μετάρσιος ᾖξα, καὶ
πλείστων ἁψάμενος λόγων
965 κρεῖσσον οὐδὲν Ἀνάγκας
ηὗρον οὐδέ τι φάρμακον

256

understand. For how shall I endure entering this house?
Whom will I greet, by whom be greeted, that my
homecoming may give me pleasure? Which way shall I
turn? For the desolation within will drive me out of doors
when I see my wife's bed and the chairs in which she sat
now empty, the floor unswept throughout the house and
the children falling about my knees weeping for their
mother, while the slaves lament that they have lost so good
a mistress from the house. That is how things stand within
the palace. But outside it, weddings of Thessalians and
gatherings full of women will drive me back indoors. I
shall not be able to endure the sight of women my wife's
age. And anyone who is my enemy will say, "Look at this
man who lives on in disgrace! He did not have the courage
to die but in cowardice escaped death by giving his wife in
his place. And after that can we think him a man? He
hates his parents though he himself is unwilling to die."
Besides my sorrows I will have to endure this kind of talk.
What profit, then, my friends, for me in living since both
my reputation and my fortunes are so ill?

CHORUS

I have soared aloft with poetry and with high thought, and
though I have laid my hand to many a reflection, I have
found nothing stronger than Necessity, nor is there any

---

[941] εἰσόδους] fort. ἀμβάσεις, cl. 943
[960] κέρδιον Purgold: κύδιον C

Θρήσσαις ἐν σανίσιν, τὰς
Ὀρφεία κατέγραψεν
γῆρυς, οὐδ' ὅσα Φοῖβος Ἀ-
970   σκληπιάδαις ἔδωκε
φάρμακα πολυπόνοις
ἀντιτεμὼν βροτοῖσιν.

ἀντ. α

μόνας δ' οὔτ' ἐπὶ βωμοὺς
ἐλθεῖν οὔτε βρέτας θεᾶς
975   ἔστιν, οὐ σφαγίων κλύει.
μή μοι, πότνια, μείζων
ἔλθοις ἢ τὸ πρὶν ἐν βίῳ.
καὶ γὰρ Ζεὺς ὅ τι νεύσῃ
σὺν σοὶ τοῦτο τελευτᾷ.
980   καὶ τὸν ἐν Χαλύβοις δαμά-
ζεις σὺ βίᾳ σίδαρον,
οὐδέ τις ἀποτόμου
λήματός ἐστιν αἰδώς.

στρ. β

καὶ σ' ἐν ἀφύκτοισι χερῶν εἷλε θεὰ δεσμοῖς.
985   τόλμα δ' · οὐ γὰρ ἀνάξεις ποτ' ἔνερθεν
κλαίων τοὺς φθιμένους ἄνω.
καὶ θεῶν σκότιοι φθίνουσι
990   παῖδες ἐν θανάτῳ.
φίλα μὲν ὅτ' ἦν μεθ' ἡμῶν,
φίλα δὲ θανοῦσ' ἔτ' ἔσται,
γενναιοτάταν δὲ πασᾶν
ἐζεύξω κλισίαις ἄκοιτιν.

cure for it in the Thracian tablets set down by the voice of Orpheus nor in all the simples which Phoebus harvested in aid of trouble-ridden mortals and gave to the sons of Asclepius.

Of that goddess alone there are no altars, no statue to approach, and to sacrifice she pays no heed. Do not, I pray you, Lady, come with greater force than heretofore in my life. For whatever Zeus ordains, with your help he brings it to fulfillment. Even the iron of the Chalybes[a] you overcome with your violence, and there is no pity in your unrelenting heart.

You also, Admetus, have been caught in the goddess's ineluctable chains. But endure! For you cannot bring up the dead from below by weeping. Even the sons of the gods perish in the darkness of death. She was loved when she was with us, she will be loved still in death, and the noblest of all women was she that you brought to your bridal bed.

[a] A people living on the Black Sea, said to have invented the working of iron.

---

992 θανοῦσ᾽ ἔτ᾽ ἔσται Prinz: καὶ θανοῦσ᾽ ἔσται C: καὶ ἐν θανοῦσι Marzullo

ἀντ. β

995 μηδὲ νεκρῶν ὡς φθιμένων χῶμα νομιζέσθω
τύμβος σᾶς ἀλόχου, θεοῖσι δ' ὁμοίως
τιμάσθω, σέβας ἐμπόρων.

1000 καί τις δοχμίαν κέλευθον
ἐμβαίνων τόδ' ἐρεῖ·
Αὕτα ποτὲ προὔθαν' ἀνδρός,
νῦν δ' ἔστι μάκαιρα δαίμων·
χαῖρ', ὦ πότνι', εὖ δὲ δοίης.

1005 τοία νιν προσεροῦσι φήμᾳ.

— καὶ μὴν ὅδ', ὡς ἔοικεν, Ἀλκμήνης γόνος,
Ἄδμητε, πρὸς σὴν ἑστίαν πορεύεται.

ΗΡΑΚΛΗΣ

φίλον πρὸς ἄνδρα χρὴ λέγειν ἐλευθέρως,
Ἄδμητε, μομφὰς δ' οὐχ ὑπὸ σπλάγχνοις ἔχειν

1010 σιγῶντ'. ἐγὼ δὲ σοῖς κακοῖσιν ἠξίουν
ἐγγὺς παρεστὼς ἐξετάζεσθαι φίλος·
σὺ δ' οὐκ ἔφραζες σῆς προκείμενον νέκυν
γυναικός, ἀλλά μ' ἐξένιζες ἐν δόμοις,
ὡς δὴ θυραίου πήματος σπουδὴν ἔχων.

1015 κἄστεψα κρᾶτα καὶ θεοῖς ἐλειψάμην
σπονδὰς ἐν οἴκοις δυστυχοῦσι τοῖσι σοῖς.
καὶ μέμφομαι μέν, μέμφομαι, παθὼν τάδε·
οὐ μήν σε λυπεῖν <γ'> ἐν κακοῖσι βούλομαι.
ὧν δ' οὕνεχ' ἥκω δεῦρ' ὑποστρέψας πάλιν

1020 λέξω· γυναῖκα τήνδε μοι σῶσον λαβών,
ἕως ἂν ἵππους δεῦρο Θρῃκίας ἄγων

260

ALCESTIS

Let not the grave of your wife be regarded as the funeral mound of the dead departed but let her be honored as are the gods, an object of reverence to the wayfarer. Someone walking a winding path past her tomb shall say, "This woman died in the stead of her husband, and now she is a blessed divinity. Hail, Lady, and grant us your blessing!" With such words will they address her.

Enter HERACLES by Eisodos A with a veiled woman.

CHORUS LEADER

But look: it seems Alcmene's son is coming to your hearth, Admetus.

HERACLES

One should speak frankly to a friend, Admetus, and not silently store up reproaches in the heart. I thought it right that I should stand by you in your misfortune and give proof that I was your friend. Yet you did not tell me your wife was laid out for burial but feasted me in the house, saying that you were busy with a grief not your own. So I garlanded my head and poured libations to the gods in your house in its hour of misfortune. I do object to this treatment, indeed I do. Yet I do not want to cause you pain in the midst of your trouble.

But I will tell you why I have returned here. Take and keep this woman for me until I have killed the king of the Bistones and come back with the Thracian mares. But if I

1005 τοίᾳ ... φήμᾳ Broadhead: τοῖαι ... φῆμαι C
1018 <γ'> Monk

261

ἔλθω, τύραννον Βιστόνων κατακτανών.
πράξας δ' ὃ μὴ τύχοιμι (νοστήσαιμι γάρ)
δίδωμι τήνδε σοῖσι προσπολεῖν δόμοις.

1025 πολλῷ δὲ μόχθῳ χεῖρας ἦλθεν εἰς ἐμάς·
ἀγῶνα γὰρ πάνδημον εὑρίσκω τινὰς
τιθέντας, ἀθληταῖσιν ἄξιον πόνον,
ὅθεν κομίζω τήνδε νικητήρια
λαβών. τὰ μὲν γὰρ κοῦφα τοῖς νικῶσιν ἦν

1030 ἵππους ἄγεσθαι, τοῖσι δ' αὖ τὰ μείζονα
νικῶσι, πυγμὴν καὶ πάλην, βουφόρβια·
γυνὴ δ' ἐπ' αὐτοῖς εἵπετ'· ἐντυχόντι δὲ
αἰσχρὸν παρεῖναι κέρδος ἦν τόδ' εὐκλεές.
ἀλλ', ὥσπερ εἶπον, σοὶ μέλειν γυναῖκα χρή·

1035 οὐ γὰρ κλοπαίαν ἀλλὰ σὺν πόνῳ λαβὼν
ἥκω· χρόνῳ δὲ καὶ σύ μ' αἰνέσεις ἴσως.

ΑΔΜΗΤΟΣ
οὔτοι σ' ἀτίζων οὐδ' ἐν ἐχθροῖσιν τιθεὶς
ἔκρυψ' ἐμῆς γυναικὸς ἀθλίους τύχας.
ἀλλ' ἄλγος ἄλγει τοῦτ' ἂν ἦν προσκείμενον,

1040 εἴ του πρὸς ἄλλου δώμαθ' ὡρμήθης ξένου·
ἅλις δὲ κλαίειν τοὐμὸν ἦν ἐμοὶ κακόν.
    γυναῖκα δ', εἴ πως ἔστιν, αἰτοῦμαί σ', ἄναξ,
ἄλλον τιν' ὅστις μὴ πέπονθεν οἷ' ἐγὼ
σῴζειν ἄνωχθι Θεσσαλῶν· πολλοὶ δέ σοι

1045 ξένοι Φεραίων· μή μ' ἀναμνήσῃς κακῶν.
οὐκ ἂν δυναίμην τήνδ' ὁρῶν ἐν δώμασιν
ἄδακρυς εἶναι· μὴ νοσοῦντί μοι νόσον

should suffer the fate I pray heaven may avert (for I pray I may return), I give her to you to be a servant in your house. It was with great labor that she came into my hands. I found some people holding a public contest, an occasion worthy of an athlete's toil. It is from there that I took this woman as a prize. Those victorious in the light events won horses as their prize, while those in the greater events, boxing and wrestling, won cattle, with a woman in addition. Since I happened to be there, it seemed a shame to let slip this chance for profit combined with glory. But as I said, you must care for the woman. For I did not steal her but won her with labor. Perhaps in time you will praise me for this.

ADMETUS

I was not slighting you or regarding you as an enemy when I concealed from you my wife's unhappy fate. Rather, it would have been pain added to pain if you had departed for some other friend's house; and it was already enough for me to lament my loss.

As for the woman, if it is possible, my lord, I beg you to ask some other Thessalian, who has not suffered as I have, to keep her. You have many guest-friends in Pherae. Do not remind me of my troubles. For if I were to see this woman in my house, I could not hold back my tears. Do not put affliction on the already afflicted. I am weighed

προσθῇς· ἅλις γὰρ συμφορᾷ βαρύνομαι.
ποῦ καὶ τρέφοιτ᾽ ἂν δωμάτων νέα γυνή;
1050 νέα γάρ, ὡς ἐσθῆτι καὶ κόσμῳ πρέπει.
πότερα κατ᾽ ἀνδρῶν δῆτ᾽ ἐνοικήσει στέγην;
καὶ πῶς ἀκραιφνὴς ἐν νέοις στρωφωμένη
ἔσται; τὸν ἡβῶνθ᾽, Ἡράκλεις, οὐ ῥᾴδιον
εἴργειν· ἐγὼ δὲ σοῦ προμηθίαν ἔχω.
1055 ἢ τῆς θανούσης θάλαμον ἐσβήσας τρέφω;
καὶ πῶς ἐπεσφρῶ τήνδε τῷ κείνης λέχει;
διπλῆν φοβοῦμαι μέμψιν, ἔκ τε δημοτῶν,
μή τίς μ᾽ ἐλέγξῃ τὴν ἐμὴν εὐεργέτιν
προδόντ᾽ ἐν ἄλλης δεμνίοις πίτνειν νέας,
1060 καὶ τῆς θανούσης (ἀξία δέ μοι σέβειν)
πολλὴν πρόνοιαν δεῖ μ᾽ ἔχειν. σὺ δ᾽, ὦ γύναι,
ἥτις ποτ᾽ εἶ σύ, ταῦτ᾽ ἔχουσ᾽ Ἀλκήστιδι
μορφῆς μέτρ᾽ ἴσθι, καὶ προσῄξαι δέμας.
οἴμοι. κόμιζε πρὸς θεῶν ἐξ ὀμμάτων
1065 γυναῖκα τήνδε, μή μ᾽ ἕλῃς ᾑρημένον.
δοκῶ γὰρ αὐτὴν εἰσορῶν γυναῖχ᾽ ὁρᾶν
ἐμήν· θολοῖ δὲ καρδίαν, ἐκ δ᾽ ὀμμάτων
πηγαὶ κατερρώγασιν· ὦ τλήμων ἐγώ,
ὡς ἄρτι πένθους τοῦδε γεύομαι πικροῦ.

ΧΟΡΟΣ

1070 ἐγὼ μὲν οὐκ ἔχοιμ᾽ ἂν εὖ λέγειν τύχην·
χρὴ δ᾽, ἥτις ἐστί, καρτερεῖν θεοῦ δόσιν.

<hr />

1071 ἥτις ἐστί Earle: ὅστις εἶ σύ C

down enough with disaster. Where in the house could a
young woman be kept? For she is young, as is evident
from her clothing and adornment. Shall she stay in the
men's quarters? And how, moving among young men,
shall she remain untouched? It is not easy, Heracles, to
rein in a young man in his prime. In this I am looking out
for your interests. Or shall I keep her in my dead wife's
room? How shall I put this woman in her bed? I fear a
double reproach: from my people, lest someone should
cast in my teeth that betraying the memory of her who
saved my life, I fall into the bed of another woman; and I
must show all care for my dead wife (she deserves my
honor). Woman, whoever you are, know that in shape you
are like Alcestis and resemble her in appearance. What
agony! Take this woman out of my sight, by the gods, do
not slay again one who is dead! For when I see her I think
I see my wife. She makes my heart pound, and tears
stream from my eyes. Oh luckless me! It is but now that I
taste the full bitterness of this grief!

CHORUS LEADER

I cannot call Fate kind. But one must endure what the
god gives, whatever it is.

ΗΡΑΚΛΗΣ

εἰ γὰρ τοσαύτην δύναμιν εἶχον ὥστε σὴν
ἐς φῶς πορεῦσαι νερτέρων ἐκ δωμάτων
γυναῖκα καί σοι τήνδε πορσῦναι χάριν.

ΑΔΜΗΤΟΣ

1075 σάφ᾽ οἶδα βούλεσθαί σ᾽ ἄν. ἀλλὰ ποῦ τόδε;
οὐκ ἔστι τοὺς θανόντας ἐς φάος μολεῖν.

ΗΡΑΚΛΗΣ

μή νυν ὑπέρβαλλ᾽ ἀλλ᾽ ἐναισίμως φέρε.

ΑΔΜΗΤΟΣ

ῥᾷον παραινεῖν ἢ παθόντα καρτερεῖν.

ΗΡΑΚΛΗΣ

τί δ᾽ ἂν προκόπτοις, εἰ θέλεις ἀεὶ στένειν;

ΑΔΜΗΤΟΣ

1080 ἔγνωκα καὐτός, ἀλλ᾽ ἔρως τις ἐξάγει.

ΗΡΑΚΛΗΣ

τὸ γὰρ φιλῆσαι τὸν θανόντ᾽ ἄγει δάκρυ.

ΑΔΜΗΤΟΣ

ἀπώλεσέν με κἄτι μᾶλλον ἢ λέγω.

ΗΡΑΚΛΗΣ

γυναικὸς ἐσθλῆς ἤμπλακες· τίς ἀντερεῖ;

ΑΔΜΗΤΟΣ

ὥστ᾽ ἄνδρα τόνδε μηκέθ᾽ ἥδεσθαι βίῳ.

ΗΡΑΚΛΗΣ

1085 χρόνος μαλάξει, νῦν δ᾽ ἔθ᾽ ἡβάσκει, κακόν.

HERACLES

I wish I had the power to convey your wife to the light
from the halls below and could do you this service.

ADMETUS

I know that you would wish to. But what is the good of
such a wish? It is not possible for the dead to come back to
the light.

HERACLES

Do not then be excessive in grief but bear your sorrow
moderately.

ADMETUS

It is easier to give advice than to endure suffering.

HERACLES

But what good will you accomplish if you lament forever?

ADMETUS

No good, I know, but longing for my wife extracts these
groans from me.

HERACLES

Yes, your love for the departed stirs up your tears.

ADMETUS

Her death has destroyed me, even more than I can say.

HERACLES

You have lost a noble wife. Who will deny it?

ADMETUS

And so I shall have no more joy in life.

HERACLES

Time will soften the pain. Now it is still intense.

ΑΔΜΗΤΟΣ

χρόνον λέγοις ἄν, εἰ χρόνος τὸ κατθανεῖν.

ΗΡΑΚΛΗΣ

γυνή σε παύσει καὶ νέοι γάμοι πόθου.

ΑΔΜΗΤΟΣ

σίγησον· οἶον εἶπας. οὐκ ἂν ᾠόμην.

ΗΡΑΚΛΗΣ

τί δ'; οὐ γαμεῖς γὰρ ἀλλὰ χηρεύσῃ λέχος;

ΑΔΜΗΤΟΣ

1090   οὐκ ἔστιν ἥτις τῷδε συγκλιθήσεται.

ΗΡΑΚΛΗΣ

μῶν τὴν θανοῦσαν ὠφελεῖν τι προσδοκᾷς;

ΑΔΜΗΤΟΣ

κείνην ὅπουπερ ἔστι τιμᾶσθαι χρεών.

ΗΡΑΚΛΗΣ

αἰνῶ μὲν αἰνῶ· μωρίαν δ' ὀφλισκάνεις.

[ΑΔΜΗΤΟΣ

ὡς μήποτ' ἄνδρα τόνδε νυμφίον καλῶν.

ΗΡΑΚΛΗΣ

1095   ἐπήνεσ' ἀλόχῳ πιστὸς οὕνεκ' εἶ φίλος.]

ΑΔΜΗΤΟΣ

θάνοιμ' ἐκείνην καίπερ οὐκ οὖσαν προδούς.

―――――

1087 νέοι γάμοι πόθου F. W. Schmidt: νέου γάμου πόθος C
1094–5 del. Dale

ADMETUS

Time, yes, if by time you mean death.

HERACLES

A woman and a new union will put an end to your longing.

ADMETUS

Hush! What a shocking thing you have said! I should never have thought it of you.

HERACLES

What? Will you never marry but keep a widower's bed?

ADMETUS

No woman shall ever lie beside me.

HERACLES

Do you suppose you are doing your dead wife any good that way?

ADMETUS

Wherever she is, she must be held in honor.

HERACLES

I commend you, truly. But you deserve the name of fool.

[ADMETUS

You will never call this man a bridegroom.

HERACLES

I commend you for being faithful to your wife.]

ADMETUS

May I die if ever I betray her, even though she is gone!

ΗΡΑΚΛΗΣ

δέχου νυν εἴσω τήνδε γενναίων δόμων.

ΑΔΜΗΤΟΣ

μή, πρός σε τοῦ σπείραντος ἄντομαι Διός.

ΗΡΑΚΛΗΣ

καὶ μὴν ἁμαρτήσῃ γε μὴ δράσας τάδε.

ΑΔΜΗΤΟΣ

1100 καὶ δρῶν γε λύπῃ καρδίαν δηχθήσομαι.

ΗΡΑΚΛΗΣ

πιθοῦ· τάχ' ἂν γὰρ ἐς δέον πέσοι χάρις.

ΑΔΜΗΤΟΣ

φεῦ.
εἴθ' ἐξ ἀγῶνος τήνδε μὴ 'λαβές ποτε.

ΗΡΑΚΛΗΣ

νικῶντι μέντοι καὶ σὺ συννικᾷς ἐμοί.

ΑΔΜΗΤΟΣ

καλῶς ἔλεξας· ἡ γυνὴ δ' ἀπελθέτω.

ΗΡΑΚΛΗΣ

1105 ἄπεισιν, εἰ χρή· πρῶτα δ' εἰ χρεὼν ἄθρει.

ΑΔΜΗΤΟΣ

χρή, σοῦ γε μὴ μέλλοντος ὀργαίνειν ἐμοί.

ΗΡΑΚΛΗΣ

εἰδώς τι κἀγὼ τήνδ' ἔχω προθυμίαν.

1097 γενναίως Lenting
1106 ἐμέ Monk

ALCESTIS

HERACLES

Take this woman, then, into your generous house.

ADMETUS

I beg you by Zeus who begot you, do not ask this!

HERACLES

And yet you will be making a mistake if you do not.

ADMETUS

And if I do, my heart will be stung with sorrow.

HERACLES

Consent, for perhaps this may prove a timely favor.

ADMETUS

Oh, how I wish you had never won her at the games!

HERACLES

But when I win, you are a sharer in my victory.

ADMETUS

Excellent sentiments, but the woman must go away.

HERACLES

She will if she must. First see if she must.

ADMETUS

She must unless you mean to get angry with me.[a]

HERACLES

I too have reasons for insisting.

[a] Or, with Monk's conjecture, "unless you intend to make me angry."

ΑΔΜΗΤΟΣ

νίκα νυν· οὐ μὴν ἁνδάνοντά μοι ποιεῖς.

ΗΡΑΚΛΗΣ

ἀλλ᾽ ἔσθ᾽ ὅθ᾽ ἡμᾶς αἰνέσεις· πιθοῦ μόνον.

ΑΔΜΗΤΟΣ

1110 κομίζετ᾽, εἰ χρὴ τήνδε δέξασθαι δόμοις.

ΗΡΑΚΛΗΣ

οὐκ ἂν μεθείην τὴν γυναῖκα προσπόλοις.

ΑΔΜΗΤΟΣ

σὺ δ᾽ αὐτὸς αὐτὴν εἴσαγ᾽, εἰ δοκεῖ, δόμους.

ΗΡΑΚΛΗΣ

ἐς σὰς μὲν οὖν ἔγωγε θήσομαι χέρας.

ΑΔΜΗΤΟΣ

οὐκ ἂν θίγοιμι· δῶμα δ᾽ εἰσελθεῖν πάρα.

ΗΡΑΚΛΗΣ

1115 τῇ σῇ πέποιθα χειρὶ δεξιᾷ μόνῃ.

ΑΔΜΗΤΟΣ

ἄναξ, βιάζῃ μ᾽ οὐ θέλοντα δρᾶν τάδε.

ΗΡΑΚΛΗΣ

τόλμα προτεῖναι χεῖρα καὶ θιγεῖν ξένης.

1115 μόνου Nauck

272

ALCESTIS

ADMETUS

Be the winner, then! But you do not act to my liking.

HERACLES

Yet some day you will praise me. Just do as I say.

ADMETUS

(to his servants) Take her in, since I must receive her into my house.

HERACLES

I will not release the woman into the hands of servants.[a]

ADMETUS

Take her into the house yourself, if you like.

HERACLES

No, I shall put her into your hands.

ADMETUS

I will not touch her. She may go into the house.

HERACLES

I trust only your right hand.

ADMETUS

My lord, you compel me to do this against my will.

HERACLES

Have the courage to stretch out your hand and touch the stranger.

[a] Proper form, when entrusting valuable property to a friend, was to put it into his very hands.

ΑΔΜΗΤΟΣ

καὶ δὴ προτείνω, Γοργόν' ὡς καρατομῶν.

ΗΡΑΚΛΗΣ

ἔχεις;

ΑΔΜΗΤΟΣ

ἔχω, ναί.

ΗΡΑΚΛΗΣ

σῷζέ νυν, καὶ τὸν Διὸς
1120 φήσεις ποτ' εἶναι παῖδα γενναῖον ξένον.
βλέψον πρὸς αὐτήν, εἴ τι σῇ δοκεῖ πρέπειν
γυναικί· λύπης δ' εὐτυχῶν μεθίστασο.

ΑΔΜΗΤΟΣ

ὦ θεοί, τί λέξω; θαῦμ' ἀνέλπιστον τόδε·
γυναῖκα λεύσσω τήνδ' ἐμὴν ἐτητύμως,
1125 ἢ κέρτομός μ' ἐκ θεοῦ τις ἐκπλήσσει χαρά;

ΗΡΑΚΛΗΣ

οὐκ ἔστιν, ἀλλὰ τήνδ' ὁρᾷς δάμαρτα σήν.

ΑΔΜΗΤΟΣ

ὅρα δὲ μή τι φάσμα νερτέρων τόδ' ᾖ.

ΗΡΑΚΛΗΣ

οὐ ψυχαγωγὸν τόνδ' ἐποιήσω ξένον.

[1118] καρατομῶν Lobeck: -τόμῳ C
[1125] μ' ἐκ Bucheler: με C
[1127] δὲ Diggle: γε C

---

[a] In order to avoid being turned to stone by the Gorgon's

He turns away as he reaches out his hand behind him and grasps her hand.

ADMETUS

There, I stretch it out, as if I were cutting off a Gorgon's head.[a]

HERACLES

Do you have her?

ADMETUS

Yes, I have her.

HERACLES

Then keep her safe, and one day you will say that Zeus's son is a noble guest-friend.

Heracles throws back the veil to reveal Alcestis.

Look at her! See whether she bears any resemblance to your wife. Now that you are fortunate, cease your grieving!

ADMETUS

O gods, what shall I say? Here is a wonder past all hoping. Is this truly my wife I see here, or does some delusive joy sent by a god steal my wits?

HERACLES

Not so: the woman you see here is your wife.

ADMETUS

Perhaps it is some ghost from the Underworld.

HERACLES

No raiser of spirits is the man you made your guest-friend.

appearance, Perseus reached behind him with his sword as he cut off her head.

275

ΑΔΜΗΤΟΣ

ἀλλ' ἣν ἔθαπτον εἰσορῶ δάμαρτ' ἐμήν;

ΗΡΑΚΛΗΣ

1130 σάφ' ἴσθ'· ἀπιστεῖν δ' οὔ σε θαυμάζω τύχῃ.

ΑΔΜΗΤΟΣ

θίγω, προσείπω ζῶσαν ὡς δάμαρτ' ἐμήν;

ΗΡΑΚΛΗΣ

πρόσειπ'· ἔχεις γὰρ πᾶν ὅσονπερ ἤθελες.

ΑΔΜΗΤΟΣ

ὦ φιλτάτης γυναικὸς ὄμμα καὶ δέμας,
ἔχω σ' ἀέλπτως, οὔποτ' ὄψεσθαι δοκῶν.

ΗΡΑΚΛΗΣ

1135 ἔχεις· φθόνος δὲ μὴ γένοιτό τις θεῶν.

ΑΔΜΗΤΟΣ

ὦ τοῦ μεγίστου Ζηνὸς εὐγενὲς τέκνον,
εὐδαιμονοίης καί σ' ὁ φιτύσας πατὴρ
σῴζοι· σὺ γὰρ δὴ τἄμ' ἀνώρθωσας μόνος.
πῶς τήνδ' ἔπεμψας νέρθεν ἐς φάος τόδε;

ΗΡΑΚΛΗΣ

μάχην συνάψας δαιμόνων τῷ κυρίῳ.

ΑΔΜΗΤΟΣ

ποῦ τόνδε Θανάτῳ φῂς ἀγῶνα συμβαλεῖν;

ΗΡΑΚΛΗΣ

τύμβον παρ' αὐτόν, ἐκ λόχου μάρψας χεροῖν.

---

¹¹³⁰ τύχῃ Reiske: -ην C

ALCESTIS

ADMETUS

But do I see my wife, whom I buried?

HERACLES

Certainly, though I am not surprised that you disbelieve
your luck.

ADMETUS

Shall I embrace and greet her as my living wife?

HERACLES

Greet her. You have all your heart's desire.

ADMETUS

O face and form of the wife I love, I have you back against
all expectation, never thinking to see you again!

HERACLES

You have her. May no ill-will come from the gods!

ADMETUS

O noble son of mighty Zeus, may good fortune attend you,
and may the father who begot you preserve your life! For
you alone have raised up my fortunes. How did you bring
her up from below to the light of day?

HERACLES

I fought with the divinity who controlled her.

ADMETUS

Where did you fight this battle with Death?

HERACLES

Lying in ambush hard by the tomb, I caught him in my
grip.

ΑΔΜΗΤΟΣ

τί γάρ ποθ᾽ ἥδ᾽ ἄναυδος ἕστηκεν γυνή;

ΗΡΑΚΛΗΣ

οὔπω θέμις σοι τῆσδε προσφωνημάτων
1145 κλύειν, πρὶν ἂν θεοῖσι τοῖσι νερτέροις
ἀφαγνίσηται καὶ τρίτον μόλῃ φάος.
ἀλλ᾽ εἴσαγ᾽ εἴσω τήνδε· καὶ δίκαιος ὢν
τὸ λοιπόν, Ἄδμητ᾽, εὐσέβει περὶ ξένους.
καὶ χαῖρ᾽· ἐγὼ δὲ τὸν προκείμενον πόνον
1150 Σθενέλου τυράννῳ παιδὶ πορσυνῶ μολών.

ΑΔΜΗΤΟΣ

μεῖνον παρ᾽ ἡμῖν καὶ ξυνέστιος γενοῦ.

ΗΡΑΚΛΗΣ

αὖθις τόδ᾽ ἔσται, νῦν δ᾽ ἐπείγεσθαί με δεῖ.

ΑΔΜΗΤΟΣ

ἀλλ᾽ εὐτυχοίης, νόστιμον δ᾽ ἔλθοις δρόμον.
ἀστοῖς δὲ πάσῃ τ᾽ ἐννέπω τετραρχίᾳ
1155 χοροὺς ἐπ᾽ ἐσθλαῖς συμφοραῖσιν ἱστάναι
βωμούς τε κνισᾶν βουθύτοισι προστροπαῖς.
νῦν γὰρ μεθηρμόσμεσθα βελτίω βίον
τοῦ πρόσθεν· οὐ γὰρ εὐτυχῶν ἀρνήσομαι.

ΧΟΡΟΣ

πολλαὶ μορφαὶ τῶν δαιμονίων,
1160 πολλὰ δ᾽ ἀέλπτως κραίνουσι θεοί·

ALCESTIS

ADMETUS
But why on earth does she stand silent?

HERACLES
You are not yet allowed to hear her speak to you, not until
she becomes purified in the sight of the nether gods when
the third day comes. But take her in. Continue, Admetus,
to show your guests the piety of a righteous man. And now
farewell. I shall go and perform for King Eurystheus the
labor that lies at hand.

ADMETUS
Stay with us and share our hearth.

HERACLES
There will be another day for that, but now I must hurry.

Exit HERACLES by Eisodos A.

ADMETUS
May you have good fortune and run your homeward
course!
     But to the citizens and to the whole region of my four
cities I now say: let there be dance and song in honor of
these happy events and let the altars of the gods be fat-
tened with the sacrifice of bulls! For the new life we have
now taken on is better than the old. I will not deny that I
am blessed by fortune.

Exit ADMETUS and ALCESTIS into the palace.

CHORUS LEADER
There are many shapes of divinity, and many things the
gods accomplish against our expectation. What men

καὶ τὰ δοκηθέντ᾽ οὐκ ἐτελέσθη,
τῶν δ᾽ ἀδοκήτων πόρον ηὗρε θεός.
τοιόνδ᾽ ἀπέβη τόδε πρᾶγμα.

look for is not brought to pass, but a god finds a way to achieve the unexpected. Such was the outcome of this story.

Exit CHORUS by Eisodos B.

MEDEA

INTRODUCTION

Medea's story is as old as Jason's, which already in Homer's *Odyssey* (12.70) was "in everyone's thoughts." As the daughter of King Aeetes of Aia, who possessed the Golden Fleece, she figured in the Argo adventure as the friendly daughter who with her knowledge of magic helps the hero to carry out his quest in a far land. At least a generation before Euripides she acquired less attractive traits. Pherecydes (mid-fifth century) knows the story that she murdered her brother Apsyrtus, and Pindar alludes to her planning of the grisly death of Jason's wicked uncle Pelias at the hands of his own daughters. (She kills and cuts up an old ram, boils the limbs with magic herbs, and then produces the ram alive and young again. The daughters are persuaded to kill Pelias and cut him up, but this time Medea withholds the magic ingredient.) For the murder of Pelias, Medea and Jason are banished from Iolcus and go to Corinth. There, according to stories certainly current before Euripides' day, Jason and Medea have two children and live in happiness until Jason, seizing the chance to improve his position, marries the daughter of Creon, the king of Corinth. Medea sends a poisoned crown to the princess, who is engulfed in flames and dies together with her father and, in one version, Jason as well. She escapes by magic chariot to Athens, where she lives with King Aegeus and tries unsuccessfully to kill his son Theseus.

285

Various stories are told about the death of Medea's and Jason's children. In one version Medea causes their death involuntarily while trying to make them immortal. In another, the Corinthians kill them in revenge for the death of their king and put the story about that Medea killed them. From the allusion at the end of our play (1381–3) we may conclude that there was in Euripides' day a cult connected with the burial place of the children in the sanctuary of Hera Akraia, a cult understood as expiation for their murder. The evidence does not permit us to say with certainty whether the death of the children by Medea's deliberate act was an innovation of Euripides. (See A. Lesky, *Greek Tragic Poetry*, New Haven, 1983, p. 457, n. 20.)

Euripides' play, put on in 431 along with his *Philoctetes*, *Dictys*, and *The Reapers*, was awarded third prize. This is frequently taken as an indication the Athenians were shocked by *Medea*. But the competition that year was extraordinarily keen. Sophocles, who never was third and who won eighteen first prizes in the City Dionysia, came in second. The first prize went to Aeschylus' son Euphorion, who may have been competing with his father's plays. (For speculation on Euphorion's offerings, see M. L. West, *Studies in Aeschylus*, Stuttgart, 1990, p. 71.) It would be rash to assume that strong antipathy to Euripides' plays was involved here (and that the reason for it was our surviving play rather than one of the other three) or that *Medea* was necessarily judged a failure.

Euripides' plot consists in the working out of Medea's revenge on Jason, who has deserted her, and on Creon, who has banished her. But unlike other tragedies of revenge, in which the avenging figure wins safety and happiness by destroying a usurper, *Medea* portrays a revenge which, if carried out to its logical conclusion, will mean Medea's ruin as well. For midway through the play, after the scene with Aegeus has established that she will have a place of refuge in Athens, Medea revises her plan: instead of killing Creon, Creon's daughter, and Jason, she now means to kill Creon's daughter (and "whoever touches her") so that Jason shall never have children by his new bride, and then Jason's two boys by Medea. Jason will then die childless, a fate whose painfulness seems to have been suggested to Medea by her encounter with Aegeus. This, in Medea's view, is a better revenge than killing Jason himself.

Yet his children are also her children, and we see at two crucial points (1021–80 and 1236–50) that the will to revenge means violating maternal feelings that are real, that can be suppressed for a time but will return to make Medea wretched later. At the end of the play Jason has been brought low and Medea is triumphant, borne aloft toward Athens on her flying chariot. But while there is no reason to feel pity for Jason, who is portrayed throughout as callous and vain, it is not easy to know what attitude Euripides wants us to take toward Medea.

The play is divided into two halves by the Aegeus scene. The prologue and parodos make it plain that Medea has been abandoned by Jason in spite of his oaths to her. The first episode contains her long speech to the Corinthian women appealing for their sympathy on the grounds that women are helpless victims and because her helplessness is much greater than theirs since she has left home and blood relations and has no one to take her part. The arrival of Creon makes this apparent helplessness still more acute, for Creon issues a decree of banishment. The episode ends with Medea's initial plans for revenge. All hinges on whether she will have a place to live after the deed: if one appears, she will kill Jason, Creon, and Creon's daughter by stealth; if not, she will take a sword to her enemies even if it means her own death immediately thereafter.

In the second episode, Jason comes to upbraid Medea for speaking ill of the royal family and getting herself banished. In the ensuing wrangle, he shows clearly that he rates his own advantage above his sense of obligation to the woman who saved his life or the sanctity of his oaths to her.

The scenes before the Aegeus episode are thus in a certain sense exposition. They show the nature of Jason's treachery and the huge disadvantages Medea labors under, having abandoned her own country and kin and being under the imminent threat of exile from her adoptive home.

Without preamble and almost as if in answer to Medea's question whether there is a place of refuge for her, Aegeus appears. Learning of Medea's desertion by Jason and her imminent exile, he promises her the refuge she needs.

As soon as Aegeus goes off, Medea sets forth her revised plan: death for the princess and then for her own children. There follows a scene of pretended reconciliation with Jason leading up to her plea that he should intercede to allow his sons to stay in Corinth. The children are sent with the poisoned robe and crown as gifts to the princess so that she too will take their part. After a choral ode the Tutor brings them back with the good news that

they have been spared exile. Medea takes her farewell of
the children, a farewell interrupted by the flaring up of the
maternal feelings her plan of revenge must outrage. After
the death of the princess and her father has been
reported, the murder can be delayed no longer: if she
waits, the Corinthians themselves will do the deed. She
steels herself and goes in. Jason arrives and learns from
the Chorus that she has killed the children. Then Medea
appears aloft for the last confrontation with Jason, the mir-
ror image of their first confrontation. The final scene hints
that punishment may be in store for Medea as well.

The unexpected appearance of Aegeus was criticized
by Aristotle, but it may be best to see it in connection with
a divine background to the action that is never overt but is
hinted at throughout the play. Jason's perjury is funda-
mental and often alluded to: Zeus and Themis, the
enforcers of oaths, are repeatedly mentioned in the early
part of the play. The commonest form of oath called down
ἐξώλεια, root-and-branch destruction with loss of all pro-
geny, on the swearer if he should fail to keep his oath.
This is what happens to Jason. Before the event Medea
swears that "a god being my helper" she will punish Jason
(802). After Aegeus has miraculously appeared and has
left, Medea cries out "O Zeus and Zeus's justice!" (764).
After the messenger's report, the Chorus say that
apparently "the divinity" or "fate" has visited justice on
Jason (1231–2). When Medea has gone in to kill the chil-
dren, the Chorus refer to her as an Erinys, one of Zeus's
agents (1260). The play ends with five anapestic lines,
whose genuineness can be established (see *TAPA* 117
[1987], 268–70), calling Zeus "the steward of many things"
(cf. the phrase ὅρκων ταμίας, lit. "steward of oaths," in

169–70) and remarking on the gods' capacity to bring about the unexpected. In the light of all this, Aegeus' appearance can be plausibly regarded as a coincidence only from the human point of view. The final speeches of Jason suggest that Zeus had his own score to settle with Medea, and Medea suggests (1013–4) that she is not in her right mind owing to divine intervention.

The divine justice of Jason's punishment does nothing to diminish, and may well increase, the horror of Medea's revenge. Aristotle (*Poetics* 1453 b 27–29) cites the child-murder in *Medea*, done in full knowledge of the tie of blood, as characteristic of the way the "old" dramatists, those of the fifth century, managed the deed of bloodshed. The play was enormously popular in the fourth century and repeatedly revived, a testimony to its searing emotional power.

SELECT BIBLIOGRAPHY

Editions

N. Wecklein (Leipzig, 1893)
D. L. Page (Oxford, 1938)
H. van Looy (Stuttgart and Leipzig, 1992)

Literary criticism

P. E. Easterling, "The Infanticide in Euripides' *Medea*," *YCS* 25 (1977), 177–91.
B. Gredley, "The Place and Time of Victory: Euripides' *Medea*," *BICS* 34 (1987), 27–39.

B. M. W. Knox, "The *Medea* of Euripides," *YCS* 25 (1977), 193–225, rpt. in Segal, *Greek Tragedy*, pp. 272–93.

D. Kovacs, "On Medea's Great Monologue (Eur. *Medea* 1021–1080)," *CQ* 36 (1986), 343–352.

——— "Zeus in Euripides' *Medea*," *AJP* 114 (1993), 45–70.

K. Reckford, "Medea's First Exit," *TAPA* 99 (1968), 329–59.

E. Schlesinger, "Zu Euripides' Medea," *Hermes* 94 (1966), 26–53, abridged translation in E. Segal, ed., *Greek Tragedy: Modern Essays in Criticism* (Oxford, 1983), pp. 294–310.

W. Steidle, *Studien zum antiken Drama* (Munich, 1968), pp. 152–68.

K. von Fritz, "Die Entwicklung der Iason-Medea-Sage und die Medea des Euripides," *Antike und Abendland* 8 (1959), 33–106.

Dramatis Personae

ΤΡΟΦΟΣ	NURSE of Medea
ΠΑΙΔΑΓΩΓΟΣ	TUTOR to Medea's children
ΜΗΔΕΙΑ	MEDEA
ΧΟΡΟΣ ΓΥΝΑΙΚΩΝ	CHORUS of Corinthian women
ΚΡΕΩΝ	CREON, King of Corinth
ΙΑΣΩΝ	JASON
ΑΙΓΕΥΣ	AEGEUS, King of Athens
ΑΓΓΕΛΟΣ	MESSENGER
ΠΑΙΔΕΣ ΜΗΔΕΙΑΣ	CHILDREN OF MEDEA

A Note on Staging

Eisodos A leads to the countryside and roads away from Corinth, Eisodos B to the royal palace. The *skene* represents Medea's house. At the end of the play the *mechane* or stage crane is used to transport Medea and her children upon a winged chariot from an imagined spot in the courtyard of her house to the roof above the central door and from there away to her imagined destination in Athens.

293

ΜΗΔΕΙΑ

ΤΡΟΦΟΣ

Εἴθ᾽ ὤφελ᾽ Ἀργοῦς μὴ διαπτάσθαι σκάφος
Κόλχων ἐς αἶαν κυανέας Συμπληγάδας,
μηδ᾽ ἐν νάπαισι Πηλίου πεσεῖν ποτε
τμηθεῖσα πεύκη, μηδ᾽ ἐρετμῶσαι χέρας
5   ἀνδρῶν ἀριστέων οἳ τὸ πάγχρυσον δέρος
Πελίᾳ μετῆλθον. οὐ γὰρ ἂν δέσποιν᾽ ἐμὴ
Μήδεια πύργους γῆς ἔπλευσ᾽ Ἰωλκίας
ἔρωτι θυμὸν ἐκπλαγεῖσ᾽ Ἰάσονος·
οὐδ᾽ ἂν κτανεῖν πείσασα Πελιάδας κόρας
10   πατέρα κατῴκει τήνδε γῆν Κορινθίαν
<φίλων τε τῶν πρὶν ἀμπλακοῦσα καὶ πάτρας.
καὶ πρὶν μὲν εἶχε κἀνθάδ᾽ οὐ μεμπτὸν βίον>
ξὺν ἀνδρὶ καὶ τέκνοισιν, ἁνδάνουσα μὲν
φυγὰς πολίταις ὧν ἀφίκετο χθόνα

---

⁵ ἀριστέων Wakefield: ἀρίστων C
¹¹ ante h. v. lacunam indicavi, 10b suppl. Willink: vide CQ 41
(1991), 30–5

MEDEA

Enter NURSE from the house.

NURSE

Would that the Argo had never winged its way to the land
of Colchis through the dark blue Symplegades![a] Would
that pine trees had never been felled in the glens of
Mount Pelion and furnished oars for the hands of the
heroes who at Pelias' command set forth in quest of the
Golden Fleece! For then my lady Medea would not have
sailed to the towers of Iolcus, her heart smitten with love
for Jason, or persuaded the daughters of Pelias to kill their
father and hence now be inhabiting this land of Corinth,
<separated from her loved ones and country. At first, to
be sure, she had, even in Corinth, a good life>[b] with her
husband and children, an exile loved by the citizens to

---

[a] The Symplegades, mobile rocks that clashed together to
crush any ships running between them, guarded the entrance to
the Black Sea and prevented passage between East and West until
the Argo managed by a clever ruse to get through.

[b] This gives the probable sense of the lacuna.

---

[12] φυγὰς πολίταις S. Harrison, praeeunte Pierson: φυγῇ
πολιτῶν (πολίταις V³) C

αὐτῷ τε πάντα ξυμφέρουσ' Ἰάσονι ·
ἥπερ μεγίστη γίγνεται σωτηρία,
15 ὅταν γυνὴ πρὸς ἄνδρα μὴ διχοστατῇ.
νῦν δ' ἐχθρὰ πάντα, καὶ νοσεῖ τὰ φίλτατα.
προδοὺς γὰρ αὑτοῦ τέκνα δεσπότιν τ' ἐμὴν
γάμοις Ἰάσων βασιλικοῖς εὐνάζεται,
γήμας Κρέοντος παῖδ', ὃς αἰσυμνᾷ χθονός.
20 Μήδεια δ' ἡ δύστηνος ἠτιμασμένη
βοᾷ μὲν ὅρκους, ἀνακαλεῖ δὲ δεξιᾶς
πίστιν μεγίστην, καὶ θεοὺς μαρτύρεται
οἵας ἀμοιβῆς ἐξ Ἰάσονος κυρεῖ.
κεῖται δ' ἄσιτος, σῶμ' ὑφεῖσ' ἀλγηδόσιν,
25 τὸν πάντα συντήκουσα δακρύοις χρόνον
ἐπεὶ πρὸς ἀνδρὸς ᾔσθετ' ἠδικημένη,
οὔτ' ὄμμ' ἐπαίρουσ' οὔτ' ἀπαλλάσσουσα γῆς
πρόσωπον · ὡς δὲ πέτρος ἢ θαλάσσιος
κλύδων ἀκούει νουθετουμένη φίλων,
30 ἢν μή ποτε στρέψασα πάλλευκον δέρην
αὐτὴ πρὸς αὑτὴν πατέρ' ἀποιμώξῃ φίλον
καὶ γαῖαν οἴκους θ', οὓς προδοῦσ' ἀφίκετο
μετ' ἀνδρὸς ὅς σφε νῦν ἀτιμάσας ἔχει.
ἔγνωκε δ' ἡ τάλαινα συμφορᾶς ὕπο
35 οἷον πατρῴας μὴ ἀπολείπεσθαι χθονός.
στυγεῖ δὲ παῖδας οὐδ' ὁρῶσ' εὐφραίνεται.
δέδοικα δ' αὐτὴν μή τι βουλεύσῃ νέον ·
βαρεῖα γὰρ φρήν, οὐδ' ἀνέξεται κακῶς
πάσχουσ' (ἐγᾦδα τήνδε), δειμαίνω τέ νιν
40 μὴ θηκτὸν ὤσῃ φάσγανον δι' ἥπατος,

whose land she had come, and lending to Jason himself all her support. This it is that most keeps a life free of trouble, when a woman is not at variance with her husband.

But now all is enmity, and love's bonds are diseased. For Jason, abandoning his own children and my mistress, is bedding down in a royal match, having married the daughter of Creon, ruler of this land. Poor Medea, finding herself thus cast aside, calls loudly on his oaths, invokes the mighty assurance of his sworn right hand, and calls the gods to witness the unjust return she is getting from Jason. She lies fasting, giving her body up to pain, spending in ceaseless weeping all the hours since she learned that she was wronged by her husband, neither raising her face nor taking her eyes from the ground. She is as deaf to the advice of her friends as a stone or a wave of the sea, saying nothing unless perchance to turn her snow-white neck and weep to herself for her dear father, her country, and her ancestral house. All these she abandoned when she came here with a man who has now cast her aside. The poor woman has learned at misfortune's hand what a good thing it is not to be cut off from one's native land.

She loathes the children and takes no joy in looking at them. I am afraid that she will hatch some sinister plan. She has a terrible temper and will not put up with bad treatment (I know her), and I fear she may thrust a whet-

---

[13] αὐτῷ Sakorraphos: αὐτή C

[σιγῇ δόμους ἐσβᾶσ᾽, ἵν᾽ ἔστρωται λέχος,]
ἢ καὶ τυράννους τόν τε γήμαντα κτάνῃ
κἄπειτα μείζω συμφορὰν λάβῃ τινά.
δεινὴ γάρ· οὔτοι ῥᾳδίως γε συμβαλὼν
45 ἔχθραν τις αὐτῇ καλλίνικος ᾄσεται.

    ἀλλ᾽ οἵδε παῖδες ἐκ τρόχων πεπαυμένοι
στείχουσι, μητρὸς οὐδὲν ἐννοούμενοι
κακῶν· νέα γὰρ φροντὶς οὐκ ἀλγεῖν φιλεῖ.

ΠΑΙΔΑΓΩΓΟΣ

παλαιὸν οἴκων κτῆμα δεσποίνης ἐμῆς,
50 τί πρὸς πύλαισι τήνδ᾽ ἄγουσ᾽ ἐρημίαν
ἕστηκας, αὐτὴ θρεομένη σαυτῇ κακά;
πῶς σοῦ μόνη Μήδεια λείπεσθαι θέλει;

ΤΡΟΦΟΣ

τέκνων ὀπαδὲ πρέσβυ τῶν Ἰάσονος,
χρηστοῖσι δούλοις ξυμφορὰ τὰ δεσποτῶν
55 κακῶς πίτνοντα καὶ φρενῶν ἀνθάπτεται.
ἐγὼ γὰρ ἐς τοῦτ᾽ ἐκβέβηκ᾽ ἀλγηδόνος
ὥσθ᾽ ἵμερός μ᾽ ὑπῆλθε γῇ τε κοὐρανῷ
λέξαι μολούσῃ δεῦρο δεσποίνης τύχας.

ΠΑΙΔΑΓΩΓΟΣ

οὔπω γὰρ ἡ τάλαινα παύεται γόων;

    41 del. Musgrave, 38–40 et 42–3 defendit Willink CQ 38
(1988), 313–23
    42 τυράννους Hermann: τύραννον C
    45 καλλίνικος Willink: καλλίνικον C   ᾄσεται Muretus:
οἴσεται C

ted sword through her vitals, [slipping quietly into the house where the bed is laid out,] or kill the royal family and the bridegroom and then win some greater calamity. For she is dangerous. I tell you, no one who clashes with her will find it easy to crow in victory.

Enter TUTOR *by Eisodos A, escorting the two sons of Jason and Medea.*

But see, her boys are coming home after their games. They have no thought of their mother's troubles: it is not usual for young minds to dwell on grief.

TUTOR

Aged slave of my mistress' household, why do you stand alone like this outside the gate, complaining of your troubles to your own ears? How can Medea spare your service?

NURSE

Old attendant to the children of Jason, to trusty servants it is a disaster when the dice of their masters' fortunes fall badly: it touches their hearts. So great is the grief I feel that the desire stole over me to come out here and speak my mistress' troubles to the earth and the sky.

TUTOR

What? Does the poor woman not yet cease from moaning?

ΤΡΟΦΟΣ

60 ζηλῶ σ᾽· ἐν ἀρχῇ πῆμα κοὐδέπω μεσοῖ.

ΠΑΙΔΑΓΩΓΟΣ

ὦ μῶρος, εἰ χρὴ δεσπότας εἰπεῖν τόδε·
ὡς οὐδὲν οἶδε τῶν νεωτέρων κακῶν.

ΤΡΟΦΟΣ

τί δ᾽ ἔστιν, ὦ γεραιέ; μὴ φθόνει φράσαι.

ΠΑΙΔΑΓΩΓΟΣ

οὐδέν· μετέγνων καὶ τὰ πρόσθ᾽ εἰρημένα.

ΤΡΟΦΟΣ

65 μή, πρὸς γενείου, κρύπτε σύνδουλον σέθεν·
σιγὴν γάρ, εἰ χρή, τῶνδε θήσομαι πέρι.

ΠΑΙΔΑΓΩΓΟΣ

ἤκουσά του λέγοντος, οὐ δοκῶν κλύειν,
πεσσοὺς προσελθών, ἔνθα δὴ παλαίτεροι
θάσσουσι, σεμνὸν ἀμφὶ Πειρήνης ὕδωρ,
70 ὡς τούσδε παῖδας γῆς ἐλᾶν Κορινθίας
σὺν μητρὶ μέλλοι τῆσδε κοίρανος χθονὸς
Κρέων. ὁ μέντοι μῦθος εἰ σαφὴς ὅδε
οὐκ οἶδα· βουλοίμην δ᾽ ἂν οὐκ εἶναι τόδε.

ΤΡΟΦΟΣ

καὶ ταῦτ᾽ Ἰάσων παῖδας ἐξανέξεται
75 πάσχοντας, εἰ καὶ μητρὶ διαφορὰν ἔχει;

ΠΑΙΔΑΓΩΓΟΣ

παλαιὰ καινῶν λείπεται κηδευμάτων,
κοὐκ ἔστ᾽ ἐκεῖνος τοῖσδε δώμασιν φίλος.

NURSE

Your ignorance is enviable. This is but the beginning of her pain: it has not yet reached its peak.

TUTOR

Poor fool (if I may speak thus of my masters), how ignorant she is of her latest trouble!

NURSE

What is it, old man? Do not begrudge me the news.

TUTOR

Nothing. I am sorry I said as much as I have.

NURSE

I beg you by your beard, do not conceal this from your fellow slave! I will keep it a secret if I must.

TUTOR

As I approached the gaming tables where the old men sit, near the holy spring of Peirene, I heard someone say (I was pretending not to listen) that Creon, this country's king, was going to exile these children and their mother from the land of Corinth. Whether the story is true I do not know. I could wish it were not so.

NURSE

But will Jason allow this to happen to his sons even if he is at odds with their mother?

TUTOR

Old marriage ties give way to new: he is no friend to this house.

---

[68] παλαίτεροι Pierson ex t: -τατοι C

EURIPIDES

ΤΡΟΦΟΣ

ἀπωλόμεσθ᾽ ἄρ᾽, εἰ κακὸν προσοίσομεν
νέον παλαιῷ, πρὶν τόδ᾽ ἐξηντληκέναι.

ΠΑΙΔΑΓΩΓΟΣ

80 ἀτὰρ σύ γ᾽, οὐ γὰρ καιρὸς εἰδέναι τόδε
δέσποιναν, ἡσύχαζε καὶ σίγα λόγον.

ΤΡΟΦΟΣ

ὦ τέκν᾽, ἀκούεθ᾽ οἷος εἰς ὑμᾶς πατήρ;
ὄλοιτο μὲν μή· δεσπότης γάρ ἐστ᾽ ἐμός·
ἀτὰρ κακός γ᾽ ὢν ἐς φίλους ἁλίσκεται.

ΠΑΙΔΑΓΩΓΟΣ

85 τίς δ᾽ οὐχὶ θνητῶν; ἄρτι γιγνώσκεις τόδε,
ὡς πᾶς τις αὑτὸν τοῦ πέλας μᾶλλον φιλεῖ,
[οἱ μὲν δικαίως, οἱ δὲ καὶ κέρδους χάριν,]
εἰ τούσδε γ᾽ εὐνῆς οὕνεκ᾽ οὐ στέργει πατήρ;

ΤΡΟΦΟΣ

ἴτ᾽, εὖ γὰρ ἔσται, δωμάτων ἔσω, τέκνα.
90 σὺ δ᾽ ὡς μάλιστα τοῦσδ᾽ ἐρημώσας ἔχε
καὶ μὴ πέλαζε μητρὶ δυσθυμουμένῃ.
ἤδη γὰρ εἶδον ὄμμα νιν ταυρουμένην
τοῖσδ᾽, ὥς τι δρασείουσαν· οὐδὲ παύσεται
χόλου, σάφ᾽ οἶδα, πρὶν κατασκῆψαί τινι.
95 ἐχθρούς γε μέντοι, μὴ φίλους, δράσειέ τι.

---

87 del. Brunck cl. Σ
94 τινι Blomfield: τινα C

302

NURSE

We are done for, then, if we add this new trouble to our old ones before we've weathered those.

TUTOR

But you, hold your peace (since it is not the right time for your mistress to know this) and say nothing of this tale.

NURSE

O children, do you hear what kind of man your father is toward you? A curse on him!—but no, he is my master. Yet he is certainly guilty of disloyalty toward his loved ones.

TUTOR

As what mortal is not? Because of his new bride, the father does not love these boys: are you only now learning that each man loves himself more than others [, some justly, others for the sake of gain]?

NURSE

Go into the house, children, all will be well! And you, keep them as far away as you can and do not bring them near their mother in her distress. I have seen her turn a savage glance at them, as if she meant to do something to them. She will not let go of her anger, I am sure, before she brings it down on someone's head. But may it be enemies, not loved ones, that feel her wrath!

ΜΗΔΕΙΑ

(ἔσωθεν)
ἰώ,
δύστανος ἐγὼ μελέα τε πόνων,
ἰώ μοί μοι, πῶς ἂν ὀλοίμαν;

ΤΡΟΦΟΣ

τόδ' ἐκεῖνο, φίλοι παῖδες· μήτηρ
κινεῖ κραδίαν, κινεῖ δὲ χόλον.
100 σπεύσατε θᾶσσον δώματος εἴσω
καὶ μὴ πελάσητ' ὄμματος ἐγγὺς
μηδὲ προσέλθητ', ἀλλὰ φυλάσσεσθ'
ἄγριον ἦθος στυγεράν τε φύσιν
φρενὸς αὐθάδους.
105 ἴτε νυν, χωρεῖθ' ὡς τάχος εἴσω·
δῆλον ἀπ' ἀρχῆς ἐξαιρόμενον
νέφος οἰμωγῆς ὡς τάχ' ἀνάψει
μείζονι θυμῷ· τί ποτ' ἐργάσεται
μεγαλόσπλαγχνος δυσκατάπαυστος
110 ψυχὴ δηχθεῖσα κακοῖσιν;

ΜΗΔΕΙΑ

αἰαῖ,
ἔπαθον τλάμων ἔπαθον μεγάλων
ἄξι' ὀδυρμῶν. ὦ κατάρατοι
παῖδες ὄλοισθε στυγερᾶς ματρὸς
σὺν πατρί, καὶ πᾶς δόμος ἔρροι.

MEDEA

MEDEA

(within, sung) Oh, what a wretch am I, how miserable in my sorrows! Ah ah, how I wish I could die!

NURSE

Just as I said, dear children. Your mother is stirring up her feelings, stirring up her anger. Go quickly into the house, and do not come into her sight or approach her, but beware of her fierce nature and the hatefulness of her wilful temper! Go inside as quickly as you can!

Exit TUTOR and children into the house.

It is plain that flashes of still greater passion will soon set alight the cloud of lament now rising from its source: what will her proud soul, so hard to check, do when stung by this injury?

MEDEA

(sung) Oh, what sufferings are mine, sufferings that call for loud lamentation! O accursèd children of a hateful mother, may you perish with your father and the whole house collapse in ruin!

ΤΡΟΦΟΣ

115 ἰώ μοί μοι, ἰώ τλήμων.
τί δέ σοι παῖδες πατρὸς ἀμπλακίας
μετέχουσι; τί τούσδ' ἔχθεις; οἴμοι,
τέκνα, μή τι πάθηθ' ὡς ὑπεραλγῶ.
δεινὰ τυράννων λήματα καί πως
120 ὀλίγ' ἀρχόμενοι, πολλὰ κρατοῦντες
χαλεπῶς ὀργὰς μεταβάλλουσιν.
τὸ γὰρ εἰθίσθαι ζῆν ἐπ' ἴσοισιν
κρεῖσσον· ἐμοὶ γοῦν ἐπὶ μὴ μεγάλοις
ὀχυρῶς τ' εἴη καταγηράσκειν.
125 τῶν γὰρ μετρίων πρῶτα μὲν εἰπεῖν
τοὔνομα νικᾷ, χρῆσθαί τε μακρῷ
λῷστα βροτοῖσιν· τὰ δ' ὑπερβάλλοντ'
οὐδένα καιρὸν δύναται θνητοῖς,
μείζους δ' ἄτας, ὅταν ὀργισθῇ
130 δαίμων οἴκοις, ἀπέδωκεν.

ΧΟΡΟΣ

ἔκλυον φωνάν, ἔκλυον δὲ βοὰν
τᾶς δυστάνου
Κολχίδος· οὐδέπω ἤπιος;
ἀλλ', ὦ γεραιά, λέξον· ἔτ' ἀμφιπύλου
135 γὰρ ἔσω μελάθροιο βοὰν ἔκλυον,
οὐδὲ συνήδομαι, ὦ γύναι, ἄλγεσι
δώματος, ἐπεί μοι φιλία κέκραται.

---

123 ἐπὶ μὴ μεγάλοις Barthold: εἰ μὴ μεγάλως fere C
134 ἔτ' Badham: ἐπ' C
135 μελάθροιο Wilamowitz: -ου C

MEDEA

NURSE

Oh, woe is me! Why do you make the children sharers in their father's sin? Why do you hate *them*? O children, how terrified I am that you may come to harm. The minds of royalty are dangerous: since they often command and seldom obey, they are subject to violent changes of mood. It is better to be accustomed to live on terms of equality. At any rate, may I be able to grow old in modest state and with security. For moderate fortune has a name that is fairest on the tongue, and in practice it is by far the most beneficial thing for mortals. But excessive riches mean no advantage for mortals, and when a god is angry at a house, they make the ruin greater.

Enter by Eisodos B a group of Corinthian women as CHORUS.

CHORUS

I have heard the voice, I have heard the cry, of the unhappy woman of Colchis: is she not yet soothed? Tell me, old woman, for still within my double-gated house I heard her lamentation. It is no joy I feel at this house's misfortunes since I have shared the cup of friendship with it.

---

138 φιλία Porson: φίλον a: φίλα b

307

ΤΡΟΦΟΣ

οὐκ εἰσὶ δόμοι· φροῦδα τάδ' ἤδη.
140 τὸν μὲν γὰρ ἔχει λέκτρα τυράννων,
ἡ δ' ἐν θαλάμοις τήκει βιοτὴν
δέσποινα, φίλων οὐδενὸς οὐδὲν
παραθαλπομένη φρένα μύθοις.

ΜΗΔΕΙΑ

αἰαῖ,
διά μου κεφαλᾶς φλὸξ οὐρανία
145 βαίη· τί δέ μοι ζῆν ἔτι κέρδος;
φεῦ φεῦ· θανάτῳ καταλυσαίμαν
βιοτὰν στυγερὰν προλιποῦσα.

ΧΟΡΟΣ

στρ.

ἄιες, ὦ Ζεῦ καὶ γᾶ καὶ φῶς,
ἀχὰν οἵαν ἁ δύστανος
150 μέλπει νύμφα;
τίς σοί ποτε τᾶς ἀπλά-
του κοίτας ἔρος, ὦ ματαία;
σπεύσει θανάτου τελευ-
τά· μηδὲν τόδε λίσσου.
155 εἰ δὲ σὸς πόσις καινὰ λέχη σεβί-
ζει, κείνῳ τόδε μὴ χαράσσου·
Ζεύς σοι τάδε συνδικήσει.
μὴ λίαν
τάκου δυρομένα σὸν εὐνάταν.

¹⁵³ τελευτά Weil: -τάν C

MEDEA

NURSE

The house is no more: it has perished. For the husband is possessed by a royal marriage, while the wife, my mistress, wastes away her life in her chamber, her heart in no way soothed by the words of any of her friends.

MEDEA

(*sung*) Oh! May a flash of lightning pierce my head! What profit any longer for me in life? Ah, ah! may I find my rest in death and leave behind my hateful life!

CHORUS

Did you hear, O Zeus and earth and light of the sun, what a wail the miserable woman utters? What is this desire you feel for the bed of death, the bed we should not approach, foolish woman? Death will come all too quickly: do not pray for it. But if your husband holds another marriage bed in honor, do not vex yourself on his account: Zeus will be your advocate in this. Do not grieve excessively or weep over your husband.

ΜΗΔΕΙΑ

160 ὦ μεγάλα Θέμι καὶ πότνι᾽ Ἄρτεμι,
λεύσσεθ᾽ ἃ πάσχω, μεγάλοις ὅρκοις
ἐνδησαμένα τὸν κατάρατον
πόσιν; ὅν ποτ᾽ ἐγὼ νύμφαν τ᾽ ἐσίδοιμ᾽
αὐτοῖς μελάθροις διακναιομένους,
165 οἷ᾽ ἐμὲ πρόσθεν τολμῶσ᾽ ἀδικεῖν.
ὦ πάτερ, ὦ πόλις, ὧν κάσιν αἰσχρῶς
τὸν ἐμὸν κτείνασ᾽ ἀπενάσθην.

ΤΡΟΦΟΣ

κλύεθ᾽ οἷα λέγει κἀπιβοᾶται
Θέμιν εὐκταίαν Ζηνός, ὃς ὅρκων
170 θνητοῖς ταμίας νενόμισται;
οὐκ ἔστιν ὅπως ἔν τινι μικρῷ
δέσποινα χόλον καταπαύσει.

ΧΟΡΟΣ

ἀντ.

πῶς ἂν ἐς ὄψιν τὰν ἁμετέραν
ἔλθοι μύθων τ᾽ αὐδαθέντων
δέξαιτ᾽ ὀμφάν,
175 εἴ πως βαρύθυμον ὀρ-
γὰν καὶ λῆμα φρενῶν μεθείη;
μήτοι τό γ᾽ ἐμὸν πρόθυ-
μον φίλοισιν ἀπέστω.
180 ἀλλὰ βᾶσά νιν δεῦρο πόρευσον οἴ-
κων ἔξω· φίλα καὶ τάδ᾽ αὔδα,

310

MEDEA

(sung) O mighty Themis and my lady Artemis, do you see what I suffer, I who have bound my accursèd husband with mighty oaths? May I one day see him and his new bride ground to destruction, and their whole house with them, so terrible are the unprovoked wrongs they dare to commit against me! O father, O my native city, from you I departed in shame, having killed my brother!

NURSE

Do you hear what she says, how she calls on Themis invoked in prayer, daughter of Zeus, who is deemed guardian of men's oaths? It is not possible that my mistress will bring her wrath to an end in some trifling deed.

CHORUS

Oh, how I wish she could come face to face with us and listen to our words, on the chance that somehow she might give up her angry temper! May my good will never desert my friends! But go now and bring her out of the house. Tell her that here are friends, and hurry before she

---

¹⁶⁵ οἴ᾽ ἐμὲ Kaibel: οἵ γέ με fere C
^{166–7} ὧν . . . ἀπενάσθην Heimsoeth: ὧν ἀπ. αἰ. τ. ἐ. κτ. κα. C
¹⁶⁹ Ζηνός Nauck: Ζῆνά θ᾽ C

σπεύσασά τι πρὶν κακῶσαι
τοὺς ἔσω·
πένθος γὰρ μεγάλως τόδ᾽ ὁρμᾶται.

ΤΡΟΦΟΣ

δράσω τάδ᾽· ἀτὰρ φόβος εἰ πείσω
185 δέσποιναν ἐμήν·
μόχθου δὲ χάριν τήνδ᾽ ἐπιδώσω.
καίτοι τοκάδος δέργμα λεαίνης
ἀποταυροῦται δμωσίν, ὅταν τις
μῦθον προφέρων πέλας ὁρμηθῇ.
190 σκαιοὺς δὲ λέγων κοὐδέν τι σοφοὺς
τοὺς πρόσθε βροτοὺς οὐκ ἂν ἁμάρτοις,
οἵτινες ὕμνους ἐπὶ μὲν θαλίαις
ἐπί τ᾽ εἰλαπίναις καὶ παρὰ δείπνοις
ηὕροντο βίῳ τερπνὰς ἀκοάς·
195 στυγίους δὲ βροτῶν οὐδεὶς λύπας
ηὕρετο μούσῃ καὶ πολυχόρδοις
ᾠδαῖς παύειν, ἐξ ὧν θάνατοι
δειναί τε τύχαι σφάλλουσι δόμους.
καίτοι τάδε μὲν κέρδος ἀκεῖσθαι
200 μολπαῖσι βροτούς· ἵνα δ᾽ εὔδειπνοι
δαῖτες, τί μάτην τείνουσι βοήν;
τὸ παρὸν γὰρ ἔχει τέρψιν ἀφ᾽ αὑτοῦ
δαιτὸς πλήρωμα βροτοῖσιν.

182 σπεύσασά Schöne: σπεῦσαι a: σπεῦσον b: σπεῦδε c
194 βίῳ Page: βίου C

harms those inside. For this grief of hers is charging powerfully forward.

NURSE

I will do so. But there is doubt whether I shall persuade my mistress. Still, I will make you a further present of my labor, though she glowers at the servants with the look of a lioness with cubs when any of them approaches her with something to say. You would be right to call men of old foolish, not at all wise: for while they invented songs for festivities, banquets, and dinners and added pleasant sounds to our life, no one has discovered how to put an end to mortals' bitter griefs with music and song sung to the lyre. It is because of these griefs that deaths and terrible disasters overthrow houses. It would have been a gain for mortals to cure these ills by song. Where there are banquets of plenty, why do they raise the loud song to no purpose? The abundance of the feast at hand provides mortals with its own pleasure.

Exit NURSE into the house.

ΧΟΡΟΣ

205 ἰαχὰν ἄιον πολύστονον
γόων, λιγυρὰ δ' ἄχεα μογερὰ
βοᾷ τὸν ἐν λέχει προδόταν κακόνυμφον ·
θεοκλυτεῖ δ' ἄδικα <πάθη>
παθοῦσα τὰν Ζηνὸς ὁρ-
κίαν Θέμιν, ἅ νιν ἔβασεν
210 Ἑλλάδ' ἐς ἀντίπορον
δι' ἅλα νύχιον ἐφ' ἁλμυρὰν
Πόντου κλῇδ' ἀπέρατον.

ΜΗΔΕΙΑ

Κορίνθιαι γυναῖκες, ἐξῆλθον δόμων
215 μή μοί τι μέμψησθ' · οἶδα γὰρ πολλοὺς βροτῶν
σεμνοὺς γεγῶτας, τοὺς μὲν ὀμμάτων ἄπο,
τοὺς δ' ἐν θυραίοις· οἱ δ' ἀφ' ἡσύχου ποδὸς
δύσκλειαν ἐκτήσαντο καὶ ῥαθυμίαν.
δίκη γὰρ οὐκ ἔνεστ' ἐν ὀφθαλμοῖς βροτῶν,
220 ὅστις πρὶν ἀνδρὸς σπλάγχνον ἐκμαθεῖν σαφῶς
στυγεῖ δεδορκώς, οὐδὲν ἠδικημένος.
χρὴ δὲ ξένον μὲν κάρτα προσχωρεῖν πόλει,
οὐδ' ἀστὸν ἤνεσ' ὅστις αὐθάδης γεγὼς
πικρὸς πολίταις ἐστὶν ἀμαθίας ὕπο.
225 ἐμοὶ δ' ἄελπτον πρᾶγμα προσπεσὸν τόδε
ψυχὴν διέφθαρκ' · οἴχομαι δὲ καὶ βίου
χάριν μεθεῖσα κατθανεῖν χρήζω, φίλαι.

208 <πάθη> Willink
212 ἀπέρατον Blaydes: ἀπέραντον C
218 δύσνοιαν Prinz

314

CHORUS

I have heard her loud groans, the shrill accusations she utters against the husband who betrayed her bed. Having suffered wrong she raises her cry to Zeus's daughter, Themis, goddess of oaths, the goddess who brought her[a] to Hellas across the sea through the dark saltwater over the briny gateway of the Black Sea, a gateway few traverse.[b]

Enter MEDEA *with the Nurse from the house.*

MEDEA

Women of Corinth, I have come out of the house lest you find fault with me. For I know that though many mortals are haughty both in private and in public, others get a *reputation* for indifference to their neighbors from their retiring manner of life. There is no justice in the eyes of mortals: before they get sure knowledge of a man's true character, they hate him on sight, although he has done them no harm. Now a foreigner must be quite compliant with the city, nor do I have any words of praise for the citizen who is self-willed and causes his fellow citizens pain by his lack of breeding. In my case, however, this sudden blow that has struck me has destroyed my life. I am undone, I have resigned all joy in life, and I want to

[a] Themis "brought her to Hellas" in that she came to Greece relying on Jason's oath.

[b] "The briny gateway" (lit. key) of the Black Sea is probably the Bosporus.

315

ἐν ᾧ γὰρ ἦν μοι πάντα, γιγνώσκω καλῶς,
κάκιστος ἀνδρῶν ἐκβέβηχ᾽ οὑμὸς πόσις.
230   πάντων δ᾽ ὅσ᾽ ἔστ᾽ ἔμψυχα καὶ γνώμην ἔχει
γυναῖκές ἐσμεν ἀθλιώτατον φυτόν·
ἃς πρῶτα μὲν δεῖ χρημάτων ὑπερβολῇ
πόσιν πρίασθαι δεσπότην τε σώματος
λαβεῖν· κακοῦ γὰρ †τοῦδ᾽ ἔτ᾽† ἄλγιον κακόν.
235 κἂν τῷδ᾽ ἀγὼν μέγιστος, ἢ κακὸν λαβεῖν
ἢ χρηστόν· οὐ γὰρ εὐκλεεῖς ἀπαλλαγαὶ
γυναιξὶν οὐδ᾽ οἷόν τ᾽ ἀνήνασθαι πόσιν.
ἐς καινὰ δ᾽ ἤθη καὶ νόμους ἀφιγμένην
δεῖ μάντιν εἶναι, μὴ μαθοῦσαν οἴκοθεν,
240 ὅπως ἄριστα χρήσεται ξυνευνέτῃ.
κἂν μὲν τάδ᾽ ἡμῖν ἐκπονουμέναισιν εὖ
πόσις ξυνοικῇ μὴ βίᾳ φέρων ζυγόν,
ζηλωτὸς αἰών· εἰ δὲ μή, θανεῖν χρεών.
ἀνὴρ δ᾽, ὅταν τοῖς ἔνδον ἄχθηται ξυνών,
245 ἔξω μολὼν ἔπαυσε καρδίαν ἄσης
[ἢ πρὸς φίλον τιν᾽ ἢ πρὸς ἥλικα τραπείς]·
ἡμῖν δ᾽ ἀνάγκη πρὸς μίαν ψυχὴν βλέπειν.
λέγουσι δ᾽ ἡμᾶς ὡς ἀκίνδυνον βίον
ζῶμεν κατ᾽ οἴκους, οἱ δὲ μάρνανται δορί,
250 κακῶς φρονοῦντες· ὡς τρὶς ἂν παρ᾽ ἀσπίδα
στῆναι θέλοιμ᾽ ἂν μᾶλλον ἢ τεκεῖν ἅπαξ.

---

[228] γιγνώσκω Canter: γιγνώσκειν C
[234] fort. κακοῦ γὰρ τῷδ᾽ ἔτ᾽ ἄλγιον κακὸν / < ἢν ζημίαν φέρῃ
τις ὑβρισθῇ θ᾽ ἅμα>
[240] ὅπως Meineke: ὅτῳ C   ἄριστα Barthold: μάλιστα C
[246] del. Wilamowitz

die. For the man in whom all I had was bound up, as I well know—my husband—has proved the basest of men.

Of all creatures that have breath and sensation, we women are the most unfortunate. First at an exorbitant price we must buy a husband and take a master for our bodies. For this is what makes one misfortune even more galling than another, <to suffer loss and be insulted to boot>.[a] The outcome of our life's striving hangs on this, whether we take a bad or a good husband. For divorce is discreditable for women and it is not possible to refuse wedlock. When a woman comes into the new customs and practices of her husband's house, she must somehow divine, since she has not learned it at home, how she shall best deal with her husband. If after we have spent great efforts on these tasks our husbands live with us without resenting the marriage yoke, our life is enviable. Otherwise, death is preferable. A man, whenever he is annoyed with the company of those in the house, goes elsewhere and thus rids his soul of its boredom [turning to some male friend or agemate]. But we must fix our gaze on one person only. Men say that we live a life free from danger at home while *they* fight with the spear. How wrong they are! I would rather stand three times with a shield in battle than give birth once.

[a] I translate my conjectural restoration.

ἀλλ᾽ οὐ γὰρ αὑτὸς πρὸς σὲ κἄμ᾽ ἥκει λόγος·
σοὶ μὲν πόλις θ᾽ ἥδ᾽ ἐστὶ καὶ πατρὸς δόμοι
βίου τ᾽ ὄνησις καὶ φίλων συνουσία,
255 ἐγὼ δ᾽ ἔρημος ἄπολις οὖσ᾽ ὑβρίζομαι
πρὸς ἀνδρός, ἐκ γῆς βαρβάρου λελῃσμένη,
οὐ μητέρ᾽, οὐκ ἀδελφόν, οὐχὶ συγγενῆ
μεθορμίσασθαι τῆσδ᾽ ἔχουσα συμφορᾶς.
τοσοῦτον οὖν σου τυγχάνειν βουλήσομαι,
260 ἤν μοι πόρος τις μηχανή τ᾽ ἐξευρεθῇ
πόσιν δίκην τῶνδ᾽ ἀντιτείσασθαι κακῶν
[τὸν δόντα τ᾽ αὐτῷ θυγατέρ᾽ ἥν τ᾽ ἐγήματο],
σιγᾶν. γυνὴ γὰρ τἆλλα μὲν φόβου πλέα
κακή τ᾽ ἐς ἀλκὴν καὶ σίδηρον εἰσορᾶν·
265 ὅταν δ᾽ ἐς εὐνὴν ἠδικημένη κυρῇ,
οὐκ ἔστιν ἄλλη φρὴν μιαιφονωτέρα.

ΧΟΡΟΣ

δράσω τάδ᾽· ἐνδίκως γὰρ ἐκτείσῃ πόσιν,
Μήδεια. πενθεῖν δ᾽ οὔ σε θαυμάζω τύχας.
ὁρῶ δὲ καὶ Κρέοντα, τῆσδ᾽ ἄνακτα γῆς,
270 στείχοντα, καινῶν ἄγγελον βουλευμάτων.

ΚΡΕΩΝ

σὲ τὴν σκυθρωπὸν καὶ πόσει θυμουμένην,
Μήδει᾽, ἀνεῖπον τῆσδε γῆς ἔξω περᾶν
φυγάδα, λαβοῦσαν δισσὰ σὺν σαυτῇ τέκνα,
καὶ μή τι μέλλειν· ὡς ἐγὼ βραβεὺς λόγου
275 τοῦδ᾽ εἰμί, κοὐκ ἄπειμι πρὸς δόμους πάλιν
πρὶν ἄν σε γαίας τερμόνων ἔξω βάλω.

But your story and mine are not the same: you have a city and a father's house, the enjoyment of life and the company of friends, while I, without relatives or city, am suffering outrage from my husband. I was carried off as booty from a foreign land and have no mother, no brother, no kinsman to shelter me from this calamity. And so I shall ask this much from you as a favor: if I find any means or contrivance to punish my husband for these wrongs [and the bride's father and the bride], keep my secret. In all other things a woman is full of fear, incapable of looking on battle or cold steel; but when she is injured in love, no mind is more murderous than hers.

CHORUS LEADER

I will do so. For you will be justified in punishing your husband, Medea, and I am not surprised that you grieve at what has happened.

Enter CREON *by Eisodos B.*

But I see Creon coming, ruler of this land. He will have some new deliberation to report.

CREON

You, Medea, scowling with rage against your husband, I order you to leave this land and go into exile, taking your two children with you, and instantly! I am the executor of this decree, and I will not return home again until I expel you from the country.

---

262 del. Lenting
272 Μήδει', ἀνεῖπον E. Harrison: Μήδειαν εἶπον C

ΜΗΔΕΙΑ

αἰαῖ· πανώλης ἡ τάλαιν' ἀπόλλυμαι·
ἐχθροὶ γὰρ ἐξιᾶσι πάντα δὴ κάλων,
κοὐκ ἔστιν ἄτης εὐπρόσοιστος ἔκβασις.
280 ἐρήσομαι δὲ καὶ κακῶς πάσχουσ' ὅμως·
τίνος μ' ἕκατι γῆς ἀποστέλλεις, Κρέον;

ΚΡΕΩΝ

δέδοικά σ' (οὐδὲν δεῖ παραμπίσχειν λόγους)
μή μοί τι δράσῃς παῖδ' ἀνήκεστον κακόν.
συμβάλλεται δὲ πολλὰ τοῦδε δείγματα·
285 σοφὴ πέφυκας καὶ κακῶν πολλῶν ἴδρις,
λυπῇ δὲ λέκτρων ἀνδρὸς ἐστερημένη.
κλύω δ' ἀπειλεῖν σ', ὡς ἀπαγγέλλουσί μοι,
τὸν δόντα καὶ γήμαντα καὶ γαμουμένην
δράσειν τι. ταῦτ' οὖν πρὶν παθεῖν φυλάξομαι.
290 κρεῖσσον δέ μοι νῦν πρός σ' ἀπεχθέσθαι, γύναι,
ἢ μαλθακισθένθ' ὕστερον μεταστένειν.

ΜΗΔΕΙΑ

φεῦ φεῦ.
οὐ νῦν με πρῶτον ἀλλὰ πολλάκις, Κρέον,
ἔβλαψε δόξα μεγάλα τ' εἴργασται κακά.
χρὴ δ' οὔποθ' ὅστις ἀρτίφρων πέφυκ' ἀνὴρ
295 παῖδας περισσῶς ἐκδιδάσκεσθαι σοφούς·
χωρὶς γὰρ ἄλλης ἧς ἔχουσιν ἀργίας
φθόνον πρὸς ἀστῶν ἀλφάνουσι δυσμενῆ.
σκαιοῖσι μὲν γὰρ καινὰ προσφέρων σοφὰ
δόξεις ἀχρεῖος κοὐ σοφὸς πεφυκέναι·

MEDEA

Oh, I am undone, wholly lost! My enemies are making full sail against me, and there is no haven from disaster that I can reach. Still, though I am ill-treated, I will ask you: Why are you exiling me, Creon?

CREON

I am afraid (no need to dissemble) that you will do some deadly harm to my daughter. Many indications of this combine: you are a clever woman and skilled in many evil arts, and you are smarting with the loss of your husband's love. And I hear that you are threatening—such is the report people bring—to harm the bride, her father, and her husband. So I shall take precautions before the event. It is better for me to incur your hatred now, woman, than to be soft now and regret it later.

MEDEA

Ah me! This is not the first time, Creon, but often before now my reputation has done me great harm. No man who is sensible ought ever to have his children educated beyond the common run. For apart from the charge of idleness they incur, they earn hostility and ill will from their fellow citizens. If you bring novel wisdom to fools, you will be regarded as useless, not wise; and if the city

---

284 τοῦδε δείγματα Wieseler: τοῦδε δείματος C
291 μεταστένειν t, sicut coni. Nauck: μέγα στένειν C

300 τῶν δ' αὖ δοκούντων εἰδέναι τι ποικίλον
κρείσσων νομισθεὶς ἐν πόλει λυπρὸς φανῇ.
ἐγὼ δὲ καὐτὴ τῆσδε κοινωνῶ τύχης·
σοφὴ γὰρ οὖσα, τοῖς μέν εἰμ' ἐπίφθονος,
[τοῖς δ' ἡσυχαία, τοῖς δὲ θατέρου τρόπου,
305 τοῖς δ' αὖ προσάντης· εἰμὶ δ' οὐκ ἄγαν σοφή,]
σὺ δ' αὖ φοβῇ με· μὴ τί πλημμελὲς πάθῃς;
οὐχ ὧδ' ἔχει μοι, μὴ τρέσῃς ἡμᾶς, Κρέον,
ὥστ' ἐς τυράννους ἄνδρας ἐξαμαρτάνειν.
σὺ γὰρ τί μ' ἠδίκηκας; ἐξέδου κόρην
310 ὅτῳ σε θυμὸς ἦγεν. ἀλλ' ἐμὸν πόσιν
μισῶ· σὺ δ', οἶμαι, σωφρονῶν ἔδρας τάδε.
καὶ νῦν τὸ μὲν σὸν οὐ φθονῶ καλῶς ἔχειν·
νυμφεύετ', εὖ πράσσοιτε· τήνδε δὲ χθόνα
ἐᾶτέ μ' οἰκεῖν. καὶ γὰρ ἠδικημένοι
315 σιγησόμεσθα, κρεισσόνων νικώμενοι.

ΚΡΕΩΝ

λέγεις ἀκοῦσαι μαλθάκ', ἀλλ' ἔσω φρενῶν
ὀρρωδία μοι μή τι βουλεύῃς κακόν,
τοσῷδε δ' ἧσσον ἢ πάρος πέποιθά σοι·
γυνὴ γὰρ ὀξύθυμος, ὡς δ' αὔτως ἀνήρ,
320 ῥᾴων φυλάσσειν ἢ σιωπηλὸς σοφή.
ἀλλ' ἔξιθ' ὡς τάχιστα, μὴ λόγους λέγε·
ὡς ταῦτ' ἄραρε κοὐκ ἔχεις τέχνην ὅπως
μενεῖς παρ' ἡμῖν οὖσα δυσμενὴς ἐμοί.

304–5 delevi: 304 om. a, del. Pierson: cf. 808, 583
317 βουλεύῃς Elmsley: -σῃς C
320 σοφή Diggle: σοφός C

322

regards you as greater than those with a reputation for cleverness, you will be thought vexatious. I myself am a sharer in this lot, for since I am clever, some regard me with ill will, [others find me retiring, others the opposite, others an obstacle, yet I am not so very wise,] while you on the other hand fear me. What harm are you afraid of? Have no fear, Creon: I am not the kind of person to commit crimes against my rulers. What injustice have you done me? You married your daughter to the man your heart bade you to. It is my husband I hate, while you, I think, acted with perfect good sense in this. And now I do not begrudge you prosperity. Make your marriage, all of you, and may good fortune attend you! But let me stay in this land. For although I have been wronged, I will hold my peace, yielding to my superiors.

CREON

Your words are soothing to listen to, but I am afraid that in your heart you are plotting some harm, and I trust you that much the less than before. A hot-tempered woman—and a hot-tempered man likewise—is easier to guard against than a clever woman who keeps her own counsel. No, go into exile at once—no more talk: my resolve is fixed and there is no way you can remain in our midst since you are hostile to me.

Medea kneels before him in the attitude of a suppliant, grasping his knees and hand.

ΜΗΔΕΙΑ

μή, πρός σε γονάτων τῆς τε νεογάμου κόρης.

ΚΡΕΩΝ

325 λόγους ἀναλοῖς· οὐ γὰρ ἂν πείσαις ποτέ.

ΜΗΔΕΙΑ

ἀλλ' ἐξελᾷς με κοὐδὲν αἰδέσῃ λιτάς;

ΚΡΕΩΝ

φιλῶ γὰρ οὐ σὲ μᾶλλον ἢ δόμους ἐμούς.

ΜΗΔΕΙΑ

ὦ πατρίς, ὥς σου κάρτα νῦν μνείαν ἔχω.

ΚΡΕΩΝ

πλὴν γὰρ τέκνων ἔμοιγε φίλτατον πολύ.

ΜΗΔΕΙΑ

330 φεῦ φεῦ, βροτοῖς ἔρωτες ὡς κακὸν μέγα.

ΚΡΕΩΝ

ὅπως ἄν, οἶμαι, καὶ παραστῶσιν τύχαι.

ΜΗΔΕΙΑ

Ζεῦ, μὴ λάθοι σε τῶνδ' ὃς αἴτιος κακῶν.

ΚΡΕΩΝ

ἕρπ', ὦ ματαία, καί μ' ἀπάλλαξον πόνων.

ΜΗΔΕΙΑ

πονοῦμεν ἡμεῖς κοὐ πόνων κεχρήμεθα.

MEDEA

MEDEA

Do not, I beg you by your knees and by your newly wed-
ded daughter!

CREON

You waste your words. You will never win me over.

MEDEA

But will you banish me without the regard due a sup-
pliant?[a]

CREON

Yes: I do not love you more than my own house.

MEDEA

O fatherland, how I think of you now!

CREON

Yes, after my children it is much the dearest thing to me.

MEDEA

Oh, what a bane to mortals is love!

CREON

I fancy that depends on the circumstances.

MEDEA

Zeus, mark well who has caused all this woe!

CREON

Go, foolish woman, and rid me of my trouble!

MEDEA

Trouble I have already. I have no need of more.

[a] The verb αἰδέομαι and the corresponding noun αἰδώς desig-
nate the response that suppliancy requires, respect for the sanctity
of the suppliant and acquiescence in what he asks.

325

ΚΡΕΩΝ

335 τάχ' ἐξ ὀπαδῶν χειρὸς ὠσθήσῃ βίᾳ.

ΜΗΔΕΙΑ

μὴ δῆτα τοῦτό γ', ἀλλά σ' ἄντομαι, Κρέον.

ΚΡΕΩΝ

ὄχλον παρέξεις, ὡς ἔοικας, ὦ γύναι.

ΜΗΔΕΙΑ

φευξούμεθ'· οὐ τοῦθ' ἱκέτευσά σου τυχεῖν.

ΚΡΕΩΝ

τί δαὶ βιάζῃ κοὐκ ἀπαλλάσσῃ χερός;

ΜΗΔΕΙΑ

340 μίαν με μεῖναι τήνδ' ἔασον ἡμέραν
καὶ ξυμπερᾶναι φροντίδ' ᾗ φευξούμεθα,
παισίν τ' ἀφορμὴν τοῖς ἐμοῖς, ἐπεὶ πατὴρ
οὐδὲν προτιμᾷ, μηχανήσασθαί τινα.
οἴκτιρε δ' αὐτούς· καὶ σύ τοι παίδων πατὴρ
345 πέφυκας· εἰκὸς δέ σφιν εὔνοιάν σ' ἔχειν.
τοὐμοῦ γὰρ οὔ μοι φροντίς, εἰ φευξούμεθα,
κείνους δὲ κλαίω συμφορᾷ κεχρημένους.

ΚΡΕΩΝ

ἥκιστα τοὐμὸν λῆμ' ἔφυ τυραννικόν,
αἰδούμενος δὲ πολλὰ δὴ διέφθορα·

336 ἄντομαι Wecklein: αἰτοῦμαι C
339 δαὶ Housman: δ' αὖ a: δ' οὖν b   χερός Wilamowitz: χθονός C
343 τινα Earle: τέκνοις C
345 δέ σφιν Vitelli: δ' ἐστὶν fere C

CREON

In a moment you will be thrown out of the country by my servants.

MEDEA

No, no, not that, I entreat you, Creon!

CREON

Woman, it seems you are bent on causing me annoyance.

MEDEA

I accept my exile: it was not exile I sought reprieve of.

CREON

Why then are you still applying force[a] and clinging to my hand?

MEDEA

Allow me to remain this one day and to complete my plans for exile and how I may provide for my children, since their father does not care to do so. Have pity on them. You too are a parent: it would be natural for you to show kindness toward them. I do not care if I myself go into exile. It is *their* experience of misfortune I weep for.

CREON

My nature is not at all a tyrant's, and by showing consideration I have often suffered loss. And now, though I

[a] The religious obligation to respect the suppliant is so great that those supplicated feel supplication as violence and constraint: cf. *Hippolytus* 325.

350 καὶ νῦν ὁρῶ μὲν ἐξαμαρτάνων, γύναι,
ὅμως δὲ τεύξῃ τοῦδε. προυννέπω δέ σοι,
εἴ σ' ἡ 'πιοῦσα λαμπὰς ὄψεται θεοῦ
καὶ παῖδας ἐντὸς τῆσδε τερμόνων χθονός,
θανῇ· λέλεκται μῦθος ἀψευδὴς ὅδε.

355 νῦν δ', εἰ μένειν δεῖ, μίμν' ἐφ' ἡμέραν μίαν·
οὐ γάρ τι δράσεις δεινὸν ὧν φόβος μ' ἔχει.

ΧΟΡΟΣ

[δύστανε γύναι,]
φεῦ φεῦ, μελέα τῶν σῶν ἀχέων.
ποῖ ποτε τρέψῃ; τίνα προξενίαν
360 ἢ δόμον ἢ χθόνα σωτῆρα κακῶν
ἐξευρήσεις;
ὡς εἰς ἄπορόν σε κλύδωνα θεός,
Μήδεια, κακῶν ἐπόρευσεν.

ΜΗΔΕΙΑ

κακῶς πέπρακται πανταχῇ· τίς ἀντερεῖ;
365 ἀλλ' οὔτι ταύτῃ ταῦτα, μὴ δοκεῖτέ πω,
<μέλλει τελευτᾶν εἴ τι τῇ τέχνῃ σθένω.>
ἔτ' εἴσ' ἀγῶνες τοῖς νεωστὶ νυμφίοις
καὶ τοῖσι κηδεύσασιν οὐ σμικροὶ πόνοι.
δοκεῖς γὰρ ἄν με τόνδε θωπεῦσαί ποτε
εἰ μή τι κερδαίνουσαν ἢ τεχνωμένην;
370 οὐδ' ἂν προσεῖπον οὐδ' ἂν ἡψάμην χεροῖν.
ὁ δ' ἐς τοσοῦτον μωρίας ἀφίκετο

357 δύστανε γύναι om. a: del. Matthiae: post 358 trai. Barthold
359 προξενίαν a: πρὸς ξενίαν b: cf. 724

see that I am making a serious mistake, nonetheless, woman, you shall have your request. But I warn you, if tomorrow's sun sees you and your children within the borders of this land, you will be put to death. I mean what I have said. Now stay, if stay you must, for one more day. You will not do the mischief I fear by then.

Exit CREON *by Eisodos B. Medea rises to her feet.*

CHORUS LEADER
[Unhappy woman,] O dear, crushed by your misfortunes, where will you turn? What protector of strangers will you find, what house, what land, to save you from calamity? A god has cast you, Medea, into a hopeless sea of troubles.

MEDEA
In every way the situation is bad: who will deny it? But it is not thus—do not imagine it—<that things will turn out in the end, if I have any power in my arts>.[a] There are still struggles for the newly wedded pair, and for the maker of the match difficulties that are not trifling. Do you think I would ever have fawned on this man unless I stood to gain, unless I were plotting? I would not even have spoken to him or touched him with my hands. But he has reached

---

[a] I give the probable sense of the lacuna.

365 post h.v. lacunam statui

ὥστ᾽, ἐξὸν αὐτῷ τἄμ᾽ ἑλεῖν βουλεύματα
γῆς ἐκβαλόντι, τήνδ᾽ ἐφῆκεν ἡμέραν
μεῖναί μ᾽, ἐν ᾗ τρεῖς τῶν ἐμῶν ἐχθρῶν νεκροὺς
375 θήσω, πατέρα τε καὶ κόρην πόσιν τ᾽ ἐμόν.
    πολλὰς δ᾽ ἔχουσα θανασίμους αὐτοῖς ὁδούς,
οὐκ οἶδ᾽ ὁποίᾳ πρῶτον ἐγχειρῶ, φίλαι·
πότερον ὑφάψω δῶμα νυμφικὸν πυρί,
[ἢ θηκτὸν ὤσω φάσγανον δι᾽ ἥπατος,]
380 σιγῇ δόμους ἐσβᾶσ᾽, ἵν᾽ ἔστρωται λέχος;
ἀλλ᾽ ἕν τί μοι πρόσαντες· εἰ ληφθήσομαι
δόμους ὑπερβαίνουσα καὶ τεχνωμένη,
θανοῦσα θήσω τοῖς ἐμοῖς ἐχθροῖς γέλων.
κράτιστα τὴν εὐθεῖαν, ᾗ πεφύκαμεν
385 σοφοὶ μάλιστα, φαρμάκοις αὐτοὺς ἑλεῖν.
    εἶεν·
καὶ δὴ τεθνᾶσι· τίς με δέξεται πόλις;
τίς γῆν ἄσυλον καὶ δόμους ἐχεγγύους
ξένος παρασχὼν ῥύσεται τοὐμὸν δέμας;
οὐκ ἔστι. μείνασ᾽ οὖν ἔτι σμικρὸν χρόνον,
390 ἢν μέν τις ἡμῖν πύργος ἀσφαλὴς φανῇ,
δόλῳ μέτειμι τόνδε καὶ σιγῇ φόνον·
ἢν δ᾽ ἐξελαύνῃ ξυμφορά μ᾽ ἀμήχανος,
αὐτὴ ξίφος λαβοῦσα, κεἰ μέλλω θανεῖν,
κτενῶ σφε, τόλμης δ᾽ εἶμι πρὸς τὸ καρτερόν.
395 οὐ γὰρ μὰ τὴν δέσποιναν ἣν ἐγὼ σέβω
μάλιστα πάντων καὶ ξυνεργὸν εἱλόμην,
Ἑκάτην, μυχοῖς ναίουσαν ἑστίας ἐμῆς,
χαίρων τις αὐτῶν τοὐμὸν ἀλγυνεῖ κέαρ.

such a pitch of folly that, while it lay in his power to check my plans by banishing me, he has permitted me to stay for this day, a day on which I shall make corpses of three of my enemies, the father, his daughter, and my husband.

Now since I possess many ways of killing them, I do not know which I should try first, my friends: shall I set the bridal chamber on fire, [or thrust a sharp sword through their vitals,] creeping into the house where the marriage bed is laid out? One thing, however, stands in my path: if I am caught entering the house and plotting its destruction, I will be killed and bring joy to my foes. Best to proceed by the direct route, in which I am the most skilled, and kill them with poison.

So be it! Now let us suppose they have been killed. What city will receive me? What friend will give me a safe country and a secure house and rescue me? There is no one. And so I shall wait a short time yet, and if some citadel of rescue appears, I shall go about this murder by stealth. But if hard circumstance forces me into the open, I shall take the sword and, even though I am sure to die for it, kill them with my own hand, going to the very utmost of daring. By the goddess I worship most of all, my chosen helper Hecate,[a] who dwells in the inner chamber of my house, none of them shall pain my heart and smile at

---

[a] Hecate, among her many functions, is connected with magic arts.

---

[373] ἐφῆκεν Nauck: ἀφ- C

[379] damnat, 380 interrogative punxit Willink, *CQ* 38 (1988), 313–23

[385] σοφοὶ Tate, Dalzel: σοφαὶ C

πικροὺς δ᾽ ἐγώ σφιν καὶ λυγροὺς θήσω γάμους,
400   πικρὸν δὲ κῆδος καὶ φυγὰς ἐμὰς χθονός.
ἀλλ᾽ εἶα φείδου μηδὲν ὧν ἐπίστασαι,
Μήδεια, βουλεύουσα καὶ τεχνωμένη·
ἕρπ᾽ ἐς τὸ δεινόν· νῦν ἀγὼν εὐψυχίας.
ὁρᾷς ἃ πάσχεις; οὐ γέλωτα δεῖ σ᾽ ὀφλεῖν
405   τοῖς Σισυφείοις τοῖσδ᾽ Ἰάσονος γάμοις,
γεγῶσαν ἐσθλοῦ πατρὸς Ἡλίου τ᾽ ἄπο.
ἐπίστασαι δέ· πρὸς δὲ καὶ πεφύκαμεν
γυναῖκες, ἐς μὲν ἐσθλ᾽ ἀμηχανώταται,
κακῶν δὲ πάντων τέκτονες σοφώταται.

ΧΟΡΟΣ

στρ. α
410   ἄνω ποταμῶν ἱερῶν χωροῦσι παγαί,
καὶ δίκα καὶ πάντα πάλιν στρέφεται·
ἀνδράσι μὲν δόλιαι βουλαί, θεῶν δ᾽
οὐκέτι πίστις ἄραρεν.

415   τὰν δ᾽ ἐμὰν εὔκλειαν ἔχειν βιοτὰν στρέψουσι φᾶμαι·
ἔρχεται τιμὰ γυναικείῳ γένει·

420   οὐκέτι δυσκέλαδος φάμα γυναῖκας ἕξει.

ἀντ. α
μοῦσαι δὲ παλαιγενέων λήξουσ᾽ ἀοιδῶν
τὰν ἐμὰν ὑμνεῦσαι ἀπιστοσύναν.
οὐ γὰρ ἐν ἁμετέρᾳ γνώμᾳ λύρας
425   ὤπασε θέσπιν ἀοιδὰν
Φοῖβος ἁγήτωρ μελέων· ἐπεὶ ἀντάχησ᾽ ἂν ὕμνον

405 τοῖσδ᾽ Herwerden: τοῖς τ᾽ C

it! Bitter and grievous will I make their union and bitter Creon's marriage alliance and his banishment of me from the land! Come, Medea, spare nothing of the arts you are mistress of as you plot and contrive! Into the fray! Now it is a contest of courage. Do you see what is being done to you? You must not suffer mockery from this Sisyphean[a] marriage of Jason, you who are sprung from a noble father and have Helios for your grandsire. You understand how to proceed. And furthermore we are women, unable to perform noble deeds, but most skilful architects of every sort of harm.

CHORUS

Backward to their sources flow the streams of holy rivers, and the order of all things is reversed: men's thoughts have become deceitful and their oaths by the gods do not hold fast. The common talk will so alter that women's ways will enjoy good repute. Honor is coming to the female sex: no more will women be maligned by slanderous rumor.

The poetry of ancient bards will cease to hymn our faithlessness. Phoebus lord of song never endowed our minds with the glorious strains of the lyre. Else I could have sounded a hymn in reply to the male sex. Time in its

[a] This wily Sisyphus, famed for dishonest trickery, was a Corinthian.

ἀρσένων γέννᾳ. μακρὸς δ᾽ αἰὼν ἔχει
430 πολλὰ μὲν ἁμετέραν ἀνδρῶν τε μοῖραν εἰπεῖν.

στρ. β

σὺ δ᾽ ἐκ μὲν οἴκων πατρίων ἔπλευσας
μαινομένᾳ κραδίᾳ διδύμους ὁρίσασα Πόν-
435 του πέτρας· ἐπὶ δὲ ξένᾳ
ναίεις χθονί, τᾶς ἀνάν-
δρου κοίτας ὀλέσασα λέκτρον,
τάλαινα, φυγὰς δὲ χώ-
ρας ἄτιμος ἐλαύνῃ.

ἀντ. β

βέβακε δ᾽ ὅρκων χάρις, οὐδ᾽ ἔτ᾽ αἰδὼς
440 Ἑλλάδι τᾷ μεγάλᾳ μένει, αἰθερία δ᾽ ἀνέ-
πτα. σοὶ δ᾽ οὔτε πατρὸς δόμοι,
δύστανε, μεθορμίσα-
σθαι μόχθων πάρα, σῶν τε λέκτρων
ἄλλα βασίλεια κρείσ-
445 σων δόμοισιν ἐπέστα.

ΙΑΣΩΝ

οὐ νῦν κατεῖδον πρῶτον ἀλλὰ πολλάκις
τραχεῖαν ὀργὴν ὡς ἀμήχανον κακόν.
σοὶ γὰρ παρὸν γῆν τήνδε καὶ δόμους ἔχειν
κούφως φερούσῃ κρεισσόνων βουλεύματα,
450 λόγων ματαίων οὕνεκ᾽ ἐκπεσῇ χθονός.
κἀμοὶ μὲν οὐδὲν πρᾶγμα· μὴ παύσῃ ποτὲ
λέγουσ᾽ Ἰάσον᾽ ὡς κάκιστός ἐστ᾽ ἀνήρ.

443 σῶν τε Porson: τῶνδε C

334

long expanse can say many things of men's lot as well as of women's.

But you sailed from your father's halls, passing with love-maddened heart between the twin rocks of the Black Sea. On strange soil you now dwell, you have lost your marriage bed, your husband's love, poor wretch, and you are being driven from this land an exile without rights.

The magical power of an oath has gone, and Shame is no more to be found in wide Hellas: she has taken wing to heaven. You have no father's home in which to find anchorage, unhappy woman, and another, a princess, greater match than yourself, holds sway in the house.

Enter JASON by Eisodos B.

JASON

Not now for the first time but often before I have seen what an impossible evil to deal with is a fierce temper. Although you could have kept this land and this house by patiently bearing with your superiors' arrangements, you will be exiled because of your foolish talk. Not that it bothers me: go on, if you like, calling Jason the basest man

ἃ δ' ἐς τυράννους ἐστί σοι λελεγμένα,
πᾶν κέρδος ἡγοῦ ζημιουμένη φυγῇ.

455 κἀγὼ μὲν αἰεὶ βασιλέων θυμουμένων
ὀργὰς ἀφῄρουν καί σ' ἐβουλόμην μένειν·
σὺ δ' οὐκ ἀνίεις μωρίας, λέγουσ' ἀεὶ
κακῶς τυράννους· τοιγὰρ ἐκπεσῇ χθονός.

ὅμως δὲ κἀκ τῶνδ' οὐκ ἀπειρηκὼς φίλοις
460 ἥκω, τὸ σὸν δὲ προσκοπούμενος, γύναι,
ὡς μήτ' ἀχρήμων σὺν τέκνοισιν ἐκπέσῃς
μήτ' ἐνδεής του· πόλλ' ἐφέλκεται φυγὴ
κακὰ ξὺν αὑτῇ. καὶ γὰρ εἰ σύ με στυγεῖς,
οὐκ ἂν δυναίμην σοὶ κακῶς φρονεῖν ποτε.

ΜΗΔΕΙΑ

465 ὦ παγκάκιστε, τοῦτο γάρ σ' εἰπεῖν ἔχω,
γλώσσῃ μέγιστον εἰς ἀνανδρίαν κακόν,
ἦλθες πρὸς ἡμᾶς, ἦλθες ἔχθιστος γεγώς
[θεοῖς τε κἀμοὶ παντί τ' ἀνθρώπων γένει];
οὔτοι θράσος τόδ' ἐστὶν οὐδ' εὐτολμία,
470 φίλους κακῶς δράσαντ' ἐναντίον βλέπειν,
ἀλλ' ἡ μεγίστη τῶν ἐν ἀνθρώποις νόσων
πασῶν, ἀναίδει'. εὖ δ' ἐποίησας μολών·
ἐγώ τε γὰρ λέξασα κουφισθήσομαι
ψυχὴν κακῶς σὲ καὶ σὺ λυπήσῃ κλύων.

475 ἐκ τῶν δὲ πρώτων πρῶτον ἄρξομαι λέγειν·
ἔσωσά σ', ὡς ἴσασιν Ἑλλήνων ὅσοι
ταὐτὸν συνεισέβησαν Ἀργῷον σκάφος,
πεμφθέντα ταύρων πυρπνόων ἐπιστάτην

alive. But as for your words against the ruling family, count yourself lucky that your punishment is exile. For my part I have always tried to soothe the king's angry temper, and I wanted you to stay. But you would not cease from your folly and always kept reviling the ruling house. For that you will be exiled.

Still, even after this I have not failed my loved ones but have come here in your interests, woman, so that you might not go into exile with your children penniless or in need of anything: exile brings many hardships with it. Even if you hate me, I could never bear you ill will.

MEDEA

Vilest of knaves—for that is the only name I can give you, the worst reproach tongue can frame against unmanly conduct—have you really come to see me when you have made yourself my worst enemy [to the gods, to me, and to the whole human race]? This is not boldness or courage—to wrong your loved ones and then look them in the face—but the worst of all mortal vices, shamelessness. But you did well to come, for it will relieve my feelings to tell you how wicked you are, and you will be stung by what I have to say.

I shall begin my speech from the beginning. I saved your life—as witness all the Greeks who went on board the Argo with you—when you were sent to master the fire-

---

[468] del. Brunck cl. 1324

ζεύγλαισι καὶ σπεροῦντα θανάσιμον γύην·
480 δράκοντά θ᾽, ὃς πάγχρυσον ἀμπέχων δέρος
σπείραις ἔσῳζε πολυπλόκοις ἄυπνος ὤν,
κτείνασ᾽ ἀνέσχον σοι φάος σωτήριον.
αὐτὴ δὲ πατέρα καὶ δόμους προδοῦσ᾽ ἐμοὺς
τὴν Πηλιῶτιν εἰς Ἰωλκὸν ἱκόμην
485 σὺν σοί, πρόθυμος μᾶλλον ἢ σοφωτέρα·
Πελίαν τ᾽ ἀπέκτειν᾽, ὥσπερ ἄλγιστον θανεῖν,
παίδων ὕπ᾽ αὐτοῦ, πάντα τ᾽ ἐξεῖλον δόμον.
καὶ ταῦθ᾽ ὑφ᾽ ἡμῶν, ὦ κάκιστ᾽ ἀνδρῶν, παθὼν
προύδωκας ἡμᾶς, καινὰ δ᾽ ἐκτήσω λέχη,
490 παίδων γεγώτων· εἰ γὰρ ἦσθ᾽ ἄπαις ἔτι,
συγγνώστ᾽ ἂν ἦν σοι τοῦδ᾽ ἐρασθῆναι λέχους.
      ὅρκων δὲ φρούδη πίστις, οὐδ᾽ ἔχω μαθεῖν
εἰ θεοὺς νομίζεις τοὺς τότ᾽ οὐκ ἄρχειν ἔτι
ἢ καινὰ κεῖσθαι θέσμι᾽ ἀνθρώποις τὰ νῦν,
495 ἐπεὶ σύνοισθά γ᾽ εἰς ἔμ᾽ οὐκ εὔορκος ὤν.
φεῦ δεξιὰ χείρ, ἧς σὺ πόλλ᾽ ἐλαμβάνου
καὶ τῶνδε γονάτων, ὡς μάτην κεχρῴσμεθα
κακοῦ πρὸς ἀνδρός, ἐλπίδων δ᾽ ἡμάρτομεν.
      ἄγ᾽, ὡς φίλῳ γὰρ ὄντι σοι κοινώσομαι
500 (δοκοῦσα μὲν τί πρός γε σοῦ πράξειν καλῶς;
ὅμως δ᾽, ἐρωτηθεὶς γὰρ αἰσχίων φανῇ)·
νῦν ποῖ τράπωμαι; πότερα πρὸς πατρὸς δόμους,
οὓς σοὶ προδοῦσα καὶ πάτραν ἀφικόμην;
ἢ πρὸς ταλαίνας Πελιάδας; καλῶς γ᾽ ἂν οὖν
505 δέξαιντό μ᾽ οἴκοις ὧν πατέρα κατέκτανον.
ἔχει γὰρ οὕτω· τοῖς μὲν οἴκοθεν φίλοις

breathing bulls with a yoke and to sow the field of death. The dragon who kept watch over the Golden Fleece, sleeplessly guarding it with his sinuous coils, I killed, and I raised aloft for you the fair light of escape from death. Of my own accord I abandoned my father and my home and came with you to Iolcus under Pelion, showing more love than prudence. I murdered Pelias by the most horrible of deaths—at the hand of his own daughters—and I destroyed his whole house. And after such benefits from me, o basest of men, you have betrayed me and have taken a new marriage, though we had children. For if you were still childless, your desire for this marriage would be understandable.

Respect for your oaths is gone, and I cannot tell whether you think that the gods of old no longer rule or that new ordinances have now been set up for mortals, since you are surely aware that you have not kept your oath to me. O right hand of mine, which you often grasped together with my knees, how profitless was the suppliant grasp upon me of a knave, and how I have been cheated of my hopes!

But come now—for I will share my thoughts with you as a friend (yet what benefit can I expect to get from *you*? Still I will do it, for you will be shown up in an uglier light by my questions)—where am I now to turn? To my father's house, which like my country I betrayed for your sake when I came here? Or to the wretched daughters of Pelias? A fine reception they would give me in their house since I killed their father! This is how things stand: to my own kin I have become an enemy, and by my services to

---

493 εἰ Reiske: ἢ vel ἤ C

ἐχθρὰ καθέστηχ᾽, οὓς δέ μ᾽ οὐκ ἐχρῆν κακῶς
δρᾶν, σοὶ χάριν φέρουσα πολεμίους ἔχω.
τοιγάρ με πολλαῖς μακαρίαν Ἑλληνίδων
510   ἔθηκας ἀντὶ τῶνδε· θαυμαστὸν δέ σε
ἔχω πόσιν καὶ πιστὸν ἡ τάλαιν᾽ ἐγώ,
εἰ φεύξομαί γε γαῖαν ἐκβεβλημένη,
φίλων ἔρημος, σὺν τέκνοις μόνη μόνοις·
καλόν γ᾽ ὄνειδος τῷ νεωστὶ νυμφίῳ,
515   πτωχοὺς ἀλᾶσθαι παῖδας ἥ τ᾽ ἔσωσά σε.
          ὦ Ζεῦ, τί δὴ χρυσοῦ μὲν ὃς κίβδηλος ᾖ
τεκμήρι᾽ ἀνθρώποισιν ὤπασας σαφῆ,
ἀνδρῶν δ᾽ ὅτῳ χρὴ τὸν κακὸν διειδέναι
οὐδεὶς χαρακτὴρ ἐμπέφυκε σώματι;

ΧΟΡΟΣ

520   δεινή τις ὀργὴ καὶ δυσίατος πέλει,
ὅταν φίλοι φίλοισι συμβάλωσ᾽ ἔριν.

ΙΑΣΩΝ

δεῖ μ᾽, ὡς ἔοικε, μὴ κακὸν φῦναι λέγειν,
ἀλλ᾽ ὥστε ναὸς κεδνὸν οἰακοστρόφον
ἄκροισι λαίφους κρασπέδοις ὑπεκδραμεῖν
525   τὴν σὴν στόμαργον, ὦ γύναι, γλωσσαλγίαν.
ἐγὼ δ᾽, ἐπειδὴ καὶ λίαν πυργοῖς χάριν,
Κύπριν νομίζω τῆς ἐμῆς ναυκληρίας
σώτειραν εἶναι θεῶν τε κἀνθρώπων μόνην.
σοὶ δ᾽ ἔστι μὲν νοῦς λεπτός — ἀλλ᾽ ἐπίφθονος
530   λόγος διελθεῖν ὡς Ἔρως σ᾽ ἠνάγκασεν
τόξοις ἀφύκτοις τοὐμὸν ἐκσῶσαι δέμας.

MEDEA

you I have made foes of those I ought not to have harmed.
That, doubtless, is why you have made me so happy in the
eyes of many Greek women, in return for these favors! I,
poor wretch, have in you a wonderful and faithful husband
if I am to flee the country, sent into exile, deprived of
friends, abandoned with my abandoned children! What a
fine reproach for a new bridegroom, that his children are
wandering as beggars, and she who saved him likewise!

O Zeus, why, when you gave to men sure signs of gold
that is counterfeit, is there no mark on the human body by
which one could identify base *men*?

CHORUS LEADER

Terrible and hard to heal is the wrath that comes when kin
join in conflict with kin.

JASON

It appears, woman, that I must be no mean speaker but
like the good helmsman of a ship reef my sail up to its hem
and run before the storm of your wearisome prattling.
Since you so exaggerate your kindness to me, I for my part
think that Aphrodite alone of gods and mortals was the
savior of my expedition. As for you, I grant you have a
clever mind—but to tell how Eros forced you with his
ineluctable arrows to save me would expose me to ill will.

341

ἀλλ' οὐκ ἀκριβῶς αὐτὸ θήσομαι λίαν·
ὅπῃ γὰρ οὖν ὤνησας οὐ κακῶς ἔχει.
μείζω γε μέντοι τῆς ἐμῆς σωτηρίας
535 εἴληφας ἢ δέδωκας, ὡς ἐγὼ φράσω.
πρῶτον μὲν Ἑλλάδ' ἀντὶ βαρβάρου χθονὸς
γαῖαν κατοικεῖς καὶ δίκην ἐπίστασαι
νόμοις τε χρῆσθαι μὴ πρὸς ἰσχύος χάριν·
πάντες δέ σ' ᾔσθοντ' οὖσαν Ἕλληνες σοφὴν
540 καὶ δόξαν ἔσχες· εἰ δὲ γῆς ἐπ' ἐσχάτοις
ὅροισιν ᾤκεις, οὐκ ἂν ἦν λόγος σέθεν.
εἴη δ' ἔμοιγε μήτε χρυσὸς ἐν δόμοις
μήτ' Ὀρφέως κάλλιον ὑμνῆσαι μέλος,
εἰ μὴ 'πίσημος ἡ τύχη γένοιτό μοι.
545 τοσαῦτα μέν σοι τῶν ἐμῶν πόνων πέρι
ἔλεξ'· ἅμιλλαν γὰρ σὺ προύθηκας λόγων.
ἃ δ' ἐς γάμους μοι βασιλικοὺς ὠνείδισας,
ἐν τῷδε δείξω πρῶτα μὲν σοφὸς γεγώς,
ἔπειτα σώφρων, εἶτα σοὶ μέγας φίλος
550 καὶ παισὶ τοῖς ἐμοῖσιν — ἀλλ' ἔχ' ἥσυχος.
ἐπεὶ μετέστην δεῦρ' Ἰωλκίας χθονὸς
πολλὰς ἐφέλκων συμφορὰς ἀμηχάνους,
τί τοῦδ' ἂν εὕρημ' ηὗρον εὐτυχέστερον
ἢ παῖδα γῆμαι βασιλέως φυγὰς γεγώς;
555 οὐχ, ᾗ σὺ κνίζῃ, σὸν μὲν ἐχθαίρων λέχος
καινῆς δὲ νύμφης ἱμέρῳ πεπληγμένος
οὐδ' εἰς ἅμιλλαν πολύτεκνον σπουδὴν ἔχων·
ἅλις γὰρ οἱ γεγῶτες οὐδὲ μέμφομαι·
ἀλλ' ὡς, τὸ μὲν μέγιστον, οἰκοῖμεν καλῶς

No, I will not make too strict a reckoning on this point. So
far as you *did* help me, you did well. But in return for sav-
ing me you got more than you gave, as I shall make clear.
First, you now live among Greeks and not barbarians, and
you understand justice and the rule of law, with no conces-
sion to force. All the Greeks have learned that you are
clever, and you have won renown. But if you lived at the
world's edge, there would be no talk of you. Neither gold
in my house nor the power to sing songs sweeter than
Orpheus is my prayer without fame to grace my lot!

Thus far I have spoken to you regarding my labors: for
it was you who started this contest of words. As for your
reproaches to me against my royal marriage, here I shall
show, first, that I am wise, second, self-controlled, and
third a great friend to you and my children.

Medea makes a gesture of impatience.

No! Hold your peace! When I first moved here from the
land of Iolcus, bringing with me many misfortunes hard to
deal with, what luckier find than this could I have made,
marriage with the daughter of the king, though I was an
exile? It was not—the point that seems to irk you—that I
was weary of your bed and smitten with desire for a new
bride, nor was I eager to rival others in the number of my
children (we have enough already and I make no com-
plaint) but my purpose was that we should live well—

343

560　καὶ μὴ σπανιζοίμεσθα, γιγνώσκων ὅτι
　　　πένητα φεύγει πᾶς τις ἐκποδὼν φίλον,
　　　παῖδας δὲ θρέψαιμ᾽ ἀξίως δόμων ἐμῶν
　　　σπείρας τ᾽ ἀδελφοὺς τοῖσιν ἐκ σέθεν τέκνοις
　　　ἐς ταὐτὸ θείην καὶ ξυναρτήσας γένος
565　εὐδαιμονοίην. σοί τε γὰρ παίδων τί δεῖ;
　　　ἐμοί τε λύει τοῖσι μέλλουσιν τέκνοις
　　　τὰ ζῶντ᾽ ὀνῆσαι. μῶν βεβούλευμαι κακῶς;
　　　οὐδ᾽ ἂν σὺ φαίης, εἴ σε μὴ κνίζοι λέχος.
　　　ἀλλ᾽ ἐς τοσοῦτον ἥκεθ᾽ ὥστ᾽ ὀρθουμένης
570　εὐνῆς γυναῖκες πάντ᾽ ἔχειν νομίζετε,
　　　ἢν δ᾽ αὖ γένηται ξυμφορά τις ἐς λέχος,
　　　τὰ λῷστα καὶ κάλλιστα πολεμιώτατα
　　　τίθεσθε. χρῆν γὰρ ἄλλοθέν ποθεν βροτοὺς
　　　παῖδας τεκνοῦσθαι, θῆλυ δ᾽ οὐκ εἶναι γένος·
575　χοὕτως ἂν οὐκ ἦν οὐδὲν ἀνθρώποις κακόν.

ΧΟΡΟΣ

　　　Ἰᾶσον, εὖ μὲν τούσδ᾽ ἐκόσμησας λόγους·
　　　ὅμως δ᾽ ἔμοιγε, κεἰ παρὰ γνώμην ἐρῶ,
　　　δοκεῖς προδοὺς σὴν ἄλοχον οὐ δίκαια δρᾶν.

ΜΗΔΕΙΑ

　　　ἦ πολλὰ πολλοῖς εἰμι διάφορος βροτῶν·
580　ἐμοὶ γὰρ ὅστις ἄδικος ὢν σοφὸς λέγειν
　　　πέφυκε πλείστην ζημίαν ὀφλισκάνει·
　　　γλώσσῃ γὰρ αὐχῶν τἄδικ᾽ εὖ περιστελεῖν
　　　τολμᾷ πανουργεῖν· ἔστι δ᾽ οὐκ ἄγαν σοφός.
　　　ὡς καὶ σύ· μή νυν εἰς ἔμ᾽ εὐσχήμων γένῃ

which is the main thing—and not be in want, knowing that everyone goes out of his way to avoid a penniless friend. I wanted to raise the children in a manner befitting my house, to beget brothers to the children born from you, and put them on the same footing with them, so that by drawing the family into one I might prosper. For your part, what need have you of any more children? For me, it is advantageous to use future children to benefit those already born. Was this a bad plan? Not even you would say so if you were not galled by the matter of sex. But you women are so far gone in folly that if all is well in bed you think you have everything, while if some misfortune in that domain occurs, you regard as hateful your best and truest interests. Mortals ought to beget children from some other source, and there should be no female sex. Then mankind would have no trouble.

CHORUS LEADER

Jason, you have marshalled your arguments very skilfully, but I think, even though it may be imprudent to say so, that in abandoning your wife you are not doing right.

MEDEA

I realize I have far different views from the majority of mortals. To my mind, the plausible speaker who is a scoundrel incurs the greatest punishment. For since he is confident that he can cleverly cloak injustice with his words, his boldness stops at no knavery. Yet he is not as wise as all that. So it is with you. Do not, therefore, give

---

561 φίλον Driver cl. *El.* 1131: φίλος C
573 τἄρ' Kirchhoff: γὰρ C
575 χοὕτως a: οὕτως δ' b: οὕτως Blaydes

585 λέγειν τε δεινός. ἓν γὰρ ἐκτενεῖ σ᾽ ἔπος·
χρῆν σ᾽, εἴπερ ἦσθα μὴ κακός, πείσαντά με
γαμεῖν γάμον τόνδ᾽, ἀλλὰ μὴ σιγῇ φίλων.

ΙΑΣΩΝ

καλῶς γ᾽ ἄν, οἶμαι, τῷδ᾽ ὑπηρέτεις λόγῳ,
εἴ σοι γάμον κατεῖπον, ἥτις οὐδὲ νῦν
590 τολμᾷς μεθεῖναι καρδίας μέγαν χόλον.

ΜΗΔΕΙΑ

οὐ τοῦτό σ᾽ εἶχεν, ἀλλὰ βάρβαρον λέχος
πρὸς γῆρας οὐκ εὔδοξον ἐξέβαινέ σοι.

ΙΑΣΩΝ

εὖ νυν τόδ᾽ ἴσθι, μὴ γυναικὸς οὕνεκα
γῆμαί με λέκτρα βασιλέων ἃ νῦν ἔχω,
595 ἀλλ᾽, ὥσπερ εἶπον καὶ πάρος, σῶσαι θέλων
σέ, καὶ τέκνοισι τοῖς ἐμοῖς ὁμοσπόρους
φῦσαι τυράννους παῖδας, ἔρυμα δώμασιν.

ΜΗΔΕΙΑ

μή μοι γένοιτο λυπρὸς εὐδαίμων βίος
μηδ᾽ ὄλβος ὅστις τὴν ἐμὴν κνίζοι φρένα.

ΙΑΣΩΝ

600 οἶσθ᾽ ὡς μετεύξῃ καὶ σοφωτέρα φανῇ;
τὰ χρηστὰ μή σοι λυπρὰ φαίνεσθαί ποτε,
μηδ᾽ εὐτυχοῦσα δυστυχὴς εἶναι δοκεῖν.

600 μέτευξαι Elmsley

346

me your specious arguments and oratory, for one word will lay you out: if you were not a knave, you ought to have gained my consent before making this marriage, not done it behind your family's back.

JASON

Fine support, I think, would you have given to my proposal if I had mentioned the marriage to you, seeing that even now you cannot bring yourself to lay aside the towering rage in your heart.

MEDEA

It was not this. You thought that in later years a barbarian wife would discredit you.

JASON

You may be quite sure of this, that it was not for the sake of a woman that I married the royal bride I now have, but as I have just said, because I wanted to save you and to beget princes as brothers to my children, to be a bulwark for the house.

MEDEA

A prosperous life that causes pain is no wish of mine, nor do I want any wealth that torments my heart!

JASON

Do you know how to change your prayer and show yourself the wiser? Pray that you may never consider advantage painful nor think yourself wretched when you are fortunate!

ΜΗΔΕΙΑ

ὕβριζ᾽, ἐπειδὴ σοὶ μὲν ἔστ᾽ ἀποστροφή,
ἐγὼ δ᾽ ἔρημος τήνδε φευξοῦμαι χθόνα.

ΙΑΣΩΝ

605 αὐτὴ τάδ᾽ εἵλου· μηδέν᾽ ἄλλον αἰτιῶ.

ΜΗΔΕΙΑ

τί δρῶσα; μῶν γαμοῦσα καὶ προδοῦσά σε;

ΙΑΣΩΝ

ἀρὰς τυράννοις ἀνοσίους ἀρωμένη.

ΜΗΔΕΙΑ

καὶ σοῖς ἀραία γ᾽ οὖσα τυγχάνω δόμοις.

ΙΑΣΩΝ

ὡς οὐ κρινοῦμαι τῶνδέ σοι τὰ πλείονα.
610 ἀλλ᾽, εἴ τι βούλῃ παισὶν ἢ σαυτῇ φυγῆς
προσωφέλημα χρημάτων ἐμῶν λαβεῖν,
λέγ᾽· ὡς ἕτοιμος ἀφθόνῳ δοῦναι χερὶ
ξένοις τε πέμπειν σύμβολ᾽, οἳ δράσουσί σ᾽ εὖ.
καὶ ταῦτα μὴ θέλουσα μωρανεῖς, γύναι·
615 λήξασα δ᾽ ὀργῆς κερδανεῖς ἀμείνονα.

ΜΗΔΕΙΑ

οὔτ᾽ ἂν ξένοισι τοῖσι σοῖς χρησαίμεθ᾽ ἂν
οὔτ᾽ ἄν τι δεξαίμεσθα, μηδ᾽ ἡμῖν δίδου·
κακοῦ γὰρ ἀνδρὸς δῶρ᾽ ὄνησιν οὐκ ἔχει.

MEDEA

Go on, insult me! You have a refuge, but I go friendless into exile.

JASON

You yourself chose that. You have no one else to blame.

MEDEA

How? By taking another wife and abandoning you?

JASON

By uttering unholy curses against the royal family.

MEDEA

Yes, and I am a curse to your house too.

JASON

I shall not argue any more of this case with you. But if you wish to get some of my money to help the children and yourself in exile, say the word, for I am ready to give with unstinting hand, and also to send tokens[a] to my friends, who will treat you well. You would be a fool not to accept this offer, woman. Forget your anger and it will be the better for you.

MEDEA

I will accept no help from your friends nor will I take anything from you, so do not offer it. The gifts of a base man bring no benefit.

[a] The *sumbolon* is a knucklebone sawed in half and used to serve as a letter of introduction. The host can recognize someone sent to enjoy his hospitality by fitting the half he has with the guest's half.

ΙΑΣΩΝ

ἀλλ' οὖν ἐγὼ μὲν δαίμονας μαρτύρομαι
620 ὡς πάνθ' ὑπουργεῖν σοί τε καὶ τέκνοις θέλω·
σοὶ δ' οὐκ ἀρέσκει τἀγάθ', ἀλλ' αὐθαδίᾳ
φίλους ἀπωθῇ· τοιγὰρ ἀλγυνῇ πλέον.

ΜΗΔΕΙΑ

χώρει· πόθῳ γὰρ τῆς νεοδμήτου κόρης
αἱρῇ χρονίζων δωμάτων ἐξώπιος.
625 νύμφευ'· ἴσως γάρ — σὺν θεῷ δ' εἰρήσεται —
γαμεῖς τοιοῦτον ὥστε θρηνεῖσθαι γάμον.

ΧΟΡΟΣ

στρ. α

ἔρωτες ὑπὲρ μὲν ἄγαν ἐλθόντες οὐκ εὐδοξίαν
630 οὐδ' ἀρετὰν παρέδωκαν ἀνδράσιν· εἰ δ' ἅλις ἔλθοι
Κύπρις, οὐκ ἄλλα θεὸς εὔχαρις οὕτως.
μήποτ', ὦ δέσποιν', ἐπ' ἐμοὶ χρυσέων
τόξων ἀφείης ἱμέρῳ
635 χρίσασ' ἄφυκτον οἰστόν.

ἀντ. α

στέργοι δέ με σωφροσύνα, δώρημα κάλλιστον θεῶν·
μηδέ ποτ' ἀμφιλόγους ὀργὰς ἀκόρεστά τε νείκη
640 θυμὸν ἐκπλήξασ' ἑτέροις ἐπὶ λέκτροις
προσβάλοι δεινὰ Κύπρις, ἀπτολέμους δ'
εὐνὰς σεβίζουσ' ὀξύφρων
κρίνοι λέχη γυναικῶν.

626 θρηνεῖσθαι Dodds: σ' ἀρνεῖσθαι C
634 ἀφείης Naber: ἐφείης fere C

JASON

At any rate I call the gods to witness that I am willing to help you and the children all I can. But you refuse good treatment and obstinately rebuff your friends. This will only make your pain the greater.

MEDEA

Go: it is clear that you are seized by longing for your new bride as you linger so long out of the palace! Go, play the bridegroom! For perhaps—and this will prove to be prophetic—you will make such a marriage as to cause you to weep.

Exit JASON by Eisodos B.

CHORUS

Loves that come to us in excess bring no good name or goodness to men. If Aphrodite comes in moderation, no other goddess brings such happiness. Never, o goddess, may you smear with desire one of your ineluctable arrows and let it fly against my heart from your golden bow!

May moderation attend me, fairest gift of the gods! May Aphrodite never cast contentious wrath and insatiate quarreling upon me and madden my heart with love for a stranger's bed! But may she honor marriages that are peaceful and wisely determine whom we are to wed!

στρ. β

ὦ πατρίς, ὦ δώματα, μὴ
δῆτ᾽ ἄπολις γενοίμαν
τὸν ἀμηχανίας ἔχουσα
δυσπέρατον αἰῶ,
οἰκτρότατον <γ᾽> ἀχέων.
650 θανάτῳ θανάτῳ πάρος δαμείην
ἁμέραν τάνδ᾽ ἐξανύσασα· μό-
χθων δ᾽ οὐκ ἄλλος ὕπερθεν ἢ
γᾶς πατρίας στέρεσθαι.

ἀντ. β

εἴδομεν, οὐκ ἐξ ἑτέρων
655 μῦθον ἔχω φράσασθαι·
σὲ γὰρ οὐ πόλις, οὐ φίλων τις
οἰκτιρεῖ παθοῦσαν
δεινότατον παθέων.
ἀχάριστος ὄλοιθ᾽ ὅτῳ πάρεστιν
660 μὴ φίλους τιμᾶν καθαρὰν ἀνοί-
ξαντα κλῇδα φρενῶν· ἐμοὶ
μὲν φίλος οὔποτ᾽ ἔσται.

ΑΙΓΕΥΣ

Μήδεια, χαῖρε· τοῦδε γὰρ προοίμιον
κάλλιον οὐδεὶς οἶδε προσφωνεῖν φίλους.

ΜΗΔΕΙΑ

665 ὦ χαῖρε καὶ σύ, παῖ σοφοῦ Πανδίονος,
Αἰγεῦ. πόθεν γῆς τῆσδ᾽ ἐπιστροφᾷ πέδον;

MEDEA

O fatherland, o house, may I never be bereft of my city,
never have a life of helplessness, a cruel life, most pitiable
of woes! In death, o in death may I be brought low ere
that, bringing my life's daylight to an end! Of troubles
none is greater than to be robbed of one's native land.

We ourselves have seen it; it is not from others' report
that we can tell this tale. No city, no friend will take pity
on you who have suffered the most grievous of sufferings.
May that man die unloved who cannot honor his friends,
unlocking to them his honest mind! To me at any rate he
shall never be friend.

Enter by Eisodos A AEGEUS, *the aged king of Athens, in
travelling costume.*

AEGEUS
Medea, I wish you joy: no one knows a better way than
this to address a friend.

MEDEA
Joy to you as well, Aegeus, son of wise Pandion! Where
have you come from to be visiting the soil of this land?

---

648 αἰῶ Stinton: αἰῶν' C
649 <γ'> Willink
657 οἰκτιρεῖ Wieseler: ᾤκτειρε(ν) C

ΑΙΓΕΥΣ

Φοίβου παλαιὸν ἐκλιπὼν χρηστήριον.

ΜΗΔΕΙΑ

τί δ' ὀμφαλὸν γῆς θεσπιῳδὸν ἐστάλης;

ΑΙΓΕΥΣ

παίδων ἐρευνῶν σπέρμ' ὅπως γένοιτό μοι.

ΜΗΔΕΙΑ

670   πρὸς θεῶν, ἄπαις γὰρ δεῦρ' ἀεὶ τείνεις βίον;

ΑΙΓΕΥΣ

ἄπαιδές ἐσμεν δαίμονός τινος τύχῃ.

ΜΗΔΕΙΑ

δάμαρτος οὔσης ἢ λέχους ἄπειρος ὤν;

ΑΙΓΕΥΣ

οὐκ ἐσμὲν εὐνῆς ἄζυγες γαμηλίου.

ΜΗΔΕΙΑ

τί δῆτα Φοῖβος εἶπέ σοι παίδων πέρι;

ΑΙΓΕΥΣ

675   σοφώτερ' ἢ κατ' ἄνδρα συμβαλεῖν ἔπη.

ΜΗΔΕΙΑ

θέμις μὲν ἡμᾶς χρησμὸν εἰδέναι θεοῦ;

ΑΙΓΕΥΣ

μάλιστ', ἐπεί τοι καὶ σοφῆς δεῖται φρενός.

ΜΗΔΕΙΑ

τί δῆτ' ἔχρησε; λέξον, εἰ θέμις κλυεῖν.

MEDEA

AEGEUS

I have come from the ancient oracle of Phoebus.

MEDEA

Why did you go to earth's prophetic center?

AEGEUS

To inquire how I might get offspring.

MEDEA

Have you really lived so long a life without children?

AEGEUS

I am childless: it is the act of some god.

MEDEA

Have you a wife, or have you no experience of marriage?

AEGEUS

I am not without a wife to share my bed.

MEDEA

What then did Phoebus tell you about children?

AEGEUS

Words too wise for mortal to interpret.

MEDEA

Is it lawful for me to hear the response?

AEGEUS

Most certainly: it calls for a wise mind.

MEDEA

What then did the god say? Tell me, if it is lawful to hear.

ΑΙΓΕΥΣ

ἀσκοῦ με τὸν προύχοντα μὴ λῦσαι πόδα . . .

ΜΗΔΕΙΑ

680   πρὶν ἂν τί δράσῃς ἢ τίν' ἐξίκῃ χθόνα;

ΑΙΓΕΥΣ

πρὶν ἂν πατρῴαν αὖθις ἑστίαν μόλω.

ΜΗΔΕΙΑ

σὺ δ' ὡς τί χρῄζων τήνδε ναυστολεῖς χθόνα;

ΑΙΓΕΥΣ

Πιτθεύς τις ἔστι, γῆς ἄναξ Τροζηνίας.

ΜΗΔΕΙΑ

παῖς, ὡς λέγουσι, Πέλοπος, εὐσεβέστατος.

ΑΙΓΕΥΣ

685   τούτῳ θεοῦ μάντευμα κοινῶσαι θέλω.

ΜΗΔΕΙΑ

σοφὸς γὰρ ἀνὴρ καὶ τρίβων τὰ τοιάδε.

ΑΙΓΕΥΣ

κἀμοί γε πάντων φίλτατος δορυξένων.

MEDEA

AEGEUS

"Do not the wineskin's salient foot untie . . ."

MEDEA

Until you do what or come to what country?

AEGEUS

". . . until you come to hearth and home again."[a]

MEDEA

And what were you in need of that you sailed to this land?

AEGEUS

There is a man named Pittheus, king of Trozen.

MEDEA

The son of Pelops and a man most pious, they say.

AEGEUS

It is with him that I wish to share the god's response.

MEDEA

The man is wise and experienced in such matters.

AEGEUS

What is more, he is closest of all my allies.

---

[a] Aegeus is bidden in the oracle's riddling terms not to have sexual intercourse before he reaches home. This oracle, which may be Euripides' own invention, clearly does not belong with the usual story, by which Aegeus has intercourse with Aethra, daughter of Pittheus, in Trozen and thus begets Theseus. For how could Aegeus beget a son if he violated the oracle's instructions? There is no indication in our play that Aegeus goes to Trozen from Corinth and some suggestion in 759–60 that he is bound directly for Athens.

EURIPIDES

ΜΗΔΕΙΑ
ἀλλ᾽ εὐτυχοίης καὶ τύχοις ὅσων ἐρᾷς.

ΑΙΓΕΥΣ
τί γὰρ σὸν ὄμμα χρώς τε συντέτηχ᾽ ὅδε;

ΜΗΔΕΙΑ
690 Αἰγεῦ, κάκιστός ἐστί μοι πάντων πόσις.

ΑΙΓΕΥΣ
τί φῇς; σαφῶς μοι σὰς φράσον δυσθυμίας.

ΜΗΔΕΙΑ
ἀδικεῖ μ᾽ Ἰάσων οὐδὲν ἐξ ἐμοῦ παθών.

ΑΙΓΕΥΣ
τί χρῆμα δράσας; φράζε μοι σαφέστερον.

ΜΗΔΕΙΑ
γυναῖκ᾽ ἐφ᾽ ἡμῖν δεσπότιν δόμων ἔχει.

ΑΙΓΕΥΣ
695 οὔ που τετόλμηκ᾽ ἔργον αἴσχιστον τόδε;

ΜΗΔΕΙΑ
σάφ᾽ ἴσθ᾽· ἄτιμοι δ᾽ ἐσμὲν οἱ πρὸ τοῦ φίλοι.

ΑΙΓΕΥΣ
πότερον ἐρασθεὶς ἢ σὸν ἐχθαίρων λέχος;

ΜΗΔΕΙΑ
μέγαν γ᾽ ἔρωτα· πιστὸς οὐκ ἔφυ φίλοις.

358

MEDEA

Well good luck attend you, and may you obtain what you
desire!

AEGEUS

(*noticing Medea's distraught demeanor*) But why is your
face dissolved in tears?

MEDEA

Aegeus, my husband is the basest of men.

AEGEUS

What is this you say? Tell me particulars of your unhappi-
ness.

MEDEA

Jason wrongs me, though he has suffered no wrong from
me.

AEGEUS

What has he done? Tell me more plainly.

MEDEA

He has put another woman over me as mistress of the
house.

AEGEUS

Surely he has not dared to do such a shameful deed?

MEDEA

He has indeed. Once he loved me, but now I am cast off.

AEGEUS

Was it some passion, or did he grow tired of your bed?

MEDEA

A great passion. He has been unfaithful to his family.

ΑΙΓΕΥΣ

ἴτω νυν, εἴπερ, ὡς λέγεις, ἐστὶν κακός.

ΜΗΔΕΙΑ

700 ἀνδρῶν τυράννων κῆδος ἠράσθη λαβεῖν.

ΑΙΓΕΥΣ

δίδωσι δ᾽ αὐτῷ τίς; πέραινέ μοι λόγον.

ΜΗΔΕΙΑ

Κρέων, ὃς ἄρχει τῆσδε γῆς Κορινθίας.

ΑΙΓΕΥΣ

συγγνωστὰ μέντἄρ᾽ ἦν σε λυπεῖσθαι, γύναι.

ΜΗΔΕΙΑ

ὄλωλα· καὶ πρός γ᾽ ἐξελαύνομαι χθονός.

ΑΙΓΕΥΣ

705 πρὸς τοῦ; τόδ᾽ ἄλλο καινὸν αὖ λέγεις κακόν.

ΜΗΔΕΙΑ

Κρέων μ᾽ ἐλαύνει φυγάδα γῆς Κορινθίας.

ΑΙΓΕΥΣ

ἐᾷ δ᾽ Ἰάσων; οὐδὲ ταῦτ᾽ ἐπήνεσα.

ΜΗΔΕΙΑ

λόγῳ μὲν οὐχί, καρτερεῖν δὲ βούλεται.
    ἀλλ᾽ ἄντομαί σε τῆσδε πρὸς γενειάδος
710 γονάτων τε τῶν σῶν ἱκεσία τε γίγνομαι,
οἴκτιρον οἴκτιρόν με τὴν δυσδαίμονα
καὶ μή μ᾽ ἔρημον ἐκπεσοῦσαν εἰσίδῃς,
δέξαι δὲ χώρᾳ καὶ δόμοις ἐφέστιον.

MEDEA

AEGEUS

Pay him no mind then since, as you say, he is base.

MEDEA

His passion was to marry a king's daughter.

AEGEUS

Who has given his daughter to him? Tell me the rest.

MEDEA

Creon, who rules this land of Corinth.

AEGEUS

But it is quite understandable, then, that you are distressed!

MEDEA

My life is ruined! Furthermore, I am being exiled from the country.

AEGEUS

By whom? This is yet another misfortune you speak of.

MEDEA

It is Creon who exiles me from Corinth.

AEGEUS

Does Jason accede to this? I do not approve of that either.

MEDEA

He pretends not to, but he is ready to put up with it.

Medea kneels before Aegeus in the posture of a suppliant.

But I beg you by your beard and by your knees and I make myself your suppliant: have pity, have pity on an unfortunate woman, and do not allow me to be cast into exile without a friend, but receive me into your land and

οὕτως ἔρως σοι πρὸς θεῶν τελεσφόρος
715 γένοιτο παίδων καὐτὸς ὄλβιος θάνοις.
εὕρημα δ' οὐκ οἶσθ' οἷον ηὕρηκας τόδε·
παύσω γέ σ' ὄντ' ἄπαιδα καὶ παίδων γονὰς
σπεῖραί σε θήσω· τοιάδ' οἶδα φάρμακα.

ΑΙΓΕΥΣ

πολλῶν ἕκατι τήνδε σοι δοῦναι χάριν,
720 γύναι, πρόθυμός εἰμι, πρῶτα μὲν θεῶν,
ἔπειτα παίδων ὧν ἐπαγγέλλῃ γονάς·
ἐς τοῦτο γὰρ δὴ φροῦδός εἰμι πᾶς ἐγώ.
οὕτω δ' ἔχει μοι· σοῦ μὲν ἐλθούσης χθόνα,
πειράσομαί σου προξενεῖν δίκαιος ὤν.
725 τοσόνδε μέντοι σοι προσημαίνω, γύναι·
ἐκ τῆσδε μὲν γῆς οὔ σ' ἄγειν βουλήσομαι,
αὐτὴ δ' ἐάνπερ εἰς ἐμοὺς ἔλθῃς δόμους,
μενεῖς ἄσυλος κοὔ σε μὴ μεθῶ τινι.
ἐκ τῆσδε δ' αὐτὴ γῆς ἀπαλλάσσου πόδα·
730 ἀναίτιος γὰρ καὶ ξένοις εἶναι θέλω.

ΜΗΔΕΙΑ

ἔσται τάδ'· ἀλλὰ πίστις εἰ γένοιτό μοι
τούτων, ἔχοιμ' ἂν πάντα πρὸς σέθεν καλῶς.

ΑΙΓΕΥΣ

μῶν οὐ πέποιθας; ἢ τί σοι τὸ δυσχερές;

ΜΗΔΕΙΑ

πέποιθα· Πελίου δ' ἐχθρός ἐστί μοι δόμος
735 Κρέων τε. τούτοις ὁρκίοισι μὲν ζυγεὶς
ἄγουσιν οὐ μεθεῖ' ἂν ἐκ γαίας ἐμέ·

your house as a suppliant. As you grant my request, so
may your longing for children be brought to fulfillment by
the gods, and may you yourself die happy! You do not
know what a lucky find you have made in me. I will put an
end to your childlessness and cause you to beget children,
for I know the medicines to do it.

AEGEUS

Dear woman, for many reasons I am eager to grant you
this favor, first, for the sake of the gods, then for the chil-
dren you promise I will beget. For on that score I am
utterly undone. But here is how matters stand with me. If
you come to my country, I shall in justice try to act as your
protector. This much, however, I tell you in advance: I
will not consent to take you from this land. But if you
manage by yourself to come to my house, you may stay
there in safety, and I will never give you up to anyone. You
must go on your own, then, from this land. I wish to be
blameless in the eyes of my hosts as well.

MEDEA

It shall be so. But if you were to give me a promise of this,
I would have all I could wish from you.

AEGEUS

Do you not trust me? What is it you find difficult?

MEDEA

I trust you. But Pelias' house is hostile to me, and Creon
as well. If you are bound by an oath, you will not give me
up to them when they come to take me out of the country.

---

717 γέ F. W. Schmidt: δέ C: v. del. Nauck
725–6 om. Π: 725–8 del. Kirchhoff   732 ἔχοι τᾱν Seyffert
735 τούτοις Wecklein: τ. δ' fere C

EURIPIDES

λόγοις δὲ συμβὰς καὶ θεῶν ἀνώμοτος
φίλος γένοι᾽ ἂν κἀπικηρυκεύμασιν
τάχ᾽ ἂν πίθοιο· τἀμὰ μὲν γὰρ ἀσθενῆ,
740 τοῖς δ᾽ ὄλβος ἐστὶ καὶ δόμος τυραννικός.

ΑΙΓΕΥΣ

πολλὴν ἔδειξας ἐν λόγοις προμηθίαν·
ἀλλ᾽, εἰ δοκεῖ σοι, δρᾶν τάδ᾽ οὐκ ἀφίσταμαι.
ἐμοί τε γὰρ τάδ᾽ ἐστὶν ἀσφαλέστερα,
σκῆψίν τιν᾽ ἐχθροῖς σοῖς ἔχοντα δεικνύναι,
745 τὸ σόν τ᾽ ἄραρε μᾶλλον· ἐξηγοῦ θεούς.

ΜΗΔΕΙΑ

ὄμνυ πέδον Γῆς πατέρα θ᾽ Ἥλιον πατρὸς
τοὐμοῦ θεῶν τε συντιθεὶς ἅπαν γένος.

ΑΙΓΕΥΣ

τί χρῆμα δράσειν ἢ τί μὴ δράσειν; λέγε.

ΜΗΔΕΙΑ

μήτ᾽ αὐτὸς ἐκ γῆς σῆς ἔμ᾽ ἐκβαλεῖν ποτε,
750 μήτ᾽, ἄλλος ἤν τις τῶν ἐμῶν ἐχθρῶν ἄγειν
χρῄζῃ, μεθήσειν ζῶν ἑκουσίῳ τρόπῳ.

ΑΙΓΕΥΣ

ὄμνυμι Γαῖαν Ἡλίου θ᾽ ἁγνὸν σέλας
θεούς τε πάντας ἐμμενεῖν ἅ σου κλύω.

ΜΗΔΕΙΑ

ἀρκεῖ· τί δ᾽ ὅρκῳ τῷδε μὴ ᾽μμένων πάθοις;

739 τάχ᾽ Wyttenbach: οὐκ C
741 ἔδειξας Sigonius et Valkenaer: ἔλεξας C

But if you have made an agreement in mere words and have not sworn by the gods, you might become their friend and comply with diplomatic requests. For I am weak, while they have wealth and royal power.

AEGEUS

You have shown much prudence in your speech. Well, if you like, I do not object to doing this. Not only is it safer for me to show your enemies that I have fair cause to refuse them but your own case is more secure. Name the gods I must swear by.

MEDEA

Swear by the plain of Earth, by Helios, my grandfather, and by the whole race of gods all together.

AEGEUS

To do what or to refrain from what? You must say.

MEDEA

That you yourself will never banish me from your land and that, if any of my enemies ask to take me, you will not willingly give me up as long as you live.

AEGEUS

I swear by Earth, by the holy light of Helios, and by all the gods that I will do as I have heard from your lips.

MEDEA

That is good. But what punishment do you call down on yourself if you do not abide by your oath?

---

752 Ἡλίου θ' ἀγνὸν σέλας a: λαμπρὸν ἡλίου τε φῶς b: λαμπρόν θ' ἡλίου φάος c

EURIPIDES

ΑΙΓΕΥΣ

755 ἃ τοῖσι δυσσεβοῦσι γίγνεται βροτῶν.

ΜΗΔΕΙΑ

χαίρων πορεύου· πάντα γὰρ καλῶς ἔχει.
κἀγὼ πόλιν σὴν ὡς τάχιστ᾽ ἀφίξομαι,
πράξασ᾽ ἃ μέλλω καὶ τυχοῦσ᾽ ἃ βούλομαι.

ΧΟΡΟΣ

ἀλλά σ᾽ ὁ Μαίας πομπαῖος ἄναξ
760 πελάσειε δόμοις ὧν τ᾽ ἐπίνοιαν
σπεύδεις κατέχων πράξειας, ἐπεὶ
γενναῖος ἀνήρ,
Αἰγεῦ, παρ᾽ ἐμοὶ δεδόκησαι.

ΜΗΔΕΙΑ

ὦ Ζεῦ Δίκη τε Ζηνὸς Ἡλίου τε φῶς,
765 νῦν καλλίνικοι τῶν ἐμῶν ἐχθρῶν, φίλαι,
γενησόμεσθα κεἰς ὁδὸν βεβήκαμεν,
νῦν ἐλπὶς ἐχθροὺς τοὺς ἐμοὺς τείσειν δίκην.
οὗτος γὰρ ἀνὴρ ᾗ μάλιστ᾽ ἐκάμνομεν
λιμὴν πέφανται τῶν ἐμῶν βουλευμάτων·
770 ἐκ τοῦδ᾽ ἀναψόμεσθα πρυμνήτην κάλων,
μολόντες ἄστυ καὶ πόλισμα Παλλάδος.
    ἤδη δὲ πάντα τἀμά σοι βουλεύματα
λέξω· δέχου δὲ μὴ πρὸς ἡδονὴν λόγους.
πέμψασ᾽ ἐμῶν τιν᾽ οἰκετῶν Ἰάσονα
775 ἐς ὄψιν ἐλθεῖν τὴν ἐμὴν αἰτήσομαι.
μολόντι δ᾽ αὐτῷ μαλθακοὺς λέξω λόγους,
ὡς καὶ δοκεῖ μοι ταὐτὰ καὶ καλῶς γαμεῖ

366

MEDEA

AEGEUS

The punishment that befalls mortals who are godless.

MEDEA

Go your way with joy! For all is well, and I shall come to your city as soon as I can, when I have accomplished what I intend and gained what I wish.

Exit AEGEUS by Eisodos A.

CHORUS LEADER

May Hermes, Maia's son, patron of travellers, bring you safely to your house, and may you accomplish what you have set your heart on, Aegeus, since in my eyes you are a generous man!

MEDEA

O Zeus and Zeus's justice, o light of the sun, now, my friends, I shall be victorious over my foes: I have set my foot on the path. Now I may confidently expect that my enemies will pay the penalty. For this man, at the very point where I was most in trouble, has appeared as a harbor for my plans: to him will I tie my cable when I go to the city of Pallas Athena.

Now I shall reveal to you my entire design. Hear, then, words that will give you no pleasure. I shall send one of my servants and ask Jason to come to see me. When he arrives, I shall speak soothing words to him, saying that I hold the same opinion as he, that the royal marriage he has

---

⁷⁶⁷ νῦν Lenting: νῦν δ' C
⁷⁷⁷ ταὐτὰ Barnes: ταῦτα C   γαμεῖ Bolkestein: ἔχει C

γάμους τυράννων οὓς προδοὺς ἡμᾶς ἔχει,
καὶ ξύμφορ᾽ εἶναι καὶ καλῶς ἐγνωσμένα.
780 παῖδας δὲ μεῖναι τοὺς ἐμοὺς αἰτήσομαι,
οὐχ ὡς λιποῦσ᾽ ἂν πολεμίας ἐπὶ χθονὸς
ἐχθροῖσι παῖδας τοὺς ἐμοὺς καθυβρίσαι,
ἀλλ᾽ ὡς δόλοισι παῖδα βασιλέως κτάνω.
πέμψω γὰρ αὐτοὺς δῶρ᾽ ἔχοντας ἐν χεροῖν,
785 [νύμφῃ φέροντας, τήνδε μὴ φεύγειν χθόνα,]
λεπτόν τε πέπλον καὶ πλόκον χρυσήλατον·
κἄνπερ λαβοῦσα κόσμον ἀμφιθῇ χροΐ,
κακῶς ὀλεῖται πᾶς θ᾽ ὃς ἂν θίγῃ κόρης·
τοιοῖσδε χρίσω φαρμάκοις δωρήματα.
790 ἐνταῦθα μέντοι τόνδ᾽ ἀπαλλάσσω λόγον.
ᾤμωξα δ᾽ οἷον ἔργον ἔστ᾽ ἐργαστέον
τοὐντεῦθεν ἡμῖν· τέκνα γὰρ κατακτενῶ
τἄμ᾽· οὔτις ἔστιν ὅστις ἐξαιρήσεται·
δόμον τε πάντα συγχέασ᾽ Ἰάσονος
795 ἔξειμι γαίας, φιλτάτων παίδων φόνον
φεύγουσα καὶ τλᾶσ᾽ ἔργον ἀνοσιώτατον.
οὐ γὰρ γελᾶσθαι τλητὸν ἐξ ἐχθρῶν, φίλαι.
ἴτω· τί μοι ζῆν κέρδος; οὔτε μοι πατρὶς
οὔτ᾽ οἶκος ἔστιν οὔτ᾽ ἀποστροφὴ κακῶν.
800 ἡμάρτανον τόθ᾽ ἡνίκ᾽ ἐξελίμπανον
δόμους πατρῴους, ἀνδρὸς Ἕλληνος λόγοις
πεισθεῖσ᾽, ὃς ἡμῖν σὺν θεῷ τείσει δίκην.
οὔτ᾽ ἐξ ἐμοῦ γὰρ παῖδας ὄψεταί ποτε
ζῶντας τὸ λοιπὸν οὔτε τῆς νεοζύγου
805 νύμφης τεκνώσει παῖδ᾽, ἐπεὶ κακὴν κακῶς

made by abandoning me is well made, that these are
beneficial and good decisions. I shall ask that the children
be allowed to stay, not with the thought that I might leave
them behind on hostile soil for my enemies to insult, but
so that I may kill the princess by guile. I shall send them
bearing gifts, [bearing them to the bride so as not to be
exiled,] a finely woven gown and a diadem of beaten gold.
If she takes this finery and puts it on, she will die a painful
death, and likewise anyone who touches her: with such
poisons will I smear these gifts.

This subject, however, I now leave behind. Ah me, I
groan at what a deed I must do next! I shall kill my chil-
dren: there is no one who can rescue them. When I have
utterly confounded the whole house of Jason, I shall leave
the land, in flight from the murder of my own dear sons,
having committed a most unholy deed. The laughter of
one's enemies is unendurable, my friends. Let that be as it
will. What do I gain by living? I have no fatherland, no
house, and no means to turn aside misfortune. My mis-
take was when I left my father's house, persuaded by the
words of a Greek. This man—a god being my helper—will
pay for what he has done to me. He shall never from this
day see his children by me alive, nor will he have children
by his new bride since that wretch must die a wretched

---

781 λιποῦσ᾽ ἄν Elmsley: λιποῦσα C
785 om. a, del. Valckenaer cl. 940, 943, 950
798-9 del. Leo

θανεῖν σφ᾿ ἀνάγκη τοῖς ἐμοῖσι φαρμάκοις.
μηδείς με φαύλην κἀσθενῆ νομιζέτω
μηδ᾿ ἡσυχαίαν, ἀλλὰ θατέρου τρόπου,
βαρεῖαν ἐχθροῖς καὶ φίλοισιν εὐμενῆ·
810 τῶν γὰρ τοιούτων εὐκλεέστατος βίος.

ΧΟΡΟΣ
ἐπείπερ ἡμῖν τόνδ᾿ ἐκοίνωσας λόγον,
σέ τ᾿ ὠφελεῖν θέλουσα καὶ νόμοις βροτῶν
ξυλλαμβάνουσα δρᾶν σ᾿ ἀπεννέπω τάδε.

ΜΗΔΕΙΑ
οὐκ ἔστιν ἄλλως· σοὶ δὲ συγγνώμη λέγειν
815 τάδ᾿ ἐστί, μὴ πάσχουσαν, ὡς ἐγώ, κακῶς.

ΧΟΡΟΣ
ἀλλὰ κτανεῖν σὸν σπέρμα τολμήσεις, γύναι;

ΜΗΔΕΙΑ
οὕτω γὰρ ἂν μάλιστα δηχθείη πόσις.

ΧΟΡΟΣ
σὺ δ᾿ ἂν γένοιό γ᾿ ἀθλιωτάτη γυνή.

ΜΗΔΕΙΑ
ἴτω· περισσοὶ πάντες οὑν μέσῳ λόγοι.
820 ἀλλ᾿ εἶα χώρει καὶ κόμιζ᾿ Ἰάσονα
(ἐς πάντα γὰρ δὴ σοὶ τὰ πιστὰ χρώμεθα)
λέξῃς δὲ μηδὲν τῶν ἐμοὶ δεδογμένων,
εἴπερ φρονεῖς εὖ δεσπόταις γυνή τ᾿ ἔφυς.

death by my poisons. Let no one think me weak, contemptible, untroublesome. No, quite the opposite, hurtful to foes, to friends kindly. Such persons live a life of greatest glory.

CHORUS LEADER
Since you have shared this plan with me, and since I wish to help you and uphold the laws of society, I urge you not to do this deed.

MEDEA
It cannot be otherwise. I excuse you for speaking thus since you have not suffered as I have.

CHORUS LEADER
Yet will you bring yourself to kill your own offspring, woman?

MEDEA
It is the way to hurt my husband most.

CHORUS LEADER
And for yourself to become the most wretched of women.

MEDEA
Be that as it may. Till then all talk is superfluous.
(to the Nurse) But you, go and fetch Jason (for I use your service on all errands of trust). Tell him nothing of my intentions, if you are loyal to your mistress and a woman.

Exit Nurse by Eisodos B, MEDEA *into the house.*

371

EURIPIDES

ΧΟΡΟΣ

στρ. α

Ἐρεχθεῖδαι τὸ παλαιὸν ὄλβιοι
825 καὶ θεῶν παῖδες μακάρων, ἱερᾶς
χώρας ἀπορθήτου τ' ἄπο, φερβόμενοι
κλεινοτάταν σοφίαν, αἰεὶ διὰ λαμπροτάτου
830 βαίνοντες ἁβρῶς αἰθέρος, ἔνθα ποθ' ἁγνὰς
ἐννέα Πιερίδας Μούσας λέγουσι
ξανθὰν Ἁρμονίαν φυτεῦσαι·

ἀντ. α

835 τοῦ καλλινάου τ' ἐπὶ Κηφισοῦ ῥοαῖς
τὰν Κύπριν κλῄζουσιν ἀφυσσαμέναν
χώρας καταπνεῦσαι μετρίους ἀνέμων
840 ἀέρας ἡδυπνόους· αἰεὶ δ' ἐπιβαλλομέναν
χαίταισιν εὐώδη ῥοδέων πλόκον ἀνθέων
τᾷ Σοφίᾳ παρέδρους πέμπειν Ἔρωτας,
845 παντοίας ἀρετᾶς ξυνεργούς.

στρ. β

πῶς οὖν ἱερῶν ποταμῶν
ἢ πόλις ἢ θεῶν
πόμπιμός σε χώρα
τὰν παιδολέτειραν ἕξει,
850 τὰν οὐχ ὁσίαν, μετ' ἀστῶν;
σκέψαι τεκέων πλαγάν,
σκέψαι φόνον οἷον αἴρῃ.
μή, πρὸς γονάτων σε πάν-
τα πάντως ἱκετεύομεν,
855 τέκνα φονεύσῃς.

372

MEDEA

CHORUS

From ancient times the sons of Erechtheus have been favored; they are children of the blessed gods sprung from a holy land never pillaged by the enemy. They feed on wisdom most glorious, always stepping gracefully through the bright air, where once, it is said, the nine Pierian Muses gave birth to fair-haired Harmonia.

Legend tells that Aphrodite, filling her pail at the streams of the Cephisus, blew down upon the land temperate and sweet breezes. And ever dressing her hair with a fragrant chaplet of roses she sends the Loves to sit at Wisdom's side, joint workers in every kind of excellence.

How then shall this city of holy rivers or this land that escorts its gods in procession lodge you, the killer of your children, stained with their blood, in the company of her citizens? Think on the slaying of your children, think what slaughter you are committing! Do not, we beseech you by your knees and in every way we can, do not kill your children!

---

838 χώρας Reiske: χώραν C
840 ἀέρας ἡδυπνόους Page: ἡδυπνόους αὔρας C
847 θεῶν scripsi: φίλων C
850 ἀστῶν Jacobs: ἄλλων C

ἀντ. β

πόθεν θράσος ἢ φρενὸς ἢ
χειρὶ †τέκνων† σέθεν
καρδίᾳ τε λήψῃ
δεινὰν προσάγουσα τόλμαν;
860 πῶς δ' ὄμματα προσβαλοῦσα
τέκνοις ἄδακρυν μοῖραν
σχήσεις φόνου; οὐ δυνάσῃ,
παίδων ἱκετᾶν πιτνόν-
των, τέγξαι χέρα φοινίαν
865 τλάμονι θυμῷ.

ΙΑΣΩΝ

ἥκω κελευσθείς· καὶ γὰρ οὖσα δυσμενὴς
οὔ τἂν ἁμάρτοις τοῦδέ γ', ἀλλ' ἀκούσομαι·
τί χρῆμα βούλῃ καινὸν ἐξ ἐμοῦ, γύναι;

ΜΗΔΕΙΑ

Ἰᾶσον, αἰτοῦμαί σε τῶν εἰρημένων
870 συγγνώμον' εἶναι· τὰς δ' ἐμὰς ὀργὰς φέρειν
εἰκός σ', ἐπεὶ νῷν πόλλ' ὑπείργασται φίλα.
ἐγὼ δ' ἐμαυτῇ διὰ λόγων ἀφικόμην
κἀλοιδόρησα· Σχετλία, τί μαίνομαι
καὶ δυσμεναίνω τοῖσι βουλεύουσιν εὖ,
875 ἐχθρὰ δὲ γαίας κοιράνοις καθίσταμαι
πόσει θ', ὃς ἡμῖν δρᾷ τὰ συμφορώτατα,
γήμας τύραννον καὶ κασιγνήτους τέκνοις
ἐμοῖς φυτεύων; οὐκ ἀπαλλαχθήσομαι
θυμοῦ — τί πάσχω; — θεῶν πορ ιζόντων καλῶς;
880 οὐκ εἰσὶ μέν μοι παῖδες, οἶδα δὲ χθόνα

374

How will you summon up the strength of purpose or the courage of hand and heart to dare this dreadful deed? When you have turned your eyes upon your children, how will you behold their fate with tearless eye? When your children fall as suppliants at your feet, you will not be hardhearted enough to drench your hand in their blood.

Enter MEDEA from the house, then JASON by Eisodos B accompanied by the Nurse.

JASON

I have come at your bidding. For though you hate me, you will not fail to obtain a hearing from me. What further do you wish from me, woman?

MEDEA

Jason, I beg you to forgive what I said: it is reasonable for you to put up with my anger since many acts of love have passed between us in the past. I have talked with myself and reproached myself thus: "Foolish creature, why am I raving and fighting those who arrange things for the best? Why am I making myself an enemy to the rulers of this land and to my husband, who is acting in my interests by marrying a princess and begetting brothers for my children? Shall I not cease from my wrath (what has come over me?) when the gods are being so kind? Do I not have

---

857 τόνον Willink: fort. μένος

φεύγοντας ἡμᾶς καὶ σπανίζοντας φίλων·
ταῦτ᾽ ἐννοηθεῖσ᾽ ᾐσθόμην ἀβουλίαν
πολλὴν ἔχουσα καὶ μάτην θυμουμένη.
νῦν οὖν ἐπαινῶ σωφρονεῖν τέ μοι δοκεῖς
885 κῆδος τόδ᾽ ἡμῖν προσλαβών, ἐγὼ δ᾽ ἄφρων,
ᾗ χρῆν μετεῖναι τῶνδε τῶν βουλευμάτων
καὶ ξυμπεραίνειν καὶ παρεστάναι λέχει
νύμφῃ τε κηδεύουσαν ἥδεσθαι σέθεν.
ἀλλ᾽ ἐσμὲν οἷόν ἐσμεν, οὐκ ἐρῶ κακόν,
890 γυναῖκες· οὔκουν χρῆν σ᾽ ὁμοιοῦσθαι φύσιν,
οὐδ᾽ ἀντιτείνειν νήπι᾽ ἀντὶ νηπίων.
παριέμεσθα καί φαμεν κακῶς φρονεῖν
τότ᾽, ἀλλ᾽ ἄμεινον νῦν βεβούλευμαι τάδε.
ὦ τέκνα τέκνα, δεῦρο, λείπετε στέγας,
895 ἐξέλθετ᾽, ἀσπάσασθε καὶ προσείπατε
πατέρα μεθ᾽ ἡμῶν καὶ διαλλάχθηθ᾽ ἅμα
τῆς πρόσθεν ἔχθρας ἐς φίλους μητρὸς μέτα·
σπονδαὶ γὰρ ἡμῖν καὶ μεθέστηκεν χόλος.
λάβεσθε χειρὸς δεξιᾶς· οἴμοι, κακῶν
900 ὡς ἐννοοῦμαι δή τι τῶν κεκρυμμένων.
ἆρ᾽, ὦ τέκν᾽, οὕτω καὶ πολὺν ζῶντες χρόνον
φίλην ὀρέξετ᾽ ὠλένην; τάλαιν᾽ ἐγώ,
ὡς ἀρτίδακρύς εἰμι καὶ φόβου πλέα.
χρόνῳ δὲ νεῖκος πατρὸς ἐξαιρουμένη
905 ὄψιν τέρειναν τήνδ᾽ ἔπλησα δακρύων.

888 νύμφῃ Verrall: νύμφην C
890 φύσιν Stadtmüller cl. Andr. 354: κακοῖς C
894 δεῦρο Elmsley: δεῦτε C

the children? Is it not true that we are exiles and in need of friends?" These reflections have made me realize that I was being very foolish and was being angry for nothing. So now I approve and I agree that you are acting with sober sense by contracting this marriage alliance for us. It is I who am the fool, since I ought to be sharing in your plans, helping you carry them out, standing by the marriage bed, and taking joy in the connection I now have with your bride. Well, we women are, I will not say bad creatures, but we are what we are. So you ought not to imitate our nature or return our childishness with childishness. I give in: I admit that I was foolish then, but now I have taken a better view of the matter.

Children, children, come here, leave the house, come out!

The children enter from the house with the Tutor.

Greet your father, speak to him with me, and join your mother in making an end to our former hostility against one dear to us! We have made a truce, and our wrath has vanished. Take his right hand. Ah, how I think of something the future keeps hid! My children, will you continue all your lives long to stretch out your dear hands so? Unhappy me! How prone to tears I am, how full of foreboding! And as I now at long last make up the quarrel with your father, my tender eyes are filled with tears.

ΧΟΡΟΣ

κἀμοὶ κατ᾽ ὄσσων χλωρὸν ὡρμήθη δάκρυ·
καὶ μὴ προβαίη μεῖζον ἢ τὸ νῦν κακόν.

ΙΑΣΩΝ

αἰνῶ, γύναι, τάδ᾽, οὐδ᾽ ἐκεῖνα μέμφομαι·
εἰκὸς γὰρ ὀργὰς θῆλυ ποιεῖσθαι γένος
910   γάμου †παρεμπολῶντος† ἀλλοίου πόσει.
ἀλλ᾽ ἐς τὸ λῷον σὸν μεθέστηκεν κέαρ,
ἔγνως δὲ τὴν νικῶσαν, ἀλλὰ τῷ χρόνῳ,
βουλήν· γυναικὸς ἔργα ταῦτα σώφρονος.
      ὑμῖν δέ, παῖδες, οὐκ ἀφροντίστως πατὴρ
915   πολλὴν ἔθηκε σὺν θεοῖς σωτηρίαν·
οἶμαι γὰρ ὑμᾶς τῆσδε γῆς Κορινθίας
τὰ πρῶτ᾽ ἔσεσθαι σὺν κασιγνήτοις ἔτι.
ἀλλ᾽ αὐξάνεσθε· τἄλλα δ᾽ ἐξεργάζεται
πατήρ τε καὶ θεῶν ὅστις ἐστὶν εὐμενής.
920   ἴδοιμι δ᾽ ὑμᾶς εὐτραφεῖς ἥβης τέλος
μολόντας, ἐχθρῶν τῶν ἐμῶν ὑπερτέρους.
      αὕτη, τί χλωροῖς δακρύοις τέγγεις κόρας,
στρέψασα λευκὴν ἔμπαλιν παρηίδα,
κοὐκ ἀσμένη τόνδ᾽ ἐξ ἐμοῦ δέχῃ λόγον;

ΜΗΔΕΙΑ

925   οὐδέν. τέκνων τῶνδ᾽ ἐννοουμένη πέρι.

---

910 fort. παρεμπεσόντος
915 σωτηρίαν a: προμηθίαν b
923 del. Hartung cl. 1148

378

MEDEA

CHORUS LEADER

(*darkly*) From my eye too a pale tear starts. May misfortune go no further than it has!

JASON

I approve this, woman. Nor do I blame your earlier resentment. It is natural for a woman to get angry when a marriage of a different sort presents itself to her husband. But your thoughts have changed for the better, and though it took time, you have recognized the superior plan. These are the acts of a prudent woman.

Children, your father has given anxious thought and has secured for you—with the gods' help—abundant prosperity. I think that some day with your new brothers you will hold the very first place in the land of Corinth. But grow to manhood. The rest your father will see to, with the help of whatever god it is that smiles on him. May I see you as fine strapping lads coming to young manhood, victorious over my enemies!

Medea turns away weeping.

You there, why do you dampen your eyes with pale tears and turn your white cheek away, and why are you not pleased to hear these words from me?

MEDEA

It is nothing. I was thinking about the children.

ΙΑΣΩΝ

929   τί δή, τάλαινα, τοῖσδ' ἐπιστένεις τέκνοις;

ΜΗΔΕΙΑ

930   ἔτικτον αὐτούς· ζῆν δ' ὅτ' ἐξηύχου τέκνα,
931   ἐσῆλθέ μ' οἶκτος εἰ γενήσεται τάδε.

ΙΑΣΩΝ

926   θάρσει νυν· εὖ γὰρ τῶνδε θήσομαι πέρι.

ΜΗΔΕΙΑ

    δράσω τάδ'· οὔτοι σοῖς ἀπιστήσω λόγοις·
928   γυνὴ δὲ θῆλυ κἀπὶ δακρύοις ἔφυ.
932   ἀλλ' ὧνπερ οὕνεκ' εἰς ἐμοὺς ἥκεις λόγους,
    τὰ μὲν λέλεκται, τῶν δ' ἐγὼ μνησθήσομαι.
    ἐπεὶ τυράννοις γῆς μ' ἀποστεῖλαι δοκεῖ
935   (κἀμοὶ τάδ' ἐστὶ λῷστα, γιγνώσκω καλῶς,
    μήτ' ἐμποδὼν σοὶ μήτε κοιράνοις χθονὸς
    ναίειν· δοκῶ γὰρ δυσμενὴς εἶναι δόμοις),
    ἡμεῖς μὲν ἐκ γῆς τῆσδ' ἀπαροῦμεν φυγῇ,
    παῖδες δ' ὅπως ἂν ἐκτραφῶσι σῇ χερί,
940   αἰτοῦ Κρέοντα τήνδε μὴ φεύγειν χθόνα.

ΙΑΣΩΝ

    οὐκ οἶδ' ἂν εἰ πείσαιμι, πειρᾶσθαι δὲ χρή.

ΜΗΔΕΙΑ

    σὺ δ' ἀλλὰ σὴν κέλευσον ἄντεσθαι πατρὸς
    γυναῖκα παῖδας τήνδε μὴ φεύγειν χθόνα.

929–31 post 925 trai. Ladewig: vide Dyson, CQ 38 (1988), 324–7
926 τῶνδε θήσομαι a: τῶνδ' ἐγὼ θήσω b

MEDEA

JASON

But why, poor soul, do you lament over these children?

MEDEA

I gave them birth, and when you prayed that they might live, I felt pity for them wondering whether this would be.

JASON

Have no fear! I shall take good care of that!

MEDEA

I shall do as you say: I will not distrust your words. Yet a woman is by nature female and prone to tears.

But of the reasons for your coming to talk to me, some have been spoken of, others I shall mention now. The rulers of this land have resolved to exile me—and it is all for the best for me, I am well aware, that I not stay where I am in your way or that of the country's rulers, for I am thought to be an enemy to this house. Therefore I for my part shall leave this land in exile. But in order that the children may be raised by you, beg Creon that they not be sent into exile.

JASON

I don't know whether I shall win him over, but I must try.

MEDEA

Well, then, tell your wife to ask her father that the children not be exiled.

---

942 ἄντεσθαι Weidner: αἰτεῖσθαι C

ΙΑΣΩΝ

μάλιστα, καὶ πείσειν γε δοξάζω σφ' ἐγώ.

ΜΗΔΕΙΑ

945 εἴπερ γυναικῶν <γ'> ἐστι τῶν ἄλλων μία.
συλλήψομαι δὲ τοῦδέ σοι κἀγὼ πόνου·
πέμψω γὰρ αὐτῇ δῶρ' ἃ καλλιστεύεται
τῶν νῦν ἐν ἀνθρώποισιν, οἶδ' ἐγώ, πολὺ
[λεπτόν τε πέπλον καὶ πλόκον χρυσήλατον]
950 παῖδας φέροντας. ἀλλ' ὅσον τάχος χρεὼν
κόσμον κομίζειν δεῦρο προσπόλων τινά.
εὐδαιμονήσει δ' οὐχ ἓν ἀλλὰ μυρία,
ἀνδρός τ' ἀρίστου σοῦ τυχοῦσ' ὁμευνέτου
κεκτημένη τε κόσμον ὅν ποθ' Ἥλιος
955 πατρὸς πατὴρ δίδωσιν ἐκγόνοισιν οἷς.
λάζυσθε φερνὰς τάσδε, παῖδες, ἐς χέρας
καὶ τῇ τυράννῳ μακαρίᾳ νύμφῃ δότε
φέροντες· οὔτοι δῶρα μεμπτὰ δέξεται.

ΙΑΣΩΝ

τί δ', ὦ ματαία, τῶνδε σὰς κενοῖς χέρας;
960 δοκεῖς σπανίζειν δῶμα βασίλειον πέπλων,
δοκεῖς δὲ χρυσοῦ; σῷζε, μὴ δίδου τάδε.
εἴπερ γὰρ ἡμᾶς ἀξιοῖ λόγου τινὸς
γυνή, προθήσει χρημάτων, σάφ' οἶδ' ἐγώ.

945 Medeae trib. a: Iasoni contin. b: om. c
<γ'> Herwerden
949 del. Bothe cl. 786
955 ἐκγόνοις ἐμός F. W. Schmidt

JASON

Most certainly, and I think I shall persuade her.

MEDEA

Yes, if she is a woman like the rest. But I too shall lend a hand in this. By the hand of my children I shall send her gifts, gifts I know well are more beautiful by far than any now among mortals [a finely woven gown and a diadem of beaten gold]. *(to her servants)* One of you servants, quick, bring the raiment out to me!

One of the servants goes into the house.

(to Jason) She will have not one happiness but countless, getting in you an excellent husband to share her bed and possessing finery which my grandfather Helios gave to his descendants.

The servant returns with the gifts.

Take this bridal dowry, children, into your hands. Take and give it to the happy royal bride. It will be no unwelcome gift she receives.

JASON

Silly woman, why do you deprive yourself of these things? Do you think the royal house has need of gowns or gold? Keep them, don't give them away! For if my wife holds me in any regard, she will value my wishes more highly than wealth, I am quite sure.

ΜΗΔΕΙΑ

μή μοι σύ· πείθειν δῶρα καὶ θεοὺς λόγος·

965 χρυσὸς δὲ κρείσσων μυρίων λόγων βροτοῖς.
κείνης ὁ δαίμων [κεῖνα νῦν αὔξει θεός,
νέα τυραννεῖ]· τῶν δ’ ἐμῶν παίδων φυγὰς
ψυχῆς ἂν ἀλλαξαίμεθ’, οὐ χρυσοῦ μόνον.

ἀλλ’, ὦ τέκν’, εἰσελθόντε πλουσίους δόμους

970 πατρὸς νέαν γυναῖκα, δεσπότιν δ’ ἐμήν,
ἱκετεύετ’, ἐξαιτεῖσθε μὴ φεύγειν χθόνα,
κόσμον διδόντες· τοῦδε γὰρ μάλιστα δεῖ,
ἐς χεῖρ’ ἐκείνην δῶρα δέξασθαι τάδε.
ἴθ’ ὡς τάχιστα· μητρὶ δ’ ὧν ἐρᾷ τυχεῖν

975 εὐάγγελοι γένοισθε πράξαντες καλῶς.

ΧΟΡΟΣ

στρ. α

νῦν ἐλπίδες οὐκέτι μοι παίδων ζόας,
οὐκέτι· στείχουσι γὰρ ἐς φόνον ἤδη.
δέξεται νύμφα χρυσέων ἀναδεσμᾶν
δέξεται δύστανος ἄταν·

980 ξανθᾷ δ’ ἀμφὶ κόμᾳ θήσει τὸν Ἅιδα
κόσμον αὐτὰ χεροῖν.

ἀντ. α

πείσει χάρις ἀμβρόσιός τ’ αὐγὰ πέπλον
χρυσότευκτον <τε> στέφανον περιθέσθαι·

966–7 κεῖνα . . . τυραννεῖ del. Nauck
982 χεροῖν Nauck: χεροῖν λαβοῦσα C
983 πέπλον Elmsley: πέπλων a: πέπλου b
984 <τε> Reiske

384

MEDEA

Not a word! They say gifts win over even the gods, and gold is more to mortals than ten thousand words. Hers is the power we must propitiate [heaven is enhancing her lot, she is young and on the throne]. And to free my children from exile I would give my life, not merely gold.

Now, children, when you have entered the rich palace, entreat your father's new wife, my mistress, and beg her that you not be exiled. And give her the finery: this is the most important thing, that she receive the gifts into her hands. Go with all speed. And may you have success and bring back to your mother the good news she longs to hear!

Exit JASON and children, accompanied by the Tutor and the Nurse, by Eisodos B.

CHORUS

Now no more can I hope that the children shall live, no more. For already they are walking the road to murder. The bride will accept, will accept, unhappy woman, ruin in the form of a golden diadem; about her fair hair with her own hand she will place the finery of Death.

Their charm and heavenly gleam will entice her to put on the gown and the circlet of fashioned gold. But the

985 νερτέροις δ᾿ ἤδη πάρα νυμφοκομήσει.
τοῖον εἰς ἕρκος πεσεῖται
καὶ μοῖραν θανάτου δύστανος· ἄταν δ᾿
οὐχ ὑπεκφεύξεται.

στρ. β

990 σὺ δ᾿, ὦ τάλαν, ὦ κακόνυμφε
κηδεμὼν τυράννων,
παισὶν οὐ κατειδὼς
ὄλεθρον βιοτᾷ προσάγεις ἀλόχῳ
τε σᾷ στυγερὸν θάνατον.

995 δύστανε, μοίρας ὅσον παροίχῃ.

ἀντ. β

μεταστένομαι δὲ σὸν ἄλγος,
ὦ τάλαινα παίδων
μᾶτερ, ἃ φονεύσεις
τέκνα νυμφιδίων ἕνεκεν λεχέων,

1000 ἅ σοι προλιπὼν ἀνόμως
ἄλλᾳ ξυνοικεῖ πόσις συνεύνῳ.

ΠΑΙΔΑΓΩΓΟΣ

δέσποιν᾿, ἀφεῖνται παῖδες οἵδε σοι φυγῆς,
καὶ δῶρα νύμφη βασιλὶς ἀσμένη χεροῖν
ἐδέξατ᾿· εἰρήνη δὲ τἀκεῖθεν τέκνοις.
ἔα·

1005 τί συγχυθεῖσ᾿ ἕστηκας ἡνίκ᾿ εὐτυχεῖς;
[τί σὴν ἔστρεψας ἔμπαλιν παρηίδα
κοὐκ ἀσμένη τόνδ᾿ ἐξ ἐμοῦ δέχῃ λόγον;]

ΜΗΔΕΙΑ

αἰαῖ.

386

bridal bed she lies in will be with the dead. Such is the snare, such the death, she will fall into. She will not escape destruction.

And you, unlucky bridegroom, married into the house of kings, all unwitting you bring destruction upon your children's life and upon your bride a dreadful death. Unhappy man, how wrong you were about your destiny!

Your sorrows next I mourn, unhappy mother of the children, who mean to kill your sons because of your marriage bed. Your husband wickedly abandoned it and now lives with another as his wife.

Enter TUTOR *with the children by Eisodos B.*

TUTOR

My lady, your sons here have been reprieved from exile, and the princess has been pleased to take the gifts into her hands. From that quarter the children have peace.

Medea turns away and weeps.

Ah! Why are you standing in distress when your fortune is good? [Why have you turned your face away and why do you show no pleasure at this news?]

MEDEA

Alas!

1006–7 del. Valckenaer cl. 923–4.

EURIPIDES

ΠΑΙΔΑΓΩΓΟΣ

τάδ' οὐ ξυνῳδὰ τοῖσιν ἐξηγγελμένοις.

ΜΗΔΕΙΑ

αἰαῖ μάλ' αὖθις.

ΠΑΙΔΑΓΩΓΟΣ

          μῶν τιν' ἀγγέλλων τύχην

1010   οὐκ οἶδα, δόξης δ' ἐσφάλην εὐαγγέλου;

ΜΗΔΕΙΑ

ἤγγειλας οἷ' ἤγγειλας· οὐ σὲ μέμφομαι.

ΠΑΙΔΑΓΩΓΟΣ

τί δαὶ κατηφὲς ὄμμα καὶ δακρυρροεῖς;

ΜΗΔΕΙΑ

πολλή μ' ἀνάγκη, πρέσβυ· ταῦτα γὰρ θεοὶ
κἀγὼ κακῶς φρονοῦσ' ἐμηχανησάμην.

ΠΑΙΔΑΓΩΓΟΣ

1015   θάρσει· κάτει τοι καὶ σὺ πρὸς τέκνων ἔτι.

ΜΗΔΕΙΑ

ἄλλους κατάξω πρόσθεν ἡ τάλαιν' ἐγώ.

ΠΑΙΔΑΓΩΓΟΣ

οὔτοι μόνη σὺ σῶν ἀπεζύγης τέκνων·
κούφως φέρειν χρὴ θνητὸν ὄντα συμφοράς.

[1012] κατηφὲς Cobet cl. *Hcld.* 633: -φεῖς C
[1015] κάτει Porson: κρατεῖς fere C

388

MEDEA

TUTOR

This is not in tune with my tidings.

MEDEA

Alas once more!

TUTOR

Do I in ignorance report some mishap and wrongly think my news is good?

MEDEA

You have reported what you have reported. It is not you I blame.

TUTOR

Why then is your face downcast? Why do you weep?

MEDEA

I have every reason, old man. The gods, and I in my madness, have contrived it so.

TUTOR

Cheer up: one day your children will bring you home.

MEDEA

Before that there are others I shall bring home,[a] wretch that I am.

TUTOR

You are not the only woman to be separated from her children. We mortals must bear misfortune with resignation.

---

[a] The grim wordplay is untranslatable: κατάγω means both "bring home (from exile)" and "bring down."

389

ΜΗΔΕΙΑ

δράσω τάδ᾽· ἀλλὰ βαῖνε δωμάτων ἔσω
1020 καὶ παισὶ πόρσυν᾽ οἷα χρὴ καθ᾽ ἡμέραν.
     ὦ τέκνα τέκνα, σφῷν μὲν ἔστι δὴ πόλις
καὶ δῶμ᾽, ἐν ᾧ λιπόντες ἀθλίαν ἐμὲ
οἰκήσετ᾽ αἰεὶ μητρὸς ἐστερημένοι·
ἐγὼ δ᾽ ἐς ἄλλην γαῖαν εἶμι δὴ φυγάς,
1025 πρὶν σφῷν ὀνάσθαι κἀπιδεῖν εὐδαίμονας,
πρὶν λουτρὰ καὶ γυναῖκα καὶ γαμηλίους
εὐνὰς ἀγῆλαι λαμπάδας τ᾽ ἀνασχεθεῖν.
ὦ δυστάλαινα τῆς ἐμῆς αὐθαδίας.
ἄλλως ἄρ᾽ ὑμᾶς, ὦ τέκν᾽, ἐξεθρεψάμην,
1030 ἄλλως δ᾽ ἐμόχθουν καὶ κατεξάνθην πόνοις,
στερρὰς ἐνεγκοῦσ᾽ ἐν τόκοις ἀλγηδόνας.
ἦ μήν ποθ᾽ ἡ δύστηνος εἶχον ἐλπίδας
πολλὰς ἐν ὑμῖν, γηροβοσκήσειν τ᾽ ἐμὲ
καὶ κατθανοῦσαν χερσὶν εὖ περιστελεῖν,
1035 ζηλωτὸν ἀνθρώποισι· νῦν δ᾽ ὄλωλε δὴ
γλυκεῖα φροντίς. σφῷν γὰρ ἐστερημένη
λυπρὸν διάξω βίοτον ἀλγεινόν τ᾽ ἐμόν.
ὑμεῖς δὲ μητέρ᾽ οὐκέτ᾽ ὄμμασιν φίλοις
ὄψεσθ᾽, ἐς ἄλλο σχῆμ᾽ ἀποστάντες βίου.
1040   φεῦ φεῦ· τί προσδέρκεσθέ μ᾽ ὄμμασιν, τέκνα;
τί προσγελᾶτε τὸν πανύστατον γέλων;
αἰαῖ· τί δράσω; καρδία γὰρ οἴχεται,
γυναῖκες, ὄμμα φαιδρὸν ὡς εἶδον τέκνων.

1026 λουτρὰ Burges: λέκτρα C
1037 ἐμόν Platnauer: ἐμοί C

MEDEA

I will do so. But go into the house and provide the children with their daily needs.

Exit TUTOR into the house.

My children, my children, you have a city and a home,[a] in which, leaving your poor mother behind, you will live henceforth, bereft of me. I shall go to another land as an exile before I have the enjoyment of you and see you happy, before I have tended to your baths[b] and your wives and marriage beds and held the wedding torches aloft. How wretched my self-will has made me! It was all in vain, I see, that I brought you up, all in vain that I labored and was wracked with toils, enduring harsh pains in childbirth! Truly, many were the hopes that I, poor fool, once had in you, that you would tend me in my old age, and when I died, dress me for burial with your own hands, an enviable lot for mortals. But now this sweet imagining has perished. For bereft of you I shall live out my life in pain and grief. And you will no longer see your mother with loving eyes but pass into another manner of life.

Oh! What is the meaning of your glance at me, children? Why do you smile at me this last smile of yours? Alas, what am I to do? My courage is gone, women, ever since I saw the bright faces of the children. I cannot do it.

[a] To the children this would mean Corinth, to Medea it means the nether world. Such veiled discourse is characteristic of this speech, with the exception of the bracketed section below.

[b] A special bath for the bride and the groom preceded the wedding.

οὐκ ἂν δυναίμην· χαιρέτω βουλεύματα
1045   τὰ πρόσθεν· ἄξω παῖδας ἐκ γαίας ἐμούς.
τί δεῖ με πατέρα τῶνδε τοῖς τούτων κακοῖς
λυποῦσαν αὐτὴν δὶς τόσα κτᾶσθαι κακά;
οὐ δῆτ' ἔγωγε· χαιρέτω βουλεύματα.

  καίτοι τί πάσχω; βούλομαι γέλωτ' ὀφλεῖν
1050   ἐχθροὺς μεθεῖσα τοὺς ἐμοὺς ἀζημίους;
τολμητέον τάδ'; ἀλλὰ τῆς ἐμῆς κάκης
τὸ καὶ προσέσθαι μαλθακοὺς λόγους φρενί.
χωρεῖτε, παῖδες, ἐς δόμους. ὅτῳ δὲ μὴ
θέμις παρεῖναι τοῖς ἐμοῖσι θύμασιν,
1055   αὐτῷ μελήσει· χεῖρα δ' οὐ διαφθερῶ.
[ἆ ἆ.

μὴ δῆτα, θυμέ, μὴ σύ γ' ἐργάσῃ τάδε·
ἔασον αὐτούς, ὦ τάλαν, φεῖσαι τέκνων·
ἐκεῖ μεθ' ἡμῶν ζῶντες εὐφρανοῦσί σε.
μὰ τοὺς παρ' Ἅιδῃ νερτέρους ἀλάστορας,
1060   οὔτοι ποτ' ἔσται τοῦθ' ὅπως ἐχθροῖς ἐγὼ
παῖδας παρήσω τοὺς ἐμοὺς καθυβρίσαι.
πάντως σφ' ἀνάγκη κατθανεῖν· ἐπεὶ δὲ χρή,
ἡμεῖς κτενοῦμεν οἵπερ ἐξεφύσαμεν.
πάντως πέπρακται ταῦτα κοὐκ ἐκφεύξεται.]

[1051] post τάδε interrogative interpunxi
[1056–64] seclusi (1056–80 iam Bergk, alii alios): vide CQ 36 (1986), 343–52

Farewell, my former designs! I shall take my children out of the land. Why should I wound their father with their pain and win for myself pain twice as great? I shall not: farewell, my designs!

But what is coming over me? Do I wish to suffer mockery, letting my enemies go unpunished? Must I put up with that? No, it is mere weakness in me even to admit such tender words into my heart. Children, go into the house. Those who are not permitted to attend my sacrifice shall worry about their welfare: I shall not weaken my hand. [Oh! Do not, my angry heart, do not do these things! Let them go, hard-hearted wretch, spare the children! If they live with me in that other place,[a] they will gladden you. By Hell's avenging furies, I shall never leave my children for my enemies to outrage![b] They must die in any case. And since they must, the one who gave them birth shall kill them. These things are settled and cannot be undone.]

The children begin to move toward the house.

[a] The author of these lines apparently means Athens. Contrast the expressively ambiguous use of ἐκεῖ to mean Hades in 1073 below.

[b] Among the reasons for considering these lines spurious is that they are internally inconsistent. The present sentence reads as if it were the vehement rejection of a plan Medea had entertained, a plan of leaving the children in Corinth, and the impossibility of doing so is treated as a reason for killing them. But the immediately preceding sentence suggested taking them to Athens, and her vehement refusal to leave them provides no reason for killing them.

1065   καὶ δὴ 'πὶ κρατὶ στέφανος, ἐν πέπλοισι δὲ
νύμφη τύραννος ὄλλυται, σάφ' οἶδ' ἐγώ.
ἀλλ', εἶμι γὰρ δὴ τλημονεστάτην ὁδὸν
καὶ τούσδε πέμψω τλημονεστέραν ἔτι,
παῖδας προσειπεῖν βούλομαι· δότ', ὦ τέκνα,
1070   δότ' ἀσπάσασθαι μητρὶ δεξιὰν χέρα.
ὦ φιλτάτη χείρ, φίλτατον δέ μοι στόμα
καὶ σχῆμα καὶ πρόσωπον εὐγενὲς τέκνων.
εὐδαιμονοῖτον, ἀλλ' ἐκεῖ· τὰ δ' ἐνθάδε
πατὴρ ἀφείλετ'. ὦ γλυκεῖα προσβολή,
1075   ὦ μαλθακὸς χρὼς πνεῦμά θ' ἥδιστον τέκνων.
χωρεῖτε χωρεῖτ'· οὐκέτ' εἰμὶ προσβλέπειν
οἵα τε †πρὸς ὑμᾶς† ἀλλὰ νικῶμαι κακοῖς.
καὶ μανθάνω μὲν οἷα τολμήσω κακά,
θυμὸς δὲ κρείσσων τῶν ἐμῶν βουλευμάτων,
1080   ὅσπερ μεγίστων αἴτιος κακῶν βροτοῖς.

ΧΟΡΟΣ

πολλάκις ἤδη διὰ λεπτοτέρων
μύθων ἔμολον καὶ πρὸς ἁμίλλας
ἦλθον μείζους ἢ χρὴ γενεὰν
θῆλυν ἐρευνᾶν·
1085   ἀλλὰ γὰρ ἔστιν μοῦσα καὶ ἡμῖν,
ἣ προσομιλεῖ σοφίας ἕνεκεν,
πάσαισι μὲν οὔ, παῦρον δὲ γένος,
<μίαν> ἐν πολλαῖς, εὕροις ἂν ἴσως

[1077] τε πρὸς ὑμᾶς vel ἡμᾶς a: τ' ἐς ὑμᾶς b: τε παῖδας Elmsley:
fort. τ' ἐναντί'

Already the crown is on her head and the royal bride is
perishing in the robe, I know it well. But—since I now go
down the road of greatest misery and send these down one
unhappier yet—I want to say farewell to the children.

The children return to Medea.

Give me your right hands to kiss, my children, give them
to me! O hands and lips so dear to me, o noble face and
bearing of my children! I wish you happiness—but in that
other place! What is here your father has taken away. Oh,
how sweet is the touch, how tender the skin, how fragrant
the breath of these children! Go in, go in! I can no longer
look at you but am overwhelmed with my pain. And I
know well what pain I am about to undergo, but my wrath
overbears my calculation, wrath that brings mortal men
their gravest hurt.

Exit the children into the house followed by MEDEA.

CHORUS LEADER

Often ere now I have engaged in discourses subtler, and
entered upon contests greater, than is right for woman to
peer into. No, we too possess a muse, who consorts with
us to bring us wisdom: not with all of us, for it is some
small clan, one woman among many, that you will find

1078 τολμήσω omnes praeter L codd.: δρᾶν μέλλω L, tt
1087 γένος Reiske: δὴ γένος a: τι γένος b
1088 <μίαν> Elmsley cl. *Hcld.* 327–8

οὐκ ἀπόμουσον τὸ γυναικῶν.
1090 καί φημι βροτῶν οἵτινές εἰσιν
πάμπαν ἄπειροι μηδ᾽ ἐφύτευσαν
παῖδας προφέρειν εἰς εὐτυχίαν
τῶν γειναμένων.
οἱ μὲν ἄτεκνοι δι᾽ ἀπειροσύνην
1095 εἴθ᾽ ἡδὺ βροτοῖς εἴτ᾽ ἀνιαρὸν
παῖδες τελέθουσ᾽ οὐχὶ τυχόντες
πολλῶν μόχθων ἀπέχονται·
οἷσι δὲ τέκνων ἔστιν ἐν οἴκοις
γλυκερὸν βλάστημ᾽, ἐσορῶ μελέτῃ
1100 κατατρυχομένους τὸν ἄπαντα χρόνον,
πρῶτον μὲν ὅπως θρέψουσι καλῶς
βίοτόν θ᾽ ὁπόθεν λείψουσι τέκνοις·
ἔτι δ᾽ ἐκ τούτων εἴτ᾽ ἐπὶ φλαύροις
εἴτ᾽ ἐπὶ χρηστοῖς
μοχθοῦσι, τόδ᾽ ἐστὶν ἄδηλον.
1105 ἓν δὲ τὸ πάντων λοίσθιον ἤδη
πᾶσιν κατερῶ θνητοῖσι κακόν·
καὶ δὴ γὰρ ἅλις βίοτόν θ᾽ ηὗρον
σῶμά τ᾽ ἐς ἥβην ἤλυθε τέκνων
χρηστοί τ᾽ ἐγένοντ᾽· εἰ δὲ κυρῆσαι
1110 δαίμων οὕτω, φροῦδος ἐς Ἅιδου
θάνατος προφέρων σώματα τέκνων.
πῶς οὖν λύει πρὸς τοῖς ἄλλοις
τήνδ᾽ ἔτι λύπην ἀνιαροτάτην
παίδων ἕνεκεν
1115 θνητοῖσι θεοὺς ἐπιβάλλειν;

396

with a share in the Muse. I say that those mortals who are utterly without experience of children and have never borne them have the advantage in good fortune over those who have. For the childless, because they do not possess children and do not know whether they are a pleasure or a vexation to mortals, hold themselves aloof from many griefs. But those who have in their house the sweet gift of children, them I see worn down their whole life with care: first, how they shall raise their children well and how they may leave them some livelihood. And after that it is unclear whether all their toil is expended on worthless or worthy objects. But the last of all misfortunes for all mortals I shall now mention. Suppose they have found a sufficient livelihood, suppose the children have arrived at young manhood and their character is good: yet if their destiny so chances, off goes death carrying the children's bodies to Hades. How then does it profit us that for the sake of heirs the gods cast upon mortals, in addition to their other troubles, this further grief most painful?

Enter MEDEA from the house.

1089 οὐκ Π, sicut coni. Reiske: κοὐκ C

1099 ἐσορῶ Π: ὁρῶ C

1110 "Αιδου Π, sicut coni. Earle: ἀίδην vel -αν C

397

ΜΗΔΕΙΑ

φίλαι, πάλαι τοι προσμένουσα τὴν τύχην
καραδοκῶ τἀκεῖθεν οἷ προβήσεται.
καὶ δὴ δέδορκα τόνδε τῶν Ἰάσονος
στείχοντ᾽ ὀπαδῶν· πνεῦμα δ᾽ ἠρεθισμένον
1120 δείκνυσιν ὥς τι καινὸν ἀγγελεῖ κακόν.

ΑΓΓΕΛΟΣ

[ὦ δεινὸν ἔργον παρανόμως εἰργασμένη,]
Μήδεια, φεῦγε φεῦγε, μήτε ναΐαν
λιποῦσ᾽ ἀπήνην μήτ᾽ ὄχον πεδοστιβῆ.

ΜΗΔΕΙΑ

τί δ᾽ ἄξιόν μοι τῆσδε τυγχάνει φυγῆς;

ΑΓΓΕΛΟΣ

1125 ὄλωλεν ἡ τύραννος ἀρτίως κόρη
Κρέων θ᾽ ὁ φύσας φαρμάκων τῶν σῶν ὕπο.

ΜΗΔΕΙΑ

κάλλιστον εἶπας μῦθον, ἐν δ᾽ εὐεργέταις
τὸ λοιπὸν ἤδη καὶ φίλοις ἐμοῖς ἔσῃ.

ΑΓΓΕΛΟΣ

τί φῄς; φρονεῖς μὲν ὀρθὰ κοὐ μαίνῃ, γύναι,
1130 ἥτις, τυράννων ἑστίαν ᾐκισμένη,
χαίρεις κλύουσα κοὐ φοβῇ τὰ τοιάδε;

ΜΗΔΕΙΑ

ἔχω τι κἀγὼ τοῖσι σοῖς ἐναντίον
λόγοισιν εἰπεῖν· ἀλλὰ μὴ σπέρχου, φίλος,

MEDEA

My friends, for a long time now I have been expecting the event, waiting to see how matters in that quarter will turn out. And look, here I see one of Jason's servants coming. His agitated breathing shows that he is about to announce some fresh disaster.

Enter servant of Jason as MESSENGER *by Eisodos B.*

MESSENGER

[You that have done a terrible deed unlawfully,] Medea, run for your life! The sea vessel and the chariot that treads the ground—do not refuse them!

MEDEA

What event calls for my fleeing thus?

MESSENGER

The princess and her father Creon have just been killed by your poisons!

MEDEA

A splendid report you bring! Henceforth I shall regard you as one of my benefactors and friends.

MESSENGER

What? Can you be in your right mind and not mad, woman? Can you commit an outrage against the royal house, and then rejoice at the news and not be afraid?

MEDEA

I too have something that I could say in reply to your words. Do not be hot and hasty, friend, but tell me: how

λέξον δέ· πῶς ὤλοντο; δὶς τόσον γὰρ ἂν
1135 τέρψειας ἡμᾶς, εἰ τεθνᾶσι παγκάκως.

ΑΓΓΕΛΟΣ

ἐπεὶ τέκνων σῶν ἦλθε δίπτυχος γονὴ
σὺν πατρὶ καὶ παρῆλθε νυμφικοὺς δόμους,
ἥσθημεν οἵπερ σοῖς ἐκάμνομεν κακοῖς
δμῶες· δι᾽ ὤτων δ᾽ εὐθὺς ἦν πολὺς λόγος
1140 σὲ καὶ πόσιν σὸν νεῖκος ἐσπεῖσθαι τὸ πρίν.
κυνεῖ δ᾽ ὁ μέν τις χεῖρ᾽, ὁ δὲ ξανθὸν κάρα
παίδων· ἐγὼ δὲ καὐτὸς ἡδονῆς ὕπο
στέγας γυναικῶν σὺν τέκνοις ἅμ᾽ ἑσπόμην.
δέσποινα δ᾽ ἣν νῦν ἀντὶ σοῦ θαυμάζομεν,
1145 πρὶν μὲν τέκνων σῶν εἰσιδεῖν ξυνωρίδα,
πρόθυμον εἶχ᾽ ὀφθαλμὸν εἰς Ἰάσονα·
ἔπειτα μέντοι προυκαλύψατ᾽ ὄμματα
λευκήν τ᾽ ἀπέστρεψ᾽ ἔμπαλιν παρηίδα,
παίδων μυσαχθεῖσ᾽ εἰσόδους. πόσις δὲ σὸς
1150 ὀργάς τ᾽ ἀφήρει καὶ χόλον νεάνιδος,
λέγων τάδ᾽· Οὐ μὴ δυσμενὴς ἔσῃ φίλοις,
παύσῃ δὲ θυμοῦ καὶ πάλιν στρέψεις κάρα,
φίλους νομίζουσ᾽ οὕσπερ ἂν πόσις σέθεν,
δέξῃ δὲ δῶρα καὶ παραιτήσῃ πατρὸς
1155 φυγὰς ἀφεῖναι παισὶ τοῖσδ᾽ ἐμὴν χάριν;
ἡ δ᾽, ὡς ἐσεῖδε κόσμον, οὐκ ἠνέσχετο,
ἀλλ᾽ ἤνεσ᾽ ἀνδρὶ πάντα, καὶ πρὶν ἐκ δόμων
μακρὰν ἀπεῖναι πατέρα καὶ παῖδας σέθεν
λαβοῦσα πέπλους ποικίλους ἠμπέσχετο,

did they die? You will give me twice the pleasure if they died in agony.

MESSENGER

When your two children came with their father and entered the bride's house, all of us servants who were troubled by your misfortunes were cheered. For our ears buzzed with the loud report that you and your husband had brought your former quarrel to an end. And someone kissed the hands and another the blond heads of the children. And I myself for very joy went along with the children into the women's quarters. Here the mistress we now honor instead of you, before she saw the two children, had eyes only for Jason. Then she veiled her eyes and turned her white cheek away, disgusted at seeing the children come in. But your husband tried to take away the young woman's wrathful mood and said, "You must not be unkind to your kin but must cease your anger and turn your face toward us again, regarding those as near and dear whom your husband so regards. Receive these gifts and ask your father to grant these children release from their exile for my sake."

When she had seen the raiment, she could not hold out but consented to all her husband asked, and before your children and their father had gone far from the house, she took the many-colored gown and put it on, and setting the

---

1139 δι' οἴκων Weil cl. Σ
1158 πατέρα] τόνδε Page

1160 χρυσοῦν τε θεῖσα στέφανον ἀμφὶ βοστρύχοις
λαμπρῷ κατόπτρῳ σχηματίζεται κόμην,
ἄψυχον εἰκὼ προσγελῶσα σώματος.
κἄπειτ' ἀναστᾶσ' ἐκ θρόνων διέρχεται
στέγας, ἁβρὸν βαίνουσα παλλεύκῳ ποδί,
1165 δώροις ὑπερχαίρουσα, πολλὰ πολλάκις
τένοντ' ἐς ὀρθὸν ὄμμασι σκοπουμένη.
τοὐνθένδε μέντοι δεινὸν ἦν θέαμ' ἰδεῖν·
χροιὰν γὰρ ἀλλάξασα λεχρία πάλιν
χωρεῖ τρέμουσα κῶλα καὶ μόλις φθάνει
1170 θρόνοισιν ἐμπεσοῦσα μὴ χαμαὶ πεσεῖν.
καί τις γεραιὰ προσπόλων, δόξασά που
ἢ Πανὸς ὀργὰς ἤ τινος θεῶν μολεῖν,
ἀνωλόλυξε, πρίν γ' ὁρᾷ διὰ στόμα
χωροῦντα λευκὸν ἀφρόν, ὀμμάτων τ' ἄπο
1175 κόρας στρέφουσαν, αἷμά τ' οὐκ ἐνὸν χροΐ·
εἶτ' ἀντίμολπον ἧκεν ὀλολυγῆς μέγαν
κωκυτόν. εὐθὺς δ' ἡ μὲν ἐς πατρὸς δόμους
ὥρμησεν, ἡ δὲ πρὸς τὸν ἀρτίως πόσιν,
φράσουσα νύμφης συμφοράν· ἅπασα δὲ
1180 στέγη πυκνοῖσιν ἐκτύπει δραμήμασιν.
    ἤδη δ' ἑλίσσων κῶλον ἐκπλέθρου δρόμου
ταχὺς βαδιστὴς τερμόνων ἂν ἥπτετο,
ὅτ' ἐξ ἀναύδου καὶ μύσαντος ὄμματος
δεινὸν στενάξασ' ἡ τάλαιν' ἠγείρετο.
1185 διπλοῦν γὰρ αὐτῇ πῆμ' ἐπεστρατεύετο·
χρυσοῦς μὲν ἀμφὶ κρατὶ κείμενος πλόκος
θαυμαστὸν ἵει νᾶμα παμφάγου πυρός,

gold crown about her locks, she arranged her hair in a bright mirror, smiling at the lifeless image of her body. And getting up from her seat she paraded about the room, her white feet making dainty steps, entranced with the gifts, glancing back again and again at the straight tendon of her leg. But then there was a terrible sight to behold. For her color changed, and with legs trembling she staggered back sidelong, and by falling on the chair barely escaped collapsing on the floor. And one old woman among the servants, thinking, I suppose, that a frenzy from Pan or one of the other gods had come upon her, raised a festal shout to the god, until she saw the white foam coming between her lips and her eyes starting out of their sockets and her skin all pale and bloodless. Then indeed she raised a wail in answer to her former shout. And at once one servant went to her father's house, another to her new husband to tell of the bride's misfortune: the whole house rang with the sound of drumming footsteps.

And by now a sprinter, putting his legs in swift motion, would be reaching the finish line of the two-hundred-yard course,[a] when the poor woman wakened from her silence, opened her eyes, and gave forth a terrible groan. For she was being attacked with a double pain. The golden circlet about her head shot forth a terrible stream of consuming

---

[a] I.e., about twenty seconds elapsed.

1180 δρα[μη]μασιν Π, sicut coni. Cobet: δρομ- C

1181 ἑλίσσων Herwerden (cf. Tro. 333, I.A. 212–5): ἀνέλκων C ἐκπλέθρου Reiske: ἔκ- vel ἔκπλεθρον C

1182 ἂν ἥπτετο Musgrave: ἀνθήπτετο C

1183 ὅτ᾽ Π: ἡ δ᾽ C

πέπλοι δὲ λεπτοί, σῶν τέκνων δωρήματα,
λευκὴν ἔδαπτον σάρκα τῆς δυσδαίμονος.
1190 φεύγει δ' ἀναστᾶσ' ἐκ θρόνων πυρουμένη,
σείουσα χαίτην κρατά τ' ἄλλοτ' ἄλλοσε,
ῥῖψαι θέλουσα στέφανον · ἀλλ' ἀραρότως
σύνδεσμα χρυσὸς εἶχε, πῦρ δ', ἐπεὶ κόμην
ἔσεισε, μᾶλλον δὶς τόσως ἐλάμπετο.
1195 πίτνει δ' ἐς οὖδας συμφορᾷ νικωμένη,
πλὴν τῷ τεκόντι κάρτα δυσμαθὴς ἰδεῖν ·
οὔτ' ὀμμάτων γὰρ δῆλος ἦν κατάστασις
οὔτ' εὐφυὲς πρόσωπον, αἷμα δ' ἐξ ἄκρου
ἔσταζε κρατὸς συμπεφυρμένον πυρί,
1200 σάρκες δ' ἀπ' ὀστέων ὥστε πεύκινον δάκρυ
γνάθοις ἀδήλοις φαρμάκων ἀπέρρεον,
δεινὸν θέαμα · πᾶσι δ' ἦν φόβος θιγεῖν
νεκροῦ · τύχην γὰρ εἴχομεν διδάσκαλον.
    πατὴρ δ' ὁ τλήμων συμφορᾶς ἀγνωσίᾳ
1205 ἄφνω παρελθὼν δῶμα προσπίτνει νεκρῷ.
ᾤμωξε δ' εὐθὺς καὶ περιπτύξας χέρας
κυνεῖ προσαυδῶν τοιάδ' · Ὦ δύστηνε παῖ,
τίς σ' ὦδ' ἀτίμως δαιμόνων ἀπώλεσεν,
τίς τὸν γέροντα τύμβον ὀρφανὸν σέθεν
1210 τίθησιν; οἴμοι, συνθάνοιμί σοι, τέκνον.
ἐπεὶ δὲ θρήνων καὶ γόων ἐπαύσατο,
χρῄζων γεραιὸν ἐξαναστῆσαι δέμας
προσείχεθ' ὥστε κισσὸς ἔρνεσιν δάφνης
λεπτοῖσι πέπλοις, δεινὰ δ' ἦν παλαίσματα ·
1215 ὁ μὲν γὰρ ἤθελ' ἐξαναστῆσαι γόνυ,

fire, and the fine-spun gown, gift of your sons, was eating
into the wretched woman's white flesh. All aflame she
leapt from the chair and fled, tossing her hair this way and
that, trying to shake off the diadem. But the gold crown
held its fastenings firmly, and when she shook her hair, the
fire merely blazed up twice as high. She fell to the floor,
overwhelmed by disaster, barely recognizable to any but
her father. Her eyes no longer kept their wonted form nor
did her shapely face. From the top of her head blood
dripped, mingled with fire, and her flesh dropped from
her bones like resin from a pine torch, torn by the unseen
jaws of the poison, a dreadful sight to behold. We were all
afraid to touch the corpse, taught well by the event we had
seen.

But her poor father, ignorant of the calamity, stumbled
upon her body unprepared as he entered the chamber.
And at once he groaned aloud and, throwing his arms
about her, kissed her and said, "O unhappy daughter,
which of the gods has destroyed you so shamefully and has
bereft me of you, me, an old man at death's door? Oh,
may I die with you, my daughter!" But when he had
ceased from his wailing and lamenting and wanted to raise
up his aged body to his feet, he was stuck fast to the fine-
spun dress, as ivy clings to laurel-shoots, and a terrible
wrestling ensued. For he wanted to get up again, but

1205 παρελθὼν Nauck: προσ- C

ἡ δ' ἀντελάζυτ'· εἰ δὲ πρὸς βίαν ἄγοι,
σάρκας γεραιὰς ἐσπάρασσ' ἀπ' ὀστέων.
χρόνῳ δ' ἀπέστη καὶ μεθῆκ' ὁ δύσμορος
ψυχήν· κακοῦ γὰρ οὐκέτ' ἦν ὑπέρτερος.
1220 κεῖνται δὲ νεκροὶ παῖς τε καὶ γέρων πατὴρ
πέλας, †ποθεινὴ δακρύοισι συμφορά†.

    καί μοι τὸ μὲν σὸν ἐκποδὼν ἔστω λόγου·
γνώσῃ γὰρ αὐτὴ ζημίας ἐπιστροφήν.
τὰ θνητὰ δ' οὐ νῦν πρῶτον ἡγοῦμαι σκιάν,
1225 οὐδ' ἂν τρέσας εἴποιμι τοὺς σοφοὺς βροτῶν
δοκοῦντας εἶναι καὶ μεριμνητὰς λόγων
τούτους μεγίστην μωρίαν ὀφλισκάνειν.
θνητῶν γὰρ οὐδείς ἐστιν εὐδαίμων ἀνήρ·
ὄλβου δ' ἐπιρρυέντος εὐτυχέστερος
1230 ἄλλου γένοιτ' ἂν ἄλλος, εὐδαίμων δ' ἂν οὔ.

ΧΟΡΟΣ

ἔοιχ' ὁ δαίμων πολλὰ τῇδ' ἐν ἡμέρᾳ
κακὰ ξυνάπτειν ἐνδίκως Ἰάσονι.
[ὦ πλῆμον, ὥς σου συμφορὰς οἰκτίρομεν,
κόρη Κρέοντος, ἥτις εἰς Ἅιδου δόμους
1235 οἴχῃ γάμων ἕκατι τῶν Ἰάσονος.]

ΜΗΔΕΙΑ

φίλαι, δέδοκται τοὔργον ὡς τάχιστά μοι
παῖδας κτανούσῃ τῆσδ' ἀφορμᾶσθαι χθονός,
καὶ μὴ σχολὴν ἄγουσαν ἐκδοῦναι τέκνα
ἄλλῃ φονεῦσαι δυσμενεστέρᾳ χερί.
1240 πάντως σφ' ἀνάγκη κατθανεῖν· ἐπεὶ δὲ χρή,

she held him fast and prevented him. And if he used force, he would rip his aged flesh from his bones. Finally the poor man gave up and breathed his last, for he could not overcome the calamity. They lie side by side in death, the daughter and her old father, a sight to make one weep.

As regards your fate, I will say nothing: you will know soon enough the punishment that will visit you. As for our mortal life, this is not the first time that I have thought it to be a shadow, and I would say without any fear that those mortals who seem to be clever and crafters of polished speeches are guilty of the greatest folly. For no mortal ever attains to blessedness. One may may be luckier than another when wealth flows his way, but blessed never.

Exit MESSENGER *by Eisodos B.*

CHORUS LEADER

It seems that fate is this day fastening calamity on Jason, and with justice. [O poor woman, daughter of Creon, how we pity your misfortune! Because of your marriage to Jason you have departed to the halls of Hades.]

MEDEA

Friends, my resolve is fixed on the deed, to kill my children with all speed and to flee from this land: I must not, by lingering, deliver my children for murder to a less kindly hand. They must die at all events, and since they

---

1218 ἀπέσβη Scaliger
1221 ποθεινὴ δυσνοοῦσι Musgrave
1223 ἐπιστροφήν Lenting: ἀπο- C
1227 μωρίαν editio Aldina: ζημίαν C
1233-5 del. Weil

ἡμεῖς κτενοῦμεν οἵπερ ἐξεφύσαμεν.
ἀλλ' εἶ' ὁπλίζου, καρδία· τί μέλλομεν
τὰ δεινὰ κἀναγκαῖα μὴ πράσσειν κακά;
ἄγ', ὦ τάλαινα χεὶρ ἐμή, λαβὲ ξίφος,
1245 λάβ', ἕρπε πρὸς βαλβῖδα λυπηρὰν βίου,
καὶ μὴ κακισθῆς μηδ' ἀναμνησθῆς τέκνων,
ὡς φίλταθ', ὡς ἔτικτες, ἀλλὰ τήνδε γε
λαθοῦ βραχεῖαν ἡμέραν παίδων σέθεν
κἄπειτα θρήνει· καὶ γὰρ εἰ κτενεῖς σφ', ὅμως
1250 φίλοι γ' ἔφυσαν· δυστυχὴς δ' ἐγὼ γυνή.

ΧΟΡΟΣ

στρ. α

ἰὼ Γᾶ τε καὶ παμφαὴς
ἀκτὶς Ἁλίου, κατίδετ' ἴδετε τὰν
ὀλομέναν γυναῖκα, πρὶν φοινίαν
τέκνοις προσβαλεῖν χέρ' αὐτοκτόνον·
1255 σᾶς γὰρ χρυσέας ἀπὸ γονᾶς
ἔβλαστεν, θεοῦ δ' αἷμα ⟨χαμαὶ⟩ πίτνειν
φόβος ὑπ' ἀνέρων.
ἀλλά νιν, ὦ φάος διογενές, κάτειρ-
γε κατάπαυσον ἔξελ' οἴκων τάλαι-
1260 ναν φονίαν τ' Ἐρινὺν ὑπαλαστόρων.

ἀντ. α

μάταν μόχθος ἔρρει τέκνων,
μάταν ἄρα γένος φίλιον ἔτεκες, ὦ
κυανεᾶν λιποῦσα Συμπληγάδων

1256 ⟨χαμαὶ⟩ Diggle
1260 ὑπαλαστόρων Willink: ὑπ' ἀ. C

must, I who gave them birth shall kill them. Come, put on your armor, my heart! Why do I put off doing the terrible deed that must be done? Come, luckless hand, take the sword, take it and go to your life's miserable goal! Do not weaken, do not remember that you love the children, that you gave them life. Instead, for this brief day forget them—and mourn hereafter: for even if you kill them, they were dear to you. Oh, what an unhappy woman I am!

Exit MEDEA *into the house.*

CHORUS

O earth, o ray of the Sun that lightens all, turn your gaze, o turn it to this ruinous woman before she lays her bloody murderous hands upon her children! They are sprung from your race of gold,[a] and it is a fearful thing for the blood of a god to be spilt upon the ground by the hands of mortal men. O light begotten of Zeus, check the cruel and murderous Fury, take her from this house plagued by spirits of vengeance.[b]

The toil of bearing your children has come to naught, it was to no purpose that you bore your dear offspring, you who left behind the inhospitable strait where the dark blue Symplegades clash. O unhappy woman, why does

[a] Helios is the children's great-grandfather.

[b] The Chorus see in the murder the work of an Erinys (Fury), one of the punishing divinities usually thought of as under the control of Zeus. That human agents may be sometimes regarded as embodying this spirit or serving as its unconscious agent is clear from Aeschylus, *Agamemnon* 749, and Euripides, *Trojan Women* 457.

409

πετρᾶν ἀξενωτάταν ἐσβολάν.
1265 δειλαία, τί σοι φρενοβαρὴς
χόλος προσπίτνει καὶ ζαμενὴς <φόνου>
φόνος ἀμείβεται;
χαλεπὰ γὰρ βροτοῖς ὁμογενῆ μιά-
σματ᾽, ἕπεται δ᾽ ἅμ᾽ αὐτοφόνταις ξυνω-
1270 δὰ θεόθεν πίτνοντ᾽ ἐπὶ δόμοις ἄχη.

<ΠΑΙΔΕΣ>
<(ἔσωθεν)>
1270a ἰώ μοι.

ΧΟΡΟΣ
στρ. β
1273 ἀκούεις βοὰν ἀκούεις τέκνων;
1274 ἰὼ τλᾶμον, ὦ κακοτυχὲς γύναι.

ΠΑΙΣ Α
1271 οἴμοι, τί δράσω; ποῖ φύγω μητρὸς χέρας;

ΠΑΙΣ Β
1272 οὐκ οἶδ᾽, ἄδελφε φίλτατ᾽· ὀλλύμεσθα γάρ.

ΧΟΡΟΣ
1275 παρέλθω δόμους; ἀρῆξαι φόνον δοκεῖ μοι τέκνοις.

1265 φρενοβαρὴς Seidler: φρενῶν βαρὺς C
1266 ζαμενὴς Porson: δυσμενὴς C   <φόνου> Wecklein
1269 ἕπεται δ᾽ ἅμ᾽ Leo: ἐπὶ γαῖαν C
1270an <Παῖδες (ἔσωθεν)> fere Murray
1270a ιωι μ[οι Π: om. C
1273–4 ante 1271–2 Seidler

wrath fall so heavy upon your mind and one rash murder succeed another? Grievous for mortals is the stain of kindred blood. For the murderers are dogged by woes harmonious with their deeds, sent by the gods upon their houses.

CHILDREN

(within) Help!

CHORUS

Do you hear the cry, the children's cry? O wretched and accursed woman!

FIRST CHILD

(within) Oh, what shall I do? How can I escape my mother's hands?

SECOND CHILD

(within) I know not, dear brother. We are done for!

CHORUS

Shall I enter the house? I am determined to stop the death of the children.

ΠΑΙΣ Α

ναί, πρὸς θεῶν, ἀρήξατ᾽· ἐν δέοντι γάρ.

ΠΑΙΣ Β

ὡς ἐγγὺς ἤδη γ᾽ ἐσμὲν ἀρκύων ξίφους.

ΧΟΡΟΣ

1280 τάλαιν᾽, ὡς ἄρ᾽ ἦσθα πέτρος ἢ σίδαρος, ἅτις τέκνων
ὃν ἔτεκες ἄροτον αὐτόχειρι μοίρᾳ κτενεῖς.

ἀντ. β

μίαν δὴ κλύω μίαν τῶν πάρος
γυναῖκ᾽ ἐν φίλοις χέρα βαλεῖν τέκνοις,
Ἰνὼ μανεῖσαν ἐκ θεῶν, ὅθ᾽ ἡ Διὸς
1285 δάμαρ νιν ἐξέπεμπε δωμάτων ἄλαις·
πίτνει δ᾽ ἁ τάλαιν᾽ ἐς ἅλμαν φόνῳ τέκνων δυσσεβεῖ,
ἀκτῆς ὑπερτείνασα ποντίας πόδα,
δυοῖν τε παίδοιν ξυνθανοῦσ᾽ ἀπόλλυται.
1290 τί δῆτ᾽ οὐ γένοιτ᾽ ἂν ἔτι δεινόν; ὦ γυναικῶν λέχος
πολύπονον, ὅσα βροτοῖς ἔρεξας ἤδη κακά.

ΙΑΣΩΝ

γυναῖκες, αἳ τῆσδ᾽ ἐγγὺς ἕστατε στέγης,
ἆρ᾽ ἐν δόμοισιν ἡ τὰ δείν᾽ εἰργασμένη
1295 Μήδεια τοισίδ᾽ ἢ μεθέστηκεν φυγῇ;
δεῖ γάρ νιν ἤτοι γῆς γε κρυφθῆναι κάτω
ἢ πτηνὸν ἆραι σῶμ᾽ ἐς αἰθέρος βάθος,
εἰ μὴ τυράννων δώμασιν δώσει δίκην.
πέποιθ᾽ ἀποκτείνασα κοιράνους χθονὸς
1300 ἀθῷος αὐτὴ τῶνδε φεύξεσθαι δόμων;

MEDEA

FIRST CHILD

(within) Yes, in heaven's name, stop it! Now is the time!

SECOND CHILD

(within) We are now close to the murderous snare!

CHORUS

Hard-hearted wretch, you are, it seems, a stone or a piece of iron! You mean to kill the children you gave birth to with a fate your own hand deals out!

One woman, only one, of all that have been, have I heard of who put her hand to her own children: Ino driven mad by the gods when Hera sent her forth from the house to wander in madness. The unhappy woman fell into the sea, impiously murdering her sons. Stepping over the sea's edge, she perished with her two children. What further horror is now impossible? O womankind and marriage fraught with pain, how many are the troubles you have already wrought for mortal men!

Enter JASON by Eisodos B.

JASON

You women who stand near the house, is Medea inside, she who has done these dreadful deeds, or has she fled? She will have to hide herself beneath the earth or soar aloft to heaven if she is not going to give satisfaction to the royal house. Does she think that having killed the land's ruling family she will escape from this house unscathed?

1277–8 om. Π   1281 ὃν Π,sicut coni. Seidler: ὧν C

1285 ἅλαις Π, sicut coni. Blaydes: ἄλῃ fere C

1290 δῆτ' Π, sicut coni. Hermann: δή ποτ' C   οὐ Π, οὖν C

1295 τοισίδ' Canter: τοῖσιν a: τοῖσδέ γ' b

ἀλλ' οὐ γὰρ αὐτῆς φροντίδ' ὡς τέκνων ἔχω·
κείνην μὲν οὓς ἔδρασεν ἔρξουσιν κακῶς,
ἐμῶν δὲ παίδων ἦλθον ἐκσώσων βίον,
μή μοί τι δράσωσ' οἱ προσήκοντες γένει,
1305 μητρῷον ἐκπράσσοντες ἀνόσιον φόνον.

ΧΟΡΟΣ
ὦ τλῆμον, οὐκ οἶσθ' οἷ κακῶν ἐλήλυθας,
Ἰᾶσον· οὐ γὰρ τοῦσδ' ἂν ἐφθέγξω λόγους.

ΙΑΣΩΝ
τί δ' ἔστιν; οὔ που κἄμ' ἀποκτεῖναι θέλει;

ΧΟΡΟΣ
παῖδες τεθνᾶσι χειρὶ μητρῴᾳ σέθεν.

ΙΑΣΩΝ
1310 οἴμοι, τί λέξεις; ὥς μ' ἀπώλεσας, γύναι.

ΧΟΡΟΣ
ὡς οὐκέτ' ὄντων σῶν τέκνων φρόντιζε δή.

ΙΑΣΩΝ
ποῦ γάρ νιν ἔκτειν'; ἐντὸς ἢ 'ξωθεν δόμων;

ΧΟΡΟΣ
πύλας ἀνοίξας σῶν τέκνων ὄψῃ φόνον.

ΙΑΣΩΝ
χαλᾶτε κλῇδας ὡς τάχιστα, πρόσπολοι,
1315 ἐκλύεθ' ἁρμούς, ὡς ἴδω διπλοῦν κακόν,

1308 οὔ που Π, sicut coni. Barthold: ἤ πω et ἤ που C

But it is not so much about her that I am concerned as about the children. *She* will be punished by those she has wronged, but I have come to save the lives of my children, that no harm may come to them from the next of kin, avenging on them their mother's impious crime.

CHORUS LEADER

Poor Jason, you have no idea how far gone you are in misfortune! Else you would not have spoken these words.

JASON

What is it? Surely she does not mean to kill me as well?

CHORUS LEADER

Your children are dead, killed by their mother's hand.

JASON

Ah, what can you mean? You have destroyed me, woman!

CHORUS LEADER

You must realize that your children are no more.

JASON

Where did she kill them? In the house or outside?

CHORUS LEADER

Open the gates and you will see your slaughtered sons.

JASON

Servants, remove the bar at once so that I may see a double disaster, these children's corpses <and her who did

1316   τοὺς μὲν θανόντας, τὴν δὲ <δράσασαν τάδε,
1316a   φόνου τε παίδων τῶνδε> τείσωμαι δίκην.

ΜΗΔΕΙΑ

τί τάσδε κινεῖς κἀναμοχλεύεις πύλας,
νεκροὺς ἐρευνῶν κἀμὲ τὴν εἰργασμένην;
παῦσαι πόνου τοῦδ'. εἰ δ' ἐμοῦ χρείαν ἔχεις,
1320   λέγ' εἴ τι βούλῃ, χειρὶ δ' οὐ ψαύσεις ποτέ·
τοιόνδ' ὄχημα πατρὸς Ἥλιος πατὴρ
δίδωσιν ἡμῖν, ἔρυμα πολεμίας χερός.

ΙΑΣΩΝ

ὦ μῖσος, ὦ μέγιστον ἐχθίστη γύναι
θεοῖς τε κἀμοὶ παντί τ' ἀνθρώπων γένει,
1325   ἥτις τέκνοισι σοῖσιν ἐμβαλεῖν ξίφος
ἔτλης τεκοῦσα κἄμ' ἄπαιδ' ἀπώλεσας.
καὶ ταῦτα δράσασ' ἥλιόν τε προσβλέπεις
καὶ γαῖαν, ἔργον τλᾶσα δυσσεβέστατον;
ὄλοι'. ἐγὼ δὲ νῦν φρονῶ, τότ' οὐ φρονῶν,
1330   ὅτ' ἐκ δόμων σε βαρβάρου τ' ἀπὸ χθονὸς
Ἕλλην' ἐς οἶκον ἠγόμην, κακὸν μέγα,
πατρός τε καὶ γῆς προδότιν ἥ σ' ἐθρέψατο.
τὸν σὸν δ' ἀλάστορ' εἰς ἔμ' ἔσκηψαν θεοί·
κτανοῦσα γὰρ δὴ σὸν κάσιν παρέστιον
1335   τὸ καλλίπρωρον εἰσέβης Ἀργοῦς σκάφος.
ἤρξω μὲν ἐκ τοιῶνδε· νυμφευθεῖσα δὲ
παρ' ἀνδρὶ τῷδε καὶ τεκοῦσά μοι τέκνα,

<hr/>

1316–16a lacunam hic statui, cl. 1185, *Hec.* 518, *Su.* 1035, etc.
1316a τείσωμαι δίκην a: τείσομαι φόνῳ b

the deed, so that for these children's murder>[a] I may exact punishment!

Jason tries to open the doors of the house. MEDEA *appears aloft in a winged chariot upon the* mechane, *which rises from behind the* skene.

MEDEA

Why do you rattle these gates and try to unbar them, in search of the corpses and me who did the deed? Cease your toil. If you need anything from me, speak if you like. But your hand can never touch me: such is the chariot Helios my grandfather has given me to ward off a hostile hand.

JASON

O detestable creature, utterly hateful to the gods, to me, and to the whole human race, you brought yourself to take the sword to your own children and destroyed my life with childlessness! Having done this can you look on the sun and the earth, when you are guilty of a most abominable deed? Death and ruin seize you! Now I am in my right mind, though I was insane before when I brought you from your home among the barbarians to a Greek house. A great curse you were even then, betrayer of your father and of the land that nourished you. But the gods have visited on me the avenging spirit meant for you. For you killed your own brother at the hearth and then stepped aboard the fair-prowed Argo.

It was with acts like these that you began. But now when you were married to me and had borne me children,

[a] I give the probable sense of the lacuna.

417

εὐνῆς ἕκατι καὶ λέχους σφ' ἀπώλεσας.
οὐκ ἔστιν ἥτις τοῦτ' ἂν Ἑλληνὶς γυνὴ
1340 ἔτλη ποθ', ὧν γε πρόσθεν ἠξίουν ἐγὼ
γῆμαι σέ, κῆδος ἐχθρὸν ὀλέθριόν τ' ἐμοί,
λέαιναν, οὐ γυναῖκα, τῆς Τυρσηνίδος
Σκύλλης ἔχουσαν ἀγριωτέραν φύσιν.
ἀλλ' οὐ γὰρ ἄν σε μυρίοις ὀνείδεσιν
1345 δάκοιμι· τοιόνδ' ἐμπέφυκέ σοι θράσος·
ἔρρ', αἰσχροποιὲ καὶ τέκνων μιαιφόνε.
ἐμοὶ δὲ τὸν ἐμὸν δαίμον' αἰάζειν πάρα,
ὃς οὔτε λέκτρων νεογάμων ὀνήσομαι,
οὐ παῖδας οὓς ἔφυσα κἀξεθρεψάμην
1350 ἔξω προσειπεῖν ζῶντας ἀλλ' ἀπώλεσα.

ΜΗΔΕΙΑ

μακρὰν ἂν ἐξέτεινα τοῖσδ' ἐναντίον
λόγοισιν, εἰ μὴ Ζεὺς πατὴρ ἠπίστατο
οἷ' ἐξ ἐμοῦ πέπονθας οἷά τ' εἰργάσω·
σὺ δ' οὐκ ἔμελλες τἄμ' ἀτιμάσας λέχη
1355 τερπνὸν διάξειν βίοτον ἐγγελῶν ἐμοὶ
οὐδ' ἡ τύραννος, οὐδ' ὅ σοι προσθεὶς γάμους
Κρέων ἀνατεὶ τῆσδέ μ' ἐκβαλεῖν χθονός.
πρὸς ταῦτα καὶ λέαιναν, εἰ βούλῃ, κάλει
καὶ Σκύλλαν ἣ Τυρσηνὸν ᾤκησεν πέτραν·
1360 τῆς σῆς γὰρ ὡς χρῆν καρδίας ἀνθηψάμην.

1356 οὐδ' . . . οὐδ' Elmsley: οὔθ' . . . οὔθ' C
1359 πέτραν Elmsley: πέδον C: v. del. Verrall

MEDEA

you killed them because of sex and the marriage bed. No Greek woman would have dared to do this, yet I married you in preference to them, and a hateful and destructive match it has proved! You are a she-lion, not a woman, with a nature more savage than Scylla the Tuscan monster! But since ten thousand insults of mine would fail to sting you—such is your native impudence—be gone, doer of disgraceful deeds and murderer of your children! Mine is a fate to bewail: I shall never have the benefit of my new bride, nor will I be able to speak to my children alive, the children I begot and raised, but have lost them.

MEDEA

Long is the speech I would have made in reply to these words of yours if Father Zeus did not know clearly what kind of treatment you have had from me and how you have repaid it. You were not going to cast aside my bed and then spend a pleasant life laughing at me, no, nor the princess either, nor was Creon, who offered you his daughter, going to exile me with impunity! Call me a she-lion, then if you like, and Scylla, dweller on the Tuscan cliff! For I have touched your heart in the vital spot.

ΙΑΣΩΝ

καὐτή γε λυπῇ καὶ κακῶν κοινωνὸς εἶ.

ΜΗΔΕΙΑ

σάφ᾽ ἴσθι· λύει δ᾽ ἄλγος, ἢν σὺ μὴ ᾽γγελᾷς.

ΙΑΣΩΝ

ὦ τέκνα, μητρὸς ὡς κακῆς ἐκύρσατε.

ΜΗΔΕΙΑ

ὦ παῖδες, ὡς ὤλεσθε πατρῴᾳ νόσῳ.

ΙΑΣΩΝ

1365   οὔτοι νιν ἡμὴ δεξιά γ᾽ ἀπώλεσεν.

ΜΗΔΕΙΑ

ἀλλ᾽ ὕβρις οἵ τε σοὶ νεοδμῆτες γάμοι.

ΙΑΣΩΝ

λέχους σφε κἠξίωσας οὕνεκα κτανεῖν;

ΜΗΔΕΙΑ

σμικρὸν γυναικὶ πῆμα τοῦτ᾽ εἶναι δοκεῖς;

ΙΑΣΩΝ

ἥτις γε σώφρων· σοὶ δὲ πάντ᾽ ἐστὶν κακά.

ΜΗΔΕΙΑ

1370   οἶδ᾽ οὐκέτ᾽ εἰσί· τοῦτο γάρ σε δήξεται.

ΙΑΣΩΝ

οἶδ᾽ εἰσίν, οἴμοι, σῷ κάρᾳ μιάστορες.

1365 οὔτοι νιν a: οὔτοι νυν vel οὐ τοίνυν b
γ᾽ Hermann: σφ᾽ C

MEDEA

JASON

Yes, and you also have grief and are a sharer in my misfortune.

MEDEA

Of course, but the pain is worthwhile if you cannot mock me.

JASON

Children, what an evil mother you got!

MEDEA

Children, how you have perished by your father's fault!

JASON

It was not my hand, you know, that killed them.

MEDEA

No: it was the outrage of your new marriage.

JASON

Did you really think it right to kill them because of a marriage?

MEDEA

Do you imagine that loss of this is a trivial grief for a woman?

JASON

For a woman of sense, yes. But you find everything a disaster.

MEDEA

But the children are dead: this will wound you to the quick.

JASON

They live, alas, as spirits to take vengeance on your crimes!

421

ΜΗΔΕΙΑ

ἴσασιν ὅστις ἦρξε πημονῆς θεοί.

ΙΑΣΩΝ

ἴσασι δῆτα σήν γ' ἀπόπτυστον φρένα.

ΜΗΔΕΙΑ

στύγει· πικρὰν δὲ βάξιν ἐχθαίρω σέθεν.

ΙΑΣΩΝ

1375 καὶ μὴν ἐγὼ σήν· ῥᾴδιοι δ' ἀπαλλαγαί.

ΜΗΔΕΙΑ

πῶς οὖν; τί δράσω; κάρτα γὰρ κἀγὼ θέλω.

ΙΑΣΩΝ

θάψαι νεκρούς μοι τούσδε καὶ κλαῦσαι πάρες.

ΜΗΔΕΙΑ

οὐ δῆτ', ἐπεί σφας τῇδ' ἐγὼ θάψω χερί,
φέρουσ' ἐς Ἥρας τέμενος Ἀκραίας θεοῦ,
1380 ὡς μή τις αὐτοὺς πολεμίων καθυβρίσῃ
τύμβους ἀνασπῶν· γῇ δὲ τῇδε Σισύφου
σεμνὴν ἑορτὴν καὶ τέλη προσάψομεν
τὸ λοιπὸν ἀντὶ τοῦδε δυσσεβοῦς φόνου.
αὐτὴ δὲ γαῖαν εἶμι τὴν Ἐρεχθέως,
1385 Αἰγεῖ συνοικήσουσα τῷ Πανδίονος.
σὺ δ', ὥσπερ εἰκός, κατθανῇ κακὸς κακῶς,
Ἀργοῦς κάρα σὸν λειψάνῳ πεπληγμένος,
πικρὰς τελευτὰς τῶν ἐμῶν γάμων ἰδών.

MEDEA

MEDEA
The gods know who struck the first blow.

JASON
Yes, they know indeed your loathesome heart.

MEDEA
Hate on! I detest the hateful sound of your voice.

JASON
And I of yours. To part will be easy.

MEDEA
How? What shall I do? For that is very much my wish as well.

JASON
Allow me to bury these dead children and to mourn them.

MEDEA
Certainly not. I shall bury them with my own hand, taking them to the sanctuary of Hera Akraia,[a] so that none of my enemies may outrage them by tearing up their graves. And I shall enjoin on this land of Sisyphus a solemn festival and holy rites for all time to come in payment for this unholy murder.[b] As for myself, I shall go to the land of Erechtheus to live with Aegeus, son of Pandion. But you, as is fitting, shall die the miserable death of a coward, struck on the head by a piece of the Argo, having seen the bitter result of your marriage to me.

[a] Hera as worshipped on the Acrocorinth.
[b] In historical times, there appears to have been such a festival, in which young boys and girls of noble family spent a year in the temple precinct.

423

ΙΑΣΩΝ

ἀλλά σ᾽ Ἐρινὺς ὀλέσειε τέκνων
1390 φονία τε Δίκη.

ΜΗΔΕΙΑ

τίς δὲ κλύει σοῦ θεὸς ἢ δαίμων,
τοῦ ψευδόρκου καὶ ξειναπάτου;

ΙΑΣΩΝ

φεῦ φεῦ, μυσαρὰ καὶ παιδολέτορ.

ΜΗΔΕΙΑ

στεῖχε πρὸς οἴκους καὶ θάπτ᾽ ἄλοχον.

ΙΑΣΩΝ

1395 στείχω, δισσῶν γ᾽ ἄμορος τέκνων.

ΜΗΔΕΙΑ

οὔπω θρηνεῖς· μένε καὶ γῆρας.

ΙΑΣΩΝ

ὦ τέκνα φίλτατα.

ΜΗΔΕΙΑ

μητρί γε, σοὶ δ᾽ οὔ.

ΙΑΣΩΝ

κἄπειτ᾽ ἔκανες;

ΜΗΔΕΙΑ

σέ γε πημαίνουσ᾽.

ΙΑΣΩΝ

ὤμοι, φιλίου χρῄζω στόματος
1400 παίδων ὁ τάλας προσπτύξασθαι.

MEDEA

JASON

May the Fury that punishes your children's death, and Justice the murderous,[a] destroy you utterly!

MEDEA

What god or power above will listen to you, who broke your oath and deceived a stranger?

JASON

Pah! Unclean wretch! Child-murderer!

MEDEA

Go home! Bury your wife!

JASON

Yes—bereft of my two sons—I go.

MEDEA

Your mourning has yet to begin. Wait until you are old!

JASON

O children most dear!

MEDEA

Yes, to their mother, not to you.

JASON

And so you killed them?

MEDEA

Yes, to cause you grief.

JASON

Alas, how I long for the dear faces of my children, to enfold them in my arms!

---

[a] Both the Erinys (Fury) and Dikê (Justice) are agents of Zeus.

EURIPIDES

ΜΗΔΕΙΑ

νῦν σφε προσαυδᾷς, νῦν ἀσπάζῃ,
τότ' ἀπωσάμενος.

ΙΑΣΩΝ

δός μοι πρὸς θεῶν
μαλακοῦ χρωτὸς ψαῦσαι τέκνων.

ΜΗΔΕΙΑ

οὐκ ἔστι· μάτην ἔπος ἔρριπται.

ΙΑΣΩΝ

1405 Ζεῦ, τάδ' ἀκούεις ὡς ἀπελαυνόμεθ'
οἷά τε πάσχομεν ἐκ τῆς μυσαρᾶς
καὶ παιδοφόνου τῆσδε λεαίνης;
ἀλλ' ὁπόσον γοῦν πάρα καὶ δύναμαι
τάδε καὶ θρηνῶ κἀπιθεάζω,
1410 μαρτυρόμενος δαίμονας ὥς μοι
τέκνα κτείνασ' ἀποκωλύεις
ψαῦσαί τε χεροῖν θάψαι τε νεκρούς,
οὓς μήποτ' ἐγὼ φύσας ὄφελον
πρὸς σοῦ φθιμένους ἐπιδέσθαι.

ΧΟΡΟΣ

1415 πολλῶν ταμίας Ζεὺς ἐν Ὀλύμπῳ,
πολλὰ δ' ἀέλπτως κραίνουσι θεοί·
καὶ τὰ δοκηθέντ' οὐκ ἐτελέσθη,
τῶν δ' ἀδοκήτων πόρον ηὗρε θεός.
τοιόνδ' ἀπέβη τόδε πρᾶγμα.

1415–19 del. Hartung, Diggle: defendi *TAPA* 117 (1987),
268–70

426

MEDEA

Now you speak to them, now you greet them, when before you thrust them from you.

JASON

By the gods, I beg you, let me touch the tender flesh of my children!

MEDEA

It cannot be. Your words are uttered in vain.

JASON

Zeus, do you hear this, how I am driven away and what treatment I endure from this unclean, child-murdering monster? But with all the strength I have, I make my lament and adjure the gods, calling the heavenly powers to witness that you killed my sons and now forbid me to touch them or to bury their bodies. Oh that I had never begotten them, never seen them dead at your hands!

MEDEA with the corpses of her children is borne aloft away from Corinth. Exit JASON by Eisodos B.

CHORUS LEADER

Zeus on Olympus has many things in his treasure house, and many are the things the gods accomplish against our expectation. What men look for is not brought to pass, but a god finds a way to achieve the unexpected. Such is the outcome of this story.

Exit CHORUS by Eisodos B.

427